Ray

ALSO BY BRIAN E. COOPER

*Red Faber: A Biography of the Hall of
Fame Spitball Pitcher* (McFarland, 2007)

Ray Schalk

A Baseball Biography

BRIAN E. COOPER

*To Gary —
Best wishes!
Brian Cooper*

McFarland & Company, Inc., Publishers
Jefferson, North Carolina, and London

LIBRARY OF CONGRESS CATALOGUING-IN-PUBLICATION DATA

Cooper, Brian E., 1954–
    Ray Schalk : a baseball biography / Brian E. Cooper.
        p.   cm.
    Includes bibliographical references and index.

    ISBN 978-0-7864-4148-8
    softcover : 50# alkaline paper ∞

    1. Schalk, Ray.   2. Baseball players — United States —
Biography.   I. Title.
GV865.S352C66   2009
796.357092 — dc22 [B]   2009027457

British Library cataloguing data are available

On the cover: Chicago White Sox catcher Ray Schalk
in 1924 (Library of Congress)

Manufactured in the United States of America

*McFarland & Company, Inc., Publishers
    Box 611, Jefferson, North Carolina 28640
    www.mcfarlandpub.com*

To my wife, Ann.
She deserves a place in the Patience Hall of Fame.

Acknowledgments

I greatly appreciate these individuals and institutions for their assistance and cooperation with this project.

First, my thanks to these individuals: Mirdza Berzins; Mark Braun; Deborah Brinson; Roy Brinson; Gene Carney; Ralph Christian; Bill Dees; Jim Eisenbarth; James Elfers; David Fletcher; Lillian Hendricks; Mary Lee Hostert; Will Hoyer; Jarrell Jarrard; Richard C. Lindberg; Peter Morris; Mike Nola; Bill Nowlin; Michelle Romanus; James Schalk; Lee Simon; Bob Sokol; Chris Steinbach; Brian Stevens; and David Valenzuela.

I also thank these institutions: Abraham Lincoln Presidential Library and Museum, Springfield, Illinois; Bottomley-Ruffing-Schalk Baseball Museum, Nokomis, Illinois; *Buffalo (New York) News*; Carnegie-Stout Public Library, Dubuque, Iowa; Center for Dubuque History, Dubuque, Iowa; Chicago History Museum; Chicago Public Library; DePauw University, Greencastle, Indiana; Elmhurst (Illinois) Public Library; Library of Congress, Washington, D.C.; *Litchfield (Illinois) News-Herald*; Litchfield Community School District; Montgomery County (Illinois) Clerk's Office; National Baseball Hall of Fame, Cooperstown, New York; Old Timers' Baseball Association of Chicago, Inc.; Retrosheet.org; Society for American Baseball Research; Shoeless Joe Jackson Virtual Hall of Fame; Telegraph Herald/Woodward Communications, Inc., Dubuque, Iowa; and Tri-County Historical Society, Cascade, Iowa.

Table of Contents

Acknowledgments. vi
Preface 1

 1. "Put in Schalk!"   5
 2. Milwaukee 15
 3. "Here is your pitcher, Doc White" 22
 4. "Cracker" 32
 5. Domesticated on the World Tour 44
 6. Sophomore Star 55
 7. "We don't serve kids in here!" 71
 8. Two Games from Glory 83
 9. Ray and Lavinia 91
10. American League Champs 96
11. Giant-Killers 105
12. A Dynasty Interrupted. 117
13. Glory Before the Fall 130
14. Black Sox 140
15. Divided We Fall. 155
16. Thrown Down 161
17. A Team to Dismember. 174
18. Rebuilding for the Second Division 181
19. "The Human Dynamo" 191
20. Ray Down and Kid Out 200
21. Passed Over, Battered and Benched 206

22. Cracker's Comeback 214
23. Transitions 223
24. Goodbye. 242
25. A New Role 250
26. Shuffle Off to Buffalo. 259
27. Indianapolis and Milwaukee 266
28. Businessman, Volunteer and Celebrity 270
29. Turmoil on the Home Front 277
30. Cooperstown Calls. 283
31. Final Inning 292

Epilogue 297
Appendix 299
Chapter Notes. 303
Bibliography. 317
Index 321

Preface

Of the nearly 200 major league players enshrined in the National Baseball Hall of Fame, few receive as much criticism as Ray "Cracker" Schalk. He is a convenient target. After all, his lifetime batting average is a mere .253, the lowest among position players in the Hall. Certainly, had Schalk been able to add another 10 or 20 points to his batting average — not playing with all those bruises, concussions and broken and dislocated fingers might have made the difference — today's critics could throw stones at Rabbit Maranville (.258) instead of Schalk. However, if earning a place in the Hall were just a matter of offensive production, selections could be left to a computer program. Additional considerations include defense, on-field leadership and other contributions to the game — all areas where Schalk excelled.

Going into this project, I did not intend to interject my opinion on the Hall of Fame Veterans Committee's 1955 decision to enshrine Schalk. This book was not written to diminish or elevate him to superstar status. I decided that his many attributes and the controversy would just be part of the biography of an outstanding player and interesting man; readers could decide for themselves whether Schalk "deserved" Cooperstown.

When Schalk broke into major-league baseball in 1912, many experts predicted that this son of a janitor wouldn't last long. At no more than 5-foot-9 and 165 pounds — many accounts said he was much shorter and lighter than that — Cracker hardly fit the mold of a big-league catcher. After all, experts wondered, how could he handle the rigors of the position — especially the bone-jarring collisions with baserunners hell-bent on reaching home plate? Though baserunners knocked him out a few times, Schalk became an expert at avoiding collisions and tagging opponents as they slid by. When it came to catching high popups, he had no peer. Would-be base-stealers thought twice when he was behind the plate. Schalk proved that speed and smarts behind the plate helped a team more than brawn. For a decade after his retirement, he held the major league record for catching appearances. So much for the argument that Schalk was too small to be durable.

I chose Schalk for my second biography as I completed my first — on Urban "Red" Faber, another White Sox star and Hall of Famer. Schalk and Faber were teammates from 1914 until 1928, when they were part of some of the best and some of the worst White Sox teams ever. Among the Hall of Fame batteries, none played as many seasons together as Red and Cracker. For four decades in retirement, the two men remained friends who resided near each other on Chicago's South Side. To me, it seemed only fitting that both be featured in full biographies for the first time.

Schalk caught my interest for other reasons. He was raised in downstate Illinois, less than an hour's drive from my birthplace. He starred in my favorite major-league city, Chicago. He caught a baseball dropped from the 36-story Tribune Tower, home of the newspaper that helped inspire my career choice. He was the first catcher known to have recorded a putout at second base. He was once robbed and held captive at gunpoint. He was known and respected by the elite of the game — to the point of being one of Ty Cobb's few friends. He coached or managed at various levels for four decades, during which time he engaged in more than one on-field fistfight.

Then there was the Black Sox scandal. Schalk had a unique perspective on the World Series of 1919, when teammates conspired with gamblers and intentionally lost to the Cincinnati Reds. Schalk was the first of the honest players — the so-called Clean Sox — to know something was up; after all, he could tell immediately when his pitchers ignored his signals and when they grooved the ball to Reds hitters. Cracker was so angry and frustrated that he physically attacked one of his hurlers after one Series game and got tossed out of another contest for getting physical with an umpire. After initially airing his complaint that teammates "threw" the Series, Schalk changed his story. He denied it all. The reversal reflected his loyalty to Sox owner Charles A. Comiskey, who hoped to clamp a lid on the conspiracy and keep his star-laden team intact. Even after the cover-up failed and Shoeless Joe Jackson and seven others received lifetime suspensions, Schalk maintained his silence. Comiskey had his reputation to protect. Further, Cracker saw what happened to his friend Buck Weaver. The infielder received the same punishment as the conspirators, even though he played his best, because he sat in on the Black Sox' discussions but didn't report it. That to his dying day Cracker refused to tell what he knew about the scandal not only frustrated fans and researchers, it diluted his prominence in baseball history.

Cracker's 18-year career spanned the Deadball and Lively Ball eras, which fell on either side of 1920. In the Deadball period, teams won with pitching, defense and speed. When he was considered the best backstop anywhere — to that point in the game's history, perhaps the best ever — any offensive contribution from the catcher was considered a bonus. He was on the field for his defense and handling of pitchers. As the Black Sox left the game, the Lively Ball period arrived, courtesy of Babe Ruth, the home-run machine.

Though it was not my intent to judge Schalk's worthiness for the Hall of Fame, after my research I concluded that the Veterans Committee made the right call in 1955. That opinion is based not on his limited offensive abilities, certainly, but because of his defense, his leadership and other attributes that — excuse the cliché — don't show up in box scores. Add to that the countless tributes and testimonials by players, umpires and sportswriters. He was usually the shortest man on the field, but Schalk was the yardstick against whom other catchers were measured.

Brian E. Cooper • Dubuque, Iowa • Summer 2009

1

❖

"Put in Schalk!"

Jake Bene was in a jam. In just a few minutes — after the local school-boys wrapped up their preliminary contest on the Olympic Park field — his Litchfield (Illinois) semi-pro team would host Divernon. But Bene had no catcher. The reason for his absence is hazy. One version of the story said the backstop had a broken finger.[1] A later account suggested that the out-of-towner missed his train to Litchfield. As the manager pondered his limited options, he heard a spectator shout, "Put in Schalk!" Bene looked toward the fans, who directed his gaze to a scrawny 15-year-old boy catching in the high school game. Bene had little choice. He recruited the kid and placed him last in the batting order. That Sunday afternoon in 1908, in Litchfield, Ray Schalk became a boy playing among men. Though he had already played nine innings that day, the teenager caught nine more in the Litchfield Arcos' 10–4 victory. All afternoon, the pitcher, a man named Zimmerman, threw nothing but spitballs — a challenging pitch for a catcher of any age.[2] Schalk rapped two hits in three at-bats, scored two runs, played errorless defense and recorded a couple of assists. "I was one tired youngster after working 18 innings that afternoon under a sizzling sun," Schalk recalled years later, adding that the Arcos gave him not a dime for his efforts.[3]

In the next day's account of the game, the local sportswriter noted the visitors' inability to mount a rally against the Litchfield nine: "The Divernon boys died on first like a crop of corn after a June frost." The paper also touted the replacement catcher with special pride. "He is superintendent of the News carriers and spends most of his time soliciting new subscribers," the article revealed. "Whether or not he has been using his baseball tactics on the citizens we do not know, but when it comes to getting new subscribers he certainly can catch them every time." Getting back to baseball, the sportswriter added, "Schalk will make an excellent player if he will go after the game earnestly. He is young and has a few years yet in which to develop into a big leaguer."[4] Few could have predicted that those "few years" would be less than four.

Schalk (here ca. 1909) got his first taste of adult baseball in 1908 when, as an undersized 15-year-old catcher, he became a last-minute fill-in for the semi-pro Arcos in his hometown of Litchfield, Illinois. After the game, a local newspaper stated, "Schalk will make an excellent player if he will go after the game earnestly." The next season, he was a catcher in demand, receiving $2.50 a game from the Arcos and other semi-pro teams (Bottomley-Ruffing-Schalk Museum, Nokomis, Illinois).

Ray Schalk lived in a time and place where boys had to grow up quickly. His native Montgomery County was a hardscrabble area in downstate Illinois, roughly 50 miles northeast of St. Louis. Young men landed jobs in the mines, reported for their labors before dawn, returned home after dark, and grew old before their time. Luckier ones landed jobs with one of the four railroads with local facilities, a rail car manufacturing enterprise, a foundry, a shoe factory, and American Radiator Company. The Illinois Central featured five round-trips between Litchfield and St. Louis; a trip required little more than two hours in electric-lighted cars. The Wabash promoted a $19.50 round-trip fare to Minneapolis-St. Paul and $32 to New York City.[5] By the late 19th and early 20th centuries, the miners, factory workers and railroad men contributed to Litchfield's hard edge. The local papers routinely carried descriptive accounts of tavern shootings, robberies and police raids on the red-light district. In addition to its proximity to railroads and their maintenance shops, Litchfield later benefited by being situated along the famed Route 66 and its successor Interstate 55, which also linked Chicago and St. Louis. In the late 19th century, after some of the railroads operating in the city languished or relocated, Litchfield Foundry & Machine Co. became a major employer. In 1904, civic leaders convinced officials of American Radiator Company to establish a manufacturing facility in Litchfield.[6] The factory sponsored a baseball team and, playing off the company name, it was known as the "Arcos."

In Litchfield, citizens of German descent, including the Schalks, settled on the north side of town. Their home was on North Van Buren, just north of Henricks Street. Meanwhile, the Irish took up residence in the south. Rivalries ran so strong that boys ventured into the "other side" of town at their own peril. However, as one of the few boys who desired to catch — and excelled at it — Ray Schalk enjoyed safe passage.[7] If they couldn't get onto the Olympic Park diamond, a mile from home and adjacent to the American Radiator plant on the southeast edge of town, he and his cohorts cut grass to fashion their own ball fields elsewhere. They often shared a single bat, a Hillerich model featuring the etching of a Bulldog. Young Ray took his mitt with him everywhere, always ready for a game.[8]

Schalk was the son of German immigrants. His father, Herman Schalk, was born in Prussia, Germany, the son of Christian and Marian Maschinski Schalk. Based on a community history book and his obituary, he was born in December 1855.[9] However, over the years various census reports fail to corroborate that birth year. His listed ages did not change consistently. Whether the discrepancy was due to enumerator errors or respondent fibbing, Herman Schalk did not age 10 years with each decennial census. Based on the handwritten entries on census logs, between 1900 and 1910, he aged 15 years;

he slowed the aging process between 1910 and 1920, when his age increased just seven years.[10] Herman Schalk took a steamship to the United States in 1875.[11] He briefly resided in Taylorville, Illinois, before moving 20 miles southwest to Harvel Township, a tiny farming community of just 670 souls on the border of Montgomery and Christian counties. The government did not determine the village of Harvel's population until the 1890 census, when the count was 246 and the township total increased to 723.[12] Herman apparently had a slightly older relative in the area — Ferdinand Schalk, born in 1852 and a U.S. resident since 1870. In 1876, Ferdinand married Carrie Wimmesberger and by 1880 they were residing and operating a saloon in Litchfield, 19 miles southwest of Harvel. He died in 1922. Herman was a day laborer (most likely on a farm) who boarded with W.S. Lorton and his young family. It was in Harvel where Herman Schalk met Sophia Brandt, who was born in January 1860 and came to the United States aboard a sailboat with her parents and sisters.[13] By 1880, she was on her own, employed as a "servant" with the R.S. Nelson family.[14] The couple married in November 1881, farmed, and started a family in Harvel. Herman and Sophia Schalk had been married 17 years when, in 1898, they moved to Litchfield, where Herman became the janitor at the local Elks Club.[15] He held the position for decades. In addition to its meeting facilities, the four-story, red brick structure offered lodging accommodations; the Classical Revival structure was added to the National Register of Historic Places in 1995.[16]

With the Schalks were their children Leo (born in 1883), Wilhelmina (1885), Theresa (1887), Walter (1890), Ray (August 12, 1892) and Clarence (1898). As the offspring of a day laborer — at one point, Herman received $35 a month as the Elks Club janitor — the Schalk children did their part to earn money for the family.[17] After grammar school and during his brief time in high school, Ray performed various odd jobs, including delivering newspapers — it involved a 3:30 A.M. wake-up call — and hauling coal. Once, he got the job of helping drive cows through the streets of Litchfield to a pasture at the north terminus of Monroe Street.[18] Though academics were not a personal priority, Ray did enjoy certain aspects of high school. He and his buddies noticed that, as soon as the students returned to their classroom after lunch, a certain girl always used the large dictionary kept on a stand at the front of the room. One day during lunch hour, Ray slipped back into the empty classroom and tampered with the book stand. When the girl, as expected, started to turn a page of the unabridged dictionary, it fell to the floor with a thud — much to the delight of the boys watching in anticipation. History did not record whether the dictionary was opened to the word "prank."

Toddler Ray Schalk poses with his older brothers Leo (center) and Walter (right), circa 1894 (Bottomley-Ruffing-Schalk Museum, Nokomis, Illinois).

Litchfield High was known more for its basketball teams than baseball squads. Though just an underclassman, Schalk was the basketball squad's captain and forward. They played in cracker-box buildings with low ceilings, and players had to adjust the trajectories of their shots accordingly. The floor in Irving angled one foot lower at one end, forcing each team to run uphill one half and downhill the other. After a game in Barnett, six miles away (via the railroad tracks), Schalk and the other Litchfield boys walked home rather than wait until the next morning to take the train.[19] In another road game, the Litchfield High squad and Raymond Athletic Club were deadlocked at the end of regulation time. In a sudden-death overtime format, the game ended when "crack player" Schalk notched a field goal. Final score: 21–19.[20]

Young Ray eventually landed an after-school position as a "printer's devil" at the *Litchfield Daily News*, handling whatever tasks he was assigned in the production department.[21] The print trade appealed to him as a career choice. He also supervised the paper's carrier force and sold subscriptions. Ray dropped out of Litchfield High School after a year or two and started working full-time at Litchfield Printing and Stationery Co.[22]

Meanwhile, Schalk's interest and proficiency in baseball increased. As a catcher, he chose two backstops as his professional idols, Jimmy Archer and Johnny Kling, both of the Chicago Cubs.[23] Though small of stature and appearing even younger than his 16 years — his youthful appearance would produce amusing situations in years to come — Schalk established himself as a talented, take-charge catcher. For a while, a booster from Barnett would drive his buggy to Litchfield each weekend, pick up Schalk and another Litchfield lad, Roy Jarrard, and take them to Barnett's games. "The diamond, if it may be dignified by that name, was in a pasture, bordered by a cornfield. The ground was rough and the bound of the ball uncertain, but it afforded just as much fun as the best groomed fields of the big leagues," Schalk said. "At intervals it became necessary to halt the battle to 'shoo away' inquisitive cows which impeded the work of the outfielders." For their time and talents, Jarrard and Schalk received one dollar each.[24] To cover the expenses, including the pay for the newly recruited talent, organizers passed the hat among the farmers and townspeople in attendance.[25] (Jarrard's son recalls his father telling a similar story about their experiences in 1910 — only it involved a Harvel farmer chauffeuring the boys from Litchfield to wherever Taylorville played. Roy Jarrard quit school after the fourth grade — his father had deserted the family — and went to work in a glass factory. By the time he was 12 years old, he was working in the coal mines. He put in 16-hour days so he could have time to play baseball on weekends.[26]) By 1909, in the season following his service as an emergency fill-in for the local semi-pro team, Schalk was fielding letters, telephone calls and telegrams from various adult teams seeking his services. A high school dropout earning $7 a week at the newspaper, Schalk was receiving $2.50 a game — plus expenses — to catch for area teams, including those in Litchfield, Carlinville, Farmersville and Harvel. In addition to their rough, cow-pasture fields, these games featured down-home moments. In the summer of 1909, after Schalk (hitless in three at-bats) and Litchfield suffered a 9–0 home loss to the Jersey Farm Dairy team of St. Louis, a local booster made a special presentation. "Frank Crabb presented Heidie Orr, the local manager, with a fine thoroughbred pig after the game because Heidie had several chances to fall down during the afternoon and he didn't fall once. The pig is a dandy and Heidie is as proud of it as a boy with his first pair of long pants. He says he is going to keep it until it gets big and then he and Mrs. Orr and all the little Orrs will have fresh pork all winter."[27]

Not yet 18, Ray Schalk continued his job as a printer's devil and carrier supervisor at the *Litchfield Daily News* and its affiliated Litchfield Printing and Stationery. The printing trade remained his career interest. (His father, Herman, suggested that Ray follow his brother Leo into the banking business.[28]) In January 1910, he traveled to Brooklyn, New York, where he spent two months learning how to operate Ottmar Mergenthaler's invention, the Linotype machine. The Linotype was a hot and clanky, but intricate, contraption. The operator sat at the 91-key keyboard on the device, which positioned type, one line at a time, to be cast in molten lead. After Linotype training, he returned to Litchfield, ready to move up in the printing industry. However, he was informed that he still faced four years of apprenticeship — at the same $7 a week — before becoming a full-fledged printer. His enthusiasm for the trade waned. "Four more years looked like a century to me," Schalk told an interviewer decades later. (An earlier article had him working in print shops in Taylorville and Farmersville.[29]) The teenager told his father that he had quit the print shop and would pursue a career in baseball instead.[30] Herman Schalk made no attempt to hide his disappointment and disapproval.

Nonetheless, the spunky catcher continued to develop on the ball field. He remained a semi-pro backstop for hire for roughly the same $2 a game. Though Schalk drew more attention for his defense and handling of pitchers, until his big league days he also represented an offensive threat of the singles and doubles variety. On the first Sunday of 1910 — it was May Day — he sparked a 10th-inning rally for the Litchfield semi-pro team in its 7–6 victory over Springfield. Other teams in the area bid for Schalk's services, and he was a regular with the Taylorville Oil Tankers of the Trolley League. In the league's championship game, Schalk stroked a seventh-inning single, stole second and scored the winning run in the 2–1 victory over Virden.[31]

As the 1911 season was to open, the 3-M League, an amalgamation of downstate Illinois semi-pro teams, faced economic and political difficulties. Just days before Opening Day, the league president, a man named Clavin, announced that he had approved a recommendation to combine the Farmersville and Litchfield teams and stage most of the team's home games in Litchfield. The merged team would host Mount Olive in a few days. "Mount Olive is making preparations to come to this city in a special car and bring the crack Mount Olive band, which will give a concert at the park and assist in the entertainment," the *Litchfield Daily News* reported. "Olympic Park will be put into first class shape and everything prepared for a good game. Ray Schalk and Lewis Doran will be the battery for this team."[32] Before "one of the largest crowds that has witnessed a ball game in this city for a long time," Farmersville-Litchfield lost, 5–3. Schalk went hitless in three at-bats and committed an error, but he also stole a base and scored a run.[33] About this time, the 18-year-old ballplayer made the acquaintance of Lavinia Graham, the 17-year-old daughter of a Farmersville carpenter.

Perhaps the first pro scout to recognize Schalk's potential was Clarence "Pants" Rowland. The former owner of the Dubuque (Iowa) entry in the Three-I League, Rowland saw Schalk playing semi-pro in 1910 and recommended him to Charles A. Comiskey, owner of the Chicago White Sox. However, Comiskey, known as "the Old Roman," did not follow through then, when he could have purchased the kid's contract for about $600. Comiskey listened to other scouts, who believed that the undersized Schalk could not withstand the rigors of baseball at the top level. In less than two years, Comiskey parted with many times that amount to win a bidding war for Schalk's services.[34] (Rowland developed a reputation for recognizing talent. He also recommended pitcher Urban "Red" Faber, a Hall of Famer, and six other major-leaguers. All this improved his standing with Comiskey and contributed to the Old Roman's decision in late 1914 to name Rowland as manager of his White Sox.)

Schalk was not long for the Farmersville-Litchfield team or the semi-pro circuit. Just up the road, Taylorville was fielding a professional team to join the fledgling Illinois-Missouri League, a Class D minor-league circuit, and Schalk was signed during the winter.[35] The I-M started in 1908, when the lone Missouri entry, the Hannibal Cannibals, finished atop the standings; the Cannibals then found another league for 1909. No city was represented all seven years of the I-M League's existence. Among the best-known players to come from the Illinois-Missouri were Grover Cleveland Alexander (Galesburg, 1909) and Schalk, of the Taylorville Christians. (The nickname might have accurately reflected the players' religious persuasion, but more likely it was derived from the team's location, Christian County.) Even before his first professional game, the youngster was pegged as an up-and-comer. A sportswriter in Decatur, not far from Taylorville, noted, "Schalk is only 19 years of age, and the improvement noted in him last season over the year before was so marked that it is believed in a year or two more he will be eligible for much faster company than there is in the I-M League."[36] However, in the season opener, Schalk, still only 18, rode the bench and watched his 46-year-old manager, Fred Donovan, do the catching. Donovan had major-league experience: three games with the 1895 Cleveland Spiders. Losing to visiting Lincoln in the bottom of the ninth, Donovan inserted Schalk as a pinch-hitter. In his first professional appearance, on May 9, 1911, the kid responded with a double. However, Taylorville lost, 7–3, on its way to a last-place finish in its only year in the league.[37] (Later that season, the Christians were managed by Joe Adams, who once reached the major leagues long enough to pitch four innings in a single afternoon for the St. Louis Cardinals.)

Schalk did not sit on the Taylorville bench long. Barely six weeks after his professional debut, he was sporting a batting average of .445 and attracting the attention of several teams higher up baseball's pyramid. "Catcher Schalk of Taylorville continues to look like the find of the season," the *Chicago Inter-Ocean* reported, "offers being received from both St. Louis teams, Louisville, and Decatur for his services."[38] Dick Kinsella, president of the Three-I League, on behalf of his own league team (Decatur) or the St. Louis Cardinals — his intentions were not spelled out — tried to buy Schalk's contract, but Taylorville officials refused. Alfred J. "Cy" Ferry, representing the Detroit Tigers, "without making his identity known," scouted Schalk in a home game and soon afterward phoned Taylorville officials from Decatur, where he was scouting another catcher, Hickory Johnson, formerly of Taylorville, who had moved up to the Three-I. Ferry, whose major-league dossier consisted of pitching 13 innings for Detroit and two innings for Cleveland, sought to sign Schalk for 1912. "No price was fixed, but Mr. Ferry was insistent and said he would come to Taylorville this afternoon to negotiate for him," noted the *Litchfield Daily News*, which added, "Schalk has it on Johnson, in the opinion of the Taylorville fans. He has a good peg, is a good receiver and has it all over Hickory in batting, baserunning and what's more, is fully 10 years younger than the Decatur man."[39] Eventually, both catchers made the big leagues, though the locals were accurate in their assessment. Johnson, eight years Schalk's senior, appeared in only 11 major-league games — all in 1914 for John McGraw's New York Giants.[40] Ferry managed to secure an option on Schalk's contract for $750, and the catcher appeared destined to wear a Tigers uniform someday.[41] Though he did not become Detroit property, Schalk never forgot Ferry's confidence in him, and two decades later they worked together in Buffalo.[42]

At the same time scouts scrambled to see and sign Schalk, the semi-pro circuit in which he got his start struggled to survive. By mid-season 1911, Litchfield had dropped out of the 3-M League and several other teams, in a money-losing situation, were on the brink of leaving.[43] Similarly, Taylorville did not remain in the I-M after its only season, 1911.

The maneuvering for Schalk ended — at least momentarily — in mid–July 1911. Just days after paying $750 for an option on the catcher's contract, Detroit owner Frank Navin sold the option to Milwaukee, of the American Association. Despite his reputation as a tight-fisted businessman, Navin reportedly let go of the option on the future Hall of Famer for the same $750.[44] Milwaukee then negotiated with the president of the Taylorville team, a man named Martin, who accepted $1,500 to release the catcher immediately. "He has been the life of the Taylorville team and they regret to lose him, but President Martin did not feel that it would be right to keep him, when there was a chance for him to go higher," a Litchfield paper noted. "He has not only been a success as a catcher, but has led the league in batting, which is one great factor in his advancement." He hit .398 and stole 13 bases.[45] Still just 18 years old, Schalk spent a day to visit with family in Litchfield, pack his bags, catch the train to join his new team and experience his next professional adventure.[46]

2

❖❖❖

Milwaukee

Though experts viewed Schalk as a rising star, the particulars were fuzzy in Milwaukee. "Illinois Boy is a Phenom," declared a headline in the *Milwaukee Sentinel*, which described the teenage backstop as a 21-year-old outfielder. "Owner (Charles) Havenor is said to have paid a big price for the youngster," stated the *Sentinel*, adding that Schalk is "touted as a second Ty Cobb." Added manager Jimmy Barrett, "We have been dickering for the youngster for a long time, and we finally landed him. He cost us a pile of money, but if he shows any of the class he has been exhibiting so far this season, he is worth it."[1] The *Milwaukee Journal* also misreported the newest player's position. "The addition of a new outfielder to the Brewers' staff at this stage of the game when almost the entire outfit is suffering from some ailment or other is more valuable than is at first supposed." The *Journal* sounded prophetic in stating, "If Schalk lives anywhere near up to his reputation, he ought to prove a valuable addition to the team."[2] Barrett used Schalk as a pinch-hitter in his Brewers debut on July 20, 1911. Perhaps still unaware of the recruit's best position, the manager the next day stuck his team's major investment in right field before relegating the kid to the bench for a couple of weeks. The Brewers had many problems — their season was chaotic — but catching was not among them. Milwaukee's backstop was 35-year-old William Riddle "Doc" Marshall, who had more than 200 major-league games at catcher, most recently with the Brooklyn Superbas in 1909. As Schalk joined the team, Marshall slammed three home runs in one week.[3]

A charter member of the American Association, which started play in 1902, the Brewers were owned by Milwaukee businessmen Harry D. Quin, who held the title of president, and Charles S. Havenor. Before the 1903 season, Havenor — a hotelier, merchant tailor, and city alderman — wrested the presidency from Quin.[4] Havenor soon afterward made more headlines due to some legal difficulties — something about taking a $100 bribe while Milwaukee's Fourth Ward alderman. In 1909, while the American Association con-

15

tinued to ponder expanding into existing major-league cities, Havenor quietly bought land in Chicago. With the American League White Sox on the South Side and the National League Cubs then on the West Side, Havenor sought a North Side site and paid $175,000 for a Lutheran seminary's eight-acre campus.[5] "This property is considered the best vacant location in Chicago for a baseball park, and the purchase on its face appears to portend the entrance of an American Association club into that city, with a big baseball war as the result," a national magazine reported.[6] But the American Association did not come, and a few years later, Havenor's widow, Agnes, sold the land that today houses a sports landmark, Wrigley Field. The Havenors owned the Brewers until 1918, when the wartime economy necessitated a sale.

On August 4, 1911, Marshall gave way to Schalk, who recorded an eighth-inning single and caught the rest of the game. "Schalk handled Marion's twisting benders like a veteran and helped the Brewers ward off a shutout by singling his only time up," the *Milwaukee Sentinel* noted.[7] After that, Schalk started to receive more playing time, but Marshall remained the starter. On August 12, his 19th birthday, Schalk entered in the ninth inning; the umpire had tossed Marshall for excessive arguing. He doubled in two at-bats during the extra-inning victory. All told, Schalk appeared in 31 games for the 1911 Brewers. But he still impressed, despite hitting .228 and stealing only two bases for the unsettled, fifth-place Brewers (79–87). "Schalk is a young catcher Manager James Barrett has been trying out for some time who has made good," *The Sporting News* reported. "Schalk is a cool-headed youngster and a hard worker."[8] The 1911 offensive star of the American Association, leading the league in batting average (.352), hits and steals, was Aurora's Charles "Casey" Stengel.

For the Brewers, 1912 was a year of change. Charles Havenor changed managers, replacing Barrett with Hugh Duffy. The team changed spring training sites when severe flooding hit Illinois' southernmost community, Cairo, at the confluence of the Mississippi and Ohio Rivers. The Brewers found new quarters 275 miles away, in the east central Illinois community of Danville. The team changed starting catchers: Schalk for Marshall. Finally, ownership changed. Pneumonia claimed Charles Havenor. His widow, Agnes, succeeded him, becoming only the second woman to own a professional baseball team. (The first was Helen Hathaway Britton, of the St. Louis Cardinals, the previous year.[9]) Widow Havenor, a Chicago native who five years earlier was making hats in a department store, not only said she was up to the baseball job, but she was also better suited for the task than a man. She said: "I think any woman who will take the pains to master the game may thus equip herself to run a ball team. A woman seems especially adapted for it. She has above all other qualities intuition much more developed than a man, which enables her to foresee things that a man never realizes could happen until they do. In baseball one must constantly look ahead. Then a woman has diplomacy, and it takes diplomacy to run ball clubs, I can tell you. These two qualities give women an advantage over men."[10] In her first season as owner, she would entertain bids from across the major leagues for her undersized catcher.

At the start, the Agnes Havenor administration enraged many Milwaukee fans by extending the Athletic Park grandstand, reducing the bleacher area and "enabling the management to get 50 cents for seats formerly sold at 25."[11] Some fans might have paid the higher price just to see how new manager Duffy and the umpires would handle new pitcher Bruce Noel, who came to Milwaukee on option from the Pittsburgh Pirates. Noel publicly stated he had never issued an intentional walk and didn't intend to. Noel said he preferred to hit the batter — "in a fatty part of his anatomy ... where the blow will not cripple him, but will give the pitcher some compensation for allowing the player a base he has not earned." Added Noel, "Consider how many games are lost by bases on balls, and I think most fans are inclined to agree with me that my theory is at least worthy of consideration."[12] Later, Noel bolted the team for Oshkosh.[13] Also joining the Brewers on option from Pittsburgh was outfielder Ralph Capron, a former halfback and punter on the University of Minnesota football team. *The Sporting News* reported that Capron was "doing Ty Cobb stunts with the Brewers and the old timers in the Association are complaining that such speed will break up the league."[14] Capron became one of the few athletes to play in the top professional leagues of both baseball and football — barely. He appeared in only three major-league games (1912–13) and, in 1920, at age 31, played for the Chicago Tigers in their American Professional Football Association loss to the Chicago Cardinals.[15] By mid–July, Milwaukee no longer wanted Noel and Capron — but Pittsburgh was not excited about taking them back, either.[16] Toward the start of the campaign, the Brewers wanted to add veteran lefty Jack Pfiester to their pitching corps. (The left-handed pitcher is the answer to the trivia question: "Who was the Chicago Cubs pitcher in the famous Merkle Game of 1908?") But Pfiester never made it to Milwaukee. In early May 1912, Western Union failed to deliver Manager Duffy's telegram to Pfiester — the offer was $300 a month — and the sidearmer retired. Three years later, a jury awarded Pfiester a $2,000 judgment against Western Union.[17]

During spring workouts, Duffy raved about Schalk, calling him "one of the greatest young catchers I have ever seen," and there was speculation that the Illinoisan would supplant Doc Marshall as the Brewers' starter.[18] Nonetheless, Duffy had Marshall catch the first few games of the season. Schalk started the next four games, including a rain-swept shellacking in the home opener, before the Brewers bought another catcher, Johnny Hughes. For the next month, Hughes and Marshall started all but a half-dozen games. Schalk's availability was hampered by a severe cold.[19] Meanwhile, the Brewers lost more often than not and sat in the second division of the American Association standings. They did more whining than winning, and seemed to register more run-ins with umpires than runs. On Memorial Day, the umpire tossed Milwaukee pitcher Tom Dougherty, but the next inning the hurler returned to the mound. He delivered several pitches before the umpire realized the situation and sent off Dougherty again — but not before the pitcher stated that the episode proved his contention that the ump was, as alleged, visually impaired.[20]

Duffy worked with his catching prospect's offense, getting Schalk to widen his batting stance and step toward pitches.[21] The changes paid dividends. The third week of May, Schalk became the regular catcher and responded immediately. In his first week in the role, he laced a home run at St. Paul and the next day, in Minneapolis, the rising star ripped a triple against a fading star, 35-year-old future Hall of Famer Rube Waddell. By mid–June, the Brewers considered their previous starting catcher expendable. On June 20 they sold Doc Marshall to St. Paul. (Marshall returned to the Brewers in 1913.)[22] "Hugh Duffy has concluded, after some disastrous experience, that all teams can not win in the Association with has-beens, and he announces he is going to build up with young blood."[23] The Brewers moved up one notch in the standings but remained in the second division — and did so amid public acrimony between the manager and everyone else associated with the team, including his players and the owner, the Widow Havenor.[24] Few could not notice that the Brewers were a dispirited bunch. "Day in and day out, Harry Clark and Phil Lewis have been the only members of the team who let any sort of chirrup out of them," complained sportswriter "Brownie" in the *Milwaukee Journal*. "Almost every inning after the third saw the fans leaving in scores," he reported. "So far this season the Milwaukee fans have been inclined to be pretty patient, but a few more exhibitions like those of yesterday and even the grass will start growing hammers. A lot of things can be overlooked when a team is fighting every inch of the way, but with a half-hearted exhibition like that of yesterday there is no excuse. Manager Duffy is still sticking to the bench with an injured leg, but even that does not excuse the lack of fighting spirit in this team."[25] The Brewers were not the center of the only controversy in Milwaukee in the summer of 1912. After a protracted debate, the city's park board relented and allowed a new type of music to be performed at public park band concerts — but only occasionally. It was called Ragtime.[26]

About the only bright spot for the 1912 Brewers was 19-year-old Ray Schalk, who in a matter of weeks progressed from promising reserve catcher to subject of a bidding war. He put on a memorable show — even when his decisions were not by the book. Batting in the fifth inning with a teammate on third, Schalk twice swung and missed. On a 1–2 count, Schalk surprised Indianapolis pitcher Ashenfelder and his infield by laying down a perfect bunt. The baserunner scored and Schalk reached first unchallenged. "Every player will tell you that it's the worst kind of baseball to try to bunt with two strikes on you, but they will also admit that anything is good if you get away with it," the *Milwaukee Journal* stated. "So we'll have to hand it to Ray. But what a panning he would have come in for it he hadn't slipped it across."[27]

By early June, Charles Comiskey's friend and associate Ted Sullivan started scouting Schalk. The White Sox had hoped to land catcher/utility man Charles "Dutch" Sterrett, but he signed with the New York Highlanders.[28] So the Sox were taking a look at a prospect recom-

As a teen, Schalk started to pursue a career in printing. He went to New York for a two-month course in typesetting machine operation. But when he learned that his apprenticeship in a Litchfield newspaper office would last longer than he expected, he decided to forgo publishing for baseball (photograph courtesy Lillian Hendricks).

mended to them two years earlier by Pants Rowland. By mid–July 1912, several major-league teams were checking out Schalk and submitting offers for the teenager's contract. His manager, Duffy, pronounced Schalk "the best catcher in the country"— a statement perhaps calculated to up the ante for the backstop.[29] Added the *Boston Globe*, "Bids for the youngster — he is only 20 [*sic*] years old — are reported to be going up fast."[30] As many as a half-dozen major-league teams — including Cincinnati, Pittsburgh, St. Louis Browns and the White Sox — entered the Schalk Sweepstakes. Meanwhile, the Brewers were anxious to make a sale; they stood to make a tidy one-year profit after purchasing the option from Detroit and Schalk's contract from Taylorville.[31] Robert L. Hedges, owner of the St. Louis American League club, traveled to Milwaukee to see Schalk for himself. "If the sample shown yesterday doesn't bring forth a substantial bid," Brownie stated, "then it's because St. Louis doesn't need a first-class catcher." Toledo was visiting the Brewers, and scouts were also checking out Mud Hens shortstop Ray Chapman, who grew up in Herrin, a Southern Illinois mining community about 120 miles from Schalk's hometown. In the July 17 contest, Schalk threw out a half-dozen would-be base stealers. From the Milwaukee point of view, he would have recorded a seventh victim — Chapman — had Umpire Irwin made a correct decision at third base in the 11th inning of a 3–3 game. "Schalk's throw was perfect; it was close to the ground and Clarke received it in such a manner that he did not have to make a move to get his man, for to reach the base Chapman had to slide over the ball," the Milwaukee sportswriter observed. "(Pitcher) Dougherty lost his temper, as did everyone else, and Burns' homer followed." Chapman, who had two hits, and the Mud Hens withstood a Milwaukee rally in the bottom of the 11th to claim a 5–4 win.[32] The next day, Chapman again tried to steal third; this time, Schalk got his man. "Perhaps Manager (Topsy) Hartsell will learn before his team leaves here that stealing bases is not quite so easy with Schalk throwing the way he is just now," Brownie mused.[33] (Schalk and Chapman were just weeks from promotion to the majors.)

The Brewers' anger with that umpire was nothing compared to that of fans the same afternoon in Wilkes-Barre, Pennsylvania, where an umpire by the name of Cleary was swarmed by about 2,000 angry home-team rooters. At the game's unhappy conclusion, seven state police officers, using their clubs, beat back the mob and rushed Cleary to his dressing room, where angry patrons milled outside for two hours. Finally, police cleared the grounds.[34]

As July turned to August 1912, bidders for Schalk's services fell by the wayside. To no one's surprise, Comiskey, owner of the Chicago White Sox, took the inside track. He had the deep pockets and personnel to maintain Milwaukee's interest. On August 9, 1912, the White Sox and Brewers struck a deal for the 19-year-old. "The details of the sale will not be given out for a few days, but will include three players, the equivalent of $15,000," the *Milwaukee Journal* reported. "This is said to be the largest price ever paid for a green catcher."[35] Comiskey, however, was not anxious to reveal the amount of cash involved, lest that detail create exceedingly high expectations among Sox fans and place undue pressure on the new acquisition. The same day they acquired Schalk, the White Sox purchased 24-year-old Dennis Berran, a little-known outfielder from St. John (New Brunswick).[36] Both made their major-league debuts two days later. While Schalk would appear in 1,755 games, Berran's major-league career started and ended the same day.[37]

When the Schalk deal was consummated, the Brewers were in Louisville.

"Schalk was the center of interest this morning and he was loaded down with advice, good and otherwise, by his teammates," noted the *Milwaukee Journal*, which quoted Manager Duffy: "I am very pleased with the deal. And I also think that the Milwaukee fans will be when they learn who the men are that we are to get, as I figure that they will be a great big help to the team." The Sox immediately sent Milwaukee reserve infielder Russell "Lena" Blackburne, back-up catcher James "Bruno" Block, and, reportedly, $10,000 in cash. Though demoted from the majors to minors, both players expressed pleasure with the deal, because it would allow them to play rather than sit the bench.[38] Blackburne had appeared in only five games for the White Sox that season, while Block had 46 appearances as the second-string backstop.[39] The deal also included two White Sox players to be named later. Later that month, Chicago sent the Brewers 32-year-old outfielder Matty McIntyre; minor leaguer Mutz Ens was thrown in during the off-season.[40]

Even after the deal was announced, Schalk played one more game for the Brewers, going hitless in a 5–2 win.[41] His final American Association batting average dipped to .271.[42] He then caught an evening train for Chicago.[43] "Of course, I am sorry to leave Milwaukee. They have always treated me fine here," Schalk told a Milwaukee sportswriter. "But I am glad to be able to advance in my profession, and you can bet that I am going to make the most of my chances."[44]

3

"Here is your pitcher, Doc White"

After his train from Louisville arrived in Chicago, Schalk found his way to 35th Street and Shields Avenue — Comiskey Park and White Sox offices. Accounts vary as to whether it was this day or the next when Schalk met his new employer, White Sox owner Charles Comiskey. In any case, the youngster received permission to return to Milwaukee, wrap up his affairs and return to Chicago in time for the next day's game. His tasks in Milwaukee included a meeting with Brewers owner Agnes Havenor, who no doubt conveyed to Schalk her sincere thanks. As well she should have. After all, the Brewers turned a tidy profit in the year (covering portions of two seasons) they held his contract. In selling Schalk's services to the White Sox, Milwaukee received roughly a ten-fold return on its investment — $15,000 in cash and personnel. That windfall helped the Brewers' war chest for the 1913 season, when they won the American Association title and went on to defeat the Denver Bears in their "little world series."

The day that Schalk arrived in Chicago, spectators braved a steady rain to line the Chicago River for the Illinois Athletic Club's fifth annual marathon, a 2.75-mile swimming event. Chicago native William R. Vosburg, a star on the University of Illinois squad, claimed the title in a grueling and dangerous endeavor that involved more than an hour of swimming. Only 19 of the 45 competitors finished. Three swimmers were pulled from the water unconscious. Two had crossed the finish line, while the third, Ottmar J. Links, suffered a blow to the head from a support boat. All survived. Another noteworthy swimming performance was turned in by a man named Evers, who placed sixth despite having but one leg. Elsewhere in Chicago, city leaders, health officials and local pastors were campaigning to reinstate ordinances setting standards for milk inspection and pasteurization. Chicagoans learned that the rise in infant deaths in the previous years was attributed to impure milk. Meanwhile, more than 2,000 street and "L" (elevated) railway workers on the brink of a strike gathered in Brand's Park. The agenda called for a picnic and protest of their shoddy treatment by their employers. However, the event suddenly became a celebration when their leaders announced a favorable contract agreement.[1]

On that soggy Saturday, Schalk's future team was to host the defending world champion Philadelphia Athletics in a doubleheader. It had also rained the previous day, when the Sox eked out a 7–6 win. The Comiskey Park playing surface, despite having its infield under canvas, showed Mother Nature's effects. The conditions notwithstanding, when some 8,000 fans showed up, Sox management labored to allow the game to be played. Rain washed out pre-game warm-ups, but when it let up, the grounds crew — complemented by a half-dozen Chicago players — dragged the cover off the infield. Still, mud lined the outer edge of the diamond and puddles marked the outfield. The crew did what it could with the field, and Sox starter Joe Benz delivered the first pitch just 15 minutes behind schedule. The A's battered Benz and held an 8–0 lead when the Sox starter departed in the top of the fifth inning. In the top of the sixth, rain returned with serious intent, bringing an end to that game — it went into the books as a weather-shortened Philadelphia victory — and postponing the day's second game until the next day, when a doubleheader would be contested.[2]

The rain ended in the early hours of Sunday, August 11. The sky turned fair and the temperature settled in the mid- to high 60s, a half-dozen degrees below average for a summer day in Chicago. Readers of the *Chicago Sunday Tribune* that morning read about the swimming competition, milk purity and labor peace. They were also enlightened with the opinions of a Chicago neurologist, who suggested that contemporary males behave more like their forebears, the cavemen. In a front-page article, "Jealous Women Need Whipping," the *Tribune* summarized an article in *Alienist and Neurologist* by Dr. William F. Waugh, dean of Bennett Medical College and chief physician at Jefferson Park Hospital. "Some women require beating," the Chicagoan wrote. "Lacking it, they escape from the husband's control and are incapable of controlling themselves." (Despite those pronouncements, and though the American Medical Association later linked his medical school to admissions fraud, Waugh was still respected in his field died six years later when he at age 69.[3])

Schalk concluded his business in Milwaukee and hopped a train back to Chicago. He took a streetcar to Comiskey Park for the doubleheader. After reporting to the team office, he was sent to the locker room. As he departed, Comiskey ordered someone to accompany him, lest the young man lose his way.[4] Some of his new teammates, gazing upon an undersized teenager — who even looked young for his age — no doubt wondered if the unfamiliar face belonged to a new batboy. Before putting him into the lineup, player-manager James "Nixey" Callahan decided to see for himself what Schalk could do. Either the day before or day of Schalk's first game, Callahan summoned Big Ed Walsh, the ironman spitballer, to throw to Schalk. Walsh, who would win 27 games and pitch nearly 400 innings in the final quality season of his Hall of Fame career, unleashed everything in his repertoire. Walsh was not particularly interested in smoothing the way for the kid. After the demonstration, however, Callahan walked up to Schalk and said, "I'll think you'll do, kid." Accounts varied with the telling and retelling over the years, but the story was that Comiskey also had his doubts about his undersized newcomer. Schalk quoted the owner asking the manager, "But can he catch Ed Walsh?" Callahan was emphatic: "Boss, he can catch Ed Walsh in a *rocking chair!*"[5] Could Comiskey really have had second thoughts about the prospect that cost him a whopping $15,000 in a bidding war? It seems doubtful, but Schalk's diminutive stature caught many baseball experts off-guard. Though the tales of the tape varied, most accounts had Schalk weighing as little as 140

pounds and no more than 150 pounds when he reported for major-league duty. In any case, Callahan believed in him.[6]

A few minutes before Schalk was to witness his first major-league game ever, he learned that he would do so as a combatant. Callahan told him, "Young man, here's your pitcher, Doc White. You're the catcher."[7] Until he entered Cooperstown, Schalk classified the afternoon of his first major-league game as his greatest thrill in baseball.[8] It was August 11, 1912 — the day before his 20th birthday. The lad from Litchfield, who at the start of the previous season was still playing as a semi-pro, was taking his position in the "Baseball Palace of the World."[9] Recalling his debut, Schalk in one instance stated, "I didn't

James "Nixey" Callahan (shown here in 1913) was Schalk's first manager (1912–14). On Schalk's first day in uniform, Callahan put the 19-year-old into the starting lineup to catch the legendary Doc White (Library of Congress, Prints & Photographs Division, Bain Collection, LC-B2-2755-11).

On his first day in a White Sox uniform (August 11, 1912), Schalk was the start-
ing catcher. The pitcher was veteran G. Harris "Doc" White. A licensed dentist,
White pitched a record five straight shutouts in 1904 (Library of Congress, Prints
& Photographs Division, Bain Collection, LC-B2-2428-4).

even have a chance to get scared."[10] Another time, he confessed that his hands shook and he was nearly paralyzed with fright.[11]

Though the rain of previous two days had departed, conditions at Comiskey Park field remained slippery and muddy. Here and there, crews dumped sawdust in hopes it would absorb the wet spots and improve traction.

In his first major-league at-bat, leading off the bottom of the third inning, Schalk faced future Hall of Fame pitcher Charles "Chief" Bender, a 6-foot-2 right-hander. Schalk ripped a hard grounder to the right of Philadelphia third baseman Frank "Home Run" Baker. However, Baker made a one-handed snag of the ball and a quick throw to nip the sprinting Schalk at first. Later, Schalk drew a walk and made another out. The ninth inning opened with trailing, 9–4. Schalk singled — his first major-league hit — and came around to score his first major-league run.[12] Though the White Sox sent Bender to the showers, their rally stalled after two runs. Final score: Philadelphia 9, Chicago 6. (In several interviews over the years, Schalk incorrectly recalled the score as being 3–1.) Defensively, he recorded two putouts and three assists and committed no errors. Reviews were positive. "Schalk made a nice debut," Matt Foley of the *Inter-Ocean* commented, and his colleague Harry Daniel, noting that Comiskey paid $15,000 for Schalk's services, added, "He did some clever work behind the bat and rapped a blow in the ninth that was worth at least $4 of the purchase price."[13]

After losing the second game of the doubleheader to the defending champions, the White Sox had to play a make-up game the next day in Cleveland and then a series in Washington. Callahan took 15 players to Cleveland. The rest — including Schalk — traveled directly to Washington under the supervision of first-year coach Kid Gleason.

Not all baseball news that day occurred on the field. Ty Cobb, the Detroit Tigers star, suffered a stab wound and bruises when attacked by three muggers in Detroit. Cobb, who was on his way to the train depot for an exhibition game in Syracuse, New York, escaped serious injury. "The ball player's agility saved him from a bad beating and perhaps death," a wire service reported.[14] Some speculated that the beating was payback for Cobb's record of unmannerly ways, but no evidence of that motive emerged. Earlier that season, in Chicago, Cobb refused to play against the White Sox after a quarrel with management of the Chicago Beach Hotel about the location of his room; it was too close to railroad tracks. His biggest on-field blowup occurred May 15 in New York. After enduring three days of abusive remarks from spectators at Hilltop Park, Cobb early in the fourth game entered the grandstand and pummeled a spectator he believed had instigated that day's flurry of insults. Cobb said the same spectator hurled insults on other occasions.[15] Like many white Americans of the day, Cobb was a lifelong racist. He finally exploded when he heard a catcall, in graphic terms, suggesting that he was half African American. Cobb leaped over the grandstand railing, waded through the crowd, found the spectator and repeatedly punched, kicked and spiked him. The patron was an office clerk named Claude Lueker.[16] A former printing press operator who had lost three fingers on one hand and the other hand entirely, Mr. Lueker claimed he did not initiate the insults but only joined in after Cobb responded with "vile language." (A few days earlier, in the same ballpark, Cobb accepted a loving cup from Yankees fans in tribute to his 1911 batting title. In that day's contest, it was umpire Silk O'Loughlin who was the target of fans' abuse. It required squads of policemen to protect the arbiter.[17])

When American League President Ban Johnson, who was in attendance at the game, suspended Cobb, the rest of the Detroit team, after taking a 6–3 win in Philadelphia, declared itself on strike until Cobb secured reinstatement. An hour before game time, after engaging in a vigorous workout, the Tigers walked off the field. In anticipation of a strike, Detroit management had lined up replacement players, who immediately put on the uniforms the strikers had removed minutes earlier. The team consisted of Philadelphia amateurs, recently released professionals and coaches. After these "Tigers" suffered a 24–2 shellacking — the defending world champions apparently took it easy on the misfits — Johnson declared that Detroit would not play again until it fielded its regulars. Cobb reportedly urged his teammates to not make it worse for themselves and to end the work stoppage. That move might have resulted in some leniency from Johnson, who adjudged Cobb at fault but limited his punishment to a 10-day suspension and $50 fine. His striking teammates were fined $100 each. However, American League owners agreed step up security in their ballparks and show less tolerance of abusive spectators.[18] As the saga played out, and there was speculation whether other teams would join the Tigers in sympathy, White Sox manager Callahan sympathized with Cobb's situation — to a point — but declared that the White Sox would not join in any strike. Noting that harassment from the stands is commonplace, Callahan added, "The gambling element is usually the one which indulge in this sort of abuse."[19]

Three months after that Cobb episode, in mid–August 1912, Callahan's team was well-stocked with catchers. Two days before they acquired Schalk — and sent one of their back-up catchers, Bruno Block, to Milwaukee in the deal — Comiskey bought 27-year-old backstop Ted Easterly from Cleveland. Chicago's regular catcher in 1912 was Walt "Red" Kuhn, a rookie who appeared in half the Sox games that season. Another back-up catcher was 37-year-old

Billy Sullivan Sr., a one-time Sox star and manager (1909) in his last season of regular service. (The next season, Schalk vaulted into the starter's role and became an ironman; Kuhn appeared in only 24 games.)[20]

Schalk's second big-league start, in Washington, featured a celebrity spectator. President William Howard Taft entered Griffith Park shortly after the game began. Taft, who a few months earlier inaugurated the tradition of throwing out the ceremonial first pitch on Opening Day, stopped at the Nationals (Senators) bench and shook hands with Manager Clark Griffith before taking his seat and watching the White Sox win, 5–3. (In the 1920s, when Taft was chief justice of the U.S. Supreme Court, the former president accorded Schalk a favor — his signature on a special baseball. Eventually, Schalk's baseball would bear the signatures of eight U.S. presidents; he donated it to the National Baseball Hall of Fame.)

White Sox management was glad to have landed Schalk toward the end of the 1912 campaign, but as far as some veterans were concerned, the highly touted kid had some things to prove. The workhorse of the Chicago pitching staff (and of the entire American League) was Ed Walsh, a product of the hard-bitten Pennsylvania coal country. From 1906 through 1912, Walsh averaged 321 innings pitched. In 1908, he went 40–15 and logged an incredible 464 innings, which a century later still stands as the American League record. Standing 6-foot-1 and weighing 193 pounds, the Big Reel dwarfed the new catcher. Walsh and Schalk started as a battery for the first time in Chicago on September 1, 1912. It is possible that this was the game when Walsh, a nine-year veteran, intended to put the 20-year-old in his place. Perhaps he had heard management's claim that Schalk could catch him while "sitting in a rocking chair." Pitch after pitch, Walsh either shook off Schalk's signs or ignored them altogether. The catcher dropped the sign for a fastball ... and Walsh delivered a spitter. If Schalk called for a curve, Walsh threw a fastball. "After the fourth inning I went to (coach) Kid Gleason about it and explained that unless Walsh and I could get together on our signals, it might cost us the ball game," Schalk wrote years later. Accounts vary on what happened next. One story had a frustrated Schalk confronting Big Ed on the mound: "Listen you big stiff! I'm not giving any more signs. You throw the ball — I'll catch it!"[21] In an article under his own byline, Schalk said Gleason advised him to just stop flashing signs. "I did that and from then on I didn't call for anything," Schalk wrote, "but just caught what he threw." Schalk handled everything the future Hall of Famer fired his way. With that episode, Schalk said, he earned Walsh's respect and trust. "From that point on Big Ed and I never had any trouble."[22] Before season's end, Walsh made it known that he wanted Schalk to catch whenever he was on the mound.[23]

When Schalk saw his first major-league game, he had a great vantage point: right behind the plate, as the starting catcher for the Chicago White Sox on August 11, 1912. He was one day shy of his 20th birthday (Library of Congress, Prints and Photographs Division, National Photo Company Collection, LC-F81-685).

Schalk had troubles of his own in one of his few starts after his promotion. In the first game of the final White Sox homestand of the season, with his team leading 3–2, he committed back-to-back errors in Detroit's half of the eighth inning. He appeared to tag out the tying run, but dropped the ball. Retrieving the sphere, he attempted to throw out a Tiger advancing to third — and tossed wildly, permitting the go-ahead run to score. Walsh allowed Detroit to extend its lead to 6–3 in the ninth by "forgetting that Schalk was neither tall nor rangy, and shooting a high one out of the kid's clutches." However, with one out in the bottom of the ninth, Chicago responded with four straight singles against starter Ed Willett to make the score 6–5. Jean Dubuc was summoned to relieve, and with a Chicago player on third, the right-hander responded with a wild pitch to send the game into extra innings. With two away in the 10th — the first out was Schalk, who went 0-for-4 — Dubuc gave up a single, a stolen base, and infield hit before unleashing another wild pitch. Final score: Chicago 7, Detroit 6. "If Schalk would apply his name to his fingers just before tagging a runner it might help him hold on to the ball," quipped the *Chicago Tribune*'s Irv Sanborn, referring to poolroom chalk, "but the youngster will learn how, never fear, without any assistance from outsiders."[24]

Though they rebounded in that contest, the White Sox had trouble closing out their 1912 campaign. At the start of the season, they were expected to be in rebuilding mode, but initially they exceeded expectations, going 23–6 and opening a 5½-game lead in the American League standings by the middle of May. However, long before Schalk arrived, the Sox started a five-month free-fall. Even the addition of Eddie Cicotte, acquired in July from the Boston Red Sox, was not enough. They went 55–70 the rest of the way — and that included a five-game win streak to conclude the regular season. Chicago fell from first to fourth and finished 28 games behind the champion Red Sox.

The White Sox' first trip to St. Louis after the Schalk acquisition was a big deal for the recruit and his supporters. Some 200 fans from the Litchfield area made the 50-mile trip for the September 26 game. They planned to present him a gold watch.[25] However, the day was frosty, and Browns officials also feared their gate would be hurt by competition from a local fair and horse races, so they postponed the game. "Only those of the White Sox who had brought overcoats or heavy sweaters ventured to accept the invitation to the races and sideshows of the St. Louis fair," Sanborn noted. The underdressed stayed in the hotel or dashed to the theater nearby. Schalk did neither. He received permission to return to Litchfield with the delegation and overnight there. The group included one person of particular interest. Sanborn had some fun with that tidbit: "Included in the Litchfield delegation was a dainty moving picture of Sweet Sixteen, who may have been Schalk's sister or cousin, but appearances indicated a possible closer relationship in the near future. However, that may be, Schalk will be on hand to catch tomorrow if needed."[26] After spending time with Miss Lavinia Graham, Schalk did rejoin the team the next day for its doubleheader sweep. He made a cameo appearance in Game 1 and went 1-for-3 in the second contest.[27]

The blow of the Sox' disappointing season was softened with a come-from-behind victory over the Cubs in the Chicago City Series. After two rainouts and two ties, including a scoreless affair in which Walsh allowed the Cubs but one hit, the Sox fell to a 3–0 deficit in the best-of-seven series. The South Siders rallied to take the last four contests, wrapping up city bragging rights with a 16–0 shellacking of the Cubs. The one-sided nature of the deciding contest fueled rumors that the Cubs gave up to punish their employer and show support for lame-duck manager Frank Chance, who forcefully defended his players against owner Charles Murphy's charges of "loose living and dissipation." Murphy announced that Chance's services would not be required after the conclusion of the season.[28] Chance, who a couple of months later became manager of the New York Yankees, vigorously denied the whispers about a thrown City Series, noting that a prolonged series helped Murphy and the loss hurt the individual Cubs' pocketbooks. No substantiation of the rumors surfaced.[29]

The offensive leaders of the 1912 White Sox were John "Shano" Collins, who batted .292 and was first in runs batted in (81) and hits (168), and Frank "Ping" Bodie (born Francesco Stephano Puzzullo), who hit .294. Bodie, who served as the inspiration for sportswriter Ring Lardner's "You Know Me Al" series, was a free spirit whose performance on the basepaths left much to be desired. In that vein, columnist Bugs Baer said of Bodie, "There was larceny in his heart, but his feet were honest."[30]

In his first taste of the major leagues — 23 regular-season games in 1912 — Schalk batted .286. It was the highest average of his White Sox career, though involving just 63 at-bats. (In his complete seasons to follow, he twice topped .280, in 1919 and 1922.) He continued to practice and develop his defense. Coach Gleason and veteran catcher Sullivan worked with him many mornings, teaching him to more effectively block pitches in the dirt and come up throwing to nail baserunners trying to steal.[31] "Ray Schalk is the cheapest ball player ever purchased, even if President Comiskey of the White Sox paid $10,000 for him," Gleason declared. "He is worth a fortune to any team, and his value will be realized as he matures in major-league experience."[32] Schalk also visited Schorling Park, home of Chicago's American Giants, a leading Negro League team, to learn from Bruce Petway, arguably the best catcher, of any color, anywhere.[33]

During the winter of 1912–13, Schalk returned to Litchfield, where he captained the town's basketball team and spent time with Lavinia.[34] Though they were optimistic about their high-priced prospect, White Sox officials considered Schalk their second-string catcher for 1913. Kuhn was to remain the starter. "The contract of Red Kuhn reminded me that I have a great little catcher in him," Callahan said, "one who will play a much improved game from that of last year because of his experience of one year in the big leagues." The manager added, "It looked as if we grabbed a live catcher in young Schalk last fall and he is bound to be better this year."[35]

4

"Cracker"

Aside from the obvious "Red" or "Lefty," or the politically incorrect "Dummy" (hearing impaired) or "Chief" (Native American), determining the origin of ballplayer nicknames is challenging. Soon after he joined the White Sox, Schalk received the nickname that would stick with him the rest of his life: "Cracker." One explanation of the nickname's origin is that John "Shano" Collins, observing the diminutive Schalk's throwing ability, exclaimed, "Look at that squirt *crack* the ball to second!"[1] Another version — and perhaps the more accurate one — is that someone in the White Sox clubhouse spied Schalk on his first day with the team and asked, "Who's the little cracker pants?"[2] Thereafter, he was known as "Cracker."

After two winters in Texas, the White Sox returned to California for their 1913 spring training. It would be Schalk's first time in a major-league preseason camp. The Sox set up shop in the resort community of Paso Robles, between Los Angeles and San Francisco, which was noted for its therapeutic hot springs and recreational opportunities. The team's hotel, El Paso de Robles Hotel (later the Paso Robles Inn), was a popular destination for notables in sports, politics and entertainment. Guests included world-renowned Polish pianist Ignace Paderewski, boxer Jack Dempsey, Theodore Roosevelt and actors Douglas Fairbanks, Boris Karloff, Bob Hope and Clark Gable. The hotel's hot springs bathhouse, decorated with marble and ceramic tile, was considered the country's most elegant facility of its type.[3] "Civilization has touched the Pacific coast," Chicago sportswriter Sam Weller told the folks back home. "In changing a $20 bill we were handed two $1 bills along with the handful of silver and gold."[4]

After the Sox defeated Oakland, the defending Pacific Coast League champion, 9–3, Weller reported, "The best part of the game was the paid attendance. Somewhere near 4,000 persons gave up silver and gold to help Comiskey pay the expenses of this elaborate training trip. There were 300 or 400 small boys spread out on the grass, but no one cared if they did crawl through the fence, for the box office had its fill of coin."[5]

The training camp featured some leisurely contests, including a split-squad affair against a Paso Robles team on a brilliant California afternoon. The Chicagoans bolstered the home team's roster with a few of their players, including catcher Billy Sullivan. Callahan kept Schalk for his team.[6] The manager had plenty of catchers: Schalk, Sullivan, Kuhn, Ted Easterly and John "Dick" Gossett. A few weeks later, in Riverside, the White Sox thrashed White Tree, starting pitcher of the Sherman Indians. Schalk was Chicago's offensive leader, collecting four hits. Nearly a century later, the meaningless tune-up game is forgotten, but the newspaper account reflected the attitude and approach of white-owned newspapers of the day. The lead headline, "White Sox Scalp Indians,"

When Schalk joined the White Sox late in 1912, the team needed a catcher to succeed aging star Billy Sullivan (above). Coach Kid Gleason and Sullivan conducted workouts with Schalk to develop his defense. Photograph dated 1911 (Library of Congress, Prints & Photographs Division, Bain Collection, LOT 13830-24).

was followed by the subheadline, "Callahans Swing War Clubs for Victory by 14–3 Score." The article opened, "Those White Sox did the war dance around the Sherman Indians this afternoon...." The reporter noted that the game could have been even more lopsided, but in the late innings the Chicagoans eased up and "decided the scalping was sufficient for one day's work."[7]

All through professional baseball, spring training was an occasion for teams to observe prospects they had not seen before — literally. Relying only on scouts' recommendations, teams often mailed or wired contract proposals and invitations to tryouts. In 1912, Manager Pennington of the Kewanee (Illinois) Boilermakers became curious about a new outfielder named George. The kid didn't look ready, not for even the low minors. Eventually, it came out that his cousin was the one who had received the mailed contract. The cousin decided he didn't want to play ball, and he turned over the contract to his relative. "The counterfeit was discovered," *The Sporting News* noted, "and George was let out with the kindly admonition not to do it again."[8]

As the White Sox departed California, ventured deep into the heart of

Texas and played their way back north for the start of the regular season, Schalk emerged as the winner of the catching derby. The team's roster — before the required in-season reduction to 25 players — still featured five back-stops, though the veteran Sullivan, expected to serve as an unofficial assistant coach to work with the young pitchers, was virtually guaranteed a roster slot. By the end of April, without seeing any playing time and as teams faced further roster cuts, the 22-year-old Gossett became Chicago's odd man out. Sold to the Yankees, he appeared in only 48 games before he and New York parted ways midway through the next season.[9]

In the season opener, a 3–1 loss at Cleveland, Schalk affirmed management's decision to put him in the starting lineup by throwing out all three baserunners who attempted to steal second.[10] Thus began his team-record streak of 15 consecutive Opening-Day starts. However, the star of the game was Naps outfielder Joe Jackson, who made two doubles, a triple and a game-saving catch. In 1913, the American League took steps to try to speed up games. After the first contest of the year, the jury remained out. The game consumed one hour, 45 minutes — right in the ballpark for duration. "No one hit any long fouls down in the corners of the field, so the new rule prohibiting the retrieving of them immediately was not tried out," the *Tribune* noted. "However, Silk O'Loughlin tossed out a new ball every time a foul tip went back to the grandstand."[11]

Though Schalk went hitless in the season opener, he immediately went on a hot streak, collecting 10 hits in his next 16 at-bats and raising his season average to .500. "If any one man was marked for the glory of the afternoon it was little Ray Schalk, who continues to do such wonderful things for the Sox that he is the talk of every game," sportswriter Weller noted after the catcher collected three hits, including two doubles, in St. Louis on April 16. Schalk's ninth-inning single broke a 1–1 tie, and the White Sox prevailed, 3–2.

The next day, the White Sox staged their 1913 home opener. It was a sun-drenched Thursday afternoon at Comiskey Park, one permitting "the boys with ice cold soda pop to open the season with big profits." A brass band and "megaphone sextet" entertained the crowd, estimated at 25,000, for more than an hour in pre-game festivities. Schalk took part in the first-pitch ceremony by accepting the toss from Chicago Mayor Carter Harrison, Jr. Thanks to two miscues by Cleveland's Ray Chapman — a fielding error and his failure to touch first base after rapping an apparent double — the hosts prevailed, 2–1. Both Chicago runs came in the second inning. With no one out and Buck Weaver, who had just batted in the initial run, on first and Wally Mattick leading off third, Schalk smashed the ball to third baseman Ivy Olson, whose snatch of the screamer surprised Mattick between third and home. Olson threw to catcher Grover Land, whose throw back to Olson was so wild that Mattick snuck back to third. Weaver high-tailed it back to second and Schalk scrambled back to first, leaving the bases loaded. Cleveland retired the next two batters without allowing a score, but then shortstop Chapman booted Morrie Rath's grounder.[12]

Though he went 0-for-3 in the home opener, then only 1-for-11 and sat out three games, Schalk warmed up again and concluded April hitting .333. That was sufficient to attract national attention for the man who had yet to reach his 21st birthday.

The *Chicago Tribune*'s Harvey T. Woodruff produced an extensive biographical piece, accompanied by an artist's portrait and cartoons. "Although the smallest backstop in the big leagues," Woodruff wrote, "he is called the most promising and smartest youngster who has come up from the minors in recent years." Another sportswriter quoted his manager, Callahan: "Schalk cost a lot of money, but he's worth it. I think he will develop into the best backstop in the country."[13]

For his *Tribune* article, Woodruff put Schalk on the spot with a few personal questions:

> "Are you married?" the writer inquired of Schalk.
> "No," he promptly replied.
> "Have a girl, I suppose?"
> Schalk blushed.
> "Going to get married soon?"
> "I don't know what you call soon," replied the catcher, and we let it go at that.

"Soon," it turned out, was three years away.

Displaced as Chicago's No. 1 catcher, Red Kuhn faced other difficulties besides losing his starting role. He "contracted a bad cold over in Cleveland, and he was in the hands of Trainer Buckner riding from Cleveland (to St. Louis)," the *Tribune* noted. "Buckner fixed up a hot toddy for Red just before tucking him in the berth, and immediately a dozen fellows in the car began to cough."[14] One of the first and few African Americans to hold a position of any responsibility in a major-league organization, William Buckner was more an equipment manager than an athletic trainer, though Buckner took great pride in developing home remedies and massaging and manipulating achy and uncooperative limbs and joints.

In this, the "Deadball Era," when runs were at a premium, teams relied on singles, sacrifices, speed and, occasionally, subterfuge. Shortstop Buck Weaver was credited with preserving a White Sox victory April 23 over vis-

Schalk shown in 1913, his first full season in the majors, when he was 20 years old. Because of his diminutive stature and youthful features, opponents and fans were frequently surprised to learn that he was a player and not the White Sox batboy (Chicago History Museum, Chicago Daily News Collection, SDN-058694).

iting Detroit due to his ability as an actor. With one out in the top of the ninth, Detroit veteran George Moriarty attempted to steal second base as Doc White's pitch escaped Ted Easterly, who had started in Schalk's place. Moriarty was unaware of the passed ball, but Weaver was. The shortstop raced to the bag and pretended that Easterly's throw would make it a close play. Moriarty slid into second and Weaver, continuing his ruse, rolled onto the ground as if the ball had slipped away. By the time Moriarty figured out what was really going on, he was unable to advance to third. "This would have pulled the Chicago infielders close to cut off the tying run at the plate and would have put Moriarity [*sic*] in a position to score on a fly ball, for there was only one out," the *Tribune* explained. "With the infielders in close, the double play which ended the game after Vitt walked might never have taken place."[15] After his playing days ended, the victim in this episode, Moriarty, umpired in the American League from 1917 through 1940 — except for 1927 and 1928, when he succeeded Ty Cobb as Detroit manager.

The May 1913 issue of *Baseball Magazine* carried the first published list of members of the Baseball Players Fraternity, a labor organization formed the previous year and headed by player-turned-lawyer David L. Fultz. The membership list included 296 names, including that of Raymond Schalk.[16] Though the organization lasted a few years, it was weakened by the collapse of the short-lived Federal League (1914–15) and done in by the disruption wreaked by U.S. involvement in World War I.

After splitting their first 16 games of the 1913 season, the White Sox went into Detroit and feasted on the Tigers. Chicago won all five games, including a one-run and two extra-inning affairs. The series finale was a 6–4 decision in 11 innings. In the fourth inning, when the Tigers had runners on first and second, Cobb led a double-steal attempt. Schalk fired the ball to third baseman Harry Lord in plenty of time, a sportswriter observed, but the crafty Cobb safely dodged the tag. Schalk played the entire game and singled in the 11th, even though he was not feeling 100 percent. It seems that first baseman Babe Borton, Shano Collins and Schalk made a poor choice for a Detroit dining establishment. The players "forgot how far they were from salt water and ate some oysters with the result they were pretty sick last night," The *Tribune* noted, adding that Kid Gleason "played the role of doctor and had them on their feet today."[17] Less than a month later, the Sox shipped the 24-year-old Borton, along with 29-year-old infielder Rollie Zeider, to the New York Yankees in exchange for Hal Chase, whose legacy included disrupting team chemistry, gambling and throwing ball games. Borton and Zeider were never Hall of Fame material, but acquiring Chase was one of Chicago owner Charles Comiskey's most ill-advised trades. Before the next season was half over, Chase had bolted the team to join Buffalo in the Federal League.

The Chase acquisition had yet to occur when the White Sox hosted Frank Chance Day at Comiskey Park on May 17, 1913. It was an opportunity for Chicago fans to pay tribute to the former manager of the Cubs in his first visit to the city since he was unceremoniously dumped by the West Siders.

Events included an automobile parade that stretched nearly two miles. Despite threatening weather, a huge crowd arrived early and massed outside the ballpark. Attendance that day would be nearly 36,000, accommodated by temporary grandstands constructed in anticipation of the event. As White Sox employee Maurice Kohn opened a heavy metal gate to admit the crowd, the crush of humanity caught his left hand in the gate. Kohn lost his index finger. Dr. James H. Blair dressed the wound and saw to it that Kohn got home.

Shortly afterward, sections of the temporary grandstands collapsed all around the ballpark. Most of the stands were no more than 27 inches above the ground. Among the spectators, Miss Mary Bain fainted and went home in an ambulance. A Mrs. Jewel suffered a bruised leg and departed. A man who refused to tell reporters his name was moved to the Sox bench; he woke up and stuck around to watch the game. A section above the Yankees dugout collapsed in the fifth inning, depositing a Miss Minnie Cummings among the visitors. Shaken and hysterical, she was escorted home. "Before the game ended all except a small section of the wooden platform out near the right field foul line was flat on the ground," the *Tribune* reported. "Inspection showed that the upright supports of the platform were wholly inadequate to stand the strain put upon them by a restless throng of baseball rooters. The contractor must have thought he was building seats for a Chautauqua lecture." Comiskey wouldn't reveal the name of the contractor but stated that he had used him for similar projects several times.

As if that weren't enough excitement, fans were entertained by acrobats, contortionists, tumblers and trained dogs and monkeys. The players were so enthralled that they neglected to practice and had to start the contest without their usual warm-up. Even the umpires, Silk O'Loughlin and Charlie Ferguson, got into the act, donning white uniforms — reportedly a first in the major leagues.[18] (Ferguson and the guest of honor, Chance, were once teammates — sort of. In his only major-league appearance, Ferguson pitched two innings of relief in a late-season contest for the 1901 Chicago Orphans. Chance, a member of the team that would soon become known as the Cubs, did not play in Ferguson's game.[19])

Governor Edward F. Dunne and Mayor Harrison also were on hand, presenting Chance and Callahan with floral tributes. Comiskey arranged to have 300 policemen on hand to keep order, but they weren't needed. The fans kept in order — except for those who furtively pocketed the baseballs hit into the crowd. At afternoon's end, the fans went home happy: They paid tribute to Chance, who started and played an inning at first base, and they saw the White Sox come from behind to beat Chance's Yankees, 6–3. Schalk was hitless in three at-bats with a sacrifice. That evening, the White Sox and the Yankees got together again — for dinner and entertainment at the Chicago Stockyards.[20] New York catcher Jeff Sweeney said of his 20-year-old opposite on the White Sox: "It's saying a lot, I know, but Schalk comes near being the best catcher in the American League today." A sportswriter added his own observation: "He is a light-haired, bright-eyed, modest fellow, who doesn't seem to realize his importance."[21]

Unlike the minors, where he held his own in the batter's box, Schalk did not master major-league pitching. However, he had his bright spots. In Boston on June 4, he collected three singles in a winning cause. Ten days later, he recorded his first major-league home run. In the fifth inning at Washington, Schalk ripped a curveball from future Hall of Famer Walter Johnson toward the left-field corner. Howie Shanks made a valiant effort to make the catch but missed by a foot. By the time the ball was recovered and heaved home, the speedy Schalk had circled the bases. He notched another hit that afternoon, but Johnson and the Nationals prevailed, 8–3.[22]

When they departed the nation's capital, the White Sox stood four games above .500 (30–26) but a dozen games behind the red-hot Philadelphia Athletics (40–12). However, the Chicago squad showed mental lapses and uninspired play. "With few exceptions, the White Sox are not a foxy team," Chicago sportswriter I. E. Sanborn observed. "They are not pulling much defensive brain work against the opposing runners or batsmen and they are being tricked too easily by their opponents. There are not enough men on the team doing any thinking, leaving too much to the manager." Sanborn cited a promising exception. "Ray Schalk is fast gaining the confidence in himself that will enable him to do some thinking for the rest of the team, and everyone around the circuit is predicting a brilliant career for him. Ever since he got his bearings in fast company Schalk has not lost his own head. He is cool, apparently, and knows why he does everything. He is beginning to tell some of the rest of the bunch what to do. But when a catcher is up against a third baseman of Lord's experience and a first sacker like Chase, it is pretty strong for a kid catcher to take the initiative in pulling stuff with men on bases."[23]

However, Schalk did not always keep his cool with the umpires. His first big-league ejection occurred midway through a 3–2 loss one hot summer afternoon in Chicago. On June 28, 1913, veteran O'Loughlin excused the rookie for constant complaining about decisions on balls and strikes. This most likely was the occasion told and retold in feature stories and columns about Schalk over the years. With each telling, some facts fell by the wayside.[24] The gist of the story was that the 20-year-old commented, critiqued and complained on virtually every one of O'Loughlin's ball-and-strike calls. Finally, the arbiter had had enough. After the third out of the sixth inning, as Schalk started to the White Sox bench, O'Loughlin called after him. "Hey kid!" he said, getting the catcher's attention. "You've been a big help to me today. I don't know whether I could have made it this far without you. But I think I can go the rest of the way without you. Don't come back for the next inning."[25] O'Loughlin did the honors again a month later in Boston, where Schalk protested too much on an eighth-inning ruling on a tag play at the plate. Six months later, as he reported for spring training, Schalk didn't need much prodding to resume his lament that O'Loughlin blew that call.[26] Though he was tossed from a handful of games in his career, Schalk had a reputation for only complaining when he had a legitimate beef.

In his mid–June 1913 analysis of the White Sox, Sanborn made special mention of Schalk's feel for the game. "In one thing Schalk seems to have few equals among catchers. He never loses track of the ball, even when it is hit sharply over his head. He starts instinctively in the right direction, no matter whether there is a chance to get the foul or not. In this way he gains a step or two on such plays."[27]

Schalk's baseball instincts were further displayed June 23 against the visiting St. Louis Browns. With no one out in the top of the eighth inning of a tight game, St. Louis' Johnny Johnston tried to advance from first base to third on Jimmy Austin's bunt. Chicago third baseman Harry Lord had dashed in to the field the bunt and, with shortstop Buck Weaver covering second, it took Johnston just an instant to see that third base was unguarded. He made his break, now with Weaver running alongside. However, Schalk had the situation sized up, and he raced up the line to third base. First baseman Chase fired the ball toward third. Schalk grabbed the throw and dived at Johnston, "getting the verdict in sensational fashion."[28] The double-play contributed to Schalk's status as the No. 1 catcher in that category. (Some sources credit him with 18 DPs, others 21.)[29]

A few days earlier, Schalk had shown not only that he possessed speed and a head for the game, he also had the mettle. In Cleveland to play the Naps, a team acquiring a reputation for rough and dirty play, the White Sox took a 3–0 lead into the ninth inning. However, the hosts put runners on first and third with no one out. Then Nap Lajoie ripped the ball into left-center field. Both baserunners believed it was a sure hit — perhaps good for four bases — and took off. However, Wally Mattick staged a spectacular run from center field and made the catch. The runner heading toward the plate, Ivy Olson, retreated to re-touch third and, apparently forgetting that his run meant nothing at that point, again dashed for home. Weaver relayed Mattick's throw to Schalk, who waited patiently for Olson's arrival. Realizing that he would be an easy out at the plate, Olson jumped into Schalk with his spikes

Schalk models the "tools of ignorance" in 1913, his first full season with the White Sox, when he appeared in 125 of 153 games (Chicago History Museum, Chicago Daily News Collection, SDN-058376).

high, hitting the catcher well above the knee. Cut badly, Schalk nonetheless refused to leave the game. Trainer Buckner took several minutes to patch up Schalk, who then put on his mask and took his position. The next batter hit a comebacker to starting pitcher Eddie Cicotte, who tossed to Chase for the game's final out. "It is possible, of course, that Olson's work was unintentional, and the spiking of Schalk wholly accidental," Sanborn observed, "but the facts are the ethics of baseball always are against going into an opponent with one's feet so high in the air as to gouge a knee cap or puncture an eye.... So unless Olson can convince us he is much thicker in the dome than he is suspected to be, we shall continue to believe he deliberately tried to disable one of the crack catchers of the country and the gamest of the bunch."[30]

Schalk survived the attack and continued to impress. Two months later, in the second game of a doubleheader in New York, a foul tip dislocated a finger on Schalk's throwing hand. He allowed it to be yanked back into place — most likely, Buckner did the honors — and continued the game. In the first game that afternoon, Schalk rapped three hits and stole home. The theft, with two outs in the ninth of a 9–3 Chicago victory, surprised substitute catcher Bill Reynolds, who had made his major-league debut just two days earlier; he dropped the ball.[31]

However, Schalk's determined play could not push the White Sox into the first division, the top half of the eight-team American League. Four games above .500 in mid–June, they finished the season there (78–74, with one tie), winding up in fifth. Connie Mack's Athletics coasted to their third pennant in four seasons, and then swept John McGraw's New York Giants in the World Series.

Meanwhile, the White Sox and Cubs staged their sixth post-season City Series. Game 1 was set for the Cubs' ballpark on the west side of town. The White Sox changed into their uniforms at Comiskey Park and took taxis to the game. They won, 6–4. Schalk contributed offensively with a double, a single, two runs and a sixth-inning squeeze bunt. He bunted directly to pitcher Larry Cheney, who tried to throw out Shano Collins at the plate; his peg to Jimmy Archer was late, and the catcher couldn't hold onto the ball. Schalk's double might have been of the ground-rule variety. With attendance of just under 17,000, spectators occupied temporary bleachers set up in the outfield; the teams agreed that any ball hit into that area on the fly would be good for two bases only. The series featured something special — a crew of four umpires. One worked home plate, one covered the bases and two worked the outfield.[32]

The Cubs won the next two contests, a 13-inning thriller at Comiskey Park and then an 8–0 shellacking on the West Side. In Game 3, Schalk struck out twice against Bert Humphries and misplayed a wind-blown pop-up. However, the Sox rebounded, coming from behind to win Game 4 and then pushing across the game's only two runs in the top of Game 5's 11th inning. In the first inning of that game, Sox starter Joe Benz lost his grip and sent a pitch flying against the press gallery screen. Noting that the pitch was a spitball, a sportswriter quipped, "A telegraph operator was nearly drowned." The writer, noting that the band hired for the occasion was positioned immediately behind the press box, also served as a concert reviewer: "The cornet player thought there might be a few folks in the big crowd who had not heard him play 'Baby Mine.' It is to be hoped that the silence which greeted his rendition of it will work for future good."[33] The White Sox made it three victories in a row — and grabbed Chicago bragging rights — with their 5–2 win in Game 6. Schalk's hitless performance in the finale dropped his City Series batting average to a paltry .103. Winning the series meant an additional $807 in each player's final paycheck — more for six ballgames than the average American earned in an entire year.[34]

Despite his lack of offense against the Cubs, Schalk made his mark in his first full season in the major leagues. He appeared in 125 of his team's 153 regular-season games, posted a .980 fielding average and hit .244.

However, Schalk's baseball season was not over yet.

5

Domesticated on the World Tour

White Sox owner Charles Comiskey and John McGraw, fiery manager of the New York Giants, agreed to take their players on a four-month worldwide tour between the 1913 and 1914 seasons. The Comiskey-McGraw tour would be more ambitious and competitive than the one staged 25 years earlier by A.G. Spalding, baseball executive and sporting goods magnate. Unlike Spalding, whose barnstormers routinely routed overmatched local squads, Comiskey and McGraw sought to recreate, as much as possible, the major-league experience. They intended to bankroll the tour, but eventually brought in Comiskey's manager, Callahan, as an investor.[1] Taking charge of tour logistics was Ted Sullivan, Comiskey's long-time friend and himself a baseball pioneer. Sullivan founded two professional leagues, the Texas and the Northwestern. (For a time, Comiskey and Sullivan, former college roommates, were married to sisters, the Kelly girls of Dubuque, Iowa.)

Comiskey and McGraw welcomed and encouraged their players to make the tour, but it was not required — and not without risks. They would give up their off-season freedom, their winter jobs and their time with friends and family. Several players who accepted invitations paid the expenses to bring along their wives. Some were newlyweds who made the tour a honeymoon. Among them were former Olympic star and Giants rookie Jim Thorpe and J. Louis Comiskey, son of the White Sox owner. Some honeymooners remained only on the domestic leg of the tour. Whether accompanied or not, each player had to come up with a $300 deposit to hold his spot on the tour. A four-month road trip, including the overseas travel and games virtually every day, posed its own risks of fatigue, illness and injury. For those and other reasons, some players declined tour invitations.

From the outset, Schalk would not commit beyond the stateside portion of the tour.[2] Comiskey and McGraw sought to round out their rosters with top major-leaguers from other teams; among the takers were future Hall of Famers "Wahoo" Sam Crawford and Tris Speaker. When they ran out of stars and regular major-leaguers, the White Sox owner and Giants manager filled the remaining gaps with untested recruits and former big-leaguers. When the tour staged its inaugural exhibition in Cincinnati on October 18, 1913, some roster spots remained in flux. Throughout the domestic tour, players came and went — sometimes by arrangement, sometimes due to changes of circumstances and sometimes because of changes of heart.

Domestically, the tour generated plenty of excitement. The Giants, 1913 National League champions, had plenty of stars, but none brighter than Christy Mathewson, arguably the most popular American athlete of the day. Matty notched 20 or more victories in all but one of the previous 13 seasons. The Giants also featured the World's Greatest Athlete, Thorpe, who crushed the field to win the decathlon and pentathlon at the 1912 Summer Olympics in Stockholm. (A Native American of the Fox and Sac tribe, Thorpe was stripped of his titles due to a professionalism charge. Decades later, Olympic officials restored Thorpe's medals posthumously).

The Giants' opponents, the White Sox, finished only in the middle of the pack in the 1913 American League race (78–74), but they and the Giants hailed from the United States' two largest cities at the time. Fans who had never seen a major-league game flocked to see the stars as they played their way west. They traveled great distances — by rail, by horse-drawn wagon or by automobile — to see the stars they had only read about in *The Sporting News*, *Baseball Magazine* and their local papers. Community boosters who wanted to host a tour game guaranteed to pay the larger of $1,000 or 80 percent of ticket receipts. Comiskey and McGraw had more prospective hosts than dates on their schedule.

Booked for three dozen games in little more than a month in the United States, the tourists rarely slept in a hotel bed. Night after night, they lodged in Pullman cars as their trains rolled from one city to the next. Day after day, cheering fans and a brass band greeted the arrival of the entourage at the local train depot. Local dignitaries made welcoming remarks. Community boosters hosted a driving tour of the area. Many cities staged a lavish luncheon for the players, who were then transported to the ball field in an auto parade. After a mid-afternoon game, which usually included more ceremony, players rushed to board the train and head to their next destination. Occasionally, there would be a banquet between the game and departure. Players repeated this exhausting routine daily.

Schalk caught the tour opener in Cincinnati, an 11–2 decision for the Giants, and then sat out a loss the next day in chilly Chicago. In the Comiskey Park contest, the White Sox unveiled the home uniforms specially designed for the tour. They featured a thread stripe and American flags on each sleeve, white socks with a stripe of blue and a stripe of red, and blue caps with red peaks and white seam stripes. Their warm-up coats were bright red with navy blue and white trim; the national seal was affixed to the breast pocket. The Giants' road grays had a blue stripe and shield emblems of red, white and blue on the sleeves. Their warm-ups sweaters also bore shield emblems, while their socks were the same purple-and-gray style they wore during the season.[3]

When the entourage left the Windy City, Comiskey stayed behind. He skipped most of the U.S. games and joined the tourists three weeks later in San Francisco.[4]

Game 3 was set for a Monday afternoon in Illinois' capital, Springfield. Unfortunately, the day was better suited for football — or, more likely, ice hockey — than baseball. A light snow fell throughout the afternoon. Organizers scratched the players' automobile parade to the ballpark, but Gov. Edward F. Dunne showed up to throw out the first pitch. It is likely that a healthy contingent of Litchfield residents made the 50-mile trip to support their hometown boy, Schalk, but only about 500 fans shivered through the proceedings. They warmed their hands by applauding a solo home run by Thorpe and a grand slam by Mickey Doolan, a Phillies shortstop playing for the Giants. In a game requiring but 90 brisk minutes, New York won, 6–4. Schalk went hitless but scored a run. After they thawed out, the players took in an evening show at a Springfield theater before their 11:30 P.M. departure for the 75-mile run to Peoria, where the next afternoon the White Sox ended the Giants' unbeaten streak at three, 6–4.[5]

The following day, in the Southeast Iowa community of Ottumwa, White Sox recruit Urban "Red" Faber joined the entourage. A right-handed pitcher, Faber was purchased for 1914 after two solid seasons with Des Moines (Western League). Entering professional baseball in 1909 at the urging of Dubuque baseball impresario Clarence Rowland, Faber received a belated invitation to join the tour when Rowland recommended the 25-year-old Iowa native to Comiskey. Faber made a less-than-favorable first impression on his future manager before even stepping onto the field. A sharp dresser, Nixey Callahan took one look at Faber's attire and decided he didn't want him.[6] Callahan apparently got over it, because Faber not only stayed on the tour but played 20 seasons with the White Sox. It was in Ottumwa where Faber and Schalk met. Over their long careers, Schalk caught most of Faber's outings. Of all batterymates enshrined in the Hall of Fame, none played more seasons together. Further, they would become lifelong friends.

Faber and Schalk's first game together occurred on October 26 in Kansas City. Cold and wet weather greeted the tourists at nearly every Midwest and

Schalk, only 20 years old, poses in what appears to be White Sox headquarters before departing for spring training in February 1913 and his first full season in the major leagues. It would be another nine months before team owner Charles Comiskey shook Schalk's hand, in November 1913 during the World Tour (Chicago History Museum, Chicago Daily News Collection, SDN-058130).

Southwest stop. Kansas City was no exception, but the contest attracted some 5,000 fans. "Their presence was a distinct sign of bravery and a healthy tribute to baseball," a sportswriter testified. Rain and snow left the field a quagmire. "It was about as tough a day as could be selected for the national sport, but the game was played sharply and the athletes went at it just as fiercely as if a world's championship affair was in progress."[7] Sent in to relieve Ewell "Reb" Russell in the fourth inning, Faber immediately gave up three runs despite allowing only one hit and a walk. As a battery, Schalk and Faber looked anything but future Hall of Famers. Their first inning together included a walk, a stolen base, a passed ball and their participation in a botched run-down play between third and the plate. A teammate's fielding error was thrown in for bad measure. After Faber held them scoreless in the fifth inning, the Giants erupted for three more runs, again while allowing only a single hit. Callahan yanked Faber in favor of Jim Scott with one out in the sixth. All of the Giants' runs in their 6–2 victory came with Faber on the mound.[8]

Faber got a chance to redeem himself the next day in Joplin, Missouri, where field conditions and weather were no better than in Kansas City — so bad that McGraw confessed that the game was a "joke." He wrote, "The boys did the best they could." Still, that could not keep 4,000 fans away. After all, the great Walter Johnson was scheduled to show up and pitch for the White Sox. The Washington star made the trip from his home in Coffeyville, Kansas. He declined money for his travel and appearance. However, when The Big Train came to bat in the second inning, the game stopped and local organizers presented him with a gold watch. "The crowd yelled with delight," McGraw observed. "It was a fine tribute to Johnson, and he enjoyed every bit of it." Johnson pitched three innings in a 13–12 win by McGraw's Giants.[9] Schalk did his part, going 3-for-5 on the raw afternoon.

The next day, in Tulsa, terrible weather was the least concern. The only two pitchers who would become charter members of the National Baseball Hall of Fame, Johnson and Mathewson, were to have their first-ever head-to-head meeting. Some 4,000 fans and dignitaries jammed South Main Street Park in anticipation of witnessing baseball history. About 700 fans crammed into the right-field bleacher section, which was designed to hold about 400. About 30 minutes before game time, those bleachers collapsed, spilling the occupants and splintered wood upon soldiers who were walking under the stands. Oklahoma Governor Lee Cruce, who was seated with his daughter and friends when the bleachers gave way, stepped in to direct the rescue effort. Schalk, the rest of the White Sox, and the Giants rushed to lend assistance. The tragedy took one life: Army Private Chester Taylor, of Little Rock,

Arkansas, died of a crushed skull. There were dozens of injuries, with at least 25 people requiring hospitalization. Local organizers started to cancel the game, but they went along with the wishes of the survivors (including Governor Cruce) and staged the game. The tragedy delayed the first pitch by a half-hour. Schalk received the nod to catch Johnson, who went the distance for the White Sox. Meanwhile, an arm-weary Mathewson departed in the fourth inning. The players apparently were anxious to get away from the tragedy in Tulsa; Chicago's 6–0 victory required 70 minutes.[10]

After a 50-mile hop to Muskogee, the White Sox the next day again beat the Giants by six runs. Schalk received a different assignment: First base. He collected two hits in four at-bats, including an RBI single during Chicago's 7–1 victory.[11] The following afternoon, October 30, in Bonham, Texas, Schalk played first and also caught; he went hitless as the Giants won, 4–1. He did not play three of the next four games, his only action being a 2-for-4 performance in Houston on November 2. That four-day period featured the best and worst in travel accommodations. Players arrived for their date in Houston at 1 A.M. — enough time for them to book nice hotel beds in place of their Pullman compartments. That helped make up for their experience on the previous leg. After riding through the night in darkened train cars — the interior lights malfunctioned — they went without any food most of the day after railroad officials somehow failed to supply their dining car.[12]

After 17 games in 17 cities in 17 days, the ballplayers finally received a day off November 4 in Abilene, Texas — but not by design. A steady, day-long rain washed out the contest. With the prospect of a game unlikely, the players planned to catch up on their rest and stay in their train berths until noon. About 9 A.M., the drowsing passengers felt the bump of another rail being hooked onto the train. Shortly afterward, Steve Evans, a St. Louis Cardinals outfielder who had just joined the tour, passed through the players' cars with an announcement. Evans, who would represent the White Sox on the tour, said that the dining car had just been attached and that railroad officials invited the tourists to enjoy a complimentary breakfast — and to not hold back. The players, perhaps thinking the railroad company desired to make amends for its foul-up a few days earlier, and apparently not fully aware of Evans' abilities as a practical joker, scrambled from their berths to partake of the full menu. "After the boys had let themselves go freely in the diner, all hands got very bulky checks," McGraw said. "Most of them found that they had eaten at least $2 worth of breakfast, and the company insisted they pay for it." There is no such thing as a free lunch, and no such thing as a free breakfast. The invitation to free rein in the dining car was an Evans prank. To make matters worse, the players, their wallets a couple of bucks lighter, returned to find their berths made up and closed for the day. "Evans did not pick up any popularity for an hour or two," McGraw said, "until he began telling some stories."[13] Thus, the players likely were out of sorts (but not hungry) when they made an appearance for the fans who converged on the Abilene depot. From the back platform of their train, McGraw and Callahan introduced each player to the crowd. Russell and Tris Speaker, both natives of Texas, received the largest ovations. Since the players couldn't entertain the locals, the locals entertained the players. A sportswriter reported, "An old fashion badger fight was staged for the benefit of the teams and proved a big success."[14]

In El Paso, the ball field was far from accommodating. The sandy surface contributed to so many scratch hits that many fans shouted their disgust, and some left before the conclusion of the proceedings, a 30-hit farce that went to the White Sox, 10–7. McGraw attributed those totals to poor field conditions, breaking balls that would not break at an elevation of 1,800 feet above sea level, and the Texas sky. He wrote, "The fielders could never get a start on the ball, and when they once were set for it, it was likely to fall 50 feet behind them, or in front, due to the high sky."[15] Yet that was not the most unusual feature of the game. In the first inning, aviator Eugene Wagner buzzed the ballpark and landed on the field. Wagner asked if any of the players wanted to go up for a ride. "Sam Crawford accepted the opportunity to add to his store of experiences by going up with Wagner for a short flight," reported the *Chicago Tribune*, which added that umpire Bill Klem, not at all amused by the disruption, threatened to call off the contest. He didn't.[16]

The town of Douglas, on the Arizona border with Mexico — shuttered its business district on November 6. Its only enterprise that day would be baseball. That morning, the players' train pulled into the station to the sound of the Ninth Cavalry Band. After dignitaries gave their welcoming speeches, they took their guests on a sight-seeing tour and feted them at a noon banquet — a meal Mathewson and Speaker skipped in favor of a round of golf. The ball field in Douglas was as good as El Paso's diamond was bad. The ball park was adjacent to an Army base, and a sportswriter thought it noteworthy that the crowd of 2,000 included "many Mexicans," whose "*vivas*" were heard amid the cheers, and several hundred "colored" soldiers, who were admitted free. After the Giants posted a 14–5 victory to take a 10–9 series lead, the players hustled for the 25-mile ride to Bisbee, where an evening banquet awaited.[17] Bisbee's miners received that Friday off so that they could witness part of baseball history. As they did in Douglas, the Giants cruised past the White Sox. The score was 9–1. Schalk's contribution was a pinch-hit single.[18]

With that, the tour headed northwest, to California. Their nine days in the state would feature some hotel stays and 10 games. Schalk tripled and stole a base in his first game in California, a 5–3 White Sox victory in Los Angeles. The next game, still in Los Angeles, was arguably the biggest dud of the tour. Physical and mental errors abounded. Buck Weaver got himself ejected by Klem, and the White Sox, already short-handed, were desperate for players. Frank Isbell couldn't continue after running out a fifth-inning single. The 39-year-old manager, Callahan, who batted just nine times in 1913, entered the game as a pinch-runner for the 38-year-old Isbell. Defensively, Schalk moved to first, Callahan to right and Tom Daly came in from right to catch. New York held a comfortable 7–1 lead entering Chicago's half of the seventh. Schalk struck out on a spitball to open the seventh, but catcher Ivy Wingo was no better at connecting with that particular pitch, and Schalk reached first on the dropped third strike. He scored immediately afterward when Callahan surprised everyone with a triple over right-fielder Thorpe's head. As the inning dragged on, the Sox loaded the bases. With one out, the batter lifted a shallow fly to left field. The runner on third, Callahan, showed no inclination to attempt to score after the catch. Outfielder Lee Magee snagged the ball for the second out, but, obviously believing it was the third out of the inning, playfully hurled the ball far over the head of center fielder Mike Donlin. As Harry A. Williams of The *Los Angeles Times* described it, "Eight thousand people sat with their mouths open and their eyes popping out while Callahan and Rath scored and Speaker went to third." Williams further observed, "Magee's from St. Louis. We understand now why baseball is not popular in that city." This turned out to be Callahan's game. In addition to his triple, he hit a single, stole a base, scored twice and drove in the tying run. Chicago's right-handed spitballer, Faber, held the Giants to one hit and one run over the final four innings. Thanks to assistance from Magee, Chicago scored six times to tie the game before it was declared a nine-inning draw. After this exhibition, sportswriter Williams told his Los Angeles readers, "If this be major league baseball, then friends, let us remain a minor league for the rest of our natural lives."[19]

Meanwhile, as the tour's domestic leg neared conclusion, speculation grew over who would and would not go overseas. Isbell, whose last official appearance in the majors was in 1909, was no longer able to meet the physical demands of a big leaguer. He quit the tour and went hunting. (However, Isbell's wife and daughter, who were traveling with him, continued on the around-the-world adventure.) Management planned to send home a few of the young players they brought along for seasoning, including Faber of the White Sox.[20] Other players were having second thoughts and citing various reasons. *Chicago American* sportswriter Bill Veeck Sr.— his pen name was Bill Bailey — revealed the unspoken concern: seasickness. Veeck reported that Schalk, John "Chief" Meyers, Hal Chase "and a few others" found the prospect of seasickness too daunting to continue on the tour. Whatever his reasons, Schalk's departure should not have surprised anyone. From the start he declined to commit beyond the domestic stops, and the White Sox already planned on two other catchers, Tom Daly and Andy Slight. Veeck also reported that the fear of seasickness caused the marquee player, Christy Mathewson, to withdraw.[21] Despite McGraw's persuasive best, the worn-out Mathewson refused to continue. That turned out to be a break for Red Faber. McGraw now had too few pitchers while the White Sox were figuring to send Faber home. The organizations struck a deal: Chicago would loan Faber to the Giants for the rest of the tour. The untested prospect from Iowa would pitch in the place of the nation's favorite athlete.

This "trade" was far from the only oddity in the first month of the tour. At the November 10 game in San Diego, most in attendance lost track of which team was the "home" team. The confused included the chief umpire, Klem. As darkness descended, Klem, believing a full nine innings had been played, declared the contest a 3–3 tie. The fans jammed the exits, and even some players departed. However, someone soon informed Klem that his declaration came after just 8½ innings; the Giants had not received their chance to bat in the bottom of the ninth. As the teams sorted out matters and got ready to resume play, the man scheduled to lead off, "Chief" Meyers, could not be found. McGraw sent a messenger or two to find the catcher. They located Meyers, who grew up in and near San Diego, visiting with friends in the parking area. He had to be persuaded to break off his conversation to resume the game. When he stepped to the plate, he let Klem know what he thought of the whole affair. The delay hardly helped the already depleted supply of daylight. McGraw wrote, "Pitcher (Jim) Scott at this time had everything in his favor, as it was really too dark to play."[22] Scott worked the count to 1 and 2. Meyers then ripped Scott's next pitch for a game-ending home run. For Meyers, a full-blooded Cahuilla, a California tribe of Native Americans, it was a most satisfying homecoming. For his heroics, Meyers received a hat from his favorite San Diego haberdashery and a tie pin from W.S. Eldredge, a fan and businessman.[23]

The community of Oxnard, California — a sugar beet capital of some sort — the next day rolled out the red carpet for the tourists. It featured a pregame barbecue that McGraw found too delicious to describe. "Even Jack London, who, I believe, is somewhat known out here, would have been lost for words with which to picture the feast...."[24] After the barbecue and before the game, there was a competition of a different sort. Hans Lobert, a Phillies infielder playing for the Giants, agreed to race a horse around the bases. Though 32 years old, Lobert remained one of the National League's leading base stealers; he still held the world record for fastest tour of the bases, 13.8 seconds, set three years earlier.[25] Lobert removed his baseball uniform jersey and, wearing his undershirt, toed the line next to the horse and jockey. When Umpire Klem signaled the start, Lobert flashed to an early lead. Around second base, still ahead, Lobert glanced to the side for a look at his opponent. The jockey inched his mount closer and closer. By third base, Lobert still held a small lead. "I do not know that I ever saw a man get over the ground faster," McGraw said, "and for a while it seemed as if Lobert might beat the four-footed rival to the goal." With the amazed crowd cheering, the man and beast raced for home plate. Just two yards from the finish, the horse finally grabbed the lead. McGraw later described it as a tie and claimed that Lobert would have prevailed if not for the enormity of the barbecue consumed just an hour or two earlier. Afterward, Lobert vowed to never again participate in such an exhibition. The danger was too great.[26]

Charles Comiskey (1859–1931), original owner of the Chicago White Sox, in 1914. Known as "Commy" and "the Old Roman," Comiskey in 1912 won a bidding war for Schalk's services (Library of Congress, Prints & Photographs Division, Bain Collection, LC-B2-2981-8).

By this time, it was well known that Schalk's tour participation would end on U.S. soil. On November 9, when Comiskey departed Chicago to join the tourists in San Francisco, the Old Roman's traveling party included catcher Andy Slight. Like Faber, another tourist who had yet to appear in a major-league game, Slight was signed by Comiskey on the recommendation of Pants Rowland. During the 1913 minor-league season, Slight and Faber were batterymates for Des Moines. The transaction caused a Chicago sportswriter to quip: "Charles Comiskey seems determined to have a Lilliputian catching staff. Ray Schalk is no bigger than a minute and now Commy has signed up Slight."[27] Slight would become the No. 2 catcher, with Tom Daly moving up when Schalk moved out in a few days.

Schalk still had some baseball to play. In San Francisco on November 14, while McGraw boycotted the game to protest umpire Klem's decisions of the previous afternoon, the White Sox trailed 2–0 entering the bottom of the ninth inning. Chicago rallied for the tying runs against starter Art Fromme. Reliever Jeff Tesreau entered to quell the uprising. His first batter, Schalk, laced a game-winning double to center field. It was Schalk's last hit of the tour.

Schalk appeared in two of the final five U.S. games. After going hitless in three at-bats (with a sacrifice) in Chicago's victory in Portland, he had a first-time experience at an elaborate post-game banquet. "Although Ray Schalk, sensational young catcher of the White Sox has been with the team for two years, he never shook hands with Charles Comiskey, president of the club, until yesterday," the local newspaper revealed. "Schalk has met with the 'Old Roman' many times and talked to him, but never had the glad hand of good fellowship extended to him before. Schalk explained that Comiskey left all dealings with the players to his manager, Jimmy Callahan, which seems somewhat strange to those not accustomed to the methods employed in the major leagues."[28] Customary or not, it is hard to believe that the Old Roman had until then failed to shake hands with the young star who had been in his employ for some 15 months — and for whom he had paid top dollar to acquire.

Plagued by poor weather throughout, the tour saw its final two domestic games rained out. Portland and Seattle were unable to see the major leaguers in action. Schalk and the others leaving the tour wished the others *bon voyage*. *The Empress of Japan*, a 298-foot-long Canadian steamer, shoved off for Japan from Victoria, British Columbia, the evening of November 19. The traveling party faced adventure and danger. As it turned out, concerns about seasickness were well-founded: Everyone aboard suffered for days at a time, and a typhoon packing snow and tremendous waves nearly sank the ship.

By then, Schalk was safely home and enjoying his winter in Litchfield.

6

❖

Sophomore Star

Having played more than 200 games — pre-season, regular season, exhibition, City Series and the domestic half of the World Tour — Schalk enjoyed his winter respite in Litchfield. He was a regular on the local basketball courts, and occasionally suited up with a local club, the Litchfield White Flyers.[1] No doubt, he also spent time with Lavinia Graham, the Farmersville girl with whom he had been acquainted since he played ball there nearly three years earlier. Now 21 years old and eligible for membership, he joined the local Elks club, the organization that employed his father as lodge custodian.[2]

Schalk in mid–February headed to Chicago to catch the team's train for California and spring training 1914. Cracker was an early arrival in the Windy City, as was outfielder Larry Chappell, who hailed from McClusky, Illinois, a community about 40 miles from Litchfield. The 24-year-old Chappell was purchased from Milwaukee for a whopping $18,000 in July 1913. Despite hurting his knee in his final game with the Brewers, Chappell appeared in 60 White Sox games over the balance of the 1913 campaign. Schalk and Chappell were teammates in Milwaukee most of the 1912 season. (Chappell never met others' lofty expectations, appearing in only 49 more major-league games from 1914 to 1917. Serving in San Francisco as a member of the Army's medical corps during The Great War, Chappell, like millions of people worldwide, came down with influenza. He died of pneumonia in November 1918.[3]) The evening of February 19, Chappell, Schalk and about five dozen others — players, team officials, wives, well-heeled boosters and sportswriters — departed Chicago's LaSalle Street station aboard their special train. About 500 fans showed up to see them off. The Rock Island Railroad provided six cars — a combination baggage and buffet car, three sleepers, one diner and one combination compartment and observation car. The railroad also assigned a representative to travel with the team until the end of its jurisdiction in Arizona. The accommodations were so ample that none of the passengers had to sleep in a dreaded upper berth. Absent were manager James Callahan, owner

Comiskey and the half-dozen Sox players still on the world tour. Another dozen players planned to catch the train along the way or to meet the team in Paso Robles. Coach Kid Gleason, team secretary Harry Grabiner and business manager Joe "Tip" O'Neill were in charge of the traveling party.

The White Sox special, scheduled to follow a limited train all the way to Los Angeles, initially made good time — almost too good. The travelers were ahead of schedule when they reached Kansas City, where railroad officials initially told them they would sit for a while because the limited had to wait for an important connecting train from Minneapolis. However, possibly because the Rock Island had a representative accompany the team, officials suddenly decided to let the White Sox move ahead of the limited and continue on its way immediately. Not everyone got the word. When their train started to pull away, a handful of players were in or around the depot, posing for a Kansas City newspaper photographer. "One of the grandest hustles ever seen resulted," sportswriter I. E. Sanborn reported. "Before the last straggler was aboard, the train had moved nearly out of the station." It was not until O'Neill carefully counted noses that it was certain that no one was still on the platform in Kansas City.[4]

The scheduled 3½-day trip provided ample time for cards and conversation. On the social scene, there were new dances. The fox trot was quickly becoming the nation's favorite. And what about the tango and its variants? Were they really improper, as critics charged? (A few weeks later, the International Dancing Congress, meeting in Paris, unanimously issued a "not guilty" for the tango, maxixe and *Trés-Moutarde*.)[5] Of all the hot topics for the baseball men, none was hotter than the new Federal League. It was aggressively pursuing players — including those already under contract or, arguably, obligated under the reserve clause in their previous contract. The Feds offered higher salaries and better contract terms, particularly to marquee players, many of whom contemplated violating their contracts in pursuit of bigger paydays. The new league also needed managerial and administrative talent. Somewhere in Kansas, a sportswriter aboard the White Sox special coaxed from Gleason an admission that during the winter Baltimore's Federal League entry unsuccessfully wooed him to become its manager. He later explained, "I can't see where those fellows have a chance." Pitcher Eddie Cicotte also turned down the Federals.[6]

While the White Sox continued westward, they no doubt discussed the uproar surrounding the cross-town Chicago Cubs. Just a few days before spring training, Charles Webb Murphy, majority owner since 1905, fired Johnny Evers as manager and named as his replacement Hank O'Day, a veteran National League umpire who had managed Cincinnati in 1912. The manner of Evers' ouster was the final straw. Though Murphy was within his rights — Evers signed the contract without reading the provision that he could be dismissed on 10 days notice — the baseball community decried the action. Even the American League went on record condemning Murphy, with President Ban Johnson stating, "We are prepared to go to any length to get rid of this influence in Chicago."[7] By the time the White Sox special reached the California border, Murphy was out, selling his 53 percent of the Cubs to Charles P. Taft. Added Murphy, "I am through with baseball and its controversies and squabbles. I'm the happiest man in the world tonight."[8] (Though Murphy was out, O'Day was in: He managed the Cubs in 1914 — they went 78–76 — before returning to umpiring for 13 more seasons.)

Poor weather negatively impacted the White Sox on two continents. The world tour stalled in Paris, where rain washed out games against the Giants on four consecutive days. Meanwhile, passengers bound for spring training experienced extensive delays due to flooding in Southern California. Their train crawled through Indio on tracks covered by water, and advanced another 48 miles to Beaumont, where they sat for nearly 24 hours due to washed-out bridges. The passengers whiled away the afternoon with hikes and sightseeing. After they made the final 80 miles to Los Angeles, arriving 26 hours behind schedule, their train passed through flooded areas on temporary tracks and bridges. Unlike Kansas City, where it received expedited service, the team's special was held in Los Angeles. (The Rock Island Railroad's jurisdiction of the special ended back in Yuma, Arizona, and the team was left with a beleaguered emergency crew.) Trains that had departed Chicago a full day after the White Sox special chugged past the team. Nonetheless, Sanborn reported, "all members of the party have survived the tough trip in good health and spirits," though the experience was likely to have Comiskey thinking twice before choosing California for future training camps.[9] While killing time in Los Angeles, Gleason and O'Neill visited Washington Park, where the Venice Tigers, an entry in the Pacific Coast League, opened their pre-season workouts. They looked up veteran left-hander Guy "Doc" White, who was seeking to extend his baseball career after leaving the White Sox the previous fall. "I am starting here on the same footing with the 'bushers.' That is, it is up to me to make good," he told a Los Angeles reporter. "I don't expect to hold my job on the strength of what I have done in the big leagues."[10] Nearly 35, White, who pitched a record five consecutive shutouts for the White Sox in 1904, pitched two seasons in the minors.

After the delays and detours due to flooded and unstable ground, the White Sox finally departed Los Angeles. The trains were so backed up and crowded that tickets on regular trains out of the city could not be had. White

Sox traveling secretary O'Neill, displaying pity and a profit motive, agreed to sell a few desperate civilians transportation on the team's special. What should have been a 12-hour trip between Los Angeles and Paso Robles was another 24-hour ordeal. It was slow-going as a steady parade of trains — some tied up for nearly a week — rumbled up the single line. Finally, three days late, the White Sox arrived in Paso Robles. Two days behind schedule for workouts, Gleason directed a practice that was considered ambitious for the first day out. It included fungo hitting, easy throwing, light batting practice and running — three whole laps of the ball field in the morning and three more in the afternoon. The next day, he ordered a five-inning intra-squad game on top of a two-hour workout. Spitballer Ed Walsh, the former ironman attempting to come back after an injury-plagued 1913, fired pitches to Schalk and Walt Kuhn and had people talking about a Walsh comeback. (The optimism was premature. Walsh, who twice pitched more than 400 innings in a regular season, appeared in only 21 games over his final four years.) Meanwhile, the resort pampered the players with post-workout baths (both hot and cold) and massages. A couple of days later, the White Sox defeated a Paso Robles amateur team — with a suspected professional "ringer" thrown in — by an 11–5 score. It could have been more one-sided, but, after scoring eight runs in the first inning, the Sox just went through the motions against the locals, whose squad included a bellhop from their resort. The ballplayers were not the only amateurs at the game. Among the spectators were musicians who produced, as a sportswriter observed, "some of the weirdest noise ever blown out of brass instruments." Schalk started the game but gave way to Kuhn. In the eighth inning, the back-up backstop suffered a badly split hand on a foul tip. With Cracker no longer available, Jack Fournier came in from first base and put on the "tools of ignorance" for the balance of the contest. Kid Gleason, 47 years old, found his glove and took Fournier's place at first.[11]

Facing the Pacific Coast League Seals in San Francisco, downstate Illinois products Schalk and Chappell stroked home runs. It was part of a three-hit afternoon for Schalk. The noteworthy event of the 5–3 Sox victory occurred with two out in the ninth. Outfielder Ping Bodie ran over to catch an easy fly ball and kept running toward the clubhouse, endeavoring to stick the baseball in his pocket. The ball dropped to the grass, and the umpires ruled Bodie failed to make the catch even though he had run at least a dozen yards. With some 5,000 hometown supporters there to support the two umpires' ruling, the White Sox remained on the field to record the fourth out of the ninth inning.[12]

After requiring a week to get there, the White Sox stayed barely a week in Paso Robles before splitting into two squads — the regulars and reserves —

for daily exhibitions. The regulars set up shop in San Francisco, 200 miles north of Paso Robles, while the reserves were based in Los Angeles, 200 miles south of the resort. After 10 days or so, they traded locations for a couple of weeks. By then, Callahan and others who completed the world tour were in California. On March 26, Schalk had a close call while tagging out Venice's Carlisle, whose spikes ripped through the catcher's uniform and scratched his knee. Had it been a regular-season contest, Schalk would have continued. But Callahan would have none of it in an exhibition, especially after seeing Larry Chappell laid up with blood poisoning due to inattention to an apparently minor foot injury. Callahan removed Cracker and had trainer William Buckner work his magic on the cut.[13]

Starting March 30, the two squads began playing their way back to Chicago. The players would not see their teammates from the other squad until they reached the Windy City for the season opener.[14] The split-squad approach might have served Comiskey's training and profit-making purposes, but seeing half of a second-division ballclub did not satisfy California fans. "Oh, Charley Comiskey," a local sportswriter complained, "how many more years do you propose to pass out this kind of stuff to Pacific Coast fans?" Chicago sportswriter Sanborn predicted that by 1916 Comiskey's team would not return for a fourth spring in California, where fans desired to see different teams after a couple of years and where teams' travel and lodging expenses ran higher than for other U.S. sites.[15] He was correct.

Some of the exhibitions were farces. Leading comfortably on an increasingly rainy afternoon in Venice, California, both teams sought to put themselves out in the fifth inning so as to make it a regulation game; after all, gate receipts were at stake. However, Sox outfielder Ping Bodie either didn't know the plan or didn't care. Bodie, it should be noted, was the slow-thinking inspiration for sportswriter Ring Lardner's "You Know Me Al" series. He slugged the ball to the center-field wall, but it was obvious to all — except Bodie — that an inside-the-park home run was impossible. Eddie Cicotte, coaching third base, waved Bodie around toward home, where Ping was a dead duck.[16]

Schalk and pitcher Jim Scott skipped the game in Yuma, Arizona — played on a sandy ball field lacking a fence — because the Sox needed to scale back their traveling contingent. The Southern Pacific railroad could not assure enough berths on the 550-mile trip between Yuma and El Paso, so a couple of players were sent ahead to Texas. The major leaguers arrived in El Paso on April 1, April Fool's Day, and they felt foolish. They learned that the team they had arranged to play was defunct, local officials were antagonistic toward professional baseball, and the city's only ball field was unavailable. The White Sox would have welcomed a day off. However, when officers stationed at the

military base in El Paso learned of the situation, they rounded up a team of
soldiers, most of them from the 20th Infantry. Few residents of El Paso even
knew the White Sox were in town; soldiers made up virtually the entire small
audience. Played on the sandy surface of a former race track, the game was a
13–1 snoozer. Schalk sat it out. It was another "hit-and-run" appearance for
which traveling secretary O'Neill was noted. Sanborn described it as "a case
of get through, take a splash, grab a bite of grub and run for the train."[17]

A few days later, Dallas was to observe "Go to Church Sunday." Callahan, on behalf of the team, accepted a pastor's special invitation to attend
services at First Presbyterian Church. "More than the usual number of Sox
athletes attended in consequence," the *Chicago Tribune* reported, "but it would
be unfair to the others to state how many went or who they were."[18]

As the White Sox closed in on Chicago, which soon would be the home
to three major-league teams, the local newspapers analyzed the teams' schedules. On 61 days the Federal League's Chicago Whales would have a home
game the same afternoon as the White Sox (29) or Cubs (32). Four Sundays
during the year all three teams would be in action in Chicago.[19]

Meanwhile, Callahan and Comiskey analyzed their team's prospects for
1914. "Without a doubt, in my mind, the White Sox are a stronger team than
they were last year," Callahan wrote. "I do not believe in making pennant
boasts on paper, but I feel confident the team that beats us this year will win
the flag." Comiskey noted that Ed Walsh might be coming back, but even if
he does not, the pitching will be strong. "I think we have a chance for the
pennant. I always think that way at the beginning of a season, for it is my
nature, but this year there seems more reason than usual for my opinion as
well as my hopes."[20] Sportswriter Sanborn, who noted that only the White
Sox and the Athletics had lost no one to the Federal League, agreed with the
prediction that the South Siders would be better than they were in 1913. After
listing areas of concern, he wrote, "Back of the bat there is nothing for Callahan to worry about as long as Ray Schalk has his health. He is an even better catcher than last year, when he had only (Wally) Schang to share the mitt
laurels with. Schalk, however, is more likely to be hurt than in previous years,
as he is absolutely fearless in the matter of blocking runners, and, since learning how to do it successfully, is more likely to take big chances than ever
before."[21]

On Tuesday, April 14, the day the White Sox opened the 1914 regular
season, Chicagoans opened their morning newspapers to read of the latest in
the tensions between the United States and Mexico's leader, General Victoriano Huerta, who in 1913 led a coup and assumed the presidency. When his
troops subsequently arrested nine U.S. sailors after they landed their small

craft at Tampico, U.S. President Woodrow Wilson turned up the heat. Though Huerta ordered the immediate release of the Americans and apologized for the incident, he balked at U.S. demands that he also conduct a 21-gun salute to the U.S. flag. By this point, Wilson was threatening a blockade of Mexico. (Eventually, U.S. forces overthrew Huerta, and the nations nearly went to war.) Closer to home, the *Tribune* reported the surrender of a suspect known as Duffy the Goat in connection with the shooting death of one Isaac Henagow during a quarrel in Roy Jones' café on the South Side of Chicago. Meanwhile, someone was plotting to tamper with the coroner's jury investigating Henagow's death. [22] While those events played out, some 23,000 fans streamed to Comiskey Park for the home opener of the 1914 White Sox.

On the street, ticket scalpers took advantage of some fans unfamiliar with the spaciousness of Comiskey Park, receiving a 50 percent premium for tickets to seats in the upper deck — even though a few thousands tickets were available for face value at the ticket window. Inside, fans and ballplayers noted

Fans jam the grandstand of Comiskey Park, home of the Chicago White Sox, ca. 1910. The ballpark was in only its third season of existence in 1912, when Ray Schalk made his major league debut (Library of Congress, Prints & Photographs Division, Bain Collection, LOT 11147-3).

that Comiskey had improved the hitter's background with a solid green wall. The White Sox took the field in new uniforms of bright white with only a faint stripe. When the pre-game ceremonies ended, fans settled in to watch the White Sox host Cleveland. Chicago pulled out a 5–2 victory. With the game tied 2–2 in the seventh, utilityman Tom Daly, appearing in only his second regular-season major-league game, stroked a pinch-hit double to push across Chicago's third run. Daly had recently demonstrated a sense for the dramatic. In the final contest of the world tour, in London, Daly hit a walk-off homer against Red Faber, the White Sox recruit loaned to the Giants. In his second consecutive Opening-Day start, Schalk had a quiet afternoon behind the bat and went hitless in three at-bats.

Schalk deservedly received plaudits for his defense, but occasionally he had a bad day. One late afternoon in April, he threw wildly to second in an attempt to pick off Doc Johnston, who took third on the play. Then Schalk tried to pick Johnston off third — and again threw wildly, allowing Johnston to score. Later that inning, Nap Lajoie engaged Cracker in a home-plate collision with such force that he separated the little catcher from the ball. As the ball rolled away, another Cleveland baserunner, Jack Graney, rounded third and headed for home. Schalk recovered the ball in time to toss it to pitcher Jim Scott, who appeared to tag out Graney. However, umpire Silk O'Loughlin saw it otherwise. Scott put up such a fuss over the call that O'Loughlin excused him from the rest of the day's proceedings. Schalk's errors were critical in the 4–2 loss.[23]

Schalk missed an opportunity to provide the heroics — and break a five-game losing streak — a few days later in an unusual defeat in Detroit. The game's first batter, White Sox outfielder Ray Demmitt, stroked a double and came around to score. However, that was it for the Chicago offense. Though they held the White Sox to just one hit all afternoon, the Tigers nearly gave the game away. Taking a 5–1 lead into the top of the ninth, Tiger pitchers issued three bases-loaded walks to make the score 5–4. Sportswriter Sanborn sarcastically suggested that the White Sox might have fared better had they stepped to the plate without their bats. Daly popped out on a bad pitch for the second out. "One more walk would knot the count, but Schalk was allowed to take his bat to the plate." After taking a ball and a strike, Schalk "foozled" the next one in front of the plate and was easily retired to end the game, catcher to first.[24]

Most major-league catchers play their entire careers without catching a no-hitter. Schalk caught two nine-inning no-hitters in little more than two weeks — but one of them did not go into the books. In Washington on May 14, Chicago veteran Jim Scott battled rookie Yancey "Doc" Ayers through nine scoreless innings. Washington had its chances, thanks to a couple of eighth-inning walks and errors by infielder Lena Blackburne in the fifth and seventh, but they could not push across a run. Blackburne's struggles were not limited to defense. Failing twice to lay down a sacrifice bunt with two men on in the second, he tapped into an inning-ending double play. In the 10th, with two out and two teammates on base, Blackburne struck out. The White Sox managed only three hits all afternoon. In the bottom of the 10th inning, Washington first baseman Chick Gandil, a former and future member of the White Sox, stroked a clean single to center field. Howie Shanks followed with a hit to right field that took a bad hop, eluded Demmitt and rolled to the wall while Gandil came around to score the game's only run. Scott went into the books as throwing a no-hitter because he completed nine innings without a blemish. Decades later, a rules change took away the no-hitter from Scott (and Schalk).

Cracker did not have to wait long to catch an undisputed no-hitter. In Chicago on May 31, Joe Benz held the Cleveland Naps hitless en route to a 6–1 victory. The Sox blew Benz' shutout in the fourth with a couple of errors. Then the White Sox buckled down. With Schalk giving the signs, Benz baffled visiting batters. "During half of that battle both Sox and Naps seemed bent on giving the 10,000 or so spectators a demonstration of why they are scrapping for the tail end berth," sportswriter Sanborn said. "Then, as if by a community hunch, both teams realized the magnificence of the battle Joe Benz was putting up in the face of everything. They started playing the baseball that was more familiar to the multitude, even if less advanced." Sanborn continued, "The fans got wise to the nature of the combat, and to the fact Benz had a clean slate as to hits in spite of the run which had been scored. They cheered him tumultuously as each inning ended without a hit. And when the ninth wound up in a dazzling electrical display — code for lightning double play — the whole assemblage stood on its hind legs and gave Benz the loud acclaim all the way to the spot where he vanished into the coop."[25]

Justification of pre-season concerns about Schalk suffering injury on tag plays at the plate came in a mid–June game in Chicago. Washington had plated three runs in the fifth inning, and with runners on first and third base with two out, the Senators were looking for more. On reliever Henry Jasper's pitch, the baserunner on third, Danny Moeller, attempted to steal home. Schalk anticipated the theft and moved to apply the tag. Moeller's spikes ripped such a deep gash in the catcher's left forearm that he had to leave the game. "It will be some time before even Schalk's phenomenal pluck will get him back into the harness," a sportswriter predicted.[26] The next day, it was revealed that the injury "was more painful than serious." Still, while the wound

Ray Schalk in 1914, when the 21-year-old caught two of his four career no-hitters: Jim Scott against Washington and Joe Benz against Cleveland. Scott's no-hitter was disallowed years later because Scott gave up two hits in the 10th inning (Library of Congress, Prints & Photographs Division, Bain Collection, LC-B2-3396-9).

healed, Schalk went home to Litchfield. "The plucky backstop promised to be back in harness in three days," Irv Sanborn reported, "but it is more likely to be a week before it will be safe for him to officiate."[27] Schalk missed three games.

He returned to Chicago in time to help rookie Red Faber experience a brush with baseball history. Schalk, already building his reputation for savvy handling of pitchers, was the better choice to guide Faber against the defending world champion Philadelphia Athletics — more so than rookie Tom Daly. In the June 17 contest, Faber dominated. Through eight innings, the Athletics had managed only two baserunners — one on a walk and one on second baseman Lena Blackburne's error. Leading off the top of the ninth, Jack Lapp hit a grounder to Blackburne's right. One sportswriter noted that instead of charging the ball, Blackburne stepped back, played the ball on the big hop and made a deliberate toss to first base. However, Lapp managed to beat the throw and spoiled Faber's no-hit bid. There was some debate in the papers over whether Blackburne could have prevented Lapp's hit. At the time, Faber was not upset with Blackburne's play but with O'Loughlin's "safe" call.[28] Faber retired the next three Athletics to close with a one-hit, 5–0 victory. "Any pitcher who can hold the Athletics to one hit," as *The Sporting News* put it, "is entitled to a seat with the mighty."[29]

Faber received a spirited welcome home in Dubuque a few days later, when the White Sox came to town for an exhibition game. He had been residing in Dubuque for nine years after moving with his parents from his native Cascade, also in Dubuque County. Faber's employer, Comiskey, had Dubuque ties as well. That Comiskey was making his first visit in six years — and bringing his White Sox along — was Big News. That his contingent included Faber, who had just one-hit the defending world champs, made it that much more special. Faber wasn't the only Sox player with Dubuque on his resume. Pitcher Henry Jasper played on Dubuque's minor-league club the previous season. Coach and emergency backstop Billy Sullivan, age 39, caught all nine innings in the Dubuque exhibition. Schalk was unavailable after wrenching a knee while running the bases a couple of days earlier. The Dubuque game came together because Forrest Plass, manager of the local Three-I League team, personally put up a $500 guarantee — plus incurred promotional expenses — to bring the White Sox to town. Playing in the city's brand-new ballpark, the Dubuque team was no challenge for the major-leaguers, who prevailed 11–2 before a record crowd of more than 6,000.[30]

Schalk remained on the shelf. Barely a week after missing three games due to the spiking, he suffered a knee injury June 21 against the Red Sox. The incident offered another example of his grit. In the bottom of the second inning, Schalk slid hard into second base, wrenched his knee and writhed on the ground until he was carried off the field. Backup catcher Wally Mayer came out to run for Schalk. However, before the game resumed, Schalk convinced manager Callahan to allow him to stay in the game. Schalk trotted gingerly from the bench and reclaimed his place at second. He stayed in the game a while longer, but the pain finally became too much in the fifth inning.[31] Cracker did not return to regular duty for another week.

Schalk's injury was about the only bad break the White Sox experienced during that period. Over the three weeks of June 18 through July 9, the Sox went 17–2 and pulled within 2½ games of the league-leading Athletics. Detroit, just two games out, was the only team to beat them during that stretch. Chicago fans' hopes for glory increased when former ironman Ed Walsh, trying to come back from arm problems, had a string of strong showings in mid-season. His first start of the year came on July 5, when he held Cleveland to three hits over seven innings. However, the comeback was short-lived. Walsh lost his place in the starting rotation within a month. He was fooling no one — not even the sportswriters. The *Chicago Tribune*'s James Crusinberry, describing Walsh's late–August relief effort against the Yankees, wrote, "In all the time Walsh was in it didn't seem that he pitched one ball with anything on it. The Yanks finally began taking toe holds and driving the ball against walls and distant fences, and the old master was waved to the clubhouse."[32] By then, the comeback was not to be. So too of Chicago's pennant hopes. From their high-water mark, the White Sox went 29–51 the rest of the way, falling from third to a sixth-place tie (with New York) in the American League standings with a 70–84 record.

Despite their collapse in the second half of 1914, the Sox still staged some exciting contests, with Schalk playing a prominent role. On July 25 in Comiskey Park, New York and Chicago went scoreless through six innings; the White Sox had yet to register a base hit. The Yankees appeared poised to break the deadlock in the seventh inning, when they had veteran William "Birdie" Cree on third with only one out. Batter Luther "Doc" Cook hit a bounder back to pitcher Joe Benz, but Cree took off for home. As Benz tossed the ball to Schalk, Cree thought better of his effort and turned to run back to third. Though encumbered by his catcher's gear, Schalk easily chased down Cree. Meanwhile, Cook rounded first and headed for second. Schalk spotted him and fired the ball to shortstop Buck Weaver, who tagged out Cook to complete a double play. The game remained scoreless until the bottom of the 13th inning, when after a couple of Yankee errors, hot-hitting Jack Fournier singled in Ray Demmitt.[33]

The August 9 game in Chicago pitted Washington pitching legend Walter Johnson against Faber, the White Sox rookie. The teams were tied entering the top half of the ninth, which Crusinberry described as "one of the great half-innings ever seen at the south side." A combination of Senators hits and White Sox errors allowed Washington to load the bases with no one out. Though only in his second full season in the majors, Schalk knew of Senators manager Clark Griffith's fondness for the bases-loaded suicide squeeze bunt. Sure enough, the runner on third, Eddie Foster, broke for home on the pitch. However, Schalk called for a pitchout, and batter Howie Shanks had no chance of making contact. Clutching the ball, Schalk moved up the line, tagged out Foster and ran toward the middle of the diamond, looking for other victims. He found one in Chick Gandil, who had dashed toward second base on the pitch. However, the original runner on second, Mike Mitchell, apparently missed the squeeze-bunt sign. He remained at second, necessitating Gandil's retreat toward first. Schalk fired to first baseman Fournier, who ran Gandil back toward second. Seeing the problem he created, Mitchell took off for third. Fournier's throw to shortstop Weaver arrived in plenty of time to retire Mitchell. When the action stopped, Gandil stood on second with two out. Shanks assumed his position in the batter's box and promptly lined a single to center, where outfielder Cecil Coombs was experiencing only his third day in the big leagues. Coombs collected the ball while Gandil rounded third and headed for home. Coombs fired a strike to Schalk, who tagged out his future teammate to end the inning. "It took minutes for the crowd to finish cheering when that one was over," Crusinberry reported. They cheered all over again the next inning, when Coombs did it again — this time throwing out Ray Morgan at the plate, with Schalk applying the tag. In the bottom of the 11th, Schalk's short sacrifice fly was deep enough to score Weaver on a close play, giving Faber and the White Sox a 2–1 decision over Walter Johnson and the Senators. Despite Coombs' heroics — the previous day, his two-run double in the sixth beat the Senators — his major-league career lasted six days. His "cup of coffee" in the majors occurred roughly midway in his 20-year career (1906–25) in the minors, where he later managed and worked in the front office.

Another tight game against the Senators ended as a 4–4 tie after 10 innings. The September 2 contest concluded not because of darkness but because both teams had trains to catch. "The Sox could have played another half-hour and still made the train for Cleveland," Crusinberry revealed. "Griffith wanted the game called at 5 o'clock so his boys wouldn't have to make a sleeper jump to New York." As the day grew longer, and the 5 P.M. cut-off approached, Schalk's patience with umpire Tommy Connolly grew shorter. The catcher no doubt was already in a foul mood after the White Sox, leading by three runs with only one more out needed for a victory, gave up three runs to force extra innings. It could have been worse: The final out of the ninth inning was recorded at home plate, where Schalk tagged out Gandil trying to complete a game-ending, inside-the-park home run. Schalk ended the top of the 10th when he popped out to the shortstop with two men on base. So, Schalk surely was not in the best of moods in the bottom of the 10th inning. Still, when Connolly ruled that Wally Smith had successfully checked his swing on a two-strike pitch, Schalk's protest was relatively mild. Crusin-berry wrote that there was no question that Smith taken a swing. Smith then rapped a double. The next batter, McBride, took what Schalk thought was a strike. Connolly called it a ball. On Joe Benz' next pitch, McBride tried to lay down a sacrifice bunt and fouled it at Schalk's feet. Connolly called it a ball. That was too much for Cracker, who ripped off his mask and unleashed his verbal fury at Connolly. The umpire removed his mask and returned the favor. Connolly and Schalk argued jaw-to-jaw. Other players swarmed around the home plate area, and the fans were about to riot. Finally, amid shouts and catcalls, Schalk left the field, having been excused for the balance of the pro-ceedings. With Schalk out of sight, the crowd settled down, and the White Sox stymied the Senators, who hurt their chances by failing to run on a dropped third strike. After 10 innings and the 5 o'clock deadline at hand, Connolly declared the tie game over. With that, the Sox headed directly from the ballpark to the railroad station and their train to Cleveland.[34] Crusin-berry took Schalk's side on the protests, noting that the lively backstop "has the reputation of never kicking without a cause." The *Washington Post*'s Stan-ley T. Milliken made no mention of questionable officiating except to report Schalk's ejection.[35]

After winning two of three in Ohio, the Sox rode the rails around Lake Erie to Detroit, where Ty Cobb was in the unfamiliar position of coming out on the short end of rough play. In the 10th inning of a 5–5 thriller, baserun-ner Cobb took off for second on a hit-and-run play. Batter Sam Crawford hit a grounder to shortstop Buck Weaver. While Weaver threw to first for the sure out, Cobb touched second and raced toward third. Sox first baseman Jack Fournier fired the ball across the diamond to young third baseman John "Jimmy" Breton. Fournier's peg was timely but low. Just as the ball bounced out of Breton's mitt, Cobb crashed into the 23-year-old, and the ball rolled about 20 feet from the point of impact. Cobb tried to scramble to his feet to score, but Breton had other plans. The 5-foot-10, 178-pound Chicago native did not run *around* Cobb to retrieve the ball; he went *over* him, "all the time acting as if in frantic effort to get to the ball, but always managing to keep his legs or arms tangled with those of Tyrus," Crusinberry reported. Finally, the men separated and Cobb dashed for home. Breton recovered the ball and fired it to Schalk when Cobb was still 20 feet from the plate. "Cobb did not try to slide in or get back. He just ran into Schalkie straight up and gave him short arm jabs in the stomach. Schalk tagged him all right, then was knocked over backwards and clear over the home plate." While the Tigers vehemently — and unsuccessfully — appealed to the umpires for an interference call, Schalk managed to regain his wind and senses. Batting in the top of the 12th, with teammates on second and third, Breton ignored the hissing, booing and taunts from Tiger fans and slammed the first pitch for a double. He then scored on Ray Demmitt's single to make Chicago's lead 8–5. They needed the insurance, as the Tigers rallied for two more runs before the White Sox nailed Crawford trying to stretch a single into a double, with right fielder Robert "Braggo" Roth providing the assist.[36]

In the first inning the next day, Cobb exacted his revenge. On another a hit-and-run effort with Cobb on first and Crawford batting, the batted ball glanced off pitcher Eddie Cicotte and bounded to shortstop Weaver. Cobb made his intentions known by not stopping at second base. Weaver tossed the ball to Breton, who waited for Cobb's arrival. "Breton tagged him easily but was cut down," Crusinberry reported. "He lay in the dirt and Cobb bounded up and stood over him as if gloating over the destruction wrought." Breton didn't say a word, acting as if the gash were just an unavoidable accident. After five minutes of attention from trainer William Buckner, Breton stayed in the game. "Cobb was tame throughout the balance of the game," Crusinberry wrote. "He had been avenged."[37] After the skirmishes, Chicago columnist Ring Lardner offered this perspective: "Admitting that Mr. Cobb isn't the gentlest ball player in the world, Ray Schalk's attitude when a base runner is hastening plateward, is hardly an effective plea for mercy. Ray came into the league with the idea that he owned that strip of property about three feet wide and ninety feet long that extends from third base to home, and Cobb is among those who realize that the only way to get the notion out of Ray's head is to knock it out. So far Cobb and the rest have failed, but we'd hate to have Schalk insured in our company."[38]

The White Sox sat in seventh place when they finished their regular season (70–84, with three ties), but they crawled up into a sixth-place tie with the Yankees, who lost two of three to the pennant-winning Athletics. By then, however, Comiskey's team was preparing for the Chicago City Series against the Cubs, who went 78–76, with two ties, good enough for fourth in the National League.

It was a tight series. The widest margin of victory was three runs — and those three came in a ninth-inning bunch when the Sox claimed the second game, 5–2. The Cubs won three of the first four contests in the best-of-seven series. But they couldn't close the deal. The White Sox won the next two to force a seventh and deciding game at Comiskey Park. The Cubs immediately jumped on Sox starter Jim Scott for two runs. Scott managed to retire only one West Sider and had two Cubs on base when he gave way to Eddie Cicotte, who two days earlier earned the Game 6 save. Meanwhile, the White Sox went down in order against Bert Humphries in the first three innings. In the fourth, an error, a walk and their only two hits of the game provided all the runs they would need. Schalk provided the game-winner — a single to center field that plated Roth, who had slammed a two-run double down the right-field line. Cicotte, meanwhile, scattered six hits over his 8⅔ innings of relief, but the Cubs threatened in the ninth. With two out and Vic Saier on second, the Cubs' Claud Derrick hit one between third baseman Breton and shortstop Weaver. As the fans in Comiskey Park rose to their feet — there were about as many Cubs "bugs" in attendance as Sox boosters — Saier appeared destined to score the tying run. But a diving Weaver managed to knock down the ball, and Saier stopped at third. Pinch-hitter Bill Sweeney worked Cicotte to a full count before he ended the series on a pop fly to Weaver in short left field. Sox fans swarmed the field to boost their heroes atop their shoulders. "While Bobby Roth was the real hero of the combat because of his timely two bagger ... the work of Eddie Cicotte and Ray Schalk was worthy of great praise," the *Tribune*'s Crusinberry wrote. Not only did Schalk have what proved to be the game-winning hit, "the battery work of Schalk and Cicotte, especially in the tight places, was beautiful."[39] The victory meant an extra $129.30 in the Sox paychecks. Each winner's share of the City Series was worth $527.30; each Cub received $398.[40] Meanwhile, the Boston Braves received $2,708.91 each for their World Series upset sweep of the Philadelphia Athletics, who took home $1,950.42 a man.[41]

With his extra pay in his pocket, Schalk returned to Litchfield for the winter. The White Sox' thrilling victory over the Cubs was not enough for manager Nixey Callahan to keep his job. Since as early as August 1914, Comiskey had been quietly considering many candidates to replace Callahan. The Old Roman's decision, announced a week before Christmas, shocked the baseball world.

7

"We don't serve kids in here!"

Watching his team collapse in the last half of 1914, White Sox owner Charles Comiskey decided to terminate Callahan's second stint as manager at season's end. Rumors abounded that Callahan was through, and Callahan resigned himself to that fate. Yet, days after the team's exciting victory over the Cubs in the City Series, Comiskey included Callahan in his 40-member party that spent a couple of weeks hunting and fishing in Wisconsin. The group traveled in the comfort of the two Pullman cars that Comiskey commissioned for the adventure. Others in the group included Ban Johnson, the American League president; veteran player Ed Walsh; and Chicago native Germany Schaefer, the funnyman and Washington infielder who amused everyone on the 1913–14 world tour.

For a successor to Callahan, the Old Roman had options. Kid Gleason, White Sox coach the previous two seasons, had nearly 2,000 games of major-league playing experience (first as a pitcher, then at second base), mostly with the National League Philadelphia Phillies, before becoming a Phillies coach in 1907. Some believed that Gleason had the inside track for manager due to his loyalty when the Old Roman's team was extremely vulnerable.[1] While Comiskey and Callahan were on the six-month world tour, and Gleason was left in charge of the team, the Federal League raided personnel from the National and American leagues. Gleason, citing his promise to Comiskey to handle matters during the owner's absence, turned down the Federal League's repeated offers to manage in the upstart league. Further, he convinced several White Sox players not to defect to the Feds — at least not before Comiskey returned and had a chance to match their offers.[2] Thanks to Gleason's perseverance and commitment, the White Sox were least affected by the Federal League's raids. Would the manager's job be Comiskey's reward to Gleason?

Speculation on prospective White Sox managers included Walsh, who was concluding his famed pitching career, and former White Sox star Fielder Jones, who was on the hot seat for having trouble delivering on his many promises to organizers of the new Federal League.[3] Also on the list was player-coach Billy Sullivan, a catcher. In terms of potential managers, catchers had the pedigree. They had to be ever-vigilant. They had to study players, game situations and strategy. They had to serve as a quarterback, positioning fielders, rallying the team and calling the pitches. There was no better example than Connie Mack, a former catcher managing the great Philadelphia Athletics teams.

The rumors also included Mack's former star second baseman, Eddie Collins, the American League's most valuable player of 1914. Mack sold Collins, a member of his "Million Dollar Infield," to Comiskey during the off-season. Asked about reports that Collins would also manage Chicago in 1915, Mack expressed doubts.[4] However, Callahan, curiously, all but installed Collins in his former job. "At this time I cannot say officially that Eddie will manage the White Sox next year," Callahan said. "Such a statement will have to come from Mr. Comiskey, who probably will make some kind of announcement tomorrow."[5]

However, the Old Roman made no announcement the next day. And when he did, his choice was not any of the candidates mentioned. On December 17, 1914, he announced his decision: Clarence "Pants" Rowland, the 35-year-old manager of Peoria of the lowly Three-I League. Few in the upper echelons of baseball knew Rowland — he had never played professionally, at any level — but Comiskey did. Their common denominator was Dubuque. Rowland had grown up in the Iowa community, where at various times he owned and managed the minor-league team. What he lacked in playing experience he made up for through close observation, study and self-assuredness. Rowland occasionally gave Comiskey recommendations on up-and-coming players. Among his suggestions was Ray Schalk, but Comiskey did not take the advice at the time.

Hearing his choice for manager, the experts wondered if the Old Roman had lost his mind. "To the utter and be-dazed surprise of all the baseball world, Charles Comiskey, instead of retaining Jimmy Callahan or appointing Eddie Collins to the position, announced the appointment of Clarence Rowland, a hitherto obscure minor leaguer, as the leader of the White Sox for 1915," *Baseball Magazine* said. "This was indeed a stunner. With veterans like Callahan, Gleason, Sullivan and Walsh at hand and with Collins just secured, Commy goes and pitchforks a Three-I man from Peoria into the place of supreme command! Can you beat it for a novelty or for a big surprise?"[6] Harry A. Williams of the *Los Angeles Times* presented it as decision of Biblical proportions: "Not since Pharaoh plucked Joseph out of obscurity and placed him on a pedestal, accompanying said move with an increase in salary, can we recall a greater sensation."[7]

Comiskey explained, "I have considered it carefully. Rowland is by no means a new man to me. I have been watching his work most carefully in the minor leagues for the past seven or eight years, and have been greatly impressed with his aggressiveness and his judgment. He is particularly good at picking ball players, and has sent up quite a few to the White Sox during that time."[8] For his part, Rowland expressed nothing but admiration for the Old Roman. "Through my career in baseball Charles A. Comiskey had been my staunchest friend and supporter. He has been my ideal. It was on his recommendations and through him that I secured the positions of handling clubs that I did. He is now placing me in a position where I can repay him for helping me in the past. I intend to give him all that I have in me."[9]

Comiskey had not rushed to this decision. As early as August 1914, he invited Rowland to Chicago for a conversation, at the conclusion of which

A virtual unknown, Clarence "Pants" Rowland (shown here in 1917) was owner Charles Comiskey's surprise pick to manage the Chicago White Sox in 1915. At the end of Rowland's third season, in 1917, Schalk and the Sox won the World Series. Comiskey fired Rowland the next season (Library of Congress, Prints & Photographs Division, Bain Collection, LC-B2-4360-5).

he said, "Tell your bosses in Peoria you won't be back next year. You're going to be with me." In what capacity, Comiskey did not state. "That's all he said," Rowland recalled four decades later. "Nothing about what he had in mind." A couple of months later, Comiskey invited Rowland back for a City Series game. "You're not afraid to take my club, are you?" Comiskey said. Rowland replied, "No. And if you think I'm kidding, I'll go down on the field and take charge right now."[10]

One of the White Sox organization's first actions under the Rowland regime was to fire Kid Gleason. Out of a job was the man who barely a year earlier put his personal word ahead of money and protected Commy's franchise against the advances of the Federal League. For Schalk, the move meant the departure of a valuable teacher — the man who helped him make the transition from top prospect to bona fide star. "For a while he had trouble in solving the delivery of Walsh," a sports reporter said of Schalk. "Gleason took pains to coach the kid. He got down on his knees back of the plate and showed Ray how to stop Walsh's low spitter."[11] Gleason expected the axe to fall, but he was fed up nonetheless. "Never again will I put on a baseball uniform," he told a sportswriter from his home in Philadelphia. "I am through with baseball." Gleason revealed that less than a month earlier he had turned down another offer from the Federal League — this time to manage Brooklyn. He explained that the fire wasn't there. Further, noting the ongoing war with the Federals, he said, "It is not much pleasure to manage a baseball team under existing conditions."[12] (Gleason returned as a Sox coach in August 1916.)

The transition in White Sox leadership might have been big American sporting news, but it was nothing compared to the news coming from Europe. The continent was roiling, with war building since late July 1914, when Austria-Hungary, seeking retribution for the assassination of Archduke Franz Ferdinand, declared war on Serbia. Within days, the larger allies of those nations — including Russia, Germany, France and Great Britain — joined in. Millions of Americans — many of them European immigrants or their children — closely followed news of The Great War. Fifteen percent of the U.S. population was foreign-born in 1915, with Germany the leading country of origin.[13] The day it reported Comiskey's hiring of Rowland, the *Chicago Tribune* headlined its top story, "Defeat Russians; Germans Rejoice." How would the conflict overseas affect or eventually involve the United States, American society and its national pastime, baseball?

While the sporting world allowed news of Rowland's appointment to sink in, accolades for his star catcher continued. "Schalk shows more life than any player I have ever seen," said Comiskey, who was not one to exceedingly praise players (particularly around contract time). "He is level-headed and his thinking and natural ability stamp him as one of the greatest catchers in the world today."[14] George C. Rice of the *Chicago Journal* affirmed Schalk as the game's best catcher. While acknowledging Schalk's fearlessness, Rice noted, "If Schalk has a fault, it is that he takes too many chances." Rice explained that Schalk had a tendency to expose himself to injury and, when injured, weakened his team. "That fact that he is daring does not lessen his ability, but it makes him something of an uncertainty."[15]

For the third and final year, the White Sox staged their spring training camp in beautiful Paso Robles, California. For Schalk, it was an unusually painful pre-season. Batting in the fourth inning against the Pacific Coast League's Los Angeles Angels, he took an Oscar Horstmann pitch in the left side and missed the better part of a week. He returned just in time to achieve the rare distinction of getting tossed out of a pre-season exhibition contest — in the first inning, no less. He vehemently and physically protested umpire

Ed Finney's "safe" call on Los Angeles Angel Harl Maggert's bid for a three-run inside-the-park homer. The *Chicago Tribune* and *Los Angeles Times* had reporters present, and their accounts of the play and its aftermath reflected their hometown perspectives. Both agreed that infielder Lena Blackburne fired an accurate relay throw to Schalk. The *Tribune* said Maggert was a dead duck, while the *Times* saw it as closer than that, adding that Finney started to signal "out" but changed the call to "safe." They agreed that Schalk exploded at the adverse ruling. The *Tribune* said Schalk hollered and poked Finney repeatedly in the chest. The *Times* said the backstop gave a two-handed shove to the umpire's stomach and then grabbed him by the arm, all the while shouting his protest. Finney, who "maintained his balance and dignity," ejected Schalk, and Rowland was barely out of the dugout before Finney ejected him, too. "It was some time before Schalk could calm himself and collect his tools," the *Times* reported. "With these things attended to, he finally departed." Exiting with him was his new manager, Rowland.[16]

The following week in Stockton, California, a foul tip struck Schalk on his right thumb, cutting it to the bone. It was the fourth time that spring that he missed action due to injury; this lay-off lasted 11 days. He put that injured thumb to some use during his rehabilitation, serving as the plate umpire during the White Sox' 6–1 win over a college squad in Redlands, California.[17] Schalk's next game as a player was an easy contest in which the White Sox loaned three players — including the battery — to their Abilene hosts. Another twist to the game was the abundance of sand burrs on the field; they attached themselves to the ball — until they transferred onto the hands of the players. Chicago trainer William Buckner had a busy afternoon removing the stickers.[18]

Clarence Rowland's first official game as a major-league manager was a road contest. Some 12,000 fans turned out at St. Louis' Sportsman's Park, where Branch Rickey's Browns seemed determined to be generous hosts. Their misplays allowed the White Sox to send the game into extra frames, where Chicago won in 13 innings, 7–6. Rowland and the White Sox won the next afternoon but lost their next six before limping into Chicago for their first homestand. Opening Day festivities included three automobile parades from the Chicago Loop south to Comiskey Park, where entertainers included a cabaret quartet and three bands. An estimated 22,000 fans jammed the ballpark. The patrons included a delegation from Dubuque, anxious to see their hometown boys Rowland and Faber. For eight innings, St. Louis starter Carl Weilman baffled the Chicagoans, who managed only one hit. The White Sox trailed 4–0 entering the bottom of the ninth. It could have been worse. In the top of the sixth, with one out and Browns on second and third, Schalk anticipated a suicide squeeze bunt. He signaled Faber, who had entered in the fourth inning, to throw a pitch-out. While Faber went into motion, so did the baserunner on third, Gus Williams. Batter Jimmy Austin couldn't reach the pitch to protect Williams, and Schalk applied the tag. A moment later, Austin lashed a run-scoring triple. In the bottom of the ninth, Schalk opened with a solid single into left field. The White Sox clawed and scratched against Weilman until they tied the contest on a Shano Collins triple. With the Comiskey Park faithful roaring, Grover Lowdermilk relieved Weilman. Buck Weaver swung at a 1–1 pitch inside and low. He missed — but so did catcher Sam Agnew. The ball rolled all the way to the screen, and Collins touched the plate in an improbable 5–4 White Sox victory.[19] The exciting comeback made reliever Faber, who pitched the final six innings, the winning pitcher and gave Rowland a home-opener win to go with his season-opening nail biter.

Everything was clicking for the White Sox on May Day 1915, when Reb Russell stymied Ty Cobb and the Detroit Tigers on two hits, 5–0. Chicago fans enjoyed giving Cobb the business all afternoon. In the seventh inning, they especially loved it when Dick Nallin called a third strike on Cobb, and the Georgia Peach lit into the rookie umpire. Nallin excused Cobb from the rest of the proceedings. The game featured a rarity — a Ray Schalk home run. He drove a Harry Coveleski pitch to the base of the Comiskey Park flagpole and raced around the bases to complete a three-run homer.[20] It was the second of his 11 career homers.

On a Sunday in May, Schalk's relatives and friends made the short trip to St. Louis' Sportsman's Park to see their favorite 22-year-old play against the Browns. They probably were not impressed. He added some extra mustard on his sixth-inning argument with umpire Silk O'Loughlin (again) over a tag decision at the plate. During the confrontation, Schalk spied the umpire's mask on the ground and gave it a kick. When O'Loughlin bent over to retrieve the mask, Schalk kicked it again. And again.[21] Telling the story years later, Cracker confessed, "I was really putting it on for those folks from home."[22] In some tellings, Schalk said the article of equipment was the umpire's small whisk broom. Whatever his target, it cost Schalk a three-game suspension.

While serving his sentence, Schalk missed out on some baseball history. On May 12, 1915, Red Faber held Washington to just three hits in a 4–1 victory. Two of the three hits came in the ninth inning, and the visitors scratched across their lone run after two were out.[23] When he was throwing well, Faber induced hitters to bat the ball into the ground. This day, the spitball pitcher was working most efficiently. He needed only three pitches to retire the Senators in the third inning. And in the fifth. Faber's longest inning was the eighth — 13 pitches. All told, Faber required just 67 pitches — 50 strikes and 17 balls — for his complete-game win. It was considered a record, besting Christy Mathewson's 72 of seven years earlier. Tom Daly, subbing for Schalk, caught Faber's gem.[24] Schalk watched again the next day, when his teammates staged a ninth-inning victory over the Nationals and Walter Johnson.

The next day, a Friday, was an open date throughout the American League. (The Washington players, in the midst of a series against the White Sox, cooled their heels in Chicago.[25]) However, the White Sox hit the rails. Comiskey took his charges to Dubuque, where they engaged the Iowa minor leaguers in their second annual exhibition game. For Rowland, the team's new manager, the trip to Dubuque was a triumphant homecoming. Sharing in the local adulation were ex–Dubuque residents Faber, Comiskey and pitcher Henry Jasper. Also in the contingent was *Chicago Tribune* sportswriter James Crusinberry, who, like Faber, was a native of nearby Cascade. "One has to visit Dubuque or Cascade to learn just how great some of the Sox athletes are," Crusinberry wrote. "Manager Rowland is about the biggest fellow in this county, and Red Faber drew a big crowd of his own from Cascade, 30 miles away. Hi Jasper, who is kept in the background, is called by his first name by every fellow he meets on the streets here. Such famed men as Eddie Collins, Ray Schalk and Jack Fournier got nothing more than a wee bit of applause."[26] A pre-game downpour cut attendance to 1,800, just one-fourth the turnout for the previous year's exhibition.[27] Despite the treacherous conditions and the contest's exhibition status, Rowland played Schalk and other regulars. However, the White Sox took it easy and coasted to a 4–1 victory. The defensive star was Shano Collins, who twice robbed Dubuque hitters of clean singles with lightning throws from right field to first base.[28]

Players — pitchers especially — received the "ironman" label for racking up many innings of work. Early in his career, Faber became the White Sox' ironman hurler. Among catchers, however, Schalk was developing a track record as an ironman receiver. On June 24 in Cleveland, he caught all 19 innings of a 5–4 victory. Faber, who entered in the ninth inning and wriggled out of a bases-loaded jam, pitched 11 scoreless innings.[29] Earlier, on May 21 in Chicago, the White Sox and Red Sox tangled for 17 innings. Schalk caught every frame, and he still had enough left to beat out an infield single in the bottom of the 17th. The hit filled the bases and made it easy for Buck Weaver to score the winning run on pinch-hitter Daly's single to left. A long-time Comiskey friend from Dubuque, Dr. William Paul Slattery, declared the 3–2 contest the greatest baseball game he had ever witnessed. That a Dubuque boy, Faber, earned the victory by pitching the last 10 innings no doubt fueled his enthusiasm.[30] The next afternoon, Schalk was back at it.

Schalk's career batting average was .253 — lowest among any position player in the Hall of Fame — but his value was in his defense and handling of pitchers. Nonetheless, he could lay down the sacrifice and squeeze bunt, and his speed contributed to the White Sox offense. Photograph dated 1917 (Library of Congress, Prints & Photographs Division, Bain Collection, LC-B2-3843-6).

He played in nearly all of Chicago's 11–3 rout over Boston, drawing three walks in four plate appearances. With the victory, their fifth straight, Rowland's White Sox sat atop the American League standings.[31] They won the next four to extend their lead over Detroit to two games.

Though 1915 was the season he was making his mark as *the* best catcher in the game, Schalk looked younger than his 22 years, and his countenance was far from the best-known face in the game. Walsh, Shano Collins and Eddie Cicotte proved that at Schalk's expense the day of a rainout in the nation's capital. They were killing time in a Washington tavern when Schalk sauntered in to join them. The bartender took one look at the new arrival and snarled, "Get out! We don't serve kids in here!" Schalk asked his teammates to vouch for him. To the young player's surprise and irritation, the trio claimed to have never before laid eyes on him, congratulated the barkeep for upholding a strict rule, and resumed sipping their brews. Schalk had no choice but to try another watering hole.[32] His teammates pulled the gag the next season, when morning practices were part of the daily routine. Rowland permitted Schalk to skip that morning's session, and the catcher, in civilian garb, relaxed in the Comiskey Park stands and watched the workout. Several teenagers had snuck into the ballpark and scattered, but a policeman working ballpark security finally shooed them out. The cop then approached Schalk, repeated his order to vacate, and moved to drag him from the premises. He didn't buy Schalk's protests that he was a Sox player. Seeing the confrontation in the stands, the Sox on the field hollered to the officer that the workout was a secret session, that they had been having problems with kids stealing baseballs, and that the young man in question was an imposter. Later, when he realized his mistake, the red-faced officer showered Schalk with apologies.[33]

Acquisitions keyed the improved White Sox. A major transaction brought to Chicago Eddie Collins, formerly of Connie Mack's "Million Dollar Infield." From Milwaukee came outfielder Oscar "Happy" Felsch. During the season, they purchased veteran outfielder Eddie Murphy from Mack. However, Comiskey's biggest catch of 1915 came late in the campaign. On August 20, he won the bidding war for a 28-year-old pure hitter from Cleveland. His name was Joseph Jefferson Jackson. He was better known as "Shoeless Joe."

During their stay in first place, the White Sox hosted the Philadelphia Athletics in a game of farcical proportions. Thunderstorms threatened Chicago the afternoon of July 14. After a 20-minute rain delay in the top of the second inning, the White Sox held a 4–2 lead after three innings. The rain returned, but it was not hard enough to call off the game. Philadelphia manager Connie Mack, assessing the skies and anticipating a game-ending rain, ordered his troops to prolong the game so that five innings — the minimum for an "official" contest — could not be completed. The Athletics used every delaying tactic they could dream of. Meanwhile, Rowland instructed the White Sox to put themselves out quickly. With thunder rumbling in the distance, the bottom of the fourth inning became a farce: Chicago batters struck out on wild pitches. The Athletics hit Faber with a pitch and allowed the slow-footed pitcher to enter the record books for "stealing" second, third and home in the same game. They dropped easy pop-ups. The inning ended only after the umpires threatened Philadelphia with a forfeit. However, the game continued, and the thunderstorm that Mack anticipated missed Comiskey Park. The game went the full nine innings: White Sox 6, Athletics 4.[34]

Chicago's home game against the Yankees was postponed, but weather was not the reason. On Saturday morning, July 24, 1915, nearly 2,600 Western Electric employees and their families boarded the excursion steamer *Eastland* docked on the Chicago River. Soon after the picnic excursion cast off, the *Eastland* listed and rolled onto its side. Men, women and children were trapped inside. The death toll reached 844. Upon learning of the tragedy, Comiskey postponed that afternoon's game. Local newspapers announced that the game would be made up with a doubleheader the next day. However, the Old Roman later called off Sunday's action after the acting mayor asked all Chicago amusements to shut down in respect to the dead. Many baseball fans did not get the word, and they complained when they arrived to find Comiskey Park's gates locked.[35]

The White Sox remained in first place through July 17, when they split a Saturday doubleheader with their closest rival, Boston, to make their record 53–20. The next day in Chicago, the Red Sox moved into the lead with a 6–2 decision. The loss marked the beginning of a White Sox fade; they went 29–31 and fell 14 games behind Boston. In a case of too little too late, the White Sox closed the regular season by winning their final 11 games to wind up 93–61, good enough for third place. Still, in Rowland's first campaign, and with a championship roster taking shape, the White Sox of 1915 posted a 23-win improvement over the previous season.

Though the weather was cold, the White Sox remained white-hot in the post-season. They took four out of five from the Cubs for another Chicago City Series title. In their final 16 contests, counting the regular season and City Series, the South Siders went 15–1. Except for their Game 2 shutout loss, the White Sox won with big innings. In each of the final three contests, they posted at least one five-run inning. In their other victory, Game 1, they had a four-run seventh and three-run eighth. As the final game ended and fans ran onto the Comiskey Park field, Cubs manager Roger Bresnahan, who had been coaching at third, dashed toward the White Sox bench and found Rowland. Shaking his hand, he said, "Congratulations, Clarence. You had the better team. And from what I have seen of you in this series I am ready to believe all the good things they have been saying about you all year."

Schalk's offensive contribution in the series was a triple and five singles in 13 at-bats for a .462 average, nearly 200 points above his regular-season .266.[36] His season fielding average was .984 — best among American League catchers. According to a retroactive calculation by baseball statistical expert Bill James, 1915 marked the third straight season Schalk would have received the American League Gold Glove Award for catcher.[37]

White Sox and Cubs players squawked when it came time to divvy the proceeds from the City Series. They complained that their owners shoved in the first four games — the only contests in which the players would receive gate proceeds — on weekdays, even when it was too cold to play, so the owners would have the big Sunday gate for Game 5 all to themselves. They had a point: Game 5 attendance was 32,666 — nearly as much as the first four games combined. Not only was the weather warmer that day, but Chicago men had fewer entertainment options that Sunday afternoon. For the first time in 43 years, under Mayor Thompson's order to enforce existing ordinances against Sunday operations, most of the city's 7,152 saloons did not serve alcohol that day. (Thus began another battle over Sunday closings.) The winners' share was $420 each while the losers received less than $300 — roughly half of what the players anticipated. "They always told me Comiskey was a friend of the ball player," said an anonymous Cub. "I understand he was responsible for our playing on the two cold days. Consequently he gets the big money from the big Sunday crowd and the ball player gets his little mite which came in on the cold days."[38] On the days in question, the temperature was 42 to 45 degrees.[39]

His work in Chicago concluded for 1915, Schalk still had some baseball to play. His hometown organized the first Schalk Day for Sunday, October 24, 1915. Schalk invited some major leaguers to join him on the Litchfield side: Sox pitcher Joe Benz; St. Louis native and Chicago Cubs infielder Joe Mulligan; and Robert "Braggo" Roth, whom the White Sox traded to Cleveland in the Joe Jackson deal two months earlier.[40] Also representing the Anchor Athletic Club of Litchfield was Walter Holke, a St. Louis native whose major-league experience to that point consisted playing a doubleheader for the New York Giants on the last day of the 1914 season. Holke in 1915 starred for Rochester of the International League.[41] In two years, Holke and Schalk would play on opposite sides in a World Series. The Wabada Graduates, an all-star team assembled by J.B. Sheridan, sports editor of the *St. Louis Globe-Demo-*

crat, provided the opposition. Sheridan's catcher was 19-year-old Herold "Muddy" Ruel, who had just made his major-league debut with 10 games for the St. Louis Browns. Ruel played 19 years in the majors, including a key role with the 1924 World Series winners, the Washington Nationals. About 2,500 fans jammed Anchor Park and stood in the outfield as Cracker stroked three hits, including two triples. "And just for good measure he stole a base on Ruel to show that it was possible, regardless of what the Metropolitan papers have been saying to the contrary," an enthusiastic Litchfield scribe wrote. Though Benz allowed only two earned runs, the Wabadas scored five en route to a 5–3 decision.[42] Schalk Day festivities concluded with a lavish evening banquet, where Sheridan heaped praise on the pride of Litchfield.[43]

With that, the nation's best catcher started his much-deserved off-season.

8

Two Games from Glory

Anxious for the 1916 season to begin, Cracker Schalk was the first White Sox player to show up in Chicago for the trip to spring training. After arriving from Litchfield, Schalk went to a Loop sporting goods shop and kept two salesmen busy for an hour. He selected one of every piece of equipment a catcher would need — and two of some. He got a new mask, glove, shin guards and a couple of pairs of shoes — one of which featured newly designed steel-toed cleats intended to improve protection against foul tips.[1]

After three springs in California, the White Sox moved their 1916 training camp to Mineral Wells, the Texas community that had hosted them in 1911. They also changed their approach to pre-season exhibitions. Instead of playing split-squad games all the way from camp back to Chicago, the Sox this year kept it "sane," playing fewer games, fewer one-day stands and on fewer substandard ball fields.[2] When the White Sox Special departed LaSalle Street Station for the Lone Star State, on hand were about 3,000 fans, some of whom had taken advantage of Comiskey's "open-house" invitation to see the inside of the special rail cars. One player did not make the departure: Red Faber came down with tonsillitis back home in Cascade, Iowa, and missed the first week of training. There were also fewer wives of players in the party. The Boston Braves and New York Giants instituted a no-wives policy, considering them a distraction and a complication to travel and accommodations. White Sox owner Charlie Comiskey did not set a policy, but he did allow the word to get around that he preferred players to leave their wives at home; all but one or two got the message.[3]

As spring training wound down, the White Sox, who won all 15 of their pre-season exhibitions (all against minor-league teams), were considered an improved team and a contender for the American League title. Sportswriter Grantland Rice gave the defending World Series champion Boston Red Sox 8–5 odds to win the pennant, followed by the Detroit Tigers at 2–1 and Chicago at 3–1.[4]

When the White Sox lost their 1916 opener at home April 12, thousands of fans were upset about more than the 4–0 loss to the Detroit Tigers. In preparation for the season, painters had applied a fresh coat of green to Comiskey Park's seats and railings — paint that had yet to dry completely. Many fans sent Charlie Comiskey bills for their garment cleaning.[5]

While some fans saw red over the green, many more were blue about the team's performance. With such high expectations, the White Sox and their fans were not prepared for the early results. On May 22, after losing to Washington 2–0, Rowland's team dropped into last place. However, at 13–19, the team was only three games out of the first division (fourth place) and just eight behind first-place Washington.

The White Sox unveiled their new style of visitors uniforms, which dropped the distinctive dark-blue garb of years past in favor of traditional gray attire.[6] That was Schalk's garb when he had a notable game. On April 23 in Detroit, on the team's first road trip of 1916, he drove in all three of Chicago's runs with a sacrifice fly and a double. Then, in the bottom of the ninth, he threw out a Tiger baserunner on a botched hit-and-run attempt to preserve a 3–2 victory. The next afternoon, he suffered a sprained left ankle when he slipped near the grandstand while chasing down an errant throw by Eddie Collins. "If you had seen Schalk's spikes catch against one of the auxiliary slabs used for the home pitchers to warm up upon, and if you had heard his plucky efforts to keep from screaming with the pain inflicted by turning his ankle on said slab, you would guess that the White Sox would be crippled for a month, with Ray Schalk on crutches," sportswriter Irv Sanborn said. "Anything less than that would be due to Schalk's nerve."[7] Schalk must have had lots of nerve, because he pinch-hit the next afternoon in Cleveland, sat out one more game and then returned to regular duty.

The pinch-hit appearance came on James Dunn Day, honoring the new owner of the Cleveland Indians. Dunn, an Iowa native who lived in Chicago, made his fortune in railroad construction. Part of White Sox owner Charlie Comiskey's old-boys club, the Woodland Bards, Dunn agreed to buy the Cleveland team at the suggestion of Ban Johnson, American League president. Comiskey headed a delegation of about 145 Bards and other Chicagoans who traveled to the Forest City for the festivities. Among them were Johnson, Secretary of War Newton D. Baker, and Charles Weeghman, owner of the Chicago Cubs. The Cleveland Chamber of Commerce hosted the Bards and others in a pre-game luncheon. Afterward, a 1½-mile-long automobile parade toured downtown Cleveland and rolled to the newly renamed Dunn Park (formerly League Park), where two bands entertained fans.[8] Six years

later, "Sunny Jim" Dunn died in his Chicago home after a months-long battle with the effects of influenza. He was 56.[9]

Schalk's ankle injury might have slowed him on a particular play in St.
Louis. The Browns had men on first and second with no one out in the seventh inning of a 1–1 game. On his second attempt to lay down a sacrifice
bunt, Burt Shotton produced a low pop-up behind the plate. Schalk scurried back and got his mitt on the ball, but couldn't hold on. Now with two
strikes on him, Shotton endeavored to hit away. He hit a line drive that shortstop Buck Weaver snared on the run toward second base. Weaver stepped on
second to record a second out and then fired to first baseman Jack Fournier
to retire the remaining baserunner and complete the triple play. His muff of
Shotton's sacrifice attempt and a run-producing error notwithstanding, Schalk
had a solid day defensively. He tagged out Eddie Plank trying to score on a
sacrifice fly — assist by Joe Jackson — threw out a baserunner going for second on a botched hit-and-run attempt and picked off a Brown who strayed
too far from third base. For good measure, he went 1-for-3 at the plate and
scored in Chicago's 3–1 victory.[10]

After the road trip, the White Sox returned to Chicago for four games
against Cleveland. The contest on the rainy afternoon of Saturday, May 6,
would not have been played except that a good crowd was on hand. The
Comiskey administration did not want to lose those ticket revenues. For the
Sox players' fortunes, it might have been better had they gotten the day off.
They played uninspired ball — with one exception. "As in many previous battles, the fighting spirit was concentrated in the person of Ray Schalk, who
had contained the only hit that counted outside the individual averages, and
who came close to starting a fist fight in the seventh inning," *Tribune* sportswriter Irv Sanborn reported. Batter Jack Graney and Schalk exchanged a few
words after the latter challenged home plate umpire Oliver Chill's decision
on a pitch. Graney, purporting to use his bat to trace the path of the pitch,
wound up pushing the end of his club into Schalk's mask. "At the same time,"
Sanborn wrote, "Graney asked Schalk why he did not join a regular ball team,
instead of catching for a bunch of misfits." Still wearing his mask, Schalk went
after Graney, and it required the assistance of Chill and players from both
benches to head off an escalation. "The incident closed with an exchange of
diplomatic notes and the promise of both to be as good as the Kaiser in the
future." Not long afterward, in the ninth inning, Schalk had an RBI single,
but it was too late in the 4–1 decision.[11]

Despite his fighting spirit, Schalk struggled at the plate. In mid–May, his
batting average was under .200, far below his .261 career average after three-
plus seasons. Still, American League pitchers dealt with Cracker Schalk cau-

tiously. "The little catching wonder is apt to break up a game whenever he gets up in a pinch," a sportswriter noted. "He seems to be at his best whenever he is placed in a position where it probably means victory for his team if he can come through with a base hit, and opposing pitchers take every precaution to give Schalk all they have in the way of deceptive deliveries."[12] Eventually, Schalk improved to end the season hitting .232, still a career low to that point.

For the third straight year, the White Sox played an exhibition in Dubuque, Iowa. Due to the departure of the city's professional team during the previous season, the White Sox played Dubuque College (previously St. Joseph's College and today Loras College). Even with Chicago providing both batteries, the White Sox had an easy time defeating the college men, 8–0. Schalk was part of neither battery; he was in Litchfield for the funeral of maternal grandfather William Brandt, 87, who died three days earlier in the Schalk home.[13] If there are silver linings in family events such as these, in Schalk's case it was that the White Sox were in St. Louis, just an hour's ride from Litchfield, when his grandfather died. Matters would have been more complicated had the team been in New York or Washington. As it happened, thanks to an open date and a rain-out, Schalk missed only one American League contest to funeral leave.

After the Dubuque exhibition, the White Sox joined the Chicago-bound train also transporting their next opponent, the Cleveland Indians, who on the same day played an exhibition in Davenport, Iowa, 70 miles south of Dubuque.[14] They returned to the Windy City, where Comiskey had arranged an innovative system to inform Chicagoans whether White Sox games were postponed when the weather was doubtful. All a baseball fan in downtown Chicago had to do was look at the Board of Trade building's flagpole. A white flag with a red ball in the center meant the game was on. A solid blue flag signaled a postponement. No flag at all indicated that no game was scheduled. The move was intended to not only be a convenience for fans but to ease the crunch on the city's telephone system.[15]

Had there been television and ESPN SportsCenter in the day, Schalk would have received airtime with a "Web Gem" on July 7, 1916. In the eighth inning in New York, Roger Peckinpaugh lifted a foul pop that drifted toward the White Sox dugout. Schalk took off in hot pursuit. As he approached the dugout, his White Sox teammates hollered for Schalk to halt his pursuit. Instead, Schalk dove, made a one-handed catch and flew into the Polo Grounds dugout. "Schalk saved himself from immediate destruction by using his other hand to prevent his favorably known head from colliding with the cement," *The New York Times* reported. "As some one remarked, any one who can dive down into the catacombs and get a foul fly is a whoop of a catcher."[16]

Added Grantland Rice, "No wonder the crowd, that always appreciates rare gameness, applauded every move he made from that point on."[17] His exploits included tagging out the apparent winning run in the 11th, taking the throw from a prostrate Buck Weaver after a botched double-steal attempt. However, the gem only forestalled defeat, as the Yankees scored twice in the 12th inning to snatch a 4–3 victory.

Even as the underperforming White Sox inched up the standings in midseason, speculation grew that Comiskey would dump Rowland; one rumor had the Old Roman naming Eddie Collins player-manager. The players read the newspapers, too, and in a clubhouse meeting, they pledged to play all-out for Rowland. They considered him a "player's manager," and he advocated for them with Comiskey, who was by no means considered a "player's owner." One who didn't read the papers, illiterate Shoeless Joe Jackson, came to his manager's defense. *The Sporting News* quoted him: "Rowland is the greatest manager I have ever had."[18] The team's renewed focus paid dividends. Soon after their meeting, the White Sox went 11–10 during a road trip that included seven doubleheaders. *Twice* they had doubleheaders three straight days. The Sox returned to Chicago and opened their 22-game homestand by winning 11 of the first 13 contests — including nine straight. The ninth victory came in the first game of an August 4 doubleheader, when Red Faber outdueled Walter Johnson, 3–2. The win pushed the White Sox atop the American League standings with a 59–42 mark. From May 22, when they occupied the league's cellar, through Faber's win over Washington, the White Sox won two-thirds of their contests (46–23). The rally occurred despite Faber missing nearly two months to various ailments, including a sore thumb and rheumatism. However, illness and injury then caught up with the White Sox, who closed the homestand 3–7 and dropped to third place.

On June 25, when Cleveland visited Chicago, the teams seemed more intent on using their spikes than bats and gloves. In the first inning, Schalk picked off an Indians baserunner on third base. Moments later, Chicago shortstop Zeb Terry, a 129-pound rookie, took a hit. Terry got it again in the third, and in the bottom of the inning the White Sox returned the favor. It happened again in the fifth, when Terry suffered spike wounds to his hand, courtesy of Ray Chapman. Matters boiled over in the eighth inning. For the second time that afternoon, Buck Weaver slid into second base with clear intent to hurt somebody, and that somebody was again Indians second baseman Ivan Howard. The pair rolled on the ground and punched each other as both benches emptied. Only quick work by umpires Dick Nallin and Billy Evans prevented a free-for-all. After the action returned to baseball, the White Sox prevailed in 11 innings, 4–3.[19]

By mid–August, Schalk's play was earning him comparisons with baseball's established greats, including Ty Cobb and Tris Speaker. Noting that Schalk executes game-changing plays virtually every day, a sportswriter stated, "Whistling, dancing, aggressive, ever alert, Schalk has no peer in the American League. He does everything just a little better than his rivals. President Comiskey couldn't afford to trade Schalk for Speaker or Cobb."[20] Schalk was on his way to his second straight season leading American League catchers in fielding percentage (.988). In Bill James' calculations, it would have been another Gold Glove season.[21]

With Schalk helping lead the charge, the White Sox stayed in the pennant race. Nonetheless, Chicago fans expected a far easier time of it, and they blamed Rowland. *Collyer's Eye*, a gambling publication in the Windy City, agreed. "If Charles A. Comiskey expects the White Sox to win the American League gonfalon he must get a manager — at once. Chicagoans, noted the length and breadth of the country for their fairness, 'pulled' for Rowland to make good, overlooked his mistakes, hoping against hope. The time, however, is past for sentiment and Clarence Rowland must make way for a successor." The newspaper called for Comiskey to fire Rowland and, if necessary, manage the team himself. In terms of a successor, the *Eye* said Comiskey has him on his roster — "one who has the makings of a great manager, one who is the greatest player in either league today. And that man is Ray Schalk."[22]

Schalk was popular among his teammates, especially the pitchers, and generally of a pleasant disposition. But he was all about winning, and he did not suffer lightly players who did not share that focus. That pleasant disposition could change abruptly. Owner Comiskey told of the time, during a tight game in Boston, a teammate asked Schalk if he intended to go on the planned boat excursion to New York the next day. Schalk curtly informed the player he didn't care to think about pleasure trips with a pennant-race game going on. "If there had been more of that spirit ... we might have won hands down," Comiskey wrote.[23]

A seven-game win streak in early September kept Rowland's crew in the hunt — still in third but only 1½ games behind the Red Sox and a half-game behind the Tigers. After their 3–2 win over Washington on September 15, the White Sox closed to within a half-game of co-leaders Boston and Detroit. The next afternoon, Chicago defeated Boston, 6–4, to pull into second place, still a half-game out of the lead, and drop the Red Sox to third. That was the closest the White Sox would get to the pennant. Boston won the following two games, pushing Chicago back into third place, 1½ games behind. While Detroit faded from the race, the two Sox squads battled on. On the penultimate day of their campaign, the White Sox swept Cleveland in a doubleheader to stay alive. But the Red Sox scored their game's only run on a sacrifice fly in the bottom of the 10th to edge New York, 1–0. The win assured Boston of no worse than a tie for the pennant. To stay alive and force a deadlock, the White Sox had to sweep for a second consecutive day in Cleveland, and Boston had to lose all three of its remaining games. Chicago did not prolong the suspense that Sunday afternoon, losing 2–0 in the opener. Tris Speaker helped preserve the victory by making a one-handed, running grab of Schalk's line drive into left center. The American League title belonged to Boston. The Red Sox would go on to defeat Brooklyn in a five-game World Series.

In his fourth full season in the majors, Schalk jumped his stolen-base output, swiping 30 bases, a record for a catcher. He was thrown out 13 times. His mark stood for a remarkable 66 years, until Kansas City's John Wathan stole 36. Schalk's stolen bases helped offset a drop in his offensive production; Cracker's batting average was .232, the lowest of his career to that point.

Rowland's players (89–65, four games worse than 1915) barely had time to lick their wounds before taking on Joe Tinker's Cubs in the City Series. The White Sox made it look easy in sweeping to their sixth straight Chicago title. The four Sox pitchers — Reb Russell, Red Faber, Claude Williams and Eddie Cicotte — all threw complete games. Sportswriters pointed to the sweep as evidence that baseball was a game played on the up-and-up. Had the series been extended by a Sox loss, an additional game would have meant a Sunday contest — particularly good money for the clubs but not the players, whose shares were calculated on receipts of the first four games only.

On the Sunday that would have been the date for Game 5 of the City

Schalk held several off-season jobs, including foundry work and sales for a metals firm, insurance sales and real estate development. For 30 years after his playing days, he owned bowling-billiards establishments in and near Chicago. He is shown here ca. 1920 (Bottomley-Ruffing-Schalk Museum, Nokomis, Illinois).

Series, Schalk joined teammates Mel Wolfgang, Buck Weaver and Joe Jackson at (where else?) a ball game. They watched the Chicago American Giants at Schorling Park, where fans were excited and honored to have the major leaguers in attendance.

Meanwhile, Schalk's hometown of Litchfield was making ready for the second annual Schalk Day event — a ball game at Anchor Park and a banquet in the Hotel Litchfield. The host team, featuring the guest of honor, took on the Alpen Braus of nearby Mount Olive. The teams loaded up with as many professionals as they could attract, many of them hailing from downstate Illinois or the St. Louis area. The Anchor team of Litchfield included Joe Slattery (Nationals) at first, Joe Mulligan (Cubs) at shortstop, Jack Roche (Browns) at third, Braggo Roth (Cleveland and formerly of the White Sox) in center, Bob Groom (Browns) pitching and, of course, Schalk behind the plate. The game attracted thousands of fans, who shivered through Litchfield's 8–0 victory. Groom struck out 15 Mount Olive batters, and Schalk contributed with three hits and a stolen base.

When he stepped toward the plate to bat in the second inning of his final baseball game of 1916, Schalk received a serenade from the Mount Olive band: Richard Wagner's "Bridal March" from the opera *Lohengrin*, commonly referred to as "Here Comes the Bride."[24] Considering Schalk's plans for later in the week, the musical selection was appropriate.

9

Ray and Lavinia

As a young man who grew up as the son of an Elks Club building custodian, Ray Schalk was no spendthrift. He didn't believe in credit. A grandson said Schalk's philosophy was, simply, "If you don't have the cash to buy it, you don't need it."[1] Family lore was that Ray would not take a bride until he had $10,000 in the bank. (The bank was probably Litchfield National Bank, where his brother Leo was a cashier and where Ray was a stockholder.) While that bank balance might sound modest to 21st century ears, consider that at the time the average price of a U.S. home was $3,200 and the average annual wage for non-farm workers was just $687. However, after four full seasons as a major-league star, the 24-year-old was ready to tie the knot.

His bride was his long-time sweetheart, 23-year-old Lavinia Graham. The daughter of carpenter James Graham and Hannah McConnell Graham, Lavinia met Ray in 1911, when he was working in a printing shop and playing semi-pro baseball in her hometown of Farmersville. Like her husband, Vin, as family and friends knew her, was of short stature, standing no more than an inch or two above the 5-foot mark. Unlike Ray and unlike most of their American peers, she was a high school graduate.

The wedding was set for October 25, 1916 — a Wednesday evening. The site was the parlor of the bride's home, across the street from St. Mary's Catholic Church in Farmersville, where the mother of the bride worshiped. It was a modest affair, attended by only a handful of friends from Farmersville, Litchfield and Chicago. Among the guests from the Windy City were businessman Sam Pass, a friend of Schalk, who served as best man; Sox manager Clarence Rowland and his wife, Ann; friend Larry Graver, who managed the box office at the Cort Theater and sold tickets at Comiskey Park; former Sox teammate Bobby Roth, now of the Cleveland Indians; and Joseph O'Neill, White Sox traveling secretary. Maid of honor was the bride's sister, Mae Graham.

Major leaguers' weddings often made fillers on the sports pages, but the

Chicago papers made Schalk's nuptials an event worth several days of articles. Sportswriter Bill Bailey — the pen name of Bill Veeck, Sr., later the owner
of the Chicago Cubs — rallied *Chicago American* readers to contribute toward
a wedding fund. The *American's* goal for the campaign was $500. Bailey
exhorted readers "to give the little catcher some concrete evidence of the
esteem in which he is held by the Chicago lovers of the national game." The
paper published the name of every contributor, most of whom gave one dollar; the list included members of the Clarence Rowland family. It also printed
a few testimonials. One came from 11-year-old Chicagoan Raymond W. Seip,
who appreciated Schalk's play and noted that his initials matched those of
the groom. "Therefore I send you $1 for the Schalk fund and wish him much
luck next year and hope he will not quarrel with this wife."[2] A three-man
committee was formed to select the gift from the *Chicago American's* fund:
White Sox owner Charlie Comiskey; sports editor Ed W. Smith; and
Comiskey pal John P. Harding, owner of the Planters Hotel. The committee
opted to purchase a bond for the couple.[3]

The Chicago newspapers also listed some of the other wedding gifts for
Ray and Vin. Comiskey sent a personal check for $500. Ed Walsh, the leg-

The October 1916 wedding of Ray Schalk and Lavinia Graham (shown here with
unidentified well-wishers) attracted lots of publicity, with newspaper reporters
from Chicago in attendance. The *Chicago American* campaigned for its readers
to donate toward a wedding gift; the goal of $500 was attained (Bottomley-
Ruffing-Schalk Museum, Nokomis, Illinois).

endary pitcher who tested the teen-age catcher when he first joined the Sox, shipped a chest of silver. Battery mates Joe Benz and Reb Russell sent "particularly accepted gifts of beauty and worth," a Litchfield paper reported in a front-page article, adding, "Presents came from scores of ball players and admiring friends scattered in every nook and corner of the country, as few individuals are better known in the United States than Schalk."

Veeck also made the trip to Farmersville. "Knowing considerable more about the recording of base hits and errors than about the modes and materials that make brides attractive, no technical description of the wedding dress will be attempted," he wrote. "It was of white, lacey and creamy, in excellent contrast to the blushing red of cheek and brilliancy of eye and it was not only the consensus of opinion, but the enthusiastic spoken belief that Schalk had this time displayed even better judgment in picking 'em off. And you know his reputation for that."[4]

The couple began their honeymoon with an automobile trip to Chicago. On Saturday evening, October 29, they were the guests of honor at the Cort Theater for a special presentation of *Fair and Warmer*, a play billed as "the biggest and best laugh in town." No doubt, Larry Graver had a hand in the arrangements. (Over at the Colonial, the theater was screening the "farewell presentation in Chicago" of D.W. Griffith's controversial and racist epic, *The Birth of a Nation*. Ticket prices ranged from 25 cents to $1.[5]) While in Chicago, the newlyweds stayed at a South Side hotel that *Tribune* sportswriter Sam Weller discreetly declined to identify. Still, the couple had a busy day accepting congratulations from "such of their friends as know where to find them." One who had hoped to personally congratulate Cracker and his bride was a player Schalk idolized as a youth, veteran catcher Jimmy Archer of the Chicago Cubs. However, Archer and the Schalks missed each other that afternoon by just a few minutes.[6] One evening, the Rowlands hosted the newlyweds for dinner in their Michigan Avenue home, "where an informal glad-hand fest was arranged to accustom them to appearing in public together."[7] Apparently, that was not much of a problem. The Schalk honeymoon carried the scent of a promotional tour. Chicago papers reported on the couple's presence in the city, and some featured a photograph of them posing in their automobile. The day of the dinner party, Rowland and Schalk made calls around the city, including a visit to the office of the *Chicago Evening Post*.[8]

After about a week in Chicago, the Schalks planned to drive east, stopping to visit friends along the way, before spending three weeks on Chesapeake Bay at Old Point Comfort, Virginia.[9] How the trip went for Mrs. Schalk was not reported, though in an interview two decades later, she revealed that she was prone to motion sickness. In any case, the newlyweds found their

Lavinia and Ray Schalk's 1916 honeymoon involved a driving tour to Chicago and parts east. Years later, Vin confessed to being prone to car-sickness, though history did not record whether she was affected on this trip (Chicago History Museum, Chicago Daily News Collection, DN-0067296).

way back to Litchfield. Sometime during the off-season, they moved to Chicago; the Windy City would be their permanent home the rest of their lives.

Before long, Lavinia carried the responsibilities of motherhood to go along with those of the spouse of an itinerant professional athlete. Pauline Schalk arrived at 1 A.M. February 27, 1918, at St. Francis Hospital in Litchfield.[10] A brother was born 3½ years later, on August 8, 1921. They named him Raymond W. Schalk, Jr.[11] Through the years, the relationship between Pauline and young Ray was full of friction, and as adults each child brought to their parents challenges, conflict and tragedy. But all that was years away.

The Schalks involved themselves in civic life. The day after Thanksgiving 1916, a month after his wedding, Ray joined the Shriners. The induction took place in Chicago's historic Medinah Temple. He remained with the Masonic organization throughout and earned Life Member status.[12] From the early 1940s through late '50s, Vin would serve as a vice president of the Martha Washington Club, which operated the Martha Washington Home for Crippled Children. The facility was at 4515 Drexel Boulevard, in the former mansion of John G. Shedd, retired president of department store Marshall Field & Co. and founder of Chicago's famous Shedd Aquarium.[13]

The joy surrounding the quiet wedding of Ray Schalk and Lavinia Graham in sleepy Farmersville, Illinois, contrasted sharply with national and world events of the day. Americans were confronted by a steep rise in food prices, which were expected to reach the astronomical heights of 60 years earlier, during the Civil War. From the markets on Chicago's South Water Street came the prediction that turkeys would be selling for the exorbitant price of 35 cents per pound and that the shortage of the birds might force Chicagoans to alter their Thanksgiving and Christmas menus. The *Chicago Tribune* compared prices of some staples with those of two years earlier and found that most had doubled. A pound of sugar now cost 8 cents, a pound of butter cost 40 cents and a dozen eggs went for 45 cents. The Republican-leaning *Tribune* blamed the spike in food prices on the Democratic administration of President Woodrow Wilson, who was soon to win re-election on the slogan, "He kept us out of war." As for the spike in food prices, the *Tribune* acknowledged that "to some degree" exports were part of the reason.[14] Many of those exports went to war-torn Europe, where events increasingly held Americans' interest and concern. For how much longer would the United States avoid being pulled into the fray? And what would U.S. involvement mean for the national pastime?

10

American League Champs

During the winter of 1916–17, as Ray and Lavinia Schalk settled into their life as newlyweds, the United States' standing as a neutral party in the Great War became increasingly unsettled. In the months following his re-election in November 1916 on the record of keeping the United States out of the European war, President Wilson positioned the nation for alliance with Great Britain against Germany, which in February had declared that it would resume unrestricted submarine warfare. In early April 1917, a month after taking the oath of office for his second term, Wilson asked for and received Congress' declaration of war on Germany. Wilson announced his plan to quadruple the size of the U.S. military — to 1.2 million men — for the war effort. If enough volunteers did not step forward, he said, he would implement conscription to make the quota.

With the start of the baseball season barely a week away, professional ball-club owners were in a quandary. How could they protect their enterprise, keeping their employees in baseball uniforms instead of military uniforms and attracting ticket-buying customers, without appearing unpatriotic? They made the case that professional baseball was vital to the psyche of Americans, civilians and military personnel alike, because it provided a respite from the tensions of wartime. Owners staged benefit games for the war effort and Red Cross support, encouraged the purchase of war bonds, saw a war tax added to ticket prices and even had their players practice and perform military drills. White Sox owner Charles Comiskey and American League President Ban Johnson arranged for thousands of copies of *The Sporting News* to be sent to servicemen overseas. After finishing his copy of *The Sporting News*, a reader could send the paper to a U.S. soldier in Europe simply by affixing a penny stamp and dropping it in a mailbox.

However, voluntary enlistments lagged, and in mid–May, Congress passed the Selective Service Act of 1917, requiring men 21 to 30 years old (later 18 to 45) to register for the draft. Exemptions were granted to men with

When Schalk (right) registered for the military draft in 1917, manager Clarence "Pants" Rowland (second from right) and "Shoeless Joe" Jackson (third from right) did the same. Taking their information personally is Chicago City Clerk James Igoe. None of the three was drafted (Chicago History Museum, Chicago Daily News Collection, SDN-061167).

dependent families, physical disabilities or indispensable duties at home. While ballclub owners continued to make the case with the Wilson administration that baseball was indispensable, sportswriters supported their cause. Keeping rosters intact and continuing play was not only advisable, it was patriotic, they argued.

Under clouds of war and uncertainty, the Chicago White Sox opened their 1917 campaign. After coming up just a couple of games short of the American League pennant in 1916, Clarence Rowland's team was no dark horse. It had its sights set on the title, and everybody knew it.

After staging spring training for the second consecutive year in Mineral Wells, Texas, the White Sox opened the regular season in St. Louis, where pre-game activities featured both teams staging military drills. When they took the field, the White Sox wore blue uniforms with faint stripes of white. On each sleeve was an American flag. In the seventh inning, with St. Louis holding a 2–0 lead, umpires halted the game. A man with a motion-picture camera stood in right field, filming the fans in the bleachers. He did not depart until physically removed by a police officer. "He got his film," *Tribune* sportswriter I. E. Sanborn noted, "but probably will occasion a rule barring all photographers from the grounds." Cracker contributed to Chicago's late-game rally with an inside-the-park homer in the ninth inning. His line drive to right center against reliever Carl Weilman scored the final two runs in the 7–2 victory. All of Chicago's runs came in the final two innings.[1]

Three days later, on April 14, 1917, Schalk caught the third of his career four no-hitters. Eddie Cicotte blanked the host Browns in an 11–0 decision. His bid for the record books received an assist when the St. Louis scorer assessed first baseman Chick Gandil an eighth-inning error on a manageable grounder. Cicotte also walked three.[2] Three weeks later, the scorer in St. Louis played a key role in another no-hitter; this time, the circumstances were questionable. On May 5, Ernie Koob blanked the White Sox, 1–0, on an apparent one-hitter. Buck Weaver reached first on a first-inning chopper; initially it was scored an infield single. Sometime after the afternoon game — late enough for the nation's morning newspapers to miss the information — the scorer changed Weaver's hit to an error and handed Koob a no-hitter. The only run of the game scored when Swede Risberg dropped a pop-up. The next afternoon, in the second game of a doubleheader, Bob Groom of the Browns recorded an undisputed no-hitter.[3]

The Browns and White Sox tangled again the next week for Chicago's home opener. The 27,000 fans who braved threatening weather inspected an improved Comiskey Park, which, Sanborn stated, was decked out with "more American flags than we supposed there were in the world." Rain halted the proceedings for a while, and the crowd started calling for the game to resume. The balance of the contest, a 6–2 victory for the home team, was played in a steady drizzle.[4]

The White Sox broke to the front of the American League pack. However, they did not always play like champions. In the top of the ninth inning of a tie game against Cleveland, Jim Scott between a single allowed walks to load the bases. He was replaced by Dave Danforth, who coaxed two Indians to pop out. Just one out away from getting out of a jam, Danforth had a full count on Jack Graney. He started his wind-up on the deciding pitch when Schalk suddenly signaled for the pitcher to stop. The stutter in the delivery made umpire Dick Nallin's ruling of a balk easy, and, due to Schalk's baffling miscue, the Indians claimed a 2–1 victory.[5]

The White Sox regained first place on June 8 and, except for two one-day dips into second position, stayed there. Their second fall from first occurred August 17, when Chicago lost a 12-inning decision to visiting Philadelphia, 9–7. The Sox had their opportunities. In the second inning, Schalk ripped a two-run double and took third on a wild throw to the plate. With pitcher Scott batting, the Sox planned a suicide squeeze. However, when Schalk broke for the plate prematurely, Philadelphia's Alexander "Rube" Schauer delivered a pitchout, and Schalk was a dead duck at the plate.[6] Not only did the Sox lose the game, but they also lost the services of Scott, who subsequently left the team to enlist in the Army.

Though they held serve for most of the final four months of the season, Rowland's White Sox encountered their battles. On a drizzly mid–June Saturday in Boston, Chicago held a 2–0 lead. The rain picked up, but it was still not hard enough to halt play. Nonetheless, the crowd started hollering, "Call the game!" In the fourth inning, the game stopped briefly while bleacher fans scurried across the outfield to shelter under the Fenway Park grandstand roof. In the fifth — the final inning necessary to have a rain-shortened game counted as official — the precipitation picked up and the Red Sox stalled. Meanwhile, Boston gamblers with money riding on the Red Sox continued the shout for the umpires to call the game. The Red Sox and gamblers desired to have the entire affair washed out before the fifth inning ended. "When they (the gamblers) saw they were likely to get another trimming and that it might be averted by breaking up the ball game," Chicago sportswriter James Crusinberry reported, "they incited the fans to riot." The next interruption involved 300–500 people jumping out of the right-field stands (where the gamblers congregated) to mill around the edge of the diamond. That situation ended peacefully after the umpires and Boston player-manager Jack Barry warned that further delay would hand Chicago a forfeit victory.

Soon afterward, the gamblers incited another interruption, and this time the trespassers became riotous. The five police officers on hand, undermanned and uninspired, were no match for the mob. Players for both teams headed beneath the stands, entering via the Red Sox bench area, pushing through the rioters. Buck Weaver, who was pegged by a pop bottle, and Fred McMullin allegedly got rough with some spectators. Schalk saw the head of the police detail and harangued him "in language not of the parlor." While the chaos (and rain) continued, a grounds crew covered home plate and the pitcher's mound with tarps. After more than a half-hour, umpire Barry McCormick, who for reasons unexplained did not declare a forfeit, announced that the game would resume. The soggy infield received a coating of sawdust, and McCormick ordered the grounds crew to remove the tarps. However, Harry Frazee, in his first season as Red Sox owner, told his crew to sit tight. Though he risked losing that afternoon's gate revenue if the game did not last at least five innings, Frazee, seated on the Red Sox bench, again refused to remove the tarps. He relented only when McCormick pulled out his watch and prepared to declare a forfeit. In sloppy conditions the rest of the afternoon — a *Boston Globe* sportswriter said the game should never have resumed — the White Sox staged a four-run rally in the ninth inning to complete a 7–2 victory.[7]

Two days later, before Chicago's next game in Boston, Weaver and McMullin received arrest warrants on the complaint of fan Augustine J.

McNally, who said that he was under the stands when attacked by the players. McNally claimed that his offense was raising three cheers for the Red Sox. Weaver, who sported a bruised neck, and McMullin denied the allegation, saying they were physical only as much as was necessary to get off the field. The legal matters were rather amicable. Authorities did not serve the warrants until they knew bail had been arranged. The players' court appearance was set aside until Chicago's next trip to Boston, in late July.[8] Meanwhile, Schalk narrowly avoided arrest. He nearly came to blows with the policeman with whom he had the earlier confrontation; the cop showed up at the clubhouse intent on either accepting the catcher's apology or arresting him. If anything further came of the prosecution of Weaver and McMullin, it did not reach the newspapers in Chicago or Boston. Most likely, considering that management of both teams wished for the situation to go away, it did. Still, the stench of gambling did not disappear. "The situation in Boston has been a scandal on which the lid has been kept long enough," Chicago sportswriter George Robbins complained in *The Sporting News*, adding that Boston gamblers have been a problem for years, both at Fenway and at the Boston Braves' National League contests.[9] That was not the first time gamblers tried to influence the outcome of baseball games and, as Schalk would painfully be aware for the rest of his days, it would not be the last.

During the summer, the government assigned military draft numbers randomly and scheduled players for physical exams. Unmarried ballplayers were the most susceptible to conscription. Among the White Sox, bachelor Red Faber came up No. 12 on the military registration record back home in Cascade Township, Iowa.[10] By July 1917, Schalk's name was among the first 100 drawn in Litchfield.[11] With a wife as a dependent, Schalk would join millions of other American husbands holding a Class 4 rating. Some Sox players did not wait to see whether the government summoned them for induction. In mid–August 1917, with his team fighting Boston for the pennant, pitcher Jim Scott enlisted and departed for officer training school.[12]

With Scott gone, the White Sox hosted Detroit in back-to-back doubleheaders over Labor Day weekend 1917. Chicago won all four games. Years afterward, questions about the integrity of baseball games brought the public's attention back to those four contests. In the opening game of the Sunday twin-bill, Chicago scored seven times in the first three innings to cruise, 7–2. In the second game, despite allowing Detroit four ninth-inning runs to tie, the Sox pulled out a 6–5 win in 10 innings. The next day, the White Sox gave up leads in both games of the Labor Day doubleheader only to come back for victories. In the morning game, the Tigers roughed up Red Faber for 11 hits in four and two-thirds innings. In the top of the third, neither he nor Schalk called for a pop fly, and the batterymates collided. Despite those and other miscues, Chicago scored three unanswered runs late to win, 7–5. In the afternoon game, Rowland sent Faber out again, but the spitballer still didn't have it. He retired only one Tiger in Detroit's four-run second inning. However, the White Sox rallied again and won again, 14–8. By the end, Rowland was out of pitchers; he warmed up Buck Weaver, who was not in the lineup, in case Eddie Cicotte failed in his relief assignment.[13] Schalk contributed offensively, hitting a triple in the morning game and slamming a three-run homer (off Bill James) and two singles in the afternoon. The four victories over two days, coupled with two Boston losses to New York on Labor Day, gave the White Sox a 6½-game lead over the Red Sox. Though ineffective in the previous day's two starts, Faber received the starting assignment for a third straight game. This time, the game was in St. Louis, and this time, Faber won. (The last of seven major leaguers since 1900 to start three straight games, Faber is the only one to have those three occur over just two days.[14]) A few years later, baseball officials scrutinized the White Sox' back-to-back doubleheader sweeps of the Tigers. Black Sox outcasts claimed that the Chicago players' agreement to assess themselves $45 a man as a gift to the Tigers was not a gift for beating Chicago's closest rival (Boston). Rather, they said, it was a bribe to get the Tigers to "lie down" against the White Sox.

With five straight wins after Labor Day, the White Sox stretched their victory streak to nine. The eighth win came on a forfeit. Chicago and Cleveland were tied 3–3 in the 10th inning. Darkness loomed. Umpire Brick Owens warned the Indians about wasting time. Still, Cleveland players argued and delayed. When Cleveland catcher Steve O'Neill expressed his disgust with an Owens decision by hurling the ball into left field, the umpire declared the game a Chicago victory by forfeit.[15]

On September 19–20, Detroit essentially doused Boston's hopes of catching the White Sox. They beat the Red Sox three straight games, the last two by 1–0 margins. The losses dropped the Red Sox nine games behind the White Sox, who, coincidentally, arrived in Boston for the next series. On September 21, only the host Red Sox stood between the White Sox and the final victory required to clinch the American League pennant. Through nine innings, the Bostonians, with Dutch Leonard on the mound, made it clear that they would not roll over against Faber and the White Sox. The game remained tied, 1–1. Chicago pushed across a run in the top of the 10th inning to take a 2–1 lead. After retiring the leadoff hitter on an infield pop-up, however, Faber gave up consecutive singles. With the potential tying run on third and winning run on first, the Red Sox sent up a pinch-hitter — Babe Ruth. Rowland had his infield play back, figuring a double-play ball was more likely than a

Boston Red Sox personnel pose with Schalk (far left) before a 1917 game in Chicago. Theater owner and producer Harry Frazee (third from left) bought the Red Sox in 1916. The Boston players are Chester "Pinch" Thomas and Harry Hooper (far right). The person standing behind Frazee might be former Chicagoan Larry Graver. A close friend of Schalk, Graver managed the box office of Frazee's Cort Theater before Frazee named him Red Sox traveling secretary (Chicago History Museum, Chicago Daily News Collection, SDN-061164).

game-tying slow roller. Ruth complied, ripping a grounder to second baseman Eddie Collins, who tossed the ball to shortstop Weaver, who relayed it to first baseman Gandil barely in time to beat Ruth.

With that double play, the White Sox became American League champions. Chicago improved its record to 97–49 with eight games to play while Boston fell to 84–57. All Chicago losses and all Boston victories the rest of the way would have produced a tie for the pennant — except that Boston would get in only 152 decisions this season, due to five ties and insufficient open dates for make-up contests. Chicago's 7–5 win over Washington on September 25 made any speculation moot. The White Sox went 3–5 after clinching, closing the regular season at 100–54, achieving the century mark in victories for the first time in the team's 17-season history.

After clinching the pennant and before the World Series, Rowland opted to keep his regulars on the field. They even played tune-up games in Buffalo and Cleveland on open dates. (Rained out was a third practice game with the Indians, who were tuning up to play Cincinnati in an Ohio Series.) Some might have questioned whether the players needed the practice more than rest, and whether they should be exposed to injury in practice games. Injury jumped to mind September 26, when Schalk took a foul tip on the hand in Washington. Had the Sox still been in a pennant race, he might have stayed in the game. Instead, he gave way to Byrd Lynn.[16] Schalk returned to the lineup a few days later but sat out the practice game in Cleveland.

Though he desperately wanted his team back in the World Series, Comiskey did not go to Boston for the clincher. He received the news of the victory over a special telephone line; telegraph reports would not be fast enough to suit him.[17] "It is no secret Commy would sacrifice almost anything to give another championship to Chicago," sportswriter Hugh S. Fullerton wrote. However, even the Old Roman's definition of sacrifice had its limits. During the pennant race, Comiskey promised his players a bonus for a pennant; after they won it, they learned that the Old Roman's "bonus" was a case of champagne donated toward the post-game celebration.[18]

The White Sox claimed the American League title, finishing the year with a nine-game lead, while the New York Giants prevailed in the National League by a similar margin. It was the fourth title in seven seasons for John McGraw's team, which finished 98–56 to outdistance Philadelphia by 10 games. The World Series combatants would be the White Sox and Giants, the nuclei of which toured the world together four years earlier.

For the first time, New York and Chicago, then the nation's two largest cities, would meet in the Fall Classic. These cities genuinely regarded each other with disdain. Chicago's nickname, the Windy City, was a moniker that had nothing to do with the weather; Chicago received the label from editors in Cincinnati (and later New York), who cited the Illinois city's boastful nature — one full of bluster. "The Broadway sport regards Chicago as a city populated by a generation of pork packers," observed Harry A. Williams in the *Los Angeles Times*, "while Chicago estimates New York as the champion boob burg of the hemisphere. Multiply this attitude several times, and you have half a glimpse of the 'spirit' of the two communities where a matter of baseball honor and prestige is involved."[19]

In his fifth full season in the major leagues, where he was regarded as the game's best catcher, Schalk was about to experience his first taste of the World Series. He caught in 139 regular-season games, his highest total, and for the third consecutive season posted the best fielding average of American League catchers (.981). He batted only .226, his lowest average to that point. Yet, what did the offensive achievements of a player in such a key defensive position matter? Perhaps pleading his own case, Schalk in 1917 told *Baseball Magazine*, "I think it is easy to tell a good outfielder. It is rather easy to choose a great shortstop from the records. But a man might be the best catcher the world ever saw or the worst, and there would be no way under heaven to gain that information from the season's statistics." He added, "Fielding averages are pretty bad, pitchers' averages rather punk, batters' averages merely fair. But the worst of all are catchers' averages." (Ironically, decades after he entered the National Baseball Hall of Fame, critics of Schalk's selection still build their argument upon Cracker's unimpressive batting average of .253, the lowest of any position player in Cooperstown). Handicapping the 1917 World Series position by position, Grantland Rice wrote, "Schalk is not only a fine mechanical catcher, arrayed with a stout young arm. He is also a tireless worker, a keen hustler, an aggressive fighter and a cool, quick thinker." He also stated, "He is no slashing hitter, but he is often a timely entry at bat."[20] Jack Veiock, sports editor of International News, opened his profile of Schalk stating that "most" baseball critics considered the White Sox star "the best catcher in baseball." He added, "Schalk's middle initial is 'W,' which stands for 'work,' and, when it comes to work, Raymond is a bear."[21]

Schalk said a catcher had to have "baseball brains"—and one did not acquire "baseball brains" in a classroom. "I used to play in the minors with a graduate of a well known university who was a brilliant scholar and a good natural athlete," he observed. "But he was positively the limit in playing baseball. He would do the most incomprehensible things. In fact he was impossible."[22]

Without a doubt, Schalk had "baseball brains," the defensive skills and the fire. Would that be enough for Cracker and his White Sox teammates against John McGraw's Giants?

11

❖❖❖

Giant-Killers

As the White Sox closed in on the 1917 American League pennant, a man named Ted Craig asked his employer for some time off. He wanted to see his favorite team, the Chicago White Sox, in the World Series. This was not a request for an afternoon or even a couple of days off. Craig lived in Los Angeles. The boss said no, so Craig said goodbye to his job. He boarded an eastbound train, arrived in the Windy City and headed for the Comiskey Park ticket window. The newly unemployed Craig had the honor of heading the line of fans wishing to buy bleacher tickets for Game 1 of the World Series against the New York Giants. However, Craig, who arrived around dinnertime the evening before the opener, gave up his place in line when rain started falling about 9 P.M. Pete Wheeler, who hopped a freight train from Sioux City, Iowa, took over the No. 1 spot and stuck it out through the brief and chilling rain — even though he was coatless. The rain soon stopped and the early arrivals rejoined the line. Eventually, as Friday night became Saturday morning and the mercury dipped to 41 degrees, hundreds of fans extended the queue. Boys sold crates — suitable for sitting — for a quarter each, while others peddled hot coffee. A Chicago funeral director collected chairs from his viewing parlors and rented them to those braving the chilly night outdoors. Five fans inserted an automobile into their spot in line, climbed inside and caught a few winks. Other fans tried to keep warm beside urban campfires, and others passed the time sitting on crates and playing poker. Hundreds — perhaps thousands — joined the four lines to the two ticket windows; one line stretched for nine blocks, snaking through a public playground in Armour Square Park, where the crush of the crowd toppled an iron fence. Not even half of the people in line got the opportunity to buy tickets. As the stadium gates were swung shut, some fans on the outside tried to bribe the gateman $10 or more to let them slip through.[1]

The White Sox were the toast of Chicago, a city gripped by baseball fever. A banquet honoring the team, organized by Comiskey's friends and fellow members of his Woodland Bards, attracted about 500 fans to the Edge-water Beach Hotel (at $10 a plate). Rowland and the players were seated in the center of the banquet hall, at a "dry" table. Promptly at 9:30 in the evening, the guests of honor entered taxis chartered to take them directly home.[2]

The demand for tickets far exceeded supply. White Sox management had orders for 300,000 more tickets, but had to return those disappointed fans' checks and money orders. Thousands of the excluded fans complained and alleged that the process was not on the up-and-up. "Nothing but favoritism pure and simple is behind the refusal of such a reasonable request, mailed in ample time," M.L. Murrin wrote to the *Tribune*, "and one who never failed to argue that everything connected with the grand old game was on the square will argue so no more." Another booster, who signed his letter, "A Sore Fan," noted how he did not get tickets but an acquaintance with "pull" who mailed his request later secured tickets through the National Commission, professional baseball's governing body. "That's how fair the national commission and Comiskey are, and as far as I am concerned ... the whole national commission can go to the land where the proverbial snowball doesn't last."[3]

Many fans unable to purchase tickets through official sources tried their luck with ticket scalpers, though Comiskey and Chicago authorities vowed to do all they could to discourage and prosecute the practice. Comiskey asked the public's assistance and announced a special phone number to accept reports of ticket scalping. Four men were arrested in the Hotel Planters — an establishment owned by Comiskey pal John P. Harding — on disorderly conduct charges for trying to sell six Series tickets in the lobby "at prohibitive prices." A judge later threw out the case, stating that the men were not being disorderly. According to the *Chicago Tribune*, as the Series opener approached, scalpers' prices tripled over just a few days. A couple of days before game time, they were getting $15 to $35 for a grandstand ticket with a face value of $4.50 (nearly $76 in 2008 dollars). As the game grew closer, scalpers offering a box-seat ticket received $60 (more than $1,000 in 2008).[4]

With tickets scarce, and World Series fans desperate to get inside Comiskey Park, the Old Roman beefed up security at the ballpark — as Schalk discovered before one of the contests. The backstop, still looking younger than his 25 years, rode a streetcar from home to the ballpark, where he found the entrance roped off by the cops checking tickets. "I had no ticket, but anticipated no difficulty," Schalk recalled. He identified himself to the officer, who responded, "Don't give us that, kid. Cracker Schalk passed here a half-hour ago." It took 15 minutes of arguing and waiting before a credible person arrived to vouch for Schalk's identity.[5]

In both Chicago and New York, as well as other places around the coun-

White Sox pitching star Eddie Cicotte and manager Clarence "Pants" Rowland pose before a 1917 World Series game. Two years later, Rowland was gone and Cicotte was betraying his honest teammates in the Black Sox scandal (Library of Congress, Prints & Photographs Division, Bain Collection, LC-B2-4360-7).

try, fans unable to attend the games headed toward a theater or auditorium presenting a simulation of the action on electronic scoreboards. The boards displayed the names of the various players, their positions on the diamond, score, and the number of balls, strikes and outs. Thus spectators followed the flow of the contests. Seats sold for as much as a dollar (worth nearly $17 in

2008). In the Windy City, it was standing-room only in the auditorium of the old *Chicago Inter-Ocean* newspaper building (capacity of more than 1,000), Dexter Park pavilion, Arcadia Hall and the Coliseum.[6] In New York, the arrangement was similar, where thousands jammed Madison Square Garden and other venues. In theaters presenting matinee performances instead of baseball simulations, management made regular announcements on the progress of the games. For this series, New York's usual bulletin board postings of the play-by-play were unavailable due to wartime restrictions on large gatherings on the streets and a torn-up Times Square.[7] The Associated Press, using its longest continuous circuit ever, tapped out the play-by-play to its 600 member newspapers using Morse Code, essentially providing "real time" coverage.[8]

Some 32,000 spectators jammed Comiskey Park — the Old Roman hurriedly expanded the capacity with temporary seating — for Game 1 on Saturday, October 6. The huge crowd roared when the White Sox players took the field to warm up. They wore new uniforms for the occasion — trimmed in red, white and blue, no doubt to highlight their patriotic support of Americans in The Great War. Still, all the effort fans exerted to get inside the ballpark several hours before the first pitch might have taken its toll. Veteran sportswriter James Crusinberry observed, "It was the quietest and most orderly crowd that ever sat in at such a big event." He contrasted the crowd's demeanor with that of 11 years earlier, when the White Sox were last in the World Series. In 1906, he said, "there were fog horns and organized bands of rooters and brigades of songsters and cheer leaders." None of that was present for this Series opener.

As the throng awaited the 2 o'clock first pitch, members of the Chicago Cubs, ex–Cub Johnny Evers, Duffy Lewis of the Red Sox and George McBride of Washington passed among the fans, collecting monetary donations to purchase baseball equipment for U.S. servicemen's recreational pursuits. During the game, a collection of a different sort occurred: Thieves outside the ballpark stole the cars of two spectators inside.[9]

In a pre-game meeting with team officials and umpires, Series officials informed managers Rowland and McGraw that excessive bench-jockeying by any player would earn that player an ejection.[10] It was an edict that went largely ignored; Artie Fletcher played a leading role among the Giants' taunters. However, there was almost as much taunting on the field as there was from the dugout.

For his Game 1 starter, Rowland selected Eddie Cicotte, who led the league in victories (28, versus 12 losses), innings (346⅔) and earned-run average (1.53). McGraw's nominee was Harry "Slim" Sallee, who went 18–7 for the Giants with a 2.17 ERA. When Cicotte threw an opening-pitch strike past outfielder George Burns, the thermometer read 58 degrees. Burns rapped a single on a 3–2 pitch and stayed at first while two teammates flied out to left-fielder Joe Jackson. With the Comiskey crowd hooting at batter Heinie Zimmerman, the former Cub, Burns tried to steal second. Schalk delivered a wide throw. Nothing further came of it, however, as Zimmerman flew out to center. The White Sox opened a 2–0 lead after four innings, the second run coming on Happy Felsch's homer over the wall in left-center field. The Giants answered in the top of the fifth when Lew McCarty tripled and Sallee singled, but they could draw no closer against Cicotte and the White Sox, who claimed the 2–1 victory. In three at-bats, Schalk never hit the ball out of the infield.

The fans who jammed Comiskey Park the next afternoon got nervous early, in the second inning, when the Giants jumped to a 2–0 lead. Schalk's excusable error contributed. He lost his grasp of the ball in a home-plate collision with Dave Robertson. The ball rolled such a distance that Walter Holke came around and scored the second run. Chicago fans' unease was eased right away, when the Sox forged a 2–2 tie in the bottom of the second. Chicago then rallied for five runs in fourth inning to make it 7–2. During the rally, Schalk contributed a single and scored a run. The White Sox might have extended their lead if not for Red Faber's baserunning blunder in the fifth inning. With two out and Buck Weaver on second, the light-hitting Faber stroked a clean single to right field. When he saw outfielder Robertson throw home to challenge Weaver, Faber set his sights on second and reached it without drawing a throw. Faber *knew* that Weaver was safe on his RBI single; after all, had Robertson's

White Sox spitballer Urban "Red" Faber and Schalk were lifelong friends who resided in the same area of Chicago. Their 15 seasons together represent the longest tenure of a Hall of Fame battery, according to the Society for American Baseball Research. Schalk long contended that had Faber's health permitted him to pitch in the 1919 World Series, the Black Sox conspiracy would have failed. Photograph date 1917 (Library of Congress, Prints & Photographs Division, Bain Collection, LC-B21-4351-27).

throw nailed Buck at the plate, the teams would now be changing sides. But the Sox pitcher did not consider the possibility that Weaver might be safely perched at third. But that is where Weaver was, and somehow Faber did not notice it. When Faber saw Giants pitcher Pol Perritt use a windup instead of the stretch to deliver his next pitch, Faber, thinking it was the reliever's lapse, took off to steal third. He slid in safely — only to find teammate Weaver occupying the base. A bemused Heinie Zimmerman applied the tag to both Sox — Faber was the one retired — to end the inning. An irritated Weaver growled at Faber, "Where the hell do you think you're going?!" An embarrassed Faber wisecracked, "Going out to pitch."[11] Besides Faber's rally-killer, another feature of the game was that every one of the game's 22 hits — Chicago had 14 — was a single. With two victories in hand, the White Sox boarded their 8 o'clock train for two games in New York, entertaining thoughts of a Series sweep. However, while exuding confidence, Rowland also candidly allowed that "we can afford to lose one game in New York and then have plenty in reserve when we come home."[12]

After a travel day and a rainout, the Giants rebounded for a 2–0 win in Game 3. Rube Benton outdueled Eddie Cicotte, going the distance and holding Chicago to five hits. Schalk went 0-for-3 and reached on a fielder's choice in the eighth inning. He was caught stealing after Strike 3 on Cicotte. The Giants made it back-to-back shutouts the next afternoon, with Ferdie Schupp beating Faber, 5–0, before 27,746 fans in the Polo Grounds. Schalk stroked two singles in three at-bats, took part in a double play and snuffed a stolen-base attempt. The teams boarded their trains for Chicago, having held serve in their respective ballparks. On their travel day, snow fell in the Windy City.

The afternoon of Game 5, the weather was raw and gray, and ticket scalpers outside Comiskey Park struggled to recoup their investments. But the Giants remained hot, grabbing a 2–0 lead before the White Sox could record an out. Rowland tried sore-armed Reb Russell as his starting pitcher and immediately learned it was "a lousy guess."[13] Russell opened the game by issuing a walk and then giving up a single and a double. With that, Rowland had seen enough. He yanked Russell in favor of Cicotte. The White Sox were fortunate to give up only two runs in the inning; twice their infielders nailed baserunners trying to score. Meanwhile, the Giants extended their mastery of Chicago to 24 shutout innings before the White Sox finally pushed across a run in the bottom of the third. Cicotte allowed two runs (one earned) over the next six innings to keep his team close (4–2). Then, the Sox rallied for three runs in the bottom of the seventh to tie, 5–5. Red Faber was sent to the mound for the eighth in relief of Cicotte. The Sox added three in the bottom of the eighth. Faber held serve in the ninth to seal Chicago's win, 8–5, and earn his second victory of the series. Cracker contributed a single, a walk and a stolen base.

The teams returned to the railroad station for another trip to New York, with the White Sox just one win from the world championship. Who would be Chicago's starting pitcher in Game 6? On the train, Rowland and Kid Gleason asked Faber, who had logged 18 innings of work, including the final two innings of Game 5, whether he felt capable of pitching the next afternoon. "Heck, I never heard of anybody refusing to pitch unless they knew something was wrong with 'em and they couldn't help the ball club," Faber said years later, adding that it is more of a strain to sit the bench in a tight game than to pitch one.[14] Rowland's battery for Game 6 in the Polo Grounds was set: Red Faber and Ray Schalk.

The Giants countered with Rube Benton and Bill Rariden.

After playing in raw conditions for Game 5, the players were treated to relatively summer-like weather for their next contest, with sunshine and temperatures in the mid–60s. Fans occupied virtually all of the 34,000 seats in the Polo Grounds, an oval-shaped stadium featuring extremely short foul lines (277 feet in left and just 258 in right) and an impossible 500 feet to the wall in dead center.

The White Sox jumped to a 3–0 lead in the fourth, an inning punctuated by one of the oddest plays in World Series history — at least since Faber tried to steal an occupied base in Game 2. The inning opened with Eddie Collins hitting a grounder to Giants third baseman Zimmerman, who unleashed a wild throw, allowing Collins to take second. Then right fielder Robertson dropped Joe Jackson's fly ball. With Collins now at third and Jackson on first, the

Eddie Collins, Hall of Fame second baseman, and Schalk, Hall of Fame catcher, were roommates on the road. Photograph dated 1922 (Library of Congress, Prints & Photographs Division, Bain Collection, LC-B2-5256-14).

Giants infield moved in, hoping to hold Collins at third and make a double play. Chicago manager Rowland had other thoughts: "Collins' strategy was to break for home to compel a throw. That would leave men on first and second with just one out instead of two men out and a man on third." The plan was put into play when Happy Felsch hit a comebacker to Benton, who ran at the trapped Collins. As the rundown developed, Collins signaled for Jackson and Felsch to advance. When Collins moved back toward third, Benton tossed the ball to Zimmerman. With that, Collins turned and dashed for home. Instead of throwing toward the plate, Zimmerman chased Collins. The baserunner won the race to notch another run for Chicago. New York fans and other observers criticized Zimmerman for trying to outrun Collins.[15] However, others pointed out home plate was left unguarded. Catcher Rariden had moved out of position during the rundown and left the plate unattended. Said Zimmerman, "Who the hell was I going to throw the ball to? Klem (the umpire)?"[16] Others agreed, but Rowland claimed that Zimmerman had called Rariden off the play.[17] As the crowd buzzed about the miscue, Chick Gandil singled to right to score Jackson and Felsch; the Giants nailed Gandil trying to take second. After Buck Weaver flew out, Schalk singled and Faber walked. But they were stranded when Shano Collins grounded out. It was Schalk's only hit in three at-bats; he allowed a passed ball in the seventh but the Giants couldn't capitalize. Those three runs were enough for Faber, who survived a two-run fifth inning and saw his mates push across an insurance run in the ninth. During that frame, New York shortstop Artie Fletcher spat at Rowland, who was coaching in the third-base box. The manager responded by challenging Fletcher to fight after the game. The altercation didn't happen. After the game Fletcher, whose on-field aggressiveness contrasted with his usual civility, stayed in the clubhouse.[18]

The Giants kept fighting in the bottom of the ninth. Lefty Dave Robertson gave the crowd a charge when he sent a liner toward the short fence in right, but the drive went foul. Robertson appeared to foul off a close pitch, and umpire Bill Klem signaled strike two. Robertson and manager McGraw protested that the batter was hit by the pitch. When Robertson showed Klem the evidence, the umpire awarded him first base. Robertson had suffered a broken finger on the play. "It was all smashed up," confirmed Faber, who saw the disfigured digit years later. With the potential game-tying run in the batter's box, Faber, a ground-ball specialist, followed Schalk's signals and coaxed a fielder's choice grounder out of Walter Holke. He then struck out Rariden looking. With Robertson on second, McGraw sent up Lew McCarty to pinch-hit. McCarty ripped a grounder to second baseman Eddie Collins. The future Hall of Famer made certain of his catch and tossed to first baseman Gandil to make Charles Comiskey's Chicago White Sox the 1917 World Champions.

As the players worked their way through the stunned New York fans who massed on the field, McGraw congratulated Faber, the pitcher whose contract he tried to purchase four seasons earlier, and other Sox players. *The New York Times, Chicago Herald* and *The Sporting News* described McGraw pushing through the crowd to locate and congratulate Rowland. "There were tears of happiness in Rowland's eyes as McGraw grasped his hand," the New York paper reported, "and he was happier still when McGraw told him he had won with as game and fair a team as he had ever played against."[19] Comiskey himself commended McGraw and captain Buck Herzog for immediately finding Rowland and Sox captain Eddie Collins to congratulate them.[20] Those accounts differ greatly from that in a McGraw biography published three decades later. Author Frank Graham stated that it was Rowland who found McGraw, and Rowland who attempted to shake the legendary manager's hand. "Mr. McGraw, I'm glad we won, but I'm sorry you had to be the one to lose." In Graham's account of the exchange, McGraw snarled, "Get away from me, you (expletive) busher!"[21]

With the World Series title Rowland appeared to shed the "busher" label. *The Sporting News* reported experts' observation that Rowland "outgenerated" McGraw and had silenced the naysayers.[22] Still, behind the scenes, there was talk that it was not Rowland but veteran coach Kid Gleason who was really the key to Chicago's success.

The World Series title boosted the bank accounts of Schalk and his mates. Reports on the winner's share ranged from $3,528 to $3,930 a man — worth about $60,000 in 2007.[23] (Ninety years later, the Series champion Boston Red Sox collected $308,236 a share.[24]) Before even receiving their checks, some of the champions purchased rings in New York, while others announced plans to buy motor cars. Schalk, who already owned a car, had other ideas. Sportswriter Crusinberry noted that Cracker, "being one of the thrifty ones, figured his share not as $3,600 but as about $250 a year added to his income, because he intends to invest it in safe securities, probably farm loans down at Litchfield."[25]

Though the World Series title was decided, the White Sox and Giants, in an unprecedented move, had agreed to play once more. After an extended overnight celebration in the Biltmore Hotel, the Sox dragged themselves to Garden City, New Jersey, where they engaged the Giants in an exhibition game for an audience of 6,000 soldiers, most of them from New York and Illinois.[26] Even hung over, the White Sox still won, 6–4. Their boss, Comiskey, did not stick around for the exhibition, returning to Chicago a day ahead of his team. He exited his train at the Englewood station, thus avoiding a substantial welcoming party waiting for him at the La Salle Street station. That night, he hosted a quiet dinner for family at the Comiskey residence. A reporter who missed the Old Roman at the train station reached him by telephone. "I always wished for a world's series between Chicago and New York, but I never thought it would come about," Comiskey said. "I knew we would win, but I know also that we would have a rough fight. We won, and there was enough of the rough stuff to satisfy anybody. But there is no hard feeling." Comiskey also praised his manager: "If they call Rowland a 'busher' after this, it will be a term of praise."[27] Nonetheless, within a year Comiskey would fire Rowland.

Soon after defeating the Giants again, the Sox boarded a regular New York Central train for Chicago. The team's three cars constituted but one-third of the train, yet the other passengers seemed to care not when the world champions' boozy celebration spilled over into other quarters. Festivities included a parade from the dining car at the front of the train to the observation car in the rear. Many passengers joined the Sox in their celebration, which, by some accounts, lasted until dawn. As their train rolled closer to Chicago, the La Salle Street station was bedlam. Fifty extra policemen had arrived for crowd control, but they were too late to do much good with the boisterous boosters of the White Sox. So many fans jammed in and around the depot that the entire area was in gridlock. At 4 o'clock sharp the afternoon of October 17, with fans lining Track 12 beyond the track platforms and overhang, the train pulled to a stop. Two brass bands — a third ensemble could not wedge inside — simultaneously (but not in unison) struck up "Hail, Hail, the Gang's All Here." The throng "let loose a yell that threatened to blow off the glass dome of the station." There was no formal welcoming ceremony, and some players — Schalk might have been among them — managed to work their way through the crush of fans without being recognized. Not as fortunate was Rowland, who was "fairly mobbed" by well-wishers, who hoisted him upon their shoulders. Meanwhile, Rowland's wife, Ann, was nearly knocked down in the crush. Louis Comiskey, the Old Roman's son and a man of substantial girth, helped several players' wives get through the crowd. As the *Chicago Herald* noted, "Dodging Polo Grounds mobs was nothing compared to the gauntlet which the returning Hose were compelled to run before they got into their taxis."[28]

The day after returning to Chicago, Cracker got into his car and started the 250-mile drive to Litchfield. (It was not reported whether Vin was with him.) Along the way, due to heavy rain, he left his car and caught a train for the balance of the trip. Time was of the essence, because Litchfield's third annual Schalk Day game was only a couple of days away. Among the current and former major leaguers invited to Litchfield were Schalk's batterymate Cicotte and former Sox star Nick Altrock, a coach and a clown prince of baseball. For the first time, motion-picture cameras would be on hand to capture the activity. Ticket prices ranged from a dime to 50 cents. The Illinois Traction System, the region's electric railroad service, put on extra cars to accommodate fans from Mount Olive, Hillsboro and Staunton.

The visiting team represented the Alpen Braus of Mount Olive. Wearing red uniforms and accompanied by their own band, the Mount Olive team, including major leaguer Ray Demmitt, marched single file onto the Anchor Park field. Meanwhile, Schalk and Altrock passed among the 3,500 spectators to solicit donations for the Clark C. Griffith Ball and Bat Fund, to provide baseball equipment for U.S. soldiers. Schalk "button-holed, pan-handled, un-buckled, ham-stringed all of his admirers for contributions," the local paper reported. Among them was Sam Pass, best man at Schalk's wedding a year earlier, who secured leave from the Fort Sheridan Army base near Chicago. Schalk and Altrock collected a healthy $166, though the paper speculated that they could have collected more had they waited until the crowd had seen more of Altrock's entertaining antics, which included staging a fight with himself, making a putout at first while prone on the field and wearing his ball cap sideways.[29]

Game organizers had asked Cicotte to "cut loose" and show how it was done in the big leagues. He complied, striking out 16 batters in eight innings. In one frame, he struck out the side on nine pitches. At bat, Cicotte blasted the ball into the parking lot for an apparent home run. However, when someone standing among the autos heaved the ball back to the field, Mount Olive relayed it to third, where a puzzled Cicotte was tagged; the umpire went along and called him out. Altrock took over in the ninth inning for Cicotte — and for the home plate umpire. The clown pitched and called his own balls and strikes — and by most accounts did both in an entertaining and equitable manner. A local paper noted, "It is impossible to say which was the greater attraction, Cicotte, Altrock or Schalk." That day was capped with a multi-course meal, including cigars, and extensive program at the Elks Club. "The lesson gained from the evening was that Ray Schalk is famous because he can fill the job of baseball catcher just a little better than can any one else in the world and tho [*sic*] all people, young men especially, can not be great ball players they do have it in them to be great in some one thing," the local reporter summarized. "That a young man choosing a career should determine to excel in that thing he undertakes, do the job just a little bit better than anyone else can or does do it. Lead a clean life and play the game of life fair and square. Because Ray Schalk has done these things he is famous. Because in spite of the honor and praise that has been heaped upon him, his hat band still fits him and he continues to know as of old, his old friends, Ray Schalk is popular."[30]

Celebrated across the nation as well as his hometown, and now a World Series champion, Schalk was on top of the world. And there was more: Soon, he would become a father. That there were so many highlights in 1917 must have made the events of 1918 especially difficult.

12

A Dynasty Interrupted

Shortly before Christmas 1917, Schalk and all the other champions received the team's gift commemorating the title: A button of solid gold, three-fourths of an inch across, with a diamond mounted in the center.[1] His button was sent to Litchfield, where Ray and Vin moved for the winter and awaited the arrival of their first-born.

Despite the world war and the tendency of other players who had just won a World Series title to show "swell-headedness" in contract negotiations for the next season, Charlie Comiskey had little trouble securing signed agreements with most of his employees.[2] However, his players might have known there was little use driving a hard bargain with the Old Roman. The owner's general approach was to offer his charges two options: (1) "Take it" or (2) "Leave it." On the last day of January 1918, Buck Weaver and Joe Benz had private audiences with Comiskey. It was a session reporter James Crusinberry described as "one of those interesting little talks," and both players emerged professing to be pleased with their terms.[3] Weaver, who was expected to move from third base to his previous position as shortstop, and Benz were among the last regulars to come to terms. Schalk was already signed.

With the war continuing in Europe, however, a signed contract was no guarantee that the player would not be wearing a military uniform instead of a baseball uniform — or that the 1918 season would be played to completion. As a married man, the chances of his being drafted into the military were remote. Schalk held Class 4 status with his draft board, a category that included men with families that were "mainly dependent on his labor for support."[4] Ray and Lavinia Schalk gained a dependent in the first hour of February 27, 1918, when Pauline came into the world. Born in St. Francis Hospital, she weighed 6½ pounds.[5]

A month before her arrival, Schalk had made a trip back to Chicago. He stopped by Rowland's office, where he caught up with Benz and Weaver, who were there to settle their contracts, and Red Faber, before taking in the Chicago auto show. However, Schalk failed to make a room reservation and discovered that the city's downtown hotels had no rooms — not even for the best catcher in the world. Finally, Schalk contacted Faber, who offered to share his hotel room in the Loop.[6]

Schalk and Faber were the first players back in town six weeks later, when the defending champions convened for their annual train trek to spring training in Mineral Wells, Texas. As was his custom, Schalk arrived early to visit a sporting goods store and pick out his catcher's equipment for the campaign. One long-time member of the Sox support staff was not on board. Comiskey fired veteran trainer and equipment manager William Buckner, one of the few African Americans in major-league baseball before Jackie Robinson broke the color barrier for players. Harry Stephenson succeeded Buckner.[7] Though the reason for Buckner's release was not given, the word was that it came at the insistence of pitcher Dave Danforth.[8] (Comiskey rehired Buckner four years later, a couple of seasons after Danforth and the White Sox parted ways. Buckner eventually became the first African American to earn a pension from a major-league team.)

The major leagues agreed to allocate proceeds from the World Series differently, allowing all teams finishing in the top half of the standings to receive a portion of the pie.[9] The decision would keep up the interest among teams out of the pennant race but in a position to battle for a finish in the first division. Further, in consideration of wartime restrictions and their financial struggles of the previous season, the teams agreed to an abbreviated 1918 spring training. It was to last just a month.

The White Sox, said to be the only team following the letter and spirit of the agreement, began another day behind schedule when their train derailed east of Weatherford, Texas, some 16 miles from their final destination. The tender car jumped the track and tore up ties for nearly 100 yards. The engineer applied the emergency brake, and the steel sleeper cars housing the White Sox nearly telescoped the other coaches. The engine and cars stayed upright, narrowly avoiding a tumble down a 25-foot embankment. The White Sox arrived in Mineral Wells just three hours behind schedule — but too late for an initial workout that afternoon. A couple of days later, the White Sox narrowly avoided another disaster. Driving to their hotel after a morning of golf, four players — Schalk, Ed Cicotte, Joe Jackson and Chick Gandil — were involved in a two-car collision. It was an odd foursome, considering that Schalk was (or soon would be) feuding with the other three.[10] Three of the players were able to participate in the afternoon workout, but Cicotte, complaining of neck pain, stayed behind and received treatment from new trainer Stephenson. News of the accident upset Comiskey. He was indignant. "Base-

Arnold "Chick" Gandil, White Sox first baseman, was the ringleader of the White Sox players linked to the Black Sox scandal of 1919. When the indictments and suspensions came down late the next season, Gandil was already retired (Library of Congress, Prints & Photographs Division, Bain Collection, LC-B2-4350-1).

ball is their game, and they are down here to get in shape to play baseball," the owner said. "Their place was on the ball field this morning if they were able to be there, not out experimenting with golf sticks and looking at scenery." Thus began the team's ban on golf during spring training.[11]

Not so lucky was pitching prospect Ed Corey, a Chicago native who broke his ankle on a botched slide during a game in Dallas. As Corey writhed in pain on the infield, teammate Fred McMullin looked over Corey's ankle for a moment and then yanked it. "McMullin's 'first aid' kept the ankle from swelling to anything like the usual size in such accidents," the *Tribune* noted.[12] Corey, still favoring the ankle three months later, made his major-league debut in the final two innings of an 11–8 loss to Detroit. The first batter he faced was Ty Cobb, who rocketed an 0–2 pitch into the glove of Shano Collins. The July 2 contest turned out to be Corey's only major-league appearance ever. As for McMullin, he stuck around three seasons — until his suspension in the Black Sox affair.

Besides the team's prohibition on extra-curriculars, *Tribune* sportswriter Irv Sanborn noted another difference in this training camp. The African American citizens of Mineral Wells treated the White Sox with an obvious coolness, effectively boycotting the traditional welcome between the train station and hotel. Sanborn reported the explanation that many of the locals had bet heavily on the New York Giants, "the most popular team in either league in Texas," to beat Chicago in the previous World Series. No mention was made of Buckner's firing.[13]

Also missing from the White Sox contingent was coach Kid Gleason, who experienced an off-season to forget. Credited with helping the team win the World Series, Gleason wound up losing his Series payoff in a business venture gone bad back home in Philadelphia. Earlier, he underwent surgery for an unspecified serious illness. Finally, he requested a leave of absence so he might straighten out his affairs.[14] However, there was also talk that Comiskey and Gleason, who four years earlier fended off Federal League overtures to White Sox players and even Gleason himself, were not on speaking terms.[15]

After barely a week of practice, the White Sox split into two squads for exhibition games. Schalk was put in charge of a group of regulars left in camp for final workouts while reserves donned their uniforms, rode by motor vehicles 35 miles for a game in Jacksboro, and rode home (in uniform) for showers and a late dinner.[16] The Chicago contingent did not have its heart in a March 22 intra-squad game (in which Schalk caught for both teams). The players did not sleep much the previous night, and they remained shaken by a tragedy at their hotel, where a 17-year-old Pennsylvania girl, trying to adjust the curtains in the room she shared with her mother, fell to her death from a third-floor window. Somehow, it fell to manager Clarence Rowland to inform the mother, confined to bed by the shock, that her daughter was dead.[17]

Meanwhile, back in Chicago, amateur baseball players were disappointed to learn that Lincoln Park was off-limits on Sunday afternoons. Bowing to complaints from patrons of the previous season's weekly band concerts, who said noise from the baseball games interfered with their enjoyment of the music, the Lincoln Park Commission announced that the baseball field could not be used after 1 P.M. on concert days.[18] Baseball fans in the Windy City also learned that the White Sox and Cubs planned to start all home games at 3 P.M., in deference to the newly instituted Daylight Saving program. While starting at 4 could have meant better gate receipts, the baseball owners believed that to do so would have been contrary to the energy-conservation intent of the wartime Daylight Saving initiative.[19]

The White Sox played their way back toward Chicago for the regular season opener. It was a spring to forget. "The training trip has been the least valuable the White Sox have ever taken, in spite of weather which has permitted work every day since they landed in Mineral Wells," Sanborn wrote. "Starting with a railroad wreck on the way to camp, things have gone wrong almost constantly." In addition, there was the auto accident, the hotel guest's fatality, the death of Buck Weaver's father, illness of Eddie Collins and absence of coach Kid Gleason." Schalk missed the final exhibition in Kansas City, where he was expected to rest anyway, after receiving word that his 7-week-old daughter, Pauline, was ill back home in Litchfield. He received permission to miss the game and check on the baby.[20]

Schalk was in uniform for the season opener April 16 in Chicago. The team marched onto the Comiskey Park field behind a military band. Part of the pre-game events included White Sox players subscribing to buy $25,500 in war bonds. In a rare occurrence, the umpires — George Hildebrand and Brick Owens — received cheers from the 25,000 fans. Hildebrand announced that the arbiters had purchased one Liberty bond and intended to secure another. However, the game itself was not as encouraging, as the St. Louis Browns battered four White Sox hurlers en route to an 8–1 victory.[21] The White Sox returned the favor the next week, spoiling the Browns' home opener, 6–2.

Though the teams were racking up wins and losses, the uncertainty of war clouded the proceedings. The status of hundreds of players depended on whether the U.S. government viewed professional baseball as an "essential" enterprise in times of war. On May 22, 1918, as the White Sox lost 1–0 in 14 innings, Gen. Enoch H. Crowder, provost marshal general, announced a "work-or-fight" order, mandating that, by July 1, every man of draft age had to be serving in the military or engaged in an occupation useful to the war effort. However, Crowder postponed a decision whether the order pertained to pro athletes. Noting that Secretary of War Newton D. Baker had exempted theatrical performers, baseball officials hoped the government would do likewise for their enterprise.[22] August Herrmann, chairman of baseball's National Commission, argued that baseball, like theater, provided entertainment vital to American society. He calculated that without the exemption major-league teams would lose 258 of their 369 players.[23] "I cannot understand that statement (by Crowder) the game is nonproductive when the two major leagues will deliver to the Government a war tax in the neighborhood of $300,000," American League President Ban Johnson said. "The ball players, umpires, club stockholders and officials have bought more than $8 million of Liberty bonds and have subscribed thousands upon thousands of dollars for the Red Cross and other war charities. Where is there another class of men earning so much for the government?"[24]

Even without a final decision on Crowder's order, organized baseball unraveled. First to feel the effects were the minor leagues, which wrestled with travel restrictions and loss of talent. Most of the players were single and thus prime candidates for the draft. Nine of the 10 minor leagues ended their seasons by July; the tenth, the International League, shut down three weeks early.

Some Sox did not wait for a final decision. Facing the virtual certainty he would be drafted into the Army, Red Faber enlisted in the Navy in early June. Comiskey gave him a going-away gift. The Old Roman was less charitable with other players. Joe Jackson, upon learning that his draft classification was raised from Class 4 to Class 1, left the team to work in a Delaware shipyard. Lefty Williams and Byrd Lynn, friends since their days in the minors, joined him there. For a while, Jackson was indeed shoeless. The day after leaving the Sox, Jackson phoned his manager, Rowland, and asked to have his baseball cleats sent to him. "He (Jackson) told the boss he thought he was doing the right thing in turning painter to protect his family,"[25] the *Tribune* reported. His action, and dozens like it, drew the attention of Crowder, who planned an investigation; authorities were especially interested in probing reports that the major leaguers were finding their way onto their wartime employers' semi-pro teams and receiving extra pay for their services.[26]

Comiskey, however, required no investigation. In the owner's view, a war-related civilian job was no substitute for military service — especially if it meant abandoning the team when they were not expected to be drafted during the 1918 season anyway. "There is no room on my ball club for players

"Shoeless" Joe Jackson, one of baseball's biggest stars, was banned for life in the Black Sox scandal. His defenders cite his .375 batting average and errorless defense in the 1919 World Series to argue that he did not participate in the conspiracy. Photograph taken 1919 (Library of Congress, Prints & Photographs Division, Bain Collection, LOT 11147-1).

who wish to evade the Army draft by entering the employ of ship concerns," Comiskey said.[27] On "Pennant Day," when the team's 1917 championship was recognized, Comiskey took away the uniforms of Williams and Lynn. Concerning uniforms, the White Sox were forced to play the next two afternoons of their homestand in their road attire; their home whites were somehow still at the laundry.[28]

Around this time, Schalk committed some blunders that were notable for their rarity. His passed ball allowed the only run of a game against Boston.[29] Two days later, he dropped Carl Mays' easy pop fly. Mays proceeded to pop up again, and this time Schalk executed a more difficult catch.[30] A few days after that, Schalk was forced to laugh at himself after he dropped an easy pop-up by Walter Johnson.[31] However, Schalk also contributed some highlights that indicated he hadn't lost his touch, such as the June 25 game in which he picked up the ball and chased down Ty Cobb halfway to first after a dropped third strike.[32]

The loss of players to the military and war-related jobs, as well as an injury to future Hall of Famer Eddie Collins, took their toll on the White Sox. Two days after Jackson jumped the team for the shipyard, Chicago and Washington battled through 17 scoreless innings. Both teams' starting pitchers, Lefty Williams and Walter Johnson, were still around in the 18th. After Johnson set down the Sox in the top of the frame, the Nationals pitcher contributed the single that pushed the potential winning run to third base with one out. Williams got two strikes on the next hitter, Burt Shotton. On his next delivery, Williams threw a pitch so wild and high that Schalk could not snare it. "Without Jackson, Eddie Collins or (Happy) Felsch in the lineup," the *Tribune* lamented, "the Sox lacked the final punch that would have landed the game easily in regulation time." (Felsch missed nearly two weeks while visiting his seriously injured brother at a Texas military base.[33]) Despite lasting 18 innings, the game, which started at 4:30 P.M. in the nation's capital, consumed less than three hours. One reporter estimated that when the game ended the teams had enough daylight for two more innings."[34]

The White Sox came out on the short end of another 1–0 marathon less than a week later in New York, where Yankee starter Hank Thormahlen outdueled Eddie Cicotte over 14 innings. About the only highlight for Schalk was nearly recording a defensive put-out at second base. With two out in the bottom of the fifth, the Yankees had Elmer Miller on second base and James "Truck" Hannah on first. Hannah lost track of the count on the batter and, believing the third ball was the fourth, sauntered toward second while Miller held his position. Ball in hand, Schalk ran from the catcher's box to confront the two baserunners convened at second. After a chase, the Sox retired Miller between second and third. A few years earlier, a sportswriter commenting on Schalk's speed and heads-up play, stated, "Recently Schalk ran to third base to make a play there when that position was open. 'I have seen Schalk do about everything on a ball field now except back up second base,' said a baseball writer, 'and I expect to watch him turn that trick before long.'"[35] Unfortunately, history did not record whether that sportswriter was present June 28, 1918, when the St. Louis Browns visited Chicago for a doubleheader. A feature of the afternoon was a thrift-stamp sale in which ladies passed among the fans to collect more than $15,000 from only 6,000 fans — rainy weather threatened — including free admissions on Ladies Day. It also was the first day as Browns manager for Jimmy Burke, who succeeded Fielder Jones, the former White Sox outfielder and World Series manager; Jones had abruptly resigned two weeks earlier.

In his managerial debut, Burke took over coaching duties at first base. His right fielder, Ray Demmitt (who had played in the Schalk Day exhibition the previous October), opened the top of the sixth inning with a walk. He was running for second on the pitch when Tim Hendryx lifted a long fly ball to left fielder Nemo Leibold, who juggled the ball but held it. Demmitt was on his way toward third when he realized that Leibold had made the catch, and he started his dash back to first. Schalk had moved toward the pitcher's mound to back up a possible throw to the infield. He — and perhaps others — noticed that on his way back to first, Demmitt failed to retouch second base, as required under the rules. Leibold threw to first in hopes of doubling up the baserunner. First baseman Chick Gandil took Leibold's throw and tossed the ball toward second base, where Schalk made the catch and completed the double play.[36] Thus did Schalk execute a baseball rarity — a catcher recording a putout at second base. In subsequent years, sportswriters asked Schalk about that unheard-of play. Schalk was happy to oblige the scribes, but his recall was not 100 percent. When he told the story, Shoeless Joe Jackson made the catch and fired the ball to Risberg, who relayed it to Schalk. According to Cracker, his accomplishment came at a price. Second baseman Eddie Collins was none too pleased to have Schalk step in to take the throw and record the put-out. But it could not have happened the way Schalk described it. Jackson was not even on the team that afternoon, having bolted for shipyard duty nearly six weeks earlier. The Leibold-Gandil-Schalk version appears in the play-by-play summary published in the *Chicago Daily News,* and the double play was noted in the *Chicago Tribune*'s box score.[37]

Regardless of who participated in that double play, Schalk's put-out established him as one of the few players to ever record an out at every base. (Johnny Roseboro of the Dodgers matched his achievement of being a catcher making a putout at second base 46 years later — to the day. He tagged out Willie Mays on a rundown play after an aborted attempted steal.[38]) Putouts at third and at first involved a bit of deception. Here is how Schalk recorded outs at third: With an opposing runner on first in a bunt situation, third baseman Harry Lord would run in to field the sacrifice and, after making the throw, appear to forget to hustle back to his position. The runner advancing to second base would notice third base unattended and try to advance an extra base. However, what the runner did not notice was Schalk dashing to third to take first baseman Hal Chase's return throw. When the runner arrived at third, Cracker was waiting to apply the tag. Schalk's putouts at first were an extension of the catcher's practice of running parallel to the first-base line to back up the first baseman after a ball is hit into play. (Some sources credit Schalk with being the first catcher to back up plays in this manner, but Harry Smith was doing it for the Philadelphia Athletics as early as 1901, nearly a dozen years before Schalk joined the majors.[39]) When an opposing batter rapped a single into right field, White Sox first baseman Chick Gandil would intentionally wander away from the bag and watch the outfielder collect the base hit. The hitter, seeing Gandil out of position, took an extra-wide turn around first. What the hitter did not see was Schalk coming from behind, positioning himself at first. Schalk received the peg from the right fielder and tagged out the surprised opponent.[40]

As the season continued, teams continued to lose players. Happy Felsch collected his June 1918 paycheck and informed Rowland that he was returning to his hometown of Milwaukee, where he would work for the natural gas utility and play semi-pro ball; he would receive $125 a month. Comiskey did not even talk with Felsch before he left, and the Old Roman was satisfied to see him go. "It has been apparent Felsch has been worrying for some time," he said, "for he hasn't been playing his regular game at all."[41] Comiskey months later indicated that there had been "some trouble" between Felsch and Eddie Collins.[42] The players nearly came to blows in the dugout one afternoon.[43] In any case, "Happy" was anything but, and he became the fifth White Sox player to depart.[44] A wire-service report on Felsch's departure flatly stated, "His loss about ruins the pennant hopes of the White Sox."[45] Even before Felsch bolted, those hopes were faint. Through June, Chicago was 30–32 and only 6½ games behind the Red Sox, but in fifth place. With so many key players missing, the White Sox were hardly positioned to defend their American League pennant.

With the departure of players and fans, and the government poised to shut down baseball operations with the work-or-fight order, major-league owners struggled to stay open for business. On a steamy afternoon in August,

with the hot wind from the Chicago stockyards wafting to the ballpark, barely 600
fans showed up at Comiskey Park.[46] Teams
took chances on unheralded and unknown
players. After spending exorbitantly on train
tickets for Frank "Kid" Willson to join,
White Sox management soon realized the
22-year-old was not major-league material.
He appeared in four games, mostly as a
pinch runner. "It seems there was some misunderstanding regarding the previous experience of the boy, for since joining the team
he has confessed he has played professional
ball only about a month and a half," the
Chicago Tribune reported. "However, he's
an athletic and ambitious fellow, and may
come up again later."[47] In Willson's case,
"later" was much later. Nine years later, he
returned to the White Sox, and again he
stayed briefly — just seven games — but long
enough to record the lone base hit of his
major-league career.[48]

On July 19, Secretary of War Baker,
with President Wilson's approval, announced

Oscar "Happy" Felsch, one of
the "Eight Men Out" in the
Black Sox scandal, in 1920
(Library of Congress, Prints &
Photographs Division, Bain
Collection, LC-B2-5278-8).

that all ball players of draft age were subject to the work-or-fight order —
immediately. Provost Marshall General Crowder had recommended that the
government allow the season to be played to completion, but Baker would
not go along. Facing the unattractive prospect of using and recruiting ballplayers age 31 and older, the major leagues prepared to shut down.[49] The
athletes, meanwhile, found themselves conflicted between obligation to
their country and to their employment contracts. Sportswriter Bill Bailey,
revealing "utter chaos" among the White Sox, said, "The players are caught
between two grinding wheels, or imagine that they are at least, and know
not which way to turn." Sox players —13 of them, including Schalk, were
subject to the order — hoped for clear direction from management as to
when they would be released from their contracts.[50] The National League
likewise considered shutdown. The remaining members of the first-place
Chicago Cubs, wishing to avoid losing the pennant due to forfeits, boarded
their train for Philadelphia.[51] Meanwhile, aggressive shipyard magnates
offered major leaguers jobs — and spots on their ball teams. The Duluth-

Mesaba League sent telegrams proposing such an arrangement to several stars, including Schalk, Ty Cobb, Walter Johnson, George Sisler and Home Run Baker.[52]

Several days later, the secretary of war granted the major leagues some additional time — but not the mid–October date they proposed. He allowed the regular season to continue through September 1, with pennant winners permitted to continue through the World Series.[53] Eventually, that deadline was extended a day, making the final afternoon of the regular season Monday, September 2 — Labor Day 1918. Each major-league team contested 123 to 131 games by the deadline. After playing in Chicago the final Sunday, Cleveland didn't bother making the trip to St. Louis. Indians officials notified the Browns they would be no-shows. The Browns staked their claim to two forfeits by taking the field at the appointed hour, making five pitches, observing the prescribed 10-minute interval between "games" and throwing five more pitches. Browns pitcher Grover Lowdermilk, who would join the White Sox the next season, was recruited to serve as the "umpire."[54]

As far as Cracker and the White Sox were concerned, the extension made little difference to their American League fortunes. With the brief exception of a few days in August, when a five-game winning streak pushed them into fourth place, the team wallowed in the second division. Their season concluded with a one-day road trip to Detroit, where Rowland took but 14 players. They went through the motions in dropping both ends of the Labor Day doubleheader to extend their losing streak to eight games. For two innings in the nightcap, Cobb took a turn at pitching.[55] World champs a season earlier, the decimated Chicago White Sox finished sixth in the eight-team league with a 57–67 record. The depressed state of baseball business was evident at the turnstiles. In their shortened season, the White Sox attracted just 195,081 fans to Comiskey Park — off the previous season's total by more than two-thirds. In 1918, total major-league attendance was worse than half what it was in 1916 and off 40 percent from the previous season.

With their major-league obligations behind them for the duration of the war, players embarked on their "essential" jobs, nearly all in war-supporting industry rather than the military. The day after Labor Day, pitchers Joe Benz and Jack Quinn started jobs in a South Chicago steel mill.[56] The greatest catcher of his day, Ray Schalk, put away his baseball uniform (and his sub-par .219 batting average) in favor of overalls. He reported to the Great Western Smelting Company at 41st and Wallace streets in Chicago. Less than two weeks after jawing with Ty Cobb on the ball field, Schalk was showing a *Chicago Tribune* reporter the ins and outs of the smelting trade. "Baseball has been pretty good to me, but now I realize how little I knew about business, so I'm glad I can learn while I'm still young," he said, adding that he played catch for about 10 minutes during his lunch hour.[57] For weekends, however, Schalk and Benz agreed to play for the Logan Squares, Chicago's leading semi-pro team. In their first game, Schalk rapped three hits and Benz allowed six hits in a 5–1 victory.[58] A couple of weeks later, the Garden City team managed to secure the services of Red Faber, still a Navy yeoman, to pitch against Benz, Schalk and the Logan Squares. Firing his best stuff to former Cubs star Jimmy Archer, Faber collected a 3–1 win.[59]

After just a few weeks of working him in the smelting plant, Schalk's employer, no doubt recognizing the value of having a star ball player call on clients, promoted him to salesman.[60] However, the move was not entirely due to his celebrity. Schalk demonstrated an affinity for the metals business and a feel for sales. By the time of his promotion the Germans had asked President Wilson for a cease-fire and terms of peace. Armistice Day came a month later, on November 11, 1918. What would happen next?

13

Glory Before the Fall

The Chicago White Sox lost more starters to military service or "essential" wartime occupations than any other major-league team during World War I. Yet manager Clarence "Pants" Rowland, hailed as a baseball genius just a year earlier, lost his job. War or no war, falling to sixth place after a World Series title was not acceptable to Comiskey. Rowland was out as White Sox manager after 1918, but he was not out of baseball. For nearly another half-century, Rowland stayed in the game as a minor-league manager and owner, major-league umpire, scout, league executive and major-league team general manager. The Pacific Coast League's president after World War II when it bid to establish itself as a third major league, Rowland is enshrined in the PCL Hall of Fame. His last association with the game was as executive vice president of the Chicago Cubs. When he died in 1969, at age 90, he was an honorary VP of the Cubs.

On the final day of 1918, Comiskey surprised baseball experts by selecting as Rowland's successor former coach William "Kid" Gleason. After serving as Rowland's able assistant during their championship season, Gleason was gone in 1918, reportedly due to a dispute with the Old Roman. The issue — as is the case with most issues — might have been money. On the day he announced the 52-year-old Gleason's hiring, Comiskey stated, "As to the report that Gleason quit because he didn't get a bonus promised, nothing was ever at any time mentioned as to a bonus, and he received everything due him from the White Sox."[1] Whatever rift existed between the baseball men, it was patched up and Gleason inherited a team that could be expected to challenge for the lofty perch it held in 1917 — if Comiskey and the "slackers" the Old Roman had lambasted, including Shoeless Joe Jackson, Happy Felsch and Lefty Williams, could come to terms. Despite Comiskey's wartime pronouncements, he signaled a willingness to take them all back. For his part, Felsch expressed disinterest in Comiskey's interest; he claimed that he had a successful season of selling Christmas trees in Milwaukee, and he could manage nicely without the Old Roman. Besides, Felsch had claimed that the Sox owed him $1,100 in wages from last season — a claim Comiskey strongly refuted. Further, the Old Roman added, he had offered Felsch additional money to abstain from alcoholic drink, and though Felsch failed to hold up his end of the deal, Comiskey paid him anyway.[2]

During the offseason of 1918–19, Schalk continued to show interest and aptitude in selling for Great Western Smelting. His clients including newspaper production departments; Schalk was familiar with their operations, thanks to his experience in the print shops back in Litchfield. Meanwhile, his contract negotiations with the White Sox were not going smoothly. Cracker's offensive statistics, never outstanding, thanks in no small measure to the various injuries and bruises accumulated while carrying his ironman defensive workload (106 of the team's 124 games), were especially unimpressive in 1918. Meanwhile, owners suffered a financial beating during the war-hampered season and were in no mood to offer big raises. Schalk made three or four visits to Comiskey's office to discuss terms before finally signing for 1919. The *Tribune* noted that, while

Gleason became White Sox manager in 1919, the year of the scandal-tainted World Series. He never quite got over the Black Sox betrayal and, unable to restore the team to its winning ways, resigned after the 1923 season. Photograph dated 1912 (Library of Congress, Prints & Photographs Division, Bain Collection, LC-B2-2794-3).

Schalk was succeeding with the metals company, the best catcher in baseball didn't think he could afford to quit the game. "After a long session in the private office with the boss Ray emerged smiling and satisfied."[3] The contract was a rare three-year deal — in those days, one-year pacts were the norm — worth $7,083 a year.[4] That was a good wage in the day — more than that paid Jackson — but less than the nearly $7,500 erstwhile Christmas tree entrepreneur Felsch accepted the same day, or the $7,664 paid to Buck Weaver in 1919.[5] On the day the White Sox departed for spring training in Texas, the Boston Red Sox came to terms with star pitcher Babe Ruth. Terms were not officially disclosed, but Ruth let it be known that it was a three-year deal for $9,000 a year.[6]

The day before the White Sox train departed for Mineral Wells, a familiar face visited team headquarters. Rowland, now managing Milwaukee (American Association), called on Gleason and team secretary Harry Grabiner to make a pitch for first pick of the players who failed their tryouts with the major-league club.[7]

Soon after their train pulled out of La Salle Street station, several players, including Buck Weaver, engaged in a pinochle game. The activity caused Weaver to forget to mention to his bosses one important fact: He had invited a prospective player to come along to training camp. The oversight was discovered a few hours later, when a Sox veteran assigned to a lower berth discovered the bed occupied by 20-year-old Roy Hansen. It seems that during the off-season Weaver and Hansen worked for the same firm in Beloit, Wisconsin, Weaver saw the boy pitch, and Buck simply invited him to spring training. Gleason and Grabiner talked with the stowaway and agreed to let him try out.[8] However, Hansen was not exactly an unknown. He had major-league experience — nine innings of decent relief work for Washington in 1918.[9] In any case, Hansen didn't make the cut with the White Sox, and he never appeared in another major-league contest. Another casualty of spring training was Jimmy Cerny. During an intra-squad game, the young Chicagoan forgot Gleason's pre-game order against sliding on the hard, sun-baked field and fractured his ankle on an attempted steal of second base.[10] Cerny's enthusiasm to do well reflected a changed tone in training camp. Sportswriter Dick Jemison reported, "Not in its pennant-winning years, say those who have seen the Sox in action, have they displayed such hustle and dash."[11] With their talent and new-found energy, the White Sox were top contenders to appear in the 1919 World Series. Coincidentally, in their penultimate exhibition game of the pre-season, the White Sox defeated the Cincinnati Reds, 5–3, with Eddie Cicotte and Lefty Williams teaming up for the victory. Those teams would make headlines the following October. Cicotte, Williams and Schalk skipped the final exhibition contest in Indianapolis; they went ahead to St. Louis for some rest before the season opener.[12] Given Schalk's relationship with the pitchers, it is doubtful Cracker had much to do with the hurlers, and he probably used the day off to visit family in Litchfield.

On the heels of the war-shortened season, during which they took their lumps financially, and unsure about fans' enthusiasm to come back to the ballpark, the major leagues shortened the 1919 season slightly —140 games instead of 154. The White Sox won three of their opening four in St. Louis, but in the fourth contest Schalk suffered a severe shake-up in a home-plate collision with a baserunner. After a day on the bench in Detroit, he returned to the lineup by rapping three singles in a 6–4 win. Despite the struggles of pitcher Red Faber, who would fight illness and injury all season long, Gleason's White Sox were every bit as formidable as the experts predicted. Yet, secretly, this was a divided and troubled team. The squad had two cliques. The nucleus of one group sowed the seeds of the Black Sox conspiracy. The other group included Schalk, Eddie Collins, Faber and Dickie Kerr.[13] There was no love lost between the cliques. Team captain Collins, the second baseman, and first baseman Chick Gandil, a gambler and ruffian, had not been on speaking terms since 1917. The infielder playing to Collins' right, Swede Risberg, likewise couldn't stand his captain.[14] Risberg also feuded with Schalk.[15] Cracker caught the deliveries of Cicotte and Williams, but he wouldn't speak to them between games; the only pitchers he associated with were Faber, Kerr and Grover Lowdermilk.[16] During between-inning warm-ups, three infielders threw a ball among themselves — and excluded Collins, whose only hope of touching the ball was when Schalk would get it and toss it his way. Players disobeyed the captain's signals so often that, when Collins complained to Gleason, the manager simply suggested that Collins flash a sign for the opposite of what he actually desired. Thinking the solution quite obvious, Gleason added, "Do I have to do ALL your thinking for you?"[17] Despite all that discord, for a team-record 134 days — all but 2½ weeks in late June and early July — Chicago owned the top spot in the American League standings.

About the time the White Sox regained first place for good, players couldn't help but notice that owners' fears about poor attendance in the first season after the war — a reason moguls gave for reduced contract offers — had not materialized. Baseball fans returned in droves. Despite having fewer home games in 1919, the White Sox were on their way to nearly matching their home attendance total of their 1917 championship season. The players, who already received just 75 percent of the $4 meal per diem paid most major leaguers and had to pay to have their uniforms laundered, wanted their cut of the windfall. In his book *Eight Men Out*, Eliot Asinof reported that in a spirited clubhouse meeting, Kid Gleason agreed to take their demands to the Old Roman. However, Comiskey would have none of it. Learning of the owner's refusal while dressing for a game, outraged players — especially Cicotte, that afternoon's scheduled pitcher — threatened to go on strike. Gleason managed to talk them out of it with the promise of post-season bonuses, but he nonetheless nicked Cicotte from the day's lineup.[18] The ill-will toward Comiskey made it easier, a couple of months later, for Gandil to recruit his clique to lose the World Series.

Off the field, Schalk and Cicotte fulfilled a May 31 commitment and made a 90-minute appearance at Marshall Field & Company's department store on State Street. Field's advertisements invited young ballplayers to the Boys Department that Saturday morning, to learn from Cicotte how to deliver the "shine ball," and give it a try by throwing to Schalk.[19] History does not record whether Cicotte and Schalk actually spoke to each other during the appearance. Afterwards, the players went to the ballpark, where Cicotte posted a complete-game victory over Cleveland, 5–2. The game featured an extended brawl between Tris Speaker of the Indians and Sox first baseman Gandil midway in the eighth inning. The fight, which required police intervention, followed by a few minutes a play in which Speaker slid toward the inside of first base, spikes high, while Gandil recorded an unassisted putout on his grounder. Words were exchanged and the conversation continued for the balance of the half-inning, with Gandil on the field and Speaker in the dugout. After the third out in the top of the eighth, Speaker and Gandil resumed their dispute. They soon came to blows and engaged in a lengthy altercation. "Baseball fights generally are stopped after about one exchange of blows. This pair were tumbling over the earth from first base halfway to the pitcher's slab, then back toward second," the *Tribune* reported, "and still nobody stopped them." Players, umpires, a few spectators and even Indians President James Dunn all stood close by, but apparently determined it detrimental to their personal welfare to intervene when the combatants were flailing and kicking so wildly. Finally, police officers from outside

Claude "Lefty" Williams (shown here in 1917) lost a record three games in the eight-game 1919 World Series. Shortly after Game 2, in which the pitcher repeatedly ignored Schalk's signals and grooved pitches to Cincinnati hitters, the incensed catcher reportedly attacked Williams. Schalk later denied the altercation ever happened (Library of Congress, Prints & Photographs Division, Bain Collection, LC-B21-4351-22).

the ballpark arrived to lend a hand. The excitement prompted some bad behavior among Sox fans in the left-field stands, who tossed pop bottles at Cleveland outfielder Jack Graney. Sox manager Gleason, accompanied by policemen, hustled to the scene of the crime and delivered a speech persuasive enough to bring an end to the uproar. After the game's final out, Gleason personally walked off the field with the opponents, just in case any fans had notions of rekindling the riot. (When the Sox called on Cleveland a month later, the series was marked by plenty of rough stuff, including police intervention.)

The altercation in Chicago was not the only incident in the American League that afternoon. In Philadelphia, Bryan Hayes, an Athletics fan sitting directly behind the Red Sox dugout, complained that during a Philadelphia rally Boston pitcher Carl Mays stepped out from the bench and angrily fired a baseball into the crowd. Hayes said the ball struck him in the head, breaking his straw hat and raising a welt. Another fan suffered a punch from veteran second baseman Dave Shean.[20]

Some unusual plays marked Chicago's run for the pennant. Batting in the bottom of the ninth inning in a losing effort June 7, Happy Felsch drove a foul ball into the ground near home plate. The ball bounced up and Felsch took another swing at it, sending the sphere over the grandstand. Yankees manager Miller Huggins argued so vehemently that Felsch should have been called out that umpire Brick Owens sent Huggins to the showers.[21] Schalk stole home June 3 in Detroit where he and Lowdermilk executed a double steal.[22] The Sox had to summon their third-string catcher in Washington on June 21 when Schalk and backup Byrd Lynn suffered injuries in the span of just a couple of minutes. In the fifth inning, Schalk twisted a knee while making a play at the plate, and right after that Lynn suffered a spike wound. Joe Jenkins, making one of his four defensive appearances all season, his last in the majors, completed the contest.[23] A limping Schalk was back in the lineup the next afternoon.

Perhaps the most unusual of Schalk's 1,345 base hits occurred June 28 in St. Louis. In the seventh inning, Schalk took a pitch by Urban Shocker, and umpire Oliver Chill called it a strike. Schalk stood in the batter's box, looked back and started to argue the call with Chill. Shocker, sensing an opportunity, attempted to hurry over another strike while Schalk wasn't looking. "But Ray turned just in time to take a wallop at the ball," the *Tribune* reported, "which probably had nothing on it," and Schalk's single helped produce the winning run in a 3–2 contest.[24]

In Chicago the afternoon of July 27, the White Sox fell to the Browns, 11–5. Meanwhile, less than two miles from Comiskey Park, Eugene Williams,

Schalk's accurate throws made baserunners think twice about stealing. However, he joked that his strategy to keep the speedy Ty Cobb from stealing third was to throw to third when the Georgia Peach tried to steal second. Photograph dated 1921 (Library of Congress, Prints & Photographs Division, Bain Collection, LC-B2-4350-3).

an African American youth, was swimming with friends in Lake Michigan near 29th Street. He strayed into an area traditionally considered a whites-only zone. Young white men began throwing stones at the youth, who was dazed by the blows and went under the surface. Whites on the beach blocked blacks from rescuing the lad, whose body was eventually pulled from the lake. Police called to the scene disregarded witness accounts and refused to make any arrests. Racial tensions, already high in post-war Chicago, erupted into a riot about 7:30 P.M. that evening. Roughly 10 square miles of the South Side, including the Comiskey Park neighborhood, became a battleground. Whites and blacks fought each other, shot each other and engaged in vandalism, looting and arson. Victims included women and children. Even the state militia struggled to stop the violence, which dragged on for nearly two weeks. When it finally ended, 38 Chicagoans (23 blacks and 15 whites) were dead, at least 500 were injured and a couple of thousand homeless. In that war zone, staging baseball games would have been impossible, but the White Sox did not have to cancel or postpone any contests. The riot started hours after their homestand concluded, and a banged-up Sox contingent — Schalk was among those limping around — was on its way to New York, Boston, Philadelphia and Washington. By the time the team returned to the Windy City after a 7–8 road trip, the emergency in Comiskey Park's environs had eased sufficiently for the White Sox to host games. However, the race riots of 1919 became part of Chicago history.

Toward the end of that road trip, in the nation's capital, Schalk had something to help him forget a bum leg. A foul tip caught him in the Adam's Apple and left him gasping for breath. Umpire Oliver Chill pounded him on the back for a time, and Schalk completed the half-inning but sat out the rest of that contest.[25] However, Schalk's misfortune was nothing to that experienced by umpire George Moriarty. A Chicago scratch hit left Boston catcher Roxy Walters holding the ball. He spied baserunner Eddie Collins straying off second base and attempted to pick off the Sox captain. Walters' peg connected with the head of the arbiter, who was laid out. Though some feared the worst for the former major-league infielder, Moriarty regained consciousness after three or four minutes.[26]

On July 21, as the White Sox battled the Yankees in the second game of a Comiskey Park doubleheader, tragedy struck in Chicago's business district. With thousands of people watching from the sidewalks, a Goodyear Tire blimp on a test flight caught fire, fell 1,200 feet and crashed through the skylight of the Illinois Trust and Savings Bank at Jackson Boulevard and La Salle Street. Eleven people died, including nine bank employees who burned to death when the aircraft's gasoline tanks exploded upon impact on the bank's floor. The other two victims were occupants of the blimp; three others on board used their parachutes and survived. Dozens of men and women, their clothing aflame, ran and crawled from the inferno.[27]

Though they held first place nearly wire to wire, the White Sox had plenty of challengers and challenges. Cleveland, New York and Detroit pursued them closely throughout the season, and they couldn't wrap up the pennant until four days remained in the season. Challenges included winning on the road (40–30) under a continual barrage of taunting and ridicule from fans who derided Sox players they considered "slackers" for pursuing "essential" civilian jobs during the Great War. Fans in the right-field stands at Washington's Griffith Park taunted Joe Jackson so incessantly that he entered the stands and went after a few of them; no injuries resulted. The fans also got a laugh the same afternoon when, while engaging Senators baserunner Joe Judge in a rundown play, Buck Weaver got mixed up and tagged his own catcher, Schalk.[28]

Sportswriters' column notes occasionally made references to gamblers, betting lines or wagers won and lost at the ballpark. As the White Sox wrapped up their late–July homestand, the *Tribune*'s Crusinberry shared this account: "Ray Schalk wasn't in the game because he has a strained muscle in his left leg. Here's how the *Tribune* reporter first heard that Ray wasn't to be in: A half hour before game, the reporter was standing in the lower part of the grand stand. A bunch of five or six well dressers were there. One of them said, 'Who do you like?' Another said, 'I like St. Louis.' 'So do I,' said another. And it was followed with: 'You can get all your money covered over in box ____ if you offer 11 to 10, and of course you know Schalk is not in the game.' A few moments later the reporter verified the words of the well dressers that Schalk was out."[29]

Still banged-up but sufficiently healed to stay in the lineup, Schalk played a key role in a mid–August victory over visiting Boston. The contest was marked by the longest home-run blast at Comiskey Park in memory; it came off the bat of Red Sox slugger Babe Ruth. In the bottom of the ninth of a tie game, the White Sox filled the bases with one out. Schalk stepped to the plate and bunted up the third-base line. The Red Sox couldn't nail Happy Felsch at the plate, and the White Sox moved another victory toward the pennant with the 7–6 victory.[30] A couple of days later, Schalk caught in his 100th game of the year. Though the 1918 and 1919 seasons were shortened due to the war and economy, Schalk had reached the century mark for the seventh straight season. "There is nothing on the ball field that 'Cracker' can't do, and do well," observed sportswriter Malcolm MacLean.[31] Schalk would catch at least 100 games the next four seasons, and five of the next six. He also rebounded from an off-year offensively, improving his batting average to .282, his career-best over a full season.

The White Sox secured their second pennant in three seasons on September 24, despite losing Eddie Collins to a short-fused umpire and Chick Gandil to illness. Chicago scored twice in the bottom of the ninth to beat St. Louis, 6–5, and confirm their ticket for the 1919 World Series against the National League champion Cincinnati Reds, who clinched the pennant by beating runner-up New York eight days earlier. Even before the clincher, New York manager John McGraw conceded the pennant to the Reds. He appointed Christy Mathewson temporary manager, left the team with a couple of weeks to play and headed to New York and Texas to attend to his business interests.[32]

With the combatants for the Fall Classic determined, speculation on the outcome began in earnest. Players, managers, sportswriters and even umpires made predictions. However, without a doubt, many fans paid attention to the opinion of another knowledgeable group, one that predicted a White Sox championship in 1919: The gamblers.

14

❖

Black Sox

As Cincinnati prepared to host its first World Series game ever, crowds jammed the sidewalks, ticket scalpers did a brisk business and brass bands played in the streets. Syndicated columnist Bugs Baer, observing the high spirits of the locals, noted, "They ought to call this town Cincin*nutty*." Added New York writer Damon Runyon, "Cincinnati is a dry town — as dry as the Atlantic Ocean."[1] The excitement in Ohio notwithstanding, most prognosticators gave the 1919 World Series, which would be a best-of-nine affair, to the White Sox.

One of their considerations was the defense and leadership demonstrated by Chicago's veteran catcher. "He is always doing something different," wrote umpire Billy Evans, a Chicago native who would take his turn calling balls and strikes in the World Series. Describing Schalk as "the original pepperpot" among catchers, Evans added, "He makes you take notice in any ball game that he works. Fans who see him perform in a big series are sure to watch a master workman." Evans, a future Hall of Fame inductee, noted Schalk "isn't still a minute. If he isn't saying kind or hard things to his pitcher he is getting after, first, Gandil, then Collins, next Risberg, and lastly Weaver. His shrill whistle after giving the signal is a bit of byplay all his own that keeps the rest of the boys on their toes. When the pitcher appears to be loafing or getting a bit careless, Schalk proceeds to return the ball with such speed that one begins to wonder who really is doing the pitching."[2] *Chicago Evening Post* sportswriter Malcolm MacLean observed, "Those who have seen Schalk block a man almost twice his size and put the ball on him have become so accustomed to the sight that it no longer causes amazement. No catcher in the world takes more chances and gets by with it than Ray."[3]

That the White Sox and Reds would meet in the World Series was not a surprise. By late August, their positions atop their respective leagues' standings appeared secure. Atlanta sportswriter Dick Jemison revealed some of the Sox players' plans for their World Series checks. Fred McMullin planned to

Umpire Billy Evans (shown here in 1914), who wrote a syndicated newspaper column, often praised Schalk and described him as the best catcher in the game. Evans' umpiring career (1906–27) spanned Schalk's playing days (Library of Congress, Prints & Photographs Division, Bain Collection, LC-B2-3225-4).

pay off his farm. Nemo Leibold was to add two lanes to his bowling alley. Swede Risberg had his designs on an auto "that will surpass Ray Schalk's."[4]

A week before the World Series opener, bookies posted odds favoring the White Sox, though the Reds were slight favorites (11–10) to win Game 1, on their home field. The *Chicago Tribune* said gamblers were giving 8–5 odds that the White Sox would win it all.[5] However, in the hours before Game 1, more money came in for the Reds, and the odds changed. As the nation would later learn, the increase in bets for Cincinnati occurred as whispers circulated that the "fix" was in and the White Sox would throw the World Series. The rumors proved true.

The presence of gambling in and around baseball was common knowledge. Gamblers tried to influence the odds, if not game outcomes, by inciting on-field riots, planting false reports about player injuries, and bribing athletes and umpires. Less than a month before the start of the World Series, three American League owners intent on ousting league President Ban Johnson — Chicago's Charles Comiskey, Boston's Harry Frazee and New York's Jacob Ruppert — called a special meeting of league directors. The main item on the agenda was Johnson's statements, as the owners described them, "that gambling exists to the menace of baseball," and other matters.[6] The owners claimed that Johnson presented no evidence to support his statement regarding the influence of gambling, and besides, the owners had done everything possible to stamp out the evil.[7] Subsequent reports had Comiskey complaining of "arbitrary" decisions by Johnson, failure to cooperate with owner inquiries and requests for information, an audit of the league's books, and Johnson's secret ownership of stock in a league franchise (Cleveland). In communication with fellow owners, Comiskey accused Johnson of drunkenness.[8]

There was some basis for the allegation. Some accounts suggested that relations between Comiskey and Johnson, once the best of friends, deteriorated over nearly 15 years until they were mortal enemies. However, Black Sox researcher Gene Carney noted that as late as 1918 Johnson was among the contingent of Comiskey's Woodland Bards making the annual fall pilgrimage to the Old Roman's resort in Wisconsin. By then, relations between Comiskey and Johnson were strained. The final straw came a few months earlier, when Comiskey came out on the short end of Johnson's ruling in a dispute with the Yankees over which team owned the contract of pitcher Jack Quinn. Little more than a year later, while maneuvering to oust Johnson, the disgruntled American League owners, in alliance with National League representatives, courted federal judge Kenesaw Mountain Landis to chair baseball's three-man National Commission.[9] Landis eventually took the job — but only after owners acceded to his demand that he hold total authority as sole commissioner.

On September 29, the day after the White Sox dropped their regular-season finale, a sloppy 10–9 decision in which Eddie Cicotte tuned up by pitching the first two innings, the *Chicago Tribune* provided an update on the World Series betting line. "Absence of Cincinnati money in any considerable amounts has forced the White Sox into favoritism in the betting on the world's series until admirers of Gleason's outfit must put up $20 to win $13 from the local handbook gentry," wrote Harvey T. Woodruff. "If you happen to fancy Moran's Reds, the bookie will lay $10 against your $7." Woodruff noted that unless more money favoring Cincinnati came in, the Sox would open the Series 2-to-1 favorites — "a false price in a series of this kind, where upsets and luck cut such a factor."[10] That night, the White Sox boarded their sleeper train and rode to Cincinnati. They arrived the next morning and sauntered into the lobby of the 10-story Hotel Sinton, the Queen City's finest lodging establishment. Hundreds of spectators jammed the lobby, wanting a closer look at the men who experts said could be the best baseball team ever. Ray and Vin Schalk and Eddie and Mabel Collins checked into rooms 702 and 704.[11]

A half-day after the White Sox' arrival, Abe Attell checked in at the Sinton. He was given the key to Room 708.[12] Having helped bribe a group of Chicago players to throw the World Series, he feverishly began getting as much money down as possible on Cincinnati. He found plenty of bettors backing the White Sox. One of them was Sam Pass, a young salesman from Chicago, who put down a whopping $3,000 — worth more than $37,000 in 2008.[13] The confident Pass was close friends with Schalk and several other Chicago players. Attell became so aggressive, he stood on a chair in the hotel lobby, amid the chaotic scene, waving thousand-dollar bills and hollering for bettors on Chicago to step forward. The scene contributed to a shift in the odds, and by the end of the day the Reds were considered less of a long-shot. Meanwhile, the day was filled with rumors raising doubts whether the series would be played on the square.[14]

The evening before Game 1, syndicated sportswriter Hugh Fullerton bumped into an acquaintance, "Sleepy" Bill Burns, a retired journeyman pitcher-turned-gambler. Burns' five years in the major leagues included appearances for both the White Sox and Reds in 1910. Sources differ on where the two men talked. *Eight Men Out* author Eliot Asinof said the men visited over a drink in the Gibson House, near the Hotel Sinton. Fullerton recalled it occurring about noon near a Cincinnati telegraph office. Susan Dellinger, granddaughter and biographer of Reds star Edd Roush, said the conversation occurred outside a roadhouse, in the Cincinnati suburb of Newport, Kentucky, where Fuller-

The Hotel Sinton in Cincinnati, circa 1910. The leading hotel in the Queen City, it lodged the Chicago White Sox as well as fans, sportswriters and gamblers during the 1919 World Series (Library of Congress, Prints & Photographs Division, Detroit Publishing Company Collection, LC-D4-70063).

ton and some fellow sportswriters went for dinner. Wherever the conversation occurred, Burns' message to Fullerton was the same: "Get wise" and bet on the Reds. Fullerton recalled, "It was not what Bill said, but the way he said it that startled me."[15] In Dellinger's account, Burns laid out for Fullerton what he knew about the fix: That St. Louis gamblers arranged for Cicotte to "lay down" and that Gandil might also be in on it.[16] That information, after a day of observing wild betting activity and hearing all the rumors, prompted Fullerton to send a dispatch to all his newspaper clients: "ADVISE ALL NOT TO BET ON THIS SERIES. UGLY RUMORS AFLOAT."[17] Most of his client editors removed the warning. Fullerton and his roommate, retired pitcher and former Reds manager Christy Mathewson, who was to provide newspaper commentary on the Series, were still awake in the wee hours, discussing the rumors of a fix, when an angry Pat Moran burst in. The Reds manager accused Fullerton of taking out one of his pitchers and getting him drunk — the night before the World Series, no less. The highly respected Matty managed to assure Moran that Fullerton was not with any Cincinnati players that evening. "As a matter of fact," Fullerton wrote years later, "Pat was right about the player — but he had the wrong reporter."[18]

The morning of Game 1, Fullerton separately told what he had heard about a fix to Comiskey, Johnson and Pittsburgh owner Barney Dreyfuss. The Old Roman had heard the rumors, too, and believed Johnson had as well, but was reluctant to call on Johnson to act. Meanwhile, the league president chalked up the talk to just Comiskey whining. Finally, Dreyfuss shrugged off the rumors as fantasy — after all, a World Series is "too complicated" to fix. A frustrated Fullerton lashed out at Dreyfuss, calling him and the rest of the baseball establishment "whitewashing bastards" interested only in protecting their financial stake in the game.[19]

Meanwhile, Cincinnati boiled with baseball fever over its first-ever World Series appearance. Redland Field, at Findlay Street and Western Avenue, the home of the Reds since 1912, was looking its best. More than 30,500 fans jammed the park. Later called Crosley Field, the spacious ballpark — 360 feet down each foul line and 420 feet to dead center — acquired a new scoreboard in right field for the big occasion.[20] On an unusually warm October afternoon, the White Sox took the field at 1:10 P.M. — 50 minutes before the opening pitch. During warm-ups, Schalk, appearing in his second World Series in three seasons, greeted Roush; they were rookies together in 1913, when Roush appeared in nine games for the White Sox and Schalk was the starting catcher.[21] Elaborate pre-game ceremonies included John Philip Sousa personally directing a band in a rendition of his "Stars and Stripes Forever." At last, it was time to play ball.

Reds left-hander Walter "Dutch" Ruether gave up a leadoff single to Shano Collins, but the Sox could make nothing of it. In the bottom of the first, Schalk signaled for an opening fastball from Chicago starter Eddie Cicotte, who complied with a blazing strike, apparently assuming that Reds leadoff man Morrie Rath would follow tradition and allow the first pitch to go by. He did. After that, Cicotte, to provide gamblers a signal that the fix was in, endeavored to walk Rath. However, his second pitch plunked Rath in the back. A seemingly upset Cicotte then gave up a single to Jake Daubert, allowing Rath to race to third. Heinie Groh's sacrifice fly to Joe Jackson plated Rath with the World Series' first run. Schalk did what he could to keep it close. With Roush at bat, Cracker threw out Daubert trying to steal second. Roush walked and succeeded in swiping second, but Louis "Pat" Duncan's groundout ended the inning.

Cicotte, who hit only 14 batters total over the previous five seasons, including two in 1919, later claimed that after plunking Rath he suffered pangs of conscience and thereafter tried to pitch his best. It is a point that has been extensively researched and debated but can never be proven. In any case, Cicotte did not need to lose the game single-handedly. Consider the fourth inning, which started with Cicotte appearing "apprehensive."[22] With Duncan on first after his one-out single, Larry Kopf rapped a pitch back to Cicotte, who seemed to hesitate before throwing to co-conspirator Swede Risberg, whose relay to first was just late enough to miss a double play.

When Eddie Cicotte (shown here in 1917) hit the first Cincinnati batter in Game 1 of the 1919 World Series, it was believed to signal gambling insiders that the fix was on. Actually, Cicotte revealed later, he intended to walk the man. Cicotte was the first Black Sox figure to confess (Library of Congress, Prints & Photographs Division, Bain Collection, LC-B21-4351-26).

On the next play, Risberg could do no better than to knock down a grounder, setting the stage for Cincinnati's big inning. Meanwhile, Mathewson, covering the Series as a newspaper analyst, moved closer to the field. There, he saw clearly that Schalk was livid with his pitcher.[23] Cicotte tended to miss with a pitch or two and then groove the next one. By the time Gleason yanked Cicotte — the manager emerged from the dugout, shouted angrily at his pitcher from the baseline and signaled the pitching change from there — the Reds had scored five runs on six hits. The game was out of reach. The Sox showed no fight after that and took the loss, 9–1. The Reds' pre-series dope, formed by a National League board of strategy, figured that the Sox would not fight — literally. The strategy included relentless bench jockeying. It went both ways, but the Reds laid it on especially thick. Cincinnati elected to send out Jimmy Smith, who had a reputation for an acidic tongue, to coach third base, where he could be closer when needling the Sox. "I have never heard such language used in a ball game since the days of the Cleveland Spiders and the Baltimore Orioles," Fullerton observed. Eddie Collins and Joe Jackson were the Reds' favorite targets; Cincinnati hoped to provoke them into fights that would result in their ejection. It nearly worked in Game 3, when Collins started after Smith. "Some of us were pulling for (Reds manager Pat) Moran because of his clean sportsmanship and honest, hard-working methods," Fullerton wrote, "and it hurt to find his team descending to the depths of muckerism to win."[24]

After Game 1, Mathewson, who was aware of (but did not disclose) the rumors of gamblers' involvement in the proceedings, wrote, "I never bet on a ball game, but if we get another warm day tomorrow and Sallee starts for Cincinnati, I think I will get down a little wager on the Reds."[25] Bettors saw it that way, too. After Game 1, the *Chicago Tribune* observed, "Lots of private cellar supplies have been tapped since the defeat of the Sox and there is more Cincinnati money in sight tonight."[26] Mathewson added a cryptic conclusion to his column: "The White Sox are supposed to be great ball club, but no team to my knowledge was ever defeated by so large a score in an opening game of the world's series *when each contender was trying its best.*"[27] (emphasis added)

Matty's roommate, Fullerton, was writing in his hotel room at the Sinton that evening when Schalk entered. Whether the visit preceded or followed the Schalks and Collinses going out together for dinner is not known, but in any case it must have been an uneasy and somber meal.[28] "Sure, I heard that the fix was on, but I looked on it as just idle gossip, and completely preposterous," Eddie Collins said years later. "I hadn't been close to some of the fellows, but, still, they were my teammates. Why shouldn't I defend them?"[29]

Still agitated, Schalk described for Fullerton the events of that afternoon, telling the sportswriter that Cicotte ignored his signals at least eight times and laid in fat pitches. Fullerton, who believed Schalk's account, nonetheless warned Cracker. "Keep your mouth shut, or go to Comiskey and Gleason," the sportswriter said. "If you make charges against anyone you'll be the goat — you can't prove them — and it would ruin you."[30] Yet Fullerton later put his neck on the line, while sports editors and other writers sat back, in publicly alleging that the World Series was not played on the square.

In addition to their own suspicions based on what they had seen on the field and heard in hotel lobbies and restaurants, Gleason and his boss, Comiskey, had received several telegrams from gamblers warning that the Series was fixed. Unable to reach Comiskey earlier in the evening, Gleason returned from dinner and an abbreviated walk; the jaunt was cut short after Reds fans on the street heckled the manager. Gleason returned to the Sinton to spot Risberg and Cicotte. The pitcher had showered and left the ballpark long before the game ended. Now, the enraged manager confronted and hollered at them. "You two think you can kid me? ... Anybody who says he can't see what you're doing out there is either blind, stupid or a goddamn liar!" Fullerton witnessed the scene and hustled Gleason from the confrontation.[31]

In 1937, Dickie Kerr told a sportswriter that before the second game of

Edd Roush couldn't believe an acquaintance's reports that some White Sox players were "laying down" in the 1919 World Series against his Cincinnati Reds. Toward the end of the series, however, he started having suspicions about some of his own teammates. Photograph dated 1923 (Library of Congress, Prints & Photographs Division, Bain Collection, LC-B2-6034-17).

the series started, he, Gleason, Schalk and Eddie Collins knew "what those fellows planned to do, but we had no proof. We wanted to do something, but we couldn't."[32]

In the biography of her grandfather Edd Roush, Dellinger reported that Gleason later interrupted a meeting of the conspirators in Cicotte's hotel room. The long-term guest in an adjoining room, a friend of Roush, observed Gleason shake hands with each player as he departed. Could one conclude that the fix was off?[33]

If Gleason was satisfied that those players were now on board, his subsequent actions did not reflect it. Later that night, he and Comiskey discussed their suspicions. Finally, in the middle of the night, the Old Roman awoke the only member of the National Commission who might give his concerns a hearing, National League President John Heydler. The other commissioners were Garry Herrmann, the owner of his Series opponent, the Reds; and Comiskey's enemy Ban Johnson. After listening to Comiskey, who acknowledged that he had no iron-clad proof of a fix, Heydler and Comiskey went to see Johnson, who dismissed the suspicion on the basis that Comiskey's complaint was "the yelp of a beaten cur."[34]

The weather for Game 2 was hotter than it had been for the opener. A Boston writer observed, "Men in the grandstands simply had to doff their coats, regardless of good manners, and the women looked as if they wished they had worn summer suits rather than the gowns in which they appeared."[35] Gleason announced Claude "Lefty" Williams as his starter. He had little choice: An ill and injured Red Faber, who won three games in the 1917 World Series, had not been available for weeks. The Sox used a three-man rotation of Cicotte, Williams and Kerr, a rookie.

Gleason took Schalk aside and, nodding in Williams' direction, told his catcher, "Watch him!" Cracker saw plenty. He was angrier with Williams than he had been with Cicotte 24 hours earlier. Williams exhibited pinpoint control — keeping his pitches just *outside* the strike zone. Schalk barked, cursed and shook his fist at Williams, who in a single inning ignored Schalk's signals three times. He also worked on home plate umpire Billy Evans about his calls. Evans, whose admiration for Schalk was well-documented in his bylined newspaper articles, patiently explained that Williams' pitches were close — but still not strikes.

The game got away in the fourth, when Williams walked three and the Reds scored three times. Schalk's anger was obvious. Cracker's whistling and cursing in the first two games became such an irritant that Gandil hollered at him to knock it off.[36] Schalk put everything he had on his return throws to Williams, and at one point, with Roush batting, raised his mask and walked to the mound, hollering at Williams the entire way. His anger aside, Cracker had to shout to be heard over the frenzied roar of the Cincinnati faithful. On his way back to his position, Schalk stopped and yelled something toward Gleason in the dugout. Williams then grooved a 2–0 pitch to Roush, who laced a single to center field and drove in Morrie Rath with the game's first run. It could have been worse: Schalk cut down Roush trying to steal. After Williams issued another walk, his troubles continued when he gave up a triple to Kopf, whose drive scored two more runs to make Cincinnati's lead 3–0. They added a run in the sixth, when Schalk cut down another would-be base stealer, future football coaching legend Alfred "Greasy" Neale, to end the frame.[37]

Moments later, the game came to a bizarre pause. An airplane buzzed the ballpark. As the plane circled, the figure of a man fell out of the aircraft and plummeted toward the ball field, arms and legs flailing. Amid gasps and shrieks from the 29,698 fans in attendance, the figure hit the ground near shortstop Kopf. The "victim" was just a dummy — a prop in a sick joke. A policeman stationed near the left-field wall removed the dummy and used it as a seat. The seventh inning began. Risberg stroked a one-out single and advanced to third on Schalk's opposite-field double. Right fielder Neale's wild throw toward second base bounded past both middle infielders, allowing Risberg to dash home. Third baseman Heinie Groh pursued the ball at a leisurely pace, assuming that Schalk would stop at third. However, Cracker kept going. Groh's throw to the plate hit Schalk and bounded away. The White Sox had cut Cincinnati's lead in half, 4–2. Did the aerial interruption change Chicago's fortunes?

The White Sox appeared to attempt a rally in the ninth against Slim Sallee, the former Giant. Chick Gandil, the ringleader in the fix, singled to bring the would-be tying run at bat. However, fellow conspirator Risberg was next. He accommodated by grounding into a double play. Representing the White Sox' final hope, Schalk worked Sallee to a full count before hitting a single to center. However, yet another fixer, pinch-hitter Fred McMullin, ended the afternoon's proceedings by grounding out to second baseman Rath. Cincinnati's 4–2 win gave the Reds a 2–0 Series lead. "Abe Attell, who cleaned up about $2,500 yesterday, repeated today, and altogether had cleaned up about $10,000 on the two days," the *Boston Globe* reported. "It is said that Abe is betting George Cohan's money."[38] If the readers only knew the whole story. Attell was hardly behind the scenes. In addition to making a demonstration of taking bets in the lobby of the Sinton, Attell appears in the background of a newspaper photo; he is the stands immediately behind several Reds posing for the photographer.[39]

While Reds fans outside the ballpark celebrated, the schism in the White Sox clubhouse was more evident than ever. When Gleason entered his small office, a dirt- and sweat-streaked Schalk was waiting. Cracker screamed, "The son of a bitch!" He told Gleason how Williams ignored signs three times in the fourth. "He wouldn't throw the curve!" Schalk shouted, "Goddamit, Kid.... You gotta do something about this!" Moments later, in the locker room, Gleason confronted Gandil, who appeared not the least disappointed with the loss, and got a choke hold on the big first baseman.[40]

In Asinof's account, a still-steaming Schalk showered, changed into his street clothes, collected his gear and waited outside the clubhouse door. When Williams emerged, Schalk called him over and walked a few steps with him under the grandstand. In an instant, the 5-foot-7 catcher flailed at the 5-foot-9 pitcher with both fists. Williams let out a yell, backed away and covered up. Teammates rushed in to break it up. Over the course of two days, Schalk accused Williams and Cicotte of repeatedly ignoring his signs and letting the Reds win. There were reports he also did battle with Cicotte.[41] Forever afterward, however, Schalk denied either altercation ever happened. Further, though he complained of a fix to reporters during and immediately after the World Series, almost as quickly he clammed up — and remained tight-lipped about the Black Sox for the rest of his life. (A possible exception: A player on a minor league team Schalk managed in 1932, Bill Werber, recalled that Schalk said that Cicotte and Joe Jackson played to win throughout the series.[42] If so, the statement is inconsistent with what he said during the brief period when he was talking, and apparently he never repeated the claim attributed to Werber. Some — including Cicotte himself— have argued that after Game 1, the pitcher tried to win.)

What fueled the events of Games 3 through 8? Various researchers have presented various accounts: That the White Sox, double-crossed by tight-fisted gamblers, thereafter tried to win. That other gamblers tried to bribe some Reds to lie down — in certain games, if not the entire series — and might have succeeded. Cincinnati pitcher Hod Eller reported being offered a payoff, and years later Roush expressed his suspicions about some teammates, especially in Games 6 and 7.[43]

However, this much is certain:

White Sox rookie Kerr pitched a masterful game in Game 3, a three-hitter, for a 3–0 victory back in Chicago. In contrast to the first two contests, the White Sox showed some fight. The only apparent exception occurred in the second inning. Fix ringleader Gandil drove in two teammates with a single and then advanced to second on a walk. Schalk bunted, more for a hit than a sacrifice. But Gandil hesitated and allowed himself to be forced at third. Had Gandil made it, the Sox would have had the bases loaded with no outs.[44] "That play stopped us in the attack," Gleason said.[45] After Swede Risberg's one-out triple in the fourth, Schalk returned to the plate. Cracker's infield hit — some accounts say it was a bunt, and others a drive off the leg of pitcher Ray Fischer — scored Risberg. Schalk then tried to swipe second but was thrown out by Bill Rariden, another ex-Giant. Schalk thought he beat the tag, and he "kicked up a lot of dust" at umpire Cy Rigler's decision. Rariden also foiled steal attempts by Joe Jackson and Happy Felsch. However, the erasure of baserunners did not deny the Sox their first victory of the series.

Aside from one inning in Game 4, Cicotte pitched a masterful contest. In eight of his nine innings of work, he faced the minimum number of batters.[46] However, his two errors in the fourth inning — including a much-discussed deflection of Jackson's attempt to cut down a baserunner at the plate — gave the Reds all the runs they needed in a 2–0 decision. Cincinnati took a 3–1 series lead. Schalk, who was 0-for-1 with two walks, continued to give his all. With two out in the top of the ninth, Groh lifted a pop-up that appeared destined for the seats. "Schalk raced bravely up to the field boxes, stretched his hand over the crowd and grabbed the ball just as it was about to nestle on the purple velvet hat of one of Chicago's fairest dames."[47] The snag earned Cracker a standing ovation from the home crowd.[48] However, the scoreboard showed what really mattered most. As Jack Lait of the *Chicago Tribune* put it, "Cicotte pitched a wonderful game — away."[49]

After giving up only one hit in the first five innings of Game 5, Lefty Williams gave the game away in the sixth. The Reds opened the frame with a double, a single, sacrifice, walk and then a triple. The three-bagger, by Roush, came with two men on. Morrie Rath easily scored on the drive to center field, and Heinie Groh raced for home. The relay throw and Groh reached the plate about the same time. Schalk thought he tagged out Groh, but umpire Rigler disagreed. Already immensely frustrated by the events of the World Series in general and current events in particular, Schalk exploded. He jumped to his feet, and while hollering about the decision, bumped Rigler and pushed the arbiter with his fists. That earned him the rest of the afternoon off, thus becoming the fifth individual (and second player) ejected in World Series history.[50]

Reds starter Eller held the White Sox to three hits, striking out six straight batters, including Schalk, in the second and third innings. After the 5–0 loss, and now trailing the Reds four games to one, Gleason told Crusinberry, "I don't know what's the matter, but I do know that something is wrong with my gang. The bunch I had fighting in August for the pennant would have trimmed this Cincinnati bunch without a struggle. This bunch I have now

When Schalk heatedly bumped and pushed umpire Charles "Cy" Rigler (shown here in 1914) in Game 5 of the 1919 World Series, the National League arbiter tossed the catcher from the game. It was only the second player ejection in World Series history (Library of Congress, Prints & Photographs Division, Bain Collection, LC-B21-3112-20).

couldn't beat a high school team." Crusinberry credited Schalk with being an exception. Allowing that perhaps Cracker did miss Groh on his tag, but possessing behind-the scenes knowledge of Schalk's allegations of a fix, Crusinberry noted, "His tantrum over this play might have been because of things in general instead of the play on Heinie Groh. It was apparent that Schalk was so wrought up that he was ready to tackle Jack Dempsey or anybody." As Lait put it, "When the heart is full the lips flow over."

The Series returned to Cincinnati for Game 6, and Kerr turned in another heroic performance, scattering 11 hits over 10 innings in a 5–4 victory. The White Sox, facing elimination in the best-of-nine series, pushed across the final run in the top of the 10th when Buck Weaver doubled, Joe Jackson bunted him to third for a single, and, after a Felsch strikeout, Gandil singled. If the conspirators were trying to lose this one, they passed up the opportunity. Schalk had an RBI single in two at-bats, two walks and a stolen base. Defensively, he cut down two of the four Reds attempting to steal and took Joe Jackson's throw to snuff Rath's effort to score on a sacrifice fly.

In Game 7, with no more than 14,000 spectators in Redland Field — the White Sox heckled the Reds that their fans had given up on them, but there was a logistical mix-up about tickets — Chicago, behind Cicotte, closed the deficit to four games to three by beating the Reds, 4–1. In this game and the previous contest Cincinnati's Edd Roush questioned whether some of HIS teammates were trying to lose. Schalk's line score included a single in four at-bats — and no ejections. "Schalk did not bite any one today," Lait quipped, "but he sure stung."[51]

With the World Series returning to Chicago, loyal White Sox fans held out hope that their boys could tie it up in Game 8 and force a ninth and deciding game. Gleason, still suspecting a lay-down, considered not pitching Williams. But he felt he had no options. According to Black Sox author Eliot Asinof, the manager sent out his team with a warning: "The minute I think any one of you ain't playing ball to win — if I think you're laying down — I'm gonna pull you out even if I have to make an infielder out of a bullpen catcher. I would use an iron on any son of a bitch who would sell out this ball club!"[52]

The manager's warning had little effect on Williams, who might or might not have been personally threatened by gamblers to take his third loss of the series. Unlike his previous two outings, when he looked sharp until pivotal moments, Williams was a disaster. He induced leadoff hitter Rath to pop out — and then failed to retire any of the next four batters he faced, allowing two singles then two doubles before Gleason yanked him. With only one out in the top of the first, the White Sox trailed, 3–0. Before reliever Bill James could stop the bleeding, Cincinnati scored again. After their three-run sixth, the Reds held a 9–1 lead after seven innings. While a four-run rally in the bottom of the eighth had some Sox fans envisioning a miracle comeback, it was not to be. Cincinnati won the world championship in a 10–5 laugher.

For Schalk, who had a dozen hits in 42 at-bats (.304), the World Series of 1919 was one he wanted to forget. But he would never forget. And never be allowed to forget.

15

✦✦✦✦

Divided We Fall

In the weeks after the 1919 World Series, a handful of sportswriters —
among them were New York writers Bill Macbeth and W.A. Farnsworth and
particularly Chicago's Hugh Fullerton — reported their doubts and suspicions
that the Series was played on the up and up. Many reporters, working for editors who feared libel suits, couched their words carefully and merely alluded
to irregularities in the series.[1] The *Chicago Tribune*'s James Crusinberry, who
hailed from the same hometown as hobbled White Sox pitcher Red Faber
(Cascade, Iowa), saw his detailed account of the corrupt series spiked by his
editor. Other *Tribune* writers had suspicions — and stronger. After Game 5,
Jack Lait sent Comiskey a telegram warning that something was amiss,[2] and
during a train trip between Cincinnati and Chicago, an intoxicated Ring
Lardner altered the lyrics of a popular song of the day, "I'm Forever Blowing
Bubbles" to make it a ditty about the Sox "forever blowing ballgames."[3]

Hours after the Reds wrapped up the World Series, Fullerton wrote:
"Today's game also means the disruption of the Chicago White Sox as a ball
club. There are seven men on the team who will not be there when the gong
sounds next spring and some of them will not be in either major league."
Fullerton, who said the better team did strange things and took the loss,
stated, "It is not up to me to decide why they (the Sox) did such things; that
all probably will come out in the wash."[4]

Thousands of Americans settled bets after the World Series, and not all
the wagers involved bookies. Former Chicagoan Larry Graver, traveling secretary of the Boston Red Sox, previously sold tickets at Comiskey Park; he
was friends with many of the White Sox. Graver won his bet on the series,
and collected a new suit of clothes, from none other than Ray Schalk.[5] For
Cracker, making good on that wager must have rubbed salt into the wound
of the World Series loss under suspicious circumstances.

During the off-season of 1919–20, rumors of a fix abated somewhat, but
they did not die — as conspirators, clean and crooked players and baseball

155

magnates might have hoped — due largely to Fullerton. The sportswriter, who moved from Chicago to New York during this period, stood virtually alone in publicly alleging that some White Sox players purposely lost. However, Fullerton was not the first to get the charge into print, and he didn't print as many details. That distinction went not to a mainstream newspaper but to *Collyer's Eye*, a Chicago-based sports and gambling tabloid. The weekly laid out what had happened and soon afterward named names.

In its October 18 edition, *Collyer's Eye* identified gambler Abe Attell as a key figure in the episode, and a week later, under the headline, "Involve White Sox Pitcher," made Lefty Williams' name part of the record. A couple of weeks after that, the tabloid's Frank Klein portrayed Eddie Collins and Schalk as "clean as a hound's tooth," adding that Schalk had cited Cicotte as being part of the fix. The next issue, dated November 15, named seven of the eight players indicted — Buck Weaver was not listed — and reported that the fix involved gamblers from New York, Pittsburgh, St. Louis and Chicago.

There were more blockbusters to come. *Collyer's Eye* on December 13 reported that Schalk indicated that seven White Sox players would not be with the team for the 1920 season — and he gave the same number as Fullerton: seven. "Schalk ... is not given to talking for publication, hence the statement carries considerably more weight." Though *Collyer's Eye* did not make it clear, it appears that Schalk might not have known that he was speaking to reporter Klein, or that whoever heard Schalk's statement would later tell Klein about it. Does that make the report more or less credible? Reminding his readers that this account was not far-fetched, Klein added that Schalk's story "also seemingly confirms the published reports of Charles Dryden of the *Examiner* and I. Sanborn of the *Tribune*. Schalk, too, it will be remembered, is reported as having trounced both Williams and Cicotte following games in which it was claimed that both pitchers deliberately double-crossed Schalk's signals."

The *Collyer's Eye* article indicated that Chick Gandil had bought a new house in California and planned to make fruit-growing his full-time endeavor. Earlier, it cited a second-hand report that Cicotte, upset that that Sox owner Charles Comiskey failed to pay him a bonus for a 30-victory season, planned to retire. Klein went on to recall that after Cicotte won his 30th, he "became more or less truculent," "fell off the wagon" and associated with "certain interests" rumored to have fixed the World Series.[6] However, Cicotte never won 30 games, coming close in 1917 (28 wins) and 1919 (29). Over the years, some contended that Comiskey denied Cicotte late-season starts to ensure the pitcher would not collect the bonus — and theorized that this gave Cicotte motivation to exact some revenge on the Old Roman in the form of the Black

Infielder Swede Risberg (shown here in 1919) was the youngest of the Black Sox outcasts — just 26 when his lifetime suspension hit. He prompted a commissioner's hearing in January 1927 after he resurfaced the allegation that the 1917 White Sox bribed the Detroit Tigers to "lay down" in back-to-back doubleheaders. Commissioner Landis found no cause to take further action except to make it clear that exchanges of "gifts" or "reward funds" between teams were prohibited (Library of Congress, Prints & Photographs Division, Bain Collection, LC-B2-4350-4).

Sox conspiracy. It is true that, in 1919, after notching victory No. 28, Cicotte did not start for a couple of weeks in the season's final month. However, after he returned and collected No. 29 on September 19, to push the White Sox within one game of the American League title, the *Chicago Tribune* revealed that Cicotte had been arm-weary. "The last previous [*sic*] time Cicotte pitched, if you remember, was in Chicago early in the month, and he gave six bases on balls, indicating that the strenuous pace was beginning to tell on him."[7] After losing a doubleheader and going three days without a game, the White Sox put Cicotte on the Comiskey Park hill September 24. However, he struggled against the Browns — five runs on 10 hits and a walk — and was trailing when he gave way to a pinch-hitter in the seventh inning. The Sox rallied for two runs in the seventh and two more in the bottom of the ninth for a 6–5 win. The pennant-clinching run scored on Shoeless Joe Jackson's single.[8]

Had the information in the *Collyer's Eye* been printed in the mainstream press — one of the leading metropolitan daily newspapers, *The Sporting News* or *Baseball Magazine*— the article linking the roster of conspirators (minus Weaver) to Schalk would have been a blockbuster. It went further than Fullerton's reporting, naming names — including that of the accuser. However, instead of picking up the ball and investigating further, the establishment publications shot at the messengers, *Collyer's Eye* and Fullerton. The tabloid's reporting was dismissed as yellow journalism by a sheet promoting an evil endeavor, gambling. As one of journalism's leading sportswriters, Fullerton was a tougher target, but that did not stop the multi-pronged attacks on his motives and reputation. It didn't help them that Schalk backtracked on his comments almost immediately.

An editorial in *The Sporting News*, noting the *Collyer's Eye* revelations attributed to Schalk, took the Sox veteran to task. "Catcher Ray Schalk of the Chicago White Sox is quoted as saying that seven members of the team will be found missing when the 1920 season opens, whereas some critic rises to remark that Schalk talks too much," opened *The Sporting News* editorial, "Out With What You Know." "But it seems to us that if he made the statement as described, Schalk talked too little, when he talked at all. Such a statement, if he made it, should have been more specific. Schalk should have told why seven members — important members — of the team will be missing." The editorial noted that the quotation was in direct conflict with public statements by Comiskey and Gleason that they could find no evidence to support stories of a World Series scandal. "Therefore, Ray Schalk either should tell what he knows, if he knows anything, or he should say nothing. We have had enough of rumors indefinite and lacking foundations that can be unearthed."

The editorial concluded, "Now what does Ray Schalk know that he should make the statement credited to him?"[9]

Two weeks later, Schalk chose the "say-nothing" option, and *The Sporting News* accommodated him. Schalk disavowed any connection to his quotations in *Collyer's Eye*. In Oscar Reichow's report, *The Sporting News*, which did not even deign to name the "certain sporting publication" that broke the story, indicated that Schalk did not initially comment on the story because, well, why dignify *Collyer's Eye* with a response? "When the yarn first came out Schalk refrained from making a statement of any kind, because he considered the source from which it came. He was literally pulling at the leash to reply, but on the advice of friends and baseball men did not do so, as it was believed he would be suspecting the integrity of his mates if he did condescend to take heed of unreliable news of that kind," Reichow explained. "I played in that World Series and played to the best of my ability," Reichow quoted Schalk as saying. "I feel that every man on our club did the same, and there was not a single moment of all the games in which we all did not try. How any one can say differently, if he saw the Series, is a mystery."[10] That, essentially, was Schalk's response for the next 10 months — if anyone was brave enough to ask him about the 1919 World Series. Even after it was all over — the indictments, the trials and lifetime bans of eight members of the 1919 White Sox — Schalk would say nothing about what he knew about the Black Sox scandal. Black Sox historian Gene Carney speculates that Schalk's about-face was due to pressure from Comiskey, who wanted to keep his team together.[11]

For the rest of his life — five long decades — Schalk refused to speak on the record about events of the 1919 World Series. His friend and teammate Red Faber in the early 1960s told Black Sox researcher Eliot Asinof, "It's tough to talk about. I see some of the boys — like Schalk, for instance — and though he was as straight as an arrow, he won't even mention the series." While researching *Eight Men Out*, Asinof secured an appointment to talk to Schalk, then a Purdue assistant coach, who cautioned that he didn't "cotton much to writers." When Cracker learned what Asinof wanted to discuss, the conversation was brief and tense. Asinof described it this way:

> He was solid granite. The first mention of the Black Sox turned him off. At first I thought this might be his sour mood, the result of yesterday's defeat of his ball club or an argument with his wife, but I was wrong.
> "Like I said, mister, you're wasting your time and mine."
> "Mr. Schalk, you're a hero to me. You represent resistance to corruption. What you had to do in that Series...."
> "...Mister, I'm not talking about it," he snapped.
> "May I ask why?"

"Forget it," he said, turning to papers on his desk.

"You dislike ALL writers?" I asked.

He refused to answer, mumbling something as he turned away, obviously wanting to be done with this. I had to get at the source of resentments, even if it meant provoking him.

"Why, Mr. Schalk? That seems like such a paranoid view. Like a black kid in the ghetto when he faces a cop — ANY cop."

He looked back at me, eyes flaring, saying nothing, for what seemed like a long time, no doubt trying to control his temper.

"What do you know what I think?" he said. "I'll tell you something: No, I don't trust writers. I've seen too many of them, they don't get as close to an umpire as to a bartender. They know nothing about baseball. They hang around picking up stories they got no right to hear, always making everything come out worse than it was. They're a bunch of old-lady gossips. What do I want to talk to you for?"[12]

Asinof reflected, "For all his hostility, I was struck by the honesty of his emotion," adding, "How many distortions and inanities would have to appear in the papers before a hard-nosed straight shooter like Schalk would be repelled by all sportswriting?"[13]

Reviewing the hundreds of articles featuring Schalk in his retirement years, and the number of times he posed for photographers at various baseball-related events, one might conclude that Cracker was not turned off by all sportswriters — just those who asked about the Black Sox.

Years after his blockbuster book was released, Asinof recalled chatting with Joe DiMaggio at a New York banquet where Schalk was the guest of honor.[14] After the writer told the Yankee Clipper about his exchange with Schalk and wondered whether he had mellowed, Asinof quickly learned the answer:

"Let's find out," DiMag suggested, volunteering to lead me to him.

"Ray, you remember Eliot Asinof?" DiMag offered. "He wrote that fine book on the Black Sox?"

Schalk barely looked up, and though I was standing behind him, I could see his body tense.

"I don't want him near me!" he snapped.[15]

Asinof noted that when Schalk died the following year, he did so "without ever saying a bloody word" about what he knew about the Black Sox scandal.[16] For the 50 years after *The Sporting News* chided him to tell all or tell nothing, Schalk did the latter.

16

Thrown Down

Downcast about the 1919 World Series and disenchanted with the unseemly aspects of professional baseball, Schalk quietly contemplated quitting the White Sox, if not baseball entirely.[1] It's not known how serious those thoughts were. Leaving Comiskey's team was problematic, given his contract's reserve clause, which bound him to the Sox as long as the Old Roman's organization desired. He was just 27 years old and arguably the best catcher in the game.

Meanwhile, Schalk's friend and teammate Red Faber, regaining his fitness after an off 1919, admitted to similar thoughts. Crusinberry reported that the spitball star said retirement or another ballclub might be best for him.[2] Years later, Faber, interviewed by Eliot Asinof, indicated that ethical breaches were not limited to a single World Series. "It was a rotten time, all right," he said. "There was so much crookedness in those days, I guess we didn't pay too much attention to it. And that's pretty terrible. That's pretty damn terrible..."[3]

For Faber and Schalk, their reservations about returning to the major leagues no doubt had less to do with on-field performance than off-field relationships. Though they could win lots of ballgames, the Chicago White Sox were deeply divided. Spending six months a year — at the ball park, on trains, in hotel and restaurants — with people they intensely disliked no doubt took its toll. Eventually, Schalk and Faber set aside their reservations. The pitcher signed for another season and his catcher, who had signed a three-year contract a year earlier, decided to continue with the team.

Schalk again held down a non-baseball job in Chicago during the off-season — most likely in sales for the same metals firm that hired him after the 1918 season. However, *Collyer's Eye* indicated he was selling cars.[4] In any case, in addition to working, exercising and spending time with Vin and their daughter, Pauline, Schalk occasionally found time for public appearances. In early February 1920, he spoke at the organizational banquet of the Chicago

Industrial Athletic League; another speaker at the Morrison Hotel that evening was Avery Brundage, former Olympian and future president of U.S. and International Olympic committees.[5]

For Comiskey and top aide Harry Grabiner, contract negotiations for 1920 were particularly challenging. The owner was certain that several of his players had thrown the recent World Series — but unsure if he knew the full story. Rather than cut the suspects loose — a move that would decimate his team and possibly expose him to litigation — the Old Roman tried to keep the mess under wraps. Because the White Sox won the 1919 pennant and baseball overall enjoyed a post–Great War resurgence, players pressed Comiskey for heftier contracts, and, uncharacteristically, generally received them. That is not to say that the Old Roman didn't put up a fight, and several players — notably the Black Sox figures — signed after spring training was under way. Eddie Collins, coming off the lucrative contract that contributed to so much dissension on the team, was another holdout.

The season of 1920 was one of significant change. There was no official pronouncement that the Deadball Era was over, but 1920 is considered the start of the Lively Ball period, when the homer and three-run rally replaced Deadball's emphasis on singles, strategy and speed. The transition rested on the broad shoulders of Babe Ruth. The day after Christmas 1919, the cash-strapped owner of the Boston Red Sox, theatrical producer Harry Frazee, and the New York Yankees finalized a deal for the slugging pitcher-turned-outfielder.[6] Ruth got his wish and was converted to a full-time outfielder.

Meanwhile, another contributor to the Lively Ball era was baseball leadership's move to eliminate the spitball and other "trick pitches." During the off-season, the Joint Rules Committee banned pitchers' use of all foreign substances — including saliva, resin, talcum powder and paraffin. The "emery ball" and "shine ball" were also out. The National League opted to let existing spitballers keep throwing the pitch — newcomers would be banned — while the American League allowed each team to designate no more than two pitchers who could throw the spitter for one more season (1920). Comiskey's designees were Red Faber and Eddie Cicotte.[7] (That effectively exiled from the majors 22-year-old Frank Shellenback, another spitball practitioner on the White Sox. Shellenback wound up taking his spitter to the Pacific Coast League, where he was "grandfathered" to throw the "freak pitch" for the balance of his career. He won 295 games during his 19 PCL seasons.[8])

However, many observers said Faber and Cicotte would have succeeded without the spitball in their repertoires. "Every once in a while I hear about a pitcher who 'has everything,'" Schalk said after his playing days ended. "Yet the only pitchers I ever saw who had everything were Faber and Cicotte—

fast ball, curve ball, three-and-two, and spitter, three-and-two. There have been a lot of names for different pitches, but Faber and Cicotte could throw 'em all, whether you called 'em fadeaways or sliders or screwballs or knucklers or forkballs."[9]

Baseball enacted other rule changes for 1920, including clarification of the infield-fly and a prohibition against the oddity of players running bases in reverse order (to distract fielders or otherwise make a travesty of the game). Off the field, January 1920 marked the beginning of Prohibition, the Great Experiment of ridding the United States of alcoholic drink, which ushered in the decade to be known as the Roaring Twenties. In a business response to Prohibition, gangsterism and bootlegging skyrocketed, and Chicago was a hotbed of this activity.

Meanwhile, White Sox owner Charles Comiskey and several cohorts continued to woo federal judge Kenesaw Mountain Landis to be an overseer of the game. After the 1920 campaign, and on the heels of the Black Sox indictments, Landis became the autocratic commissioner of baseball, replacing the weak National Commission. Within a year, after the Black Sox trial, the full extent of his power would become dramatically clear.

Though the Black Sox indictments would not come until only a few games remained in the 1920 regular season, the unsavory link between gamblers, ballplayers and baseball games received increasing scrutiny. Hal Chase, who had escaped punishment in 1918 despite Christy Mathewson having the goods on him, was finally out of baseball in 1920. The Cubs fired Lee Magee, a buddy of Chase who admitted betting on baseball and playing to lose in 1919. Magee did not go quietly, suing for the salary remaining on his contract — he lost — and sparked increased doubts about the honesty of the games. There was also speculation that the 1919 Pacific Coast League pennant race was decided not by clean play but by bribes. Going into the 1920 season, various publications opined that organized baseball needed to wipe out the scourge of professional gambling. The *New York Times* referred to "rumors" surrounding the previous World Series and repeated Schalk's disavowal of the *Collyer's Eye* article. "Any blot of this sort (the charges after the Series) on the good name of the national game would weaken the confidence of the fans," the *Times* stated.[10] In addition to stepping up police presence in the ballparks, major-league owners agreed to hire private detectives to root out the gamblers.[11]

After four years in Mineral Wells, Texas, the White Sox moved their 1920 training camp 125 miles southeast to Waco. Eventually, the roster included six of the seven players Schalk had predicted would no longer be with the team. The seventh was Chick Gandil, the ringleader of the 1919 Series fix, who kept to his word and retired from the majors. A California resident, he played the next several years in outlaw leagues in the West and Southwest.

The White Sox already had cliques and discord. It only got worse after the 1919 World Series. "Even during batting practice our gang stood in one group waiting our turn to hit and the other gang had their own group," Eddie Collins revealed after the indictments.[12] In previous seasons, members of the Gandil-Risberg clique provoked and argued with the Collins-Faber-Schalk group. Now, they erected a wall of silence, acting as if the other group didn't exist.[13] Writing in *The Sporting News* after the cover was blown off the scandal, John B. Sheridan said, "What puzzled me most is how did the White Sox, honest men and crooks, get through the season of 1920 as they did. Half the team knew the other half was crooked. Half the team knew the other half had robbed them. Half the team knew they were crooked. Half the team knew they had robbed their fellows."[14] Explained Collins: "We went along and gritted our teeth and played ball. We had to trail along with those fellows all summer, and all the time felt that they had thrown us down."[15]

But all that would not become public for another six months. The 1920 season approached. Noting the return to championship form of Faber, whose absence hurt the Sox in the 1919 post-season, and the return of all the regulars but Gandil, Chicago sportswriters happily predicted that not only would the 1920 White Sox repeat as American League champs, but they also would be better than the 1919 squad. Outside the Windy City, prognosticators predicted that the Cleveland Indians, featuring Tris Speaker, and the New York Yankees, with the newly acquired slugger Babe Ruth, would provide plenty of competition for the White Sox.

Black Sox ringleader Arnold "Chick" Gandil in 1918 (Library of Congress, Prints & Photographs Division, Bain Collection, LC-B2-2465-5).

If White Sox fans harbored any hard feelings or suspicions about their boys' performance in the World Series, it was not evident when some 25,000 fans jammed Comiskey Park for Opening Day 1920. "Among those thousands were the countless bugs who, after the deplorable world series of last fall had raised a right hand and sworn, 'Never again,'" Crusinberry observed. "They simply forgot all about the nasty rumors, the unexpected series defeats, the bum playing, and all the other things, and went back for more." The fans didn't even seem to mind that the price for a seat in the bleachers had doubled — to 50 cents.

The opening ceremony featured both teams marching, with Marines and a band, to the Comiskey Park flagpole, where they hoisted the Stars and Stripes. The game turned out to be one of the most exciting contests of the season. The visitors were Ty Cobb and the Detroit Tigers. A contract holdout, Cobb had engaged in his first baseball activity of the year just four days earlier, when he showed up for an exhibition game in Indianapolis, borrowed a pair of shoes, and singled his first time up. In the first inning of the season opener, Cobb stepped to the plate, shook hands with Umpire Brick Owens and his friend Schalk, and promptly recorded a single against Lefty Williams. The Sox starter hardly looked like a man who couldn't retire a Reds batter in the previous World Series. The White Sox held a 2–1 lead with two out in the top of the ninth. The Tigers had no one on base, and the fans started for the exits. Detroit's Harry Heilmann stopped them in their tracks when he smashed a no-doubt home run into the left-field bleachers. It was only the fourth hit against Williams all afternoon. The next batter, Ira Flagstead, threatened the outfield wall with a long drive, but Happy Felsch snared the ball with a one-handed grab. The game extended into the 11th inning, when Buck Weaver reached on a scratch single, stole second and raced home on Eddie Collins' drive to the power alley in left.[16] The 3–2 victory started a six-game streak.

In the second game of the season, Eddie Cicotte, though rulesmakers denied him the use of his alleged "shine ball," looked masterful in shutting out the Tigers. He enjoyed solid defensive support. With one out in the fourth and Donie Bush on third and Ty Cobb on first, Bobby Veach lofted a fly ball to Jackson. Shoeless Joe's throw to Schalk caused Bush to retreat to third. However, Cobb tagged up and ran for second base. When Schalk threw to head off Cobb, Bush again took off for home. Chicago second baseman Eddie Collins' return throw to Schalk arrived in time for Cracker to apply the tag and complete an unusual double play.[17]

April showers hit Chicago so hard that the Sox managed only two games in the first week of the season. The field was still soggy for Game 3, when

Schalk turned in another crowd-pleasing defensive effort. Running toward the seats in pursuit of Jimmy Austin's pop up, Schalk skidded when he tried to stop. While falling flat on his back, Cracker made the catch. The Sox prevailed over St. Louis, 7–4.[18] Game 4 featured some comical turns on the basepaths. Schalk opened a four-run seventh inning with a double. Cicotte laid down a sacrifice bunt, and Detroit pitcher Herb Dauss fired to third. Schalk retreated and engaged the Tigers in a spirited rundown play while Cicotte dashed for second. The Sox teammates arrived at second together, but infielder Ralph Young tagged the wrong opponent. Cicotte proceeded to head back for first base, but Young's throw to retire Cicotte went wild. When the mud settled, Schalk stood at third and Cicotte at second. They both then scored on Eddie Collins' double.[19]

With that sort of luck and solid play, the White Sox were poised to win their seventh straight to open the season. But the residue of the World Series scandal surfaced. Faber, nursing a 2–1 lead in Cleveland, retired the first two batters in the bottom of the eighth. The next hitter, Larry Gardner, rifled a Faber pitch over Jackson. As Gardner cruised into third, shortstop Swede Risberg caught Jackson's throw, turned and threw so wildly to third base that it got past infielder Buck Weaver and Faber, who was backing up the play. Gardner trotted home to tie the game, 2–2. "Risberg never should have made the peg," the *Tribune*'s Irving Vaughan wrote, "as there was no chance to beat the runner to the far bag."[20] Cleveland won the game in bottom of the ninth with two singles and a sacrifice fly.

In *Eight Men Out*, Asinof cited that particular game — and that particular play — as an example of Black Sox principals continuing to throw games in 1920. Asinof said the crooked players feared blackmail or physical harm by the gamblers.[21] Little more than a week later Faber lost another 3–2 decision to Cleveland, and again Red paid the price for questionable defense. Center fielder Felsch turned a clean single into a three-bagger, setting the table for a Cleveland victory. Decades afterward, Faber told Asinof, "The hoodlums had some of the boys in their pocket all through the 1920 season too, throwing ball games right up to the last week of the pennant." The Hall of Famer said, "I could feel it out there when I pitched — Risberg letting an easy ground ball go by, or Happy Felsch letting a runner take an extra base. You want to scream at them but you don't because you can see how scared they are."[22] Scared of the gamblers.

Even with a possible thrown game or two, the White Sox burst out of the gate, winning 10 of their first 12 games. They then reversed direction, losing seven of eight. The final loss in that stretch was a 14–8 decision in New York. In the fifth, Babe Ruth deposited a Lefty Williams pitch into the Polo

Grounds' right-field upper deck for his fifth round-tripper of 1920. Sox manager Kid Gleason and his charges vehemently argued that Ruth's drive curved foul, but umpire Brick Owens could not be persuaded to reverse his call. The next inning, the Yankees broke open the contest, scoring seven times with Grover Lowdermilk on the mound. The 6-foot-4 reliever had a particularly rocky outing. He gave up three hits, issued a walk, uncorked a wild pitch and committed an error when he dropped a throw from Schalk.[23] It was the 35-year-old journeyman's final major-league game. White Sox officials had just turned down $5,000 — then an American Association record — from Columbus for Lowdermilk's contact when they learned that the pitcher was secretly negotiating with an industrial league. Within two days, the Sox sold Lowdermilk to Minneapolis (American Association), where he appeared in 56 games, mostly as a starter, over the next two seasons.[24]

On a Friday afternoon in mid–May, the Sox were rained out in New York. That postponement might have afforded Schalk a chance to partake in his favorite recreational pursuits — bowling and billiards. He enjoyed both sports — bowling especially — and built his off-the-field business enterprises around them.

Meanwhile, while the Sox watched the rain in New York, the city of Chicago dedicated and officially opened a Michigan Avenue drawbridge over the Chicago River. The span, just an outfielder's throw from the present site of Tribune Tower, greatly represented welcome relief to traffic congestion downtown and at the Rush Street bridge. The ceremony was an elaborate affair, including bands, fireworks, a ribbon-cutting by Mayor William Hale Thompson and decorated autos — but without the usually speechifying. Amid the din of the celebration, an approaching lumber steamer signaled the bridge tender, who complied by starting to raise the bridge. However, four cars remained on the bridge and started to slide toward the river. The bridge tender could not hear the shouts of warning from onlookers or the potential victims, and only the quick thinking of police officers, who fired gunshots into the air, averted a tragedy.[25]

When the U.S. Census enumerator called upon the Schalk residence in 1920, the family consisted of Ray, Lavinia and their 2-year-old daughter Pauline. They resided in Chicago's Third Ward, southeast of downtown. The city's population had increased by more than 23 percent since the 1910 count, with the percentage of African American residents doubling in that time. Not coincidentally, it was in 1920 that the Negro Leagues were established, with Rube Foster and his Chicago American Giants playing a prominent role.

The *Chicago Tribune* in those days published a daily feature, "The Inquiring Reporter," in which five people on the street were asked a simple question. In early June 1920, the paper asked, "Who is the most valuable player on the White Sox team?" Two of the five named Schalk. One, a high school student named Dodo Lehman, added, "Perhaps you think because I'm a girl I don't know, eh? Well, I do. Ask Commy who his best player is. He'll say Schalk, and so will I."[26]

The Yankees' acquisition, Babe Ruth, was well on his way to a record 54-homer season. Who knows what his totals might have been had he received better offerings from opposing pitchers. Managers regularly ordered their pitchers to walk the Bambino. Fans of Yankees' opponents, including White Sox fans, hated it. Red Faber walked the Bambino under protest and under threat of discipline; he wanted to challenge Ruth. No doubt, Schalk had to walk to the mound to convince his friend to follow orders.

In August, a chorus of boos from some 25,000 fans rained down on Faber — in his own ballpark — each of the three times he walked Ruth.[27] Several fans complained to the *Chicago Tribune* about the tactic. One wrote, "When the Sox pitchers here deliberately refused to give Ruth a chance to make a hit by passing him I felt that my admission money had been obtained by false pretenses." However, a fan from Detroit preferred White Sox victories to Ruth homers: "What a pity! The Yanks lost three of four to the Sox, so little (manager) Miller Huggins cries, 'Don't be so hard on us. We have Babe Ruth. Please groove the ball to him so he can hit more home runs and give the fans a run for their money while we win the games.'"[28] Noted the *Tribune's* Harvey T. Woodruff, "Faber wanted to take a chance, and it required imperative orders, cajolery, and finally threats from Manager Gleason to force Red to carry out instructions, but the Sox won a game (3–1) which they might not have won if Ruth had clouted another homer."[29] A *Tribune* reader submitted this ditty:

> If I were pitching to Babe Ruth,
> I don't believe I'd mind him;
> I'd peg that pellet straight and true–
> And fifteen feet behind him.[30]

In another White Sox-Yankees contest, a walk to Ruth played to Chicago's advantage. Trailing 3–1 in the ninth inning, Sox lefty Dickie Kerr issued Ruth his pass. Bob Meusel's sacrifice bunt went skyward. Schalk snared the ball with one hand and, seeing Ruth spectating about 20 feet off first, fired the ball to Shano Collins to complete a double play.[31] That embarrassment notwithstanding, Ruth commanded great respect from his opponents, including Schalk, who described him as "the most terrific slugger who ever lived." He said, "There isn't any way to fool Babe Ruth. If he has a batting weakness, I don't know what it is."[32] (Decades later, Schalk said the only bat-

Slugger Babe Ruth, a charter member of the Hall of Fame, rated Schalk as the best catcher in the game. Photograph dated 1921 (Library of Congress, Prints & Photographs Division, Bain Collection, LC-B2-5463-15).

ter whose weakness he couldn't spot was Cobb.) Some of Ruth's popularity was his accommodating nature with the public, especially children. The morning before a game on Chicago's South Side, the Bambino visited St. Mary's Training School in northwest suburban Des Plaines, where he told of his boyhood days at the St. Mary's school in Baltimore.[33]

On the first day of July 1920, a Wednesday, the White Sox hosted Ray Schalk Day and officially raised their 1919 American League pennant. Tributes poured in for Schalk, who that season reached the 1,000 mark for major-league appearances. "If there were nine Schalks in Manager's Gleason's lineup," a *Tribune* columnist observed, "we'd be asking reservations for the world's series right now." The ceremony's planning committee included Schalk's first two managers, Jimmy Callahan and Clarence Rowland, and Cracker's friend Sam Pass. With temperatures in the low 80s and a doubleheader against St. Louis on the agenda, some 20,000 fans made their way to Comiskey Park for Schalk Day. Among the dignitaries were Mayor "Big Bill" Thompson, who made the presentation speech, and representatives from Litchfield. Gifts included a silver service and a "large chest of silver." Pass said the gift was purchased with contributions by Schalk's many admirers. After the Schalk tribute, the team raised the 1919 pennant — no doubt, players thought about the more prestigious banner flying in Cincinnati — and split the twin-bill with the Browns. The honoree rapped a double in four at-bats on the afternoon.[34]

Independence Day apparently inspired a *Tribune* sportswriter to turn nostalgic. "Can you remember away back when the fans at the Fourth of July games whipped out their revolvers and fired a cylinder full of shots on the first base hit of the game?"[35] Gunplay was not involved, but the White Sox fired off a 6–3 victory over the Browns on July 4. The next day, Chicago won both ends of a morning-afternoon doubleheader over Cleveland to move within 3½ games of the Indians and Yankees, who lost twice in Washington. They were still 3½ back — but now ahead of the Yankees — on August 9 after taking two close contests against Washington. In the fifth inning of the second game, with his team losing by a run, Schalk belted a Harry Courtney delivery into Comiskey Park's left-field bleachers. Of Cracker's five home runs to that point in his career, it was the first not of the inside-the-park variety.[36]

The American League pennant remained a three-team affair, with Cleveland, Chicago and New York unable to pull away. Going into the games of August 16, the standings showed Cleveland and the White Sox tied for first and the Yankees a mere half-game behind, with New York and Cleveland about to begin a three-game set in the Polo Grounds. The importance of the series gave way to tragedy that afternoon, when a pitch from Carl Mays, a submarine-style pitcher and one of the game's least-liked players, slammed into the skull of batter Ray Chapman — ironically one of the best-liked men on any ball field. Chapman's death a few hours later sparked grief across the country and outrage in some quarters, where a few major-league teams discussed going on strike if Mays, who had a reputation for throwing beanballs, were not banned from the game. The White Sox did not make that threat. Such talk soon dissipated, and the players resumed their labors, albeit with bitterness. Cleveland was given one day off for mourning. However, how would the grieving Indians, in the heat of a pennant drive, respond to the loss of their popular shortstop? Initially, it did not look promising. Cleveland lost seven of the next 10 games and fell out of first.

The White Sox pulled into a first-place tie after a doubleheader sweep in Philadelphia on August 20. The second victory went into the books as a forfeit, though Chicago held a 5–2 lead with two out in the ninth and no one on base. Pinch-hitter William "Lena" Styles topped the ball along the first base line. Pitcher Dickie Kerr picked up the sphere and tagged the batter for the apparent final out. At least it was apparent to the fans occupying Shibe Park's right-field stands. Believing the game to be over, they headed for home in their customary manner — walking across the playing field toward the grandstand exits. However, just before Kerr picked up the ball, it rolled foul. The umpires' efforts to clear the field so that the game might continue were met by indifference by the policemen in attendance and even Athletics manager Connie Mack. After five minutes of this, during which fans in the grandstand began hurling seat cushions at people on the field, umpire Oliver Chill declared the game a Chicago victory by forfeit.[37]

Ten days after Chapman's death, the first-place White Sox faced Mays in New York. It was Mays' second start since the beaning. In the third inning, Fred McMullin and Yankees outfielder Ping Bodie engaged in an on-field argument and mutually agreed to settle the score off-campus — right then. "The two umpires, Manager Gleason and several players dissuaded them," the *Tribune* reported. "Of course, the argument was about Mays, although neither belligerent would admit it." A few innings later, a foul tip hit Schalk and knocked him out momentarily. When he came to, despite urging from Gleason and backup catcher Byrd Lynn (who probably would have appreciated the playing time), Schalk refused to come out of the game. Mays pitched 10 innings and hit no batsmen before giving way to a pinch hitter. He earned a no-decision for his trouble, but the Yankees prevailed in 12 innings, 6–5, to cut Chicago's lead to 2½ games over Cleveland and three over New York. "The White Sox were so anxious to beat him (Mays) they beat themselves," observed the *Tribune*'s I.E. Sanborn.[38]

Worse, the defeat was the first in a seven-game losing streak — a dry spell in which the gambler-blackmailers had a hand. Among them was Faber's 3–0 loss to the Yankees, in which errors by Risberg and Weaver contributed to all the scoring. All the losses in Boston were particularly suspect.[39] The crooked play became so evident to Schalk and his fellow Clean Sox that the team virtually disintegrated. On a rainy August 31 in Boston, Jackson allowed a fly ball to get over his head.[40] Risberg "missed" Jackson's return throw to the infield, allowing two runs to cross, and later botched a sure double play, allowing another run in the 7–3 loss.[41] In the first two games of the series, Schalk yelled and screamed at Cicotte and Williams for not throwing the pitches he signaled. The next day, after watching Jackson and Felsch let another fly ball fall harmlessly to the ground, and having Buck Weaver drop his perfect throw on a forceout, an enraged Kerr flung his glove across the field and, in the dugout afterward, engaged Risberg and Weaver in an altercation.[42]

The losing streak continued when the Sox returned home to host St. Louis in a doubleheader. The *Tribune* reporter noted unusual behavior in the stands. "The crowd numbered more than 25,000," he wrote, "and, judging by the rooting, a considerable minority of those present wagered on the Browns to win both games."[43] If so, they lost their bets. After dropping the first game, the Sox started a four-game winning streak. But, after seven straight losses, would it be too little too late?

Only a half-game separated the top three teams in the American League standings entering Sunday, September 12, when the White Sox faced second-division Washington. The game at Comiskey Park featured the unheard-of occurrence of a batter ending his own team's inning on a home run. With two out in the fourth of a scoreless contest and teammate Frank Ellerbe on first, Washington catcher Edward "Patsy" Gharrity sent a Lefty Williams pitch into left-field bleachers. Ellerbe, in his first full season in the majors, was running with the crack of the bat and did not see the ball reach the seats. As he approached third base, Ellerbe misread the gleeful noise emanating from the Sox fans in the bleachers, who most likely were excited to witness an over-the-wall home run. However, Ellerbe took the sound to mean that Chicago left fielder Joe Jackson had made a spectacular, inning-ending catch. With that, Ellerbe turned back to take his defensive position at shortstop. Gharrity, in his home-run trot, passed Ellerbe on the infield. With that, both umpires, Bill Dinneen and Oliver Chill, signaled Gharrity out for passing a baserunner who had yet to be retired. As the bemused White Sox headed off the field, manager Clark Griffith and most of his Nationals surrounded the umpires to argue that it shouldn't have mattered because the ball was out of play. The umps held firm. No home run. Inning over. Nonetheless, Washington scored once in the fifth and three times in the sixth to chase Williams, who was ineffective all afternoon, en route to a 5–0 victory.[44] Was it just a bad afternoon for Lefty, or was this another one of those 1920 games in which gamblers exerted their control over the Black Sox? The next afternoon, while the Senators and White Sox battled in the fifth inning, Chicago detectives arrested five men in the bleachers on gambling charges. Each posted bond of $25 and was released.[45]

Schalk had a baserunning blunder of his own a couple of weeks earlier in Boston's Fenway Park. With two out in the eighth and Schalk on first, teammate Amos Strunk sent a fly ball into deep center field. Schalk raced around second and, still running hard, tried to watch the outfielder. Cracker slipped on a soft spot on the infield and fell flat on his face. It was small consolation that the miscue did not factor in the game's outcome, a 4–0 Boston victory. Chicago's losing streak continued.[46]

The day of Schalk's stumble, far more serious events were in motion behind the scenes — events that would involve a bigger fall and would impact not only the 1920 American League pennant race but also baseball history.

17

A Team to Dismember

With a dozen games to play in the 1920 regular season, still close on the tail of the league-leading Indians, the White Sox and Yankees battled in Comiskey Park. A Saturday date, the pennant race and the opportunity to see Babe Ruth contributed to a huge turnout of some 43,000 fans, a record for a ballgame in Chicago. Spectators filled every seat, and the overflow crowd stood 10-deep along the outer edges of the outfield; as a result, the ground rule stated that a fly ball hit into the crowd would be worth two bases. The patrons went home happy after the White Sox outslugged New York, 15–9. Schalk went 3-for-5, including a double, and scored twice. Cicotte, making his first start in 10 days, limited Ruth to a single in four at-bats.[1]

Entering Cleveland for a pivotal three-game series, the White Sox learned of blockbuster news from Chicago. A grand jury would investigate whether Detroit gamblers bribed one or more players of the Chicago Cubs to lose their home game against the Phillies on August 31. Team officials had received pre-game tips to that effect and scratched starter Claude Hendrix from the lineup. Grover Cleveland Alexander pitched in Hendrix' place but the Cubs lost anyway, 3–0. No evidence of a fix emerged, yet the Cubs released Hendrix; he never returned to the major leagues. However, convening a grand jury concerning the Cubs-Phillies contest created a convenient opening to look into the White Sox and their 1919 World Series. (Was the Cubs-Phillies warning planted just to create an opportunity to look into the White Sox affair? Hendrix was 33 years old and struggling; even against the Phillies, a Hendrix victory would not have been a sure thing.) Cook County (Illinois) Assistant State's Attorney Hartley Replogle secured subpoenas for several men to testify before the grand jury; among those summoned were James Crusinberry, *Tribune* sportswriter; Schalk; and Cracker's good friend Sam Pass, who lost more than $3,000 betting on one World Series game.[2]

American League President Ban Johnson, who gave testimony before the grand jury, made public the whispers that that the White Sox would not "dare" win the 1920 pennant because they were being blackmailed by gamblers who wanted them to lose.[3] Meanwhile, Charles Comiskey was holding to his official line that he investigated and could find no evidence of crookedness in the World Series of 1919. In mid–September 1920, New York sportswriter Joe Vila wrote that the 1919 Series was fixed. Representing his 61-year-old father, Louis Comiskey, treasurer of the White Sox, publicly dared Vila to submit his proof to the Chicago grand jury.[4]

Though distracted by these developments, and desperately wanting to prove Johnson wrong, the White Sox (the honest ones at least) redoubled their efforts and dared to claim the pennant. Despite appearing overeager at times — sportswriters cited miscues by Schalk and Eddie Collins as evidence — the Sox beat the Indians two out of three and cut Cleveland's lead to a half-game. As the grand jury investigation commanded the headlines, the White Sox returned to Chicago. They had five games left in the regular season — two at home against Detroit and three in St. Louis. Chicago won both from the Tigers. In the second contest, Dickie Kerr pitched a 2–0 shutout for his 20th victory of the year and made the White Sox the first major-league team ever with four 20-game winners — Faber (23 wins), Williams (22) and Cicotte (21). Kerr would win once more to finish 21–9. (Since then, only the 1971 Baltimore Orioles have had four hurlers win 20 games in a season.) But Cleveland kept pace, maintained its half-game lead over the Sox and eliminated the Yankees from the pennant chase. Cleveland was in the driver's seat: Its "magic number" was 4 — the combination of Indians wins and Sox losses — and had six games remaining on its schedule. The White Sox, meanwhile, had three open dates before they resumed action. That left plenty of time for Comiskey attorney Alfred Austrian to interview some players and for the grand jury to hear more testimony. There was plenty to discuss. As Kerr was wrapping up his 20th, Chicago's afternoon newspapers reported an expose in the *Philadelphia North American*, courtesy of small-time gambler Bill Maharg. He admitted that he and "Sleepy" Bill Burns performed the legwork in the World Series fix. The crooked Sox intentionally lost games 1, 2 and 8, Maharg said, adding that it was Cicotte who proposed the fix to Burns.[5]

While the Sox rode the rails between Philadelphia and Cleveland, Replogle declared that the 1919 World Series was fixed. According to United News writer James L. Kilgallen, Replogle wasn't making much headway regarding the World Series probe — until Crusinberry recommended that the prosecutor put Pass on the stand. Pass, in turn, suggested that Replogle hear from Henrietta Kelley. According to Kilgallen, Pass and Kelley provided the breakthrough to the indictments. For decades, it was understood that Mrs. Kelley was the landlady of Cicotte and several Sox players. In fact, she was

Cicotte's sister.[6] She hosted the pitcher's daughter and their brother during the series. She overheard the White Sox star tell their brother, "Well, what do I care? I got mine."[7] Her testimony — and that of Pass — closed the noose on Cicotte. He became the first to confess.

How it happened that the pitcher wound up in Comiskey's private office at the ballpark was never established. Some accounts had him showing up on his own volition. Others said Austrian sent for him and then directed Cicotte to Comiskey. Another is that Gleason, who heard that Cicotte was ready to talk, appeared at the player's hotel room and accompanied him to Comiskey's office.[8] In any case, it did not take much more than a "hello" for Cicotte to give in to the pressure — a year's buildup — and admit that, yes, he was "crooked." Soon he was testifying to that effect before the grand jury. He entered the criminal courts building with Austrian, unknowingly signed a waiver of immunity, and spent more than two hours telling the grand jury his role in the affair. In 1963, Eliot Asinof wrote that Cicotte told grand jurors, "Schalk was wise the moment I started pitching (in Game 1)."[9] Maybe so, but 21st century Black Sox expert Gene Carney notes that he was unable to find another instance when Cicotte repeated that admission.[10] In any case, Cicotte did confirm Schalk's accusations that he and Lefty Williams crossed up Schalk on his signals.[11]

Meanwhile, Schalk sat outside the grand jury room much of the morning, at first unaware that it was Cicotte who was inside. Asinof said Schalk still was unsure what to tell the grand jury. If he didn't disclose, could he be considered an accessory? If he did talk — as he already had to sportswriters, before he recanted — would he be considered a snitch? The question became moot when a news bulletin burned through the courthouse: Cicotte confessed! The grand jury never heard Schalk's testimony; it wouldn't need to. As Cracker left the courthouse, reporters swarmed around him. Schalk at first said he'd have plenty to tell after the baseball season ended; after all, the Sox were still in a pennant race with three games to go. But when a reporter asked him about rumors that some games in the current season had been fixed, Cracker's tone changed. He declared, "I won't say anything at all now!"[12]

Two decades afterward, Schalk described a clubhouse scene when the indictments and suspensions became official. "As long as I live, I'll never forget the day Charles A. Comiskey came into the clubhouse and told eight of the boys they had been exposed and were through forever. It was a shocking scene and my mixed emotions never have been straightened out since I watched several of the ruined athletes break down and cry like babies. I never have worried about the guys who were hard-boiled, but those tears got me."[13] He described an emotional and dramatic scene, but did it really happen? Time might have clouded Schalk's memory. First, only seven of the eight players were still with the club at the time; Chick Gandil had departed, refusing to come back for the 1920 season. Further, contemporary newspaper accounts said initially that only three players, unaware of the indictments, had been served suspension notices. The other four had yet to be located, as the White Sox had an open date on their schedule. As for Schalk, he was about 25 miles away, in Gary, Indiana, where his 21-year-old brother Clarence lived. It is possible that Comiskey confronted the other four in the clubhouse the next day, but even if they showed up after seeing the indictments reported in the morning papers, the suspension notices could not have been a surprise.

Pass accompanied several players who drove to the courthouse neighborhood. While the players waited in the car, Pass went in. He learned of the indictments and ran out to tell the Clean Sox. Their hopes for the 1920 pennant were effectively crushed, but the news sparked a celebration. "Little Nemo Leibold hugged Eddie Collins. Eddie swatted Amos Strunk on the back. Amos swung his left into Mike (Eddie) Murphy's ribs," the *Tribune* reported. The players rushed to find pay phones so they could call Schalk, Red Faber, Dickie Kerr, John Collins and the others who had endured the dissension and the thrown games of 1919 and 1920. That evening, the celebrants, including former Sox players and current Cubs Zeb Terry and Tom Daly, gathered at a downtown restaurant. Schalk drove back from Gary "at top speed" to join the party, which moved to Eddie Collins' apartment. The *Tribune* quoted an anonymous player: "No one ever will know what we put up with all this summer. I don't know how we ever got along. I know there were many times when things were about to break into a fight, but it never got that far."[14] The speaker might have been Eddie Collins, who subsequently said much the same in an on-the-record interview.[15] In Boston, the Roosevelt Newsboys Club condemned the indicted and praised the honest players — Schalk and Dickie Kerr specifically — "for their manly stand against the Benedict Arnolds of baseball."[16]

With the suspended players gone and their unusual break in the schedule over, the remaining White Sox needed to regroup and play the last three games of the season in St. Louis. Some players made confident statements about still winning the pennant without the crooks, but there were doubts whether, if the depleted White Sox somehow managed to sweep St. Louis while Cleveland faltered, there would even be a World Series.

It soon became a moot point. The Browns beat Red Faber and the White Sox, 8–6. Playing near his hometown and appearing in his first game after the indictments, Schalk stepped to the plate for his first at-bat to a fine ovation from the St. Louis fans, who presented him a large floral arrangement.[17]

Meanwhile, Cleveland split its doubleheader with Detroit. Ahead by two games with two to play, the Indians now could do no worse than tie for the pennant. Both teams won the next day, but Cleveland's 10–1 romp over Detroit settled the matter. His team broken up, the pennant lost, and feeling the effects of a punishing season, Schalk nonetheless played in the final game of the regular season to bring his total appearances to 151 games in the 154-game campaign, then a major-league record. It was later reported that he might have played in ALL the contests if not for a terrible case of sunburn suffered after an off-day visit to an Atlantic City beach.[18] In the finale, Schalk singled in his only at-bat before taking a seat in favor of Clarence "Bubber" Jonnard, who joined the team after the suspensions and was appearing in only his second major-league game. Over the season, Schalk hit .270, and topped the league's catchers in fielding percentage (.986), putouts (581) and games played.

In a year full of surprises, Schalk received one more: A $1,500 check from the Old Roman. The accompanying letter explained that the amount represented the difference between the winner's and loser's shares from the 1919 World Series. It would not be fair for the honest players to be deprived of the larger amount due to the dishonesty of others, Comiskey explained. In addition to Schalk, others who signed a public thank-you to Comiskey were Faber, Eddie Collins, John Collins, Leibold, Dickie Kerr, Eddie Murphy, Roy Wilkinson, Harvey McClellan and Byrd Lynn.[19]

Chicago's City Series was cancelled — games between a depleted and disgraced White Sox squad and a Cubs team with its own gambling-related issues would only call more attention to their respective troubles. Yet, after workouts, dozens of pre-season games and 151 regular-season contests, Schalk kept playing baseball. The weekend after the regular season closed, he and Kerr competed in semi-pro exhibitions in Chicago on back-to-back days. The weekend after that, they traveled to Litchfield for the annual Schalk Day game. The event took on extra significance in light of the Black Sox indictments, and the record turnout of an estimated 10,000 reflected it. Chicago Mayor William Hale Thompson headed a delegation of some 65 Chicagoans who made the trip. Schalk's Litchfield squad featured Kerr's pitching and a homer by Montgomery County native and future Hall of Famer Jim Bottomley, whose major-league debut (with the St. Louis Cardinals) was two years away. Litchfield defeated Mount Olive, 8–1. Afterward, the day's events concluded with a banquet and festivities at the Litchfield Hotel and Elks Club.[20]

The Kerr-Schalk battery participated in yet another exhibition the following weekend, traveling to Springfield, where they represented Litchfield's Brown Shoe Company against the Illinois Sangamos. They drew big crowds.

RAY SCHALK.   DICK KERR.   GEORGE SISLER.   JOHNNY TOBIN.
RAY RICHMOND.   MAYOR THOMPSON.

SIXTH ANNUAL

Schalk DAY!

LITCHFIELD

Sunday, Oct. 17

At 2:30 P. M. at the LITCHFIELD PARK ASSOCIATION PARK
On South State Street.

BROWN SHOE PLANT TEAM
—vs—
MT. OLIVE

BATTERIES:

LITCHFIELD:—"Dick" Kerr, Chicago White Sox; Russell Pence, White
Sox next season and Ray Schalk.
MT. OLIVE:—Ray Richmond, St. Louis Browns and Frank Fedor.

Johnny Tobin and George Sisler of the St. Louis Browns will be in the
Mt. Olive line up. Litchfield will have Newell Bote, Jimmie Bottomly,
Jocko Hughes and Harry Collenberger, all league players in their line-up.
"Brick" Owens of the American League; Turk Doolin of Litchfield and
Deitiker of Staunton will be umpires.

Mayor William Hale Thompson of Chicago and his official family will be
here. Mayor Thompson will pitch the first ball.

ADMISSION ADULTS 50cts.   Children 25c. Grand Stand and Autos 25c.

1000 Grand Stand Seats   Litchfield Daily Union   25 Acres To Park Autos

Ray Schalk Day became an October tradition in his hometown of Litchfield, Illinois. The event took on added significance in 1920, coming on the heels of the Black Sox indictments. A record crowd turned out to support Schalk as one of the "Clean Sox" (Bottomley-Ruffing-Schalk Museum, Nokomis, Illinois).

At the same time, Red Faber Day, in the pitcher's hometown of Cascade, Iowa, saw a similar boost in turnout. Their status as Clean Sox made them all the more popular with fans. The same could not be said for Buck Herzog, the Cubs infielder whose name surfaced in connection with the attempted fix of a game involving his team a month earlier. After an exhibition game in Joliet, Illinois, a fan stepped onto the running board of the auto in which Herzog was sitting, poked his head in the window and said, "You're one of those crooked Chicago ball players. When are you going to confess?" Herzog bolted out of the vehicle and wrestled with the man. A friend of the fan pulled out a knife and slashed Herzog three times. The ballplayer suffered minor injuries.[21] Herzog's major-league career was over, due not to this slashing but because no team wanted him after his link to fixed games became known.

Schalk and the other "Clean Sox" were relieved by the indictments and suspensions of the other faction of the team. However, what kind of team would the White Sox field for 1921?

18

Rebuilding for the Second Division

White Sox management spent the off-season of 1920–21 scouring minor-league rosters for suitable replacements for the seven players suspended in the Black Sox scandal, including four position players and two pitchers. The only regulars still available were pitcher Dickie Kerr, outfielder-infielder Shano Collins, outfielder Nemo Leibold and future Hall of Famers Eddie Collins, Red Faber and Ray Schalk.

Meanwhile, Schalk changed off-season careers. After two winters working for a metals business, Schalk announced in late November 1920 that he had become an insurance salesman in the Franklin J. Neuberger office, 39 S. LaSalle St. Just weeks later, he grabbed the attention of Chicago insurance men by writing a huge accident and health policy on meatpacker Nelson Morris, chairman of the board of Morris & Co. Worth a half-million dollars, the policy was so large that it had to be divided among several companies. "Ray goes after the big fellows the same as the little ones, and his commission on this big policy should amount to a neat sum. Mr. Schalk goes out and earns money," noted the *Tribune*, adding with an allusion to the Black Sox, "He never looks for it under his pillow."[1] For such a prominent businessman to buy such a large insurance policy through an agent with less than two months of experience, one might conclude that the insured was a White Sox fan.

Shortly before training camp, three players changed Sox: Shano Collins and Leibold were traded to the Red Sox while the White Sox received veteran outfielder and future Hall of Famer Harry Hooper.[2] Meanwhile, the White Sox invited about 50 prospects to try out in Waxahachie (Texas) Jungle Park before spring training. Schalk, Faber and Kerr reported early to help Manager Kid Gleason evaluate the horde of 17 pitchers.[3]

Schalk had interest in another professional prospect: his brother Clarence. As a 21-year-old, he drew notice in an industrial league in Gary, Indiana. Clarence scored a minor-league tryout with Joe Cantillon, an owner and manager with interests in St. Joseph, Missouri, and Minneapolis.[4] Cantillon said young Schalk would work out in Missouri, and, if he showed promise, try out with Minneapolis (American Association). Cantillon no doubt figured that a sibling of the game's leading catcher was at least worth a look. That was about all Clarence received. He was released outright before the season began. Ray would be the only member of his family in professional baseball. (He was no relation to Roy Schalk, who played for the White Sox in 1944 and 1945.[5])

If Gleason and the White Sox were unsure about their roster, their fans were without a clue. "It's almost impossible to talk to a man five minutes these days without his asking about the prospects of the White Sox," Crusinberry observed before tryouts. "No one can answer the question at present. All one can say is that Gleason has a tough job on his hands."[6]

After spring training in Texas, Gleason brought his reconstructed team north. In light of the Black Sox suspensions, and boasting a roster full of unfamiliar names, the White Sox were unsure how fans would respond to them. They got a hint when the team worked out in Comiskey Park before traveling to Detroit for the season opener. Some 500 fans watched the practice and tried to identify the many new players.[7]

Fans' low expectations were almost immediately realized. After 13 games, the reconstituted White Sox dropped into last in the eight-team American League. They rose to seventh — thanks to perennial cellar-dweller Philadelphia (last place every season from 1915 to 1921) — and spent the bulk of the season there. Even 13 Chicago losses in the final 17 games could not evict the Athletics from the basement. The Sox finished 62–92, nearly opposite of their 1920 record. At least they came by their losses honestly.

Events surrounding the dishonest World Series of 1919 finally came to trial in the summer of 1921. The prosecution entered the proceedings at a disadvantage; key documents, including players' confessions and waivers of immunity, had mysteriously disappeared. The discovery coincided with a change of Cook County state's attorneys following the November 1920 election. (Many of the missing documents resurfaced, conveniently, three years later when Comiskey needed them in his defense against Joe Jackson's lawsuit for back pay.) With that development, the players denied confessing to anything. Prosecutors needed more time to reconstruct their case, and the original indictments were tossed out. The suspects held out hope that this might end the affair, permit them to report for spring training and allow them get on with their lives. But baseball's new commissioner, Judge Kenesaw Mountain Landis, had other intentions; he placed them on the "ineligible" list.

Then, prosecutors, prodded by Ban Johnson, secured new indictments against the White Sox players and 11 others, including former major leaguer Hal Chase and a handful of gamblers. Among the counts were conspiring to defraud the public, conspiring to defraud team owner Charles Comiskey and conspiring to defraud Ray Schalk. Cracker's name was used as a representative of the players who lost the chance to earn the larger World Series share. For good measure, prosecutors added the charge of conspiracy to defraud White Sox fan Sam Pass, Schalk's friend who had lost $3,000 betting on the 1919 South Siders.[8] Later, prosecutors sent Pass to New York to identify a jailed Abe Attell as the man who fleeced him. Noted lawyer William J. Fallon was in Grand Central Station to greet Pass. Known as The Great Mouthpiece, Fallon represented Arnold Rothstein, major New York gambler, hoodlum and — just coincidentally — Attell's employer. After Pass and Fallon visited over a couple of drinks, $3,000 changed hands. Now made "whole" for his gambling loss, Schalk's friend returned to Chicago and testified that there was some mistake. He said the man sitting in a New York jail was not the Abe Attell who took his bet in Cincinnati.[9] Attell had wriggled off the hook. Hal Chase likewise beat extradition efforts. Fred McMullin was not re-indicted. The only gamblers to go to trial were small-time players David Zelser of Des Moines and Carl Zork of St. Louis.

After his 27 years as charter president of the American League, Ban Johnson (shown here in 1914) went from friend of White Sox owner Charles Comiskey to his enemy. Their acrimonious relationship impacted how the Black Sox scandal was investigated, prosecuted and, for a while, covered up (Library of Congress, Prints & Photographs Division, Bain Collection, LC-B2-3225-7).

As the trial was to begin with jury selection, the White Sox were hosting Detroit and in the middle of a six-game losing streak. The White Sox and Tigers also had a rainout to make up, and the schedule included open dates for both teams, but they did not play because the Sox and Cubs agreed

to not both stage home games the same afternoon unless they appeared on
their original schedules. After the day of rest, the White Sox whipped a semi-
pro team in Sullivan, Indiana, near the border with downstate Illinois. Yam
Yaryan caught most of the contest and went 4-for-4 at the plate, but Schalk
did play long enough to appear in the box score and register four putouts.[10]
With that, the Sox traveled to St. Louis, where they resumed their major-
league season and their losing streak.

A couple of weeks later, jury selection in the Black Sox trial trudged
along. In Chicago for another homestand, Schalk, several teammates and
Gleason reported to the court as ordered in subpoenas. Before the day's proceedings, in a scene that belied the rift that had so divided the White Sox the
previous couple of seasons, several Clean Sox and Black Sox greeted each
other warmly, shook hands and slapped each other on the back. Gleason's chat
with ex-infielder Buck Weaver was interrupted when Faber and Kerr tested
Weaver's reputation for being ticklish.[11] "The only mention of the baseball
scandal was when some of the men now on the team wished the others good
luck in their trial," *The New York Times* reported.[12] Newspaper accounts made
no mention whether Schalk participated in the joviality.[13] Public reaction to
the show of friendliness was so negative that Comiskey assigned spin control
to Gleason, who tried to explain to people that their eyes had deceived them.[14]
Gleason renewed his denial after the trial. "Wish them well? Not much!"[15]
That tactic is consistent with the contention that the Old Roman tried to cover
up the fix in hopes of eventually regaining the services of his star players. After
all, Comiskey went so far as to protest Johnson's use of league funds to help
the state's attorney investigate the matter.[16]

Judge Hugo Friend initially told Schalk and the others not to leave the
jurisdiction of the court — no small order for a major-league baseball team —
but later allowed them to travel provided that they return when the court required
their presence — even if they were on a road trip. That is what happened. It
appeared that the court's call would come while the White Sox were in Washington. The question was whether Chicago's game would be postponed while
the subpoenaed players were in court. After playing two games of their series,
when the court summoned the witnesses back to Chicago, the White Sox and
Nationals petitioned American League President Ban Johnson to postpone the
final three games. Officially at least, Washington concurred. Johnson, seeing an
opportunity to stick it to his enemy Comiskey, denied the request. Among the
delegation leaving Washington for Chicago were Schalk, Gleason, Faber, Eddie
Collins, Harvey McClellan, Kerr, Roy Wilkinson and trainer Harry Stephenson. In Washington, Sox shortstop Ernie Johnson, who had managed in
the minors, was left in charge of the remaining Sox players. Moving rookie

outfielder Johnny Mostil to second base and fielding a handful of reserves, Johnson and the depleted Sox lost two games. Rain fell before the second game, yet Washington owner Clark Griffith would not postpone. The game was played in a steady rain. The third game also started in rain. Only 300 fans showed up. The umpires had enough; they called it off in the second inning with Washington ahead, 5–1. Crusinberry criticized Griffith for pushing to play against the understaffed Sox: "It takes a cloudburst to stop Griff when there is a 'set up' game for him. Sometimes it looks as if there's no sportsmanship in baseball."[17] Added *Daily News* sportswriter Oscar C. Reichow, "President Comiskey did not ask for sympathy from Griffith or any one else. He said his club would play if all the pitchers had to be placed on the field, but down in his heart he knew there was only one thing Griffith should have done, and that was agree to call off the series."[18]

Back in Chicago, Friend convened a night session of the Black Sox trial to minimize the active players' time away from the team. Most of the July 28 session involved testimony from Gleason and Schalk, who primarily answered questions about what time the players left for practice and who they did and did not see in the team's hotel. The issue was the whereabouts of the defendants when the gamblers alleged they were meeting with the Black Sox. Gleason and Schalk testified that the eight accused players were at practice. Their statements boosted the defense.

A curious turn occurred when the manager and star catcher were asked whether they believed the accused players had performed to the best of their abilities. Was not that question central to the entire affair? Yet, it was the *defense* that posed the question. And it was the prosecution that objected! Judge Friend sustained the objections, and thus the two men who were first to suspect the fix were not compelled to answer. Had they responded, and responded truthfully, Comiskey's scheme to obstruct the investigation and subsequent prosecution might have come to light.[19] Everyone would have known when Comiskey became aware of the fix — after he claimed to have found no evidence of anything of the sort. Earlier that day, the prosecution objected to the defense's attempts to ask the same question of former Cincinnati pitcher Dutch Ruether and White Sox players Shano Collins and Nemo Leibold.[20] Faber, who watched the series from the dugout, did not take the stand at all. Collins, Wilkinson and Kerr testified only briefly, prompting an angry Kerr to growl as he departed the courtroom, "I came 900 miles to tell this!"[21]

After testimony, closing arguments and instructions to the jury finally concluded, jurors began deliberations about 8 P.M. August 2. Less than three hours later, three loud knocks from inside the jury room startled people lounging in the courtroom, signaling a verdict. Court officials hurriedly sent a messenger to retrieve Judge Friend from the Cooper Carlton Hotel. About 40 minutes later, at 11:22 P.M., the judge presided as jurors entered and handed their verdict slip to chief clerk Edward Myers. Chatter in the courtroom ceased. Myers read the first verdict. "We, the jury, find the defendant, Claude Williams, not guilty." The assemblage erupted as if the venue were Comiskey Park after a game-ending home run. Bailiffs tried to hush the gallery. Myers resumed reading verdicts: Not guilty. Not guilty. Not guilty. With each exoneration, the volume in the courtroom increased. When bailiffs noticed even Judge Friend breaking into a smile, they abandoned all hope of maintaining decorum.

The jurors "grinned like schoolboys" as the defendants and their attorneys rushed to shake their hands and pose with them for pictures. The jurors then adjourned to a restaurant's private room for a farewell party. The defendants and their entourage did the same — at the same restaurant. Allegedly, it took a few hours for the groups to realize that they were celebrating in adjacent rooms. In any case, two parties became one and carried on far into the morning.

If the defendants hoped that their exoneration would allow their return to organized baseball, Commissioner Landis swiftly buried those notions: "Regardless of the verdict of juries, no player that throws a game, no player that entertains proposals of promises to throw a game, no player that sits in a conference with a bunch of crooked gamblers, where the ways and means of throwing games are discussed, and does not promptly tell his

George "Buck" Weaver received a lifetime suspension from Commissioner Landis in the Black Sox scandal, even though no one doubted that he tried his best in the 1919 World Series. Weaver's offense was attending some of the conspirators' meetings and not reporting it. The rest of his life, Weaver tried in vain to win reinstatement. He and Schalk remained friends throughout, and Schalk served as his pallbearer in 1956. Photograph taken 1917 (Library of Congress, Prints & Photographs Division, Bain Collection, LC-B21-4351-21).

club about it, will ever play professional baseball."[22] The eight men were out — permanently. The White Sox would not get back their disgraced stars.

Schalk and the other current members of the White Sox read of the verdicts while riding the rails into Boston. The *Tribune* sportswriter accompanying the team observed, "There wasn't much comment." Though Schalk rarely spoke of the scandal, he did open up to the *Tribune*'s Ed Burns two decades later. "I never have contended that those who confessed did not get what they deserved when they were driven out of organized baseball in disgrace," Burns quoted Schalk as saying. "But I know that some of the fellows branded as vicious criminals were far from that. Terribly misguided, yes; but not vicious."[23] The afternoon after the trial, Schalk collected three hits in four at-bats but the Red Sox enjoyed some favorable bounces and won, 3–2. The game lasted 84 minutes.[24]

After losing two of their next three in Boston, the White Sox entourage — almost all of it, at least — boarded a midnight train at Back Bay Station and headed for New York and a date with the Yankees the next afternoon. The guy who missed the Saturday midnight departure happened to be the one responsible for the trunks containing the Chicago uniforms. The Yankees accommodated their guests by loaning their road uniforms. Some fits were better than others. "Ray Schalk's head was half hidden under a blue cap that completed an almost perfect disguise for the Chicago backstop," *The New York Times* noted, "and (Dickie) Kerr had to punch a few new holes in a New York belt." Swimming inside their borrowed garb, Schalk went hitless in two at-bats and Kerr sat on the bench in a rain-shortened, 2–0 victory for the Yankees.[25]

After that, Schalk missed three days of action. He had a good excuse. Ray and Lavinia Schalk were to be parents again. The day the Sox split a doubleheader in the Polo Grounds, where Babe Ruth blasted his 40th and 41st homers of the season, Vin gave birth to a son. His parents named him Raymond William Schalk, Jr. The *Chicago Tribune* printed a squib: "White Sox hopes of 1941 received a boost last night. Catcher Ray Schalk became the daddy of a lusty son."[26] The proud papa missed four regular-season games over three days. Catching duties were assigned to rookie George Lees, whose one-season major-league career included but 16 more games. Schalk also missed an exhibition game against the local team of Oneonta, New York, whose manager was former White Sox pitching great Ed Walsh. The old spitballer took a turn on the mound, and the White Sox went easy on him.[27] Schalk rejoined the team the next day in Cleveland.

Meanwhile, eight of his former teammates — the Black Sox — were denied the opportunity to play an exhibition in Sheboygan, Wisconsin. The bid by a Chicago promoter, E.L. Siekmeyer, to stage a game involving the Sheboygan Chairmakers of the semi-pro Lake Shore League was soundly rejected. "We realize that a game between the Chairmakers and the 'Black Sox' would be a big financial drawing card here," the team said in a statement. "But we refused to sign for such a game. It is true that a jury has acquitted these players, they are still under the shadow of shame, as far as the principles of organized baseball are concerned, and until that stigma has been removed we will not permit our team to play with them."[28]

Compared to the drama in the courtroom, Schalk's season on the field was uneventful. He was banged up for a while, and did not threaten his games-played mark of 151 set the previous year. He appeared in 126 contests, but if he had his way it would have been more. For example, the day after Independence Day, when Gleason kept Schalk out of the lineup, Cracker was observed pacing the ground near the bench while the Indians manhandled the Sox. "Ray ought to be tied outside the park when he's to have a day of rest," the *Tribune* observed.[29] Nonetheless, he led the league's backstops in defense (.985) and double plays (19). His .252 batting mark virtually matched his career average. Schalk, a regular on various lists citing the best players in baseball, was a clear-cut choice on an All-American League team presented by Irwin M. Howe, league statistician. "Few persons who are informed will dispute the selection of Ray Schalk to head the catchers," Howe wrote. "The White Sox 'Pepper Box' has set a record never approached in baseball for endurance. In mechanical excellence he has certainly had no superiors and it is doubtful there has been his equal behind the bat, when the ability to break up opposing plays, handle difficult and uncertain pitching and to inject a fighting, winning spirit in lagging fellow players are considered."[30]

Though he hit no home runs in 1921, Schalk did earn himself an ejection for protesting too much and sparking insurrection over a Babe Ruth homer August 18 at Comiskey Park. In the seventh inning, Ruth's towering shot left the ballpark entirely, the ball passing just inside the flagpole on the left-field line. Schalk, who argued that the drive was a foul ball, instigated a near-riot. Cracker, Gleason, other Sox players and bat-carrying Yankees surrounded umpire Frank Wilson, shouting at the rookie arbiter as well as opposing players, several of whom nearly came to blows. When order was restored, Schalk had been ordered out of the game. The three-run homer was Ruth's 46th of the season and put the Yankees ahead. However, the inspired White Sox rallied for three runs in the bottom of the eighth and prevailed, 7–6, giving Red Faber his 23rd victory (on the way to 25).[31] When Faber was at his best, batters would hit grounders. He must have had good stuff in the season's final weekend, when, in a rarity, Schalk threw out three straight Cleveland batters. In the eighth inning, all three topped Faber offerings in front of the plate. To that point, it was believed to be the first time a major-league catcher recorded three assists in a single inning. Nonetheless, Cleveland, holding out hope to catch the Yankees for the pennant, held on for a 3–2 win.[32] The Yankees held a two-game lead over the Indians, who had just two games to play. The next afternoon, minutes before the White Sox took the field against Cleveland, a telegraph message reached Comiskey Park: The Yankees won again to clinch the pennant. With that, Indians player-manager Tris Speaker removed himself from the lineup and watched the now-meaningless game from the team owner's box. In the other dugout, aware that the White Sox' duty to play the spoiler had expired, Gleason benched Schalk and had rookie Clarence "Yam" Yaryan catch.[33]

After an interruption of four straight Octobers — three due a Chicago team's involvement in the World Series and one because of the Black Sox indictments — the City Series pitting the White Sox and Cubs resumed. In anticipation, a writer with the initials HMS provided this verse to the *Chicago Tribune*:

> Of ball games I have seen but few
> Since gambling roused my dander;
> But I shall watch Kid Gleason's crew
> Hook up with Alexander.
> I'd leave my home, I'd leave my friends,
> I'd leave my daily labor,
> To see the Cubs combat the bends
> Served up by Urban Faber.[34]

As for the featured pitchers, the great Grover Cleveland Alexander lost two games as the White Sox swept the best-of-nine series. Faber took the win in Game 2 but suffered a season-ending knee injury. Trailing 3–0 in the bottom of the ninth inning of Game 3, the Sox scored three times to force extra innings, and then stunned the Cubs in 10 innings, 4–3. However, Schalk was not around for the excitement. A foul tip earlier caught the middle finger of his throwing hand. It must have been a particularly nasty injury. Schalk, who suffered broken fingers many times in his career and was loathe to leave a game, departed that contest and missed the final two games of the City Series.

A couple of weeks later, Schalk recovered sufficiently to appear in the annual Schalk Day game in Litchfield, where the home team handled Gillespie, 6–1. Attendance was down slightly from the previous year's contest, but the game attracted some 5,000 fans, including train cars of fans from Chicago.[35]

   With his baseball commitments for 1921 completed, Schalk returned to Chicago, where he underwent a tonsillectomy and an unspecified "minor throat operation."[36] He spent some of his convalescence time back in Litchfield.[37]

19

"The Human Dynamo"

During the Great War, Chicago's New Year's Eve celebrations were subdued compared to previous years. The Windy City's second celebration during the restrictions of Prohibition was quieter still. The traditional massing place, State Street, was free of the noise, confetti and serpentine parades. It was also free of alcohol — officially so, at least. An untold number of detectives positioned inside various establishments and some 2,000 uniformed policemen enforced the ban. Meanwhile, federal agents, tipped that booze-minded revelers would eschew downtown hotels for roadhouses on the city's outskirts, conducted dozens of raids. At The House That Jack Built, for example, agents arrested the manager when they discovered a half-gallon of liquor and a dozen quarts of real whiskey packed in a suitcase. They found other spirits at the Avenue Tavern and Lincoln Tavern. Before the stroke of 1922, police downtown had arrested nearly three dozen party-goers found wearing "hip toters" for their hooch.[1] Just a quiet New Year's Eve in "Roaring Twenties" Chicago.

How (or whether) Schalk celebrated the arrival of 1922 was not a matter for the newspapers or history books. Twenty-nine years old, Cracker prepared to begin his second decade as a member of the White Sox and his 10th year as the starting catcher. Unfortunately, after two American League pennants and a couple of close calls (1916 and 1920), the White Sox faced an extended period of being among the major leagues' worst teams. Ripped apart by scandal, and beset by years of mismanagement and misfortune, the White Sox would not appear in another World Series until 1959 and would not win one until 2005. For Schalk, a star for whom the competitive fire always burned, the reversal of his team's status — from contender to doormat — was a constant source of frustration. Before the season opener — when *every* team is in first place — even the *Chicago Tribune*, which usually generated the most optimistic predictions it could possibly justify, carried headlines such as "Dismal Outlook for White Sox" and "Gleason Job to Escape Cellar."[2]

Unlike many of his teammates, whose off-season routines were mostly sedentary, Schalk used the winter for regular visits to gymnasiums. Schalk and other batterymen — except Dickie Kerr, who was holding out in an unsuccessful attempt to wring $500 more from Comiskey — reported for early workouts in Marlin, Texas. Spring training followed in Seguin. One day, when freezing weather was expected to hit the Lone Star State, new Sox coach Johnny Evers (of Tinkers-to-Evers-to-Chance fame) and Schalk received the day off. Evers wanted to look into an investment opportunity. They traveled on a "dinkey," a small-locomotive train, about 40 miles to Mexia, Texas, where owner Charles A. Stoneham and manager John McGraw of the New York Giants had invested in an oil operation. "(Evers) wished to inspect the place out of which his fortune may gush," the *Tribune* noted. "Schalk is just naturally interested in things, so he went along to keep Johnny company."[3]

As training camp wound down, the Giants, defending World Series champs, and White Sox barnstormed a dozen pre-season games. The exhibitions brought good money; games featuring two major-league teams drew bigger crowds than White Sox contests against minor-league and semi-pro teams.

The White Sox had only three catchers in camp when one of them took out another. A foul tip off Schalk's bat struck recruit Roy V. Graham's right thumb with such force that bone broke through the skin. Graham recovered sufficiently to make his White Sox debut less than two months later, but he appeared in only five games in 1922 and concluded his major-league career the next season with 36 more appearances. Meanwhile, Schalk, with 100 or more catching appearances for a record nine seasons — he was averaging 129 games — planned to reach the century mark a 10th straight year. "If Comiskey's prize were timid at the plate, we might ascribe his figures, in part, to the fact that he took no chances and thus escaped injuries," the *Tribune*'s Harvey T. Woodruff noted. "But Schalk, despite his small stature, is one of the most daring men in baseball in standing his ground when baserunners come in to the home plate feet first in desperate slides. Ray just seems to have a knack of avoiding spikes, and he holds his position so stoutly that often he is accused of blocking the runner off the home pan."[4] Schalk's aggressive play was not limited to the plate. For example, in Chicago's fourth official game of 1922, visiting Detroit threatened to break a ninth-inning tie. The Tigers had the potential go-ahead run on third. With two out, Detroit's Ira Flagstead hit a short pop fly that came within a foot of the backstop. Schalk ran after the ball and grabbed it an instant before crashing into the screen. Detroit did not score, and in the bottom of the 10th the Sox pushed across a run for their first victory of the year.[5]

Though never an offensive threat, Schalk had one of his best seasons

Schalk poses in 1922, the best offensive season of his career, when he batted .281 and hit four of his 11 career home runs (Library of Congress, Prints & Photographs Division, Bain Collection, LC-B2-5278-14).

with the bat in 1922. He batted .281, drove in 60 runs and hit four of his 11 career homers. His first home run of the year came May 19, when he stroked an Eddie Rommel pitch into the left-field stands at Philadelphia's Shibe Park. The third occurred July 15, when he drove one over the left-field wall of the Polo Grounds against Carl Mays of the Yankees. The fourth was an inside-the-park to center field in Detroit on August 31 against Bert Cole. However, his most memorable round-tripper was his second of 1922. It took place in Detroit on June 27, when he put himself into the record books. After driving a Howard Ehmke offering into the seats in the third inning, Schalk in the fourth inning hit a triple. Batting again in the fifth, Schalk singled against Cole. In the ninth inning, with the Sox clinging to a 6–5 lead, Schalk contributed to a three-run rally with a double against Cole. With his single, double, triple and homer in the same game, Schalk became the first White Sox player — and the first American League catcher — to hit for the cycle.

Schalk played a key role in another historic event. On the last day of April, a sunny, 60-degree afternoon in Detroit, Ty Cobb's Tigers hosted the White Sox. Chicago pitched rookie Charlie Robertson, who was making his third start of the season and fourth of his major-league career. (Before this season, his only major league appearance occurred three years earlier, when he started and allowed two runs in two innings.) With some 25,000 fans booing and howling at him, the 26-year-old Robertson kept throwing whatever Schalk signaled. And he kept retiring Tigers, setting down the first dozen batters in order. The Sox scored twice in the second inning. In the bottom of the fifth, the Tigers tried to rattle the Texan. Batter Harry Heilmann complained to umpire Dick Nallin that Robertson was doctoring the baseball. Nallin found no evidence, and the game continued. Later, Cobb himself interrupted the proceedings, walked to the mound and boldly inspected Robertson's uniform for foreign substances or a device to scuff the ball.[6] Cobb then walked over to first baseman Earl Sheely and did the same. Irving Vaughan of the *Tribune* wrote, "He (Cobb) was foiled again, but even after it was all over, he still insisted there was something wrong. To a spectator it sounded like the squawk of a trimmed sucker." Decades afterward, Schalk recalled the scene. "They did everything they could to upset Charlie," he recalled. "But it didn't bother him a bit. I could have caught every pitch sitting in a rocking chair."[7]

Following Schalk's signals, Robertson continued to mow down each Detroit batter. The Chicago defense was not particularly challenged; batted balls rarely left the infield. By the time Robertson stepped on the mound in the eighth inning, the spectators in Navin Field were well aware that they might witness something special. Though their allegiance was with the Tigers, they were baseball fans first and foremost. Though they booed him just an inning earlier, Detroit fans in the eighth started cheering Robertson to keep it going. With two out in the bottom of the ninth, having retired 26 straight opponents, Robertson faced pinch-hitter Johnny Bassler. The Tigers' regular catcher, Bassler lifted a fly to left fielder Johnny Mostil, who squeezed the ball for the historic final out. Charlie Robertson had thrown only the fifth perfect game in major-league history, and the first no-hitter ever by an American League rookie. Robertson, who had six strikeouts and only six outfield outs, received an "ovation that an athlete seldom is granted on a foreign field." The perfect game was the first since Addie Joss of Cleveland outdueled Ed Walsh of the White Sox, who struck out 15 Naps in eight innings, on October 2, 1908. Probably the only man to have witnessed two of the five major-league perfect games was the rehired White Sox trainer William Buckner, who also saw Joss' gem 14 years earlier.[8]

A few days later, *Chicago Tribune* reader "R.F." made this observation: "All praise to Pitcher Robertson of the White Sox for his perfect game — he surely deserves it — but I have not read one word of commendation for the wonderful little player who caught him. Schalk probably called, as a conservative estimate, 90 percent of the balls pitched. Why not give him a share of the glory? Think the result would have been the same with a second- or third-rate catcher?" Throughout his life, Schalk made it his habit to contact the catcher of a no-hitter to extend his personal congratulations. As for Schalk, it was the fourth and final no-hitter he would catch.[9]

The White Sox exceeded expectations in 1922. They fought for a place in the first division of the American League, which would have earned them a share of World Series proceeds. Injuries to Schalk dimmed those prospects. Midway in an August 6 game against Philadelphia, a foul tip hit Schalk's right hand. He tried to play through it, but had to come out the next inning and didn't return for a week. A month later, another foul tip put out Cracker in the top of the 10th inning. The first batter in the bottom of the 10th was Schalk's replacement, Yam Yaryan, who hit a walk-off homer to beat Cleveland.[10]

In between those injuries, in mid–August, Schalk and the White Sox visited Boston. In the bottom of the eighth, the Red Sox scored twice to lead 5–1 and threatened to get more, with runners on first and second and nobody out. Gleason sent in reliever Clarence "Shovel" Hodge, a 6-foot-4, 190-pounder in his second full season with the team. After recording one out, Hodge apparently failed to keep a close enough eye on the baserunners, who proceeded to execute a double steal. This upset Schalk greatly, and he strode to the mound and he proceeded, in so many words, to call Hodge "yellow."

This in turn upset Hodge, who barked several well-chosen words at Schalk while the catcher walked back to his position. Second baseman Eddie Collins had to come over to settle down Hodge. On Hodge's first pitch after that, the Red Sox attempted another double steal; they failed, with Schalk and Company retiring the side. Hodge and Schalk had barely reached the dugout when the pitcher took the first swing. He missed. Though outsized by at least 50 pounds and eight inches, Cracker did not back down. "Schalk leaped up like a tiger and crashed his fist squarely on Shovel's nose," reported the *Tribune*'s Vaughan. "It was a healthy wallop." Manager Kid Gleason and Mostil separated the combatants.[11] Writing a few days before the altercation, Oscar C. Reichow said of Schalk, "The American League never had as hard a loser, whether the club be first or last. He is a human dynamo behind the plate, and can get more efficient work out of a pitcher than any other catcher in the ranks."[12] Hodge probably held a different opinion. In any case, within three weeks of the fight, the White Sox shoveled Hodge to San Francisco of the Pacific Coast League.

Aside from fistfights, one of the White Sox' most unusual games of 1922 was one that did not wind up in the final standings. On August 1 in Chicago, as a rainstorm threatened, the White Sox held a 5–1 lead going into the bottom of the fourth inning. The White Sox needed only to hold their lead after retiring the Yankees in the top of the fifth to make it an official game. The White Sox tried to make outs quickly in the fourth, to try to get in New York's turn in the fifth before the rain arrived. However, the Yankees wanted to prevent the top of the fifth from starting. Miller Huggins' team wasted time with wild throws, pitching changes and arguments with the umpires. When White Sox pitcher Red Faber hit an easy two-out grounder to Everett Scott, the shortstop missed the ball on purpose. Faber tried to put himself out by leisurely trotting from first base to third, while the Yankees tossed the ball among themselves. Just one out from a rain-shortened victory, the White Sox had to leave the field under a cloudburst. The home team did all it could to make the field playable after the half-hour delay, to the point of sweeping the infield with brooms, but before the game could resume, another round of rain cancelled baseball for the rest of the afternoon. "Not fewer than four Yankees should have been put out of the game and it should have been forfeited on at least two charges to the Sox," complained Ed Sullivan of the *Chicago Herald-Examiner*. "What has become of the old-fashioned umpire with some nerve?"[13] The White Sox protested to league President Ban Johnson — still the nemesis of Charles Comiskey — and said they deserved a forfeit victory. Four weeks later, Johnson ordered the game replayed. He also fined Huggins $100 and Scott, Bob Meusel, Waite Hoyt and Wally Schang $25 each for "the disgraceful exhibition of stalling." But he also fined three Chicago players — Faber, Schalk and Bib Falk — $25 each for contributing to the farce by quickly putting themselves out in the fourth inning.[14]

Before the final weekend of the regular season, major league teams had a half-week break for make-up games or exhibition contests. After games in Galva, Illinois, and Battle Creek, Michigan, the White Sox made their way toward St. Louis to resume their American League schedule. Before they got there, however, they stopped for an exhibition in Schalk's hometown. During the festivities, Litchfield's favorite son graciously accepted local admirers' gift of a pearl necklace, which he planned to give to Pauline. The White Sox crushed a bunch of semi-pros, 7–0, and headed for St. Louis in hopes of finishing in the first division. It was not to be.

Chicago dropped all three games against the Browns — two losses were by one-run margins — to wind up 77–77 and in fifth place, just one game behind Cleveland and two games behind Detroit. Still, they recorded 15 more wins than the previous season. Faber was the pitching staff's workhorse and star. He led the American League in innings (352) and earned-run average (2.81) while completing 31 of his 38 starts en route to a 21–17 record. His strikeout total of 148 ranked second, one behind Urban Shocker. Throughout Faber's 20-year career with the White Sox, no catcher handled more of his games than Ray Schalk. During the years they were teammates, Schalk caught 307 of Faber's 487 games.[15] They are among just 13 batteries enshrined in the National Baseball Hall of Fame.

The batterymates contributed to a key victory in the City Series. Entering Game 6, in Comiskey Park, the Cubs held a 3–2 lead in the best-of-seven series. In a do-or-die assignment, Faber held the Cubs scoreless through nine innings. However, Ernie Osborne did the same against the Sox through eight innings. In the bottom of the ninth, the White Sox had two men on and just one out. The Cubs issued an intentional walk to fill the bases and bring Schalk to the plate. He made a winner of Faber and forced a Game 7 when he bunted hard to shortstop Charlie Hollocher, whose throw home was too late to force Earl Sheely. In the deciding contest, however, the Cubs' Grover Cleveland Alexander shut out the Sox for a 2–0 win and Chicago bragging rights.

As the season wound down, baseball writers and non-playing managers voted on the American League's most valuable players. George Sisler of St. Louis won, easily outpointing Eddie Rommel and Schalk, who posted his record-extending 10th straight season of catching at least 100 games. However, for reasons not made public, none of the voters awarded a single point to Babe Ruth, who hit 35 homers and batted .315 for the pennant-winning Yankees.[16]

Chicago Cubs manager Bill Killefer (left) and Schalk relax at the Cubs Park batting cage before a 1922 City Series game. Killefer, a former star catcher, managed the Cubs until 1925. He then coached both St. Louis teams and managed
the St. Louis Browns (1930–33). After Schalk served as interim manager in Milwaukee in 1940, Killefer succeeded him (Chicago History Museum, Chicago
Daily News Collection, SDN-063131).

Schalk and other current members of the White Sox had hoped to put
the gambling scandal behind them, but another reminder of the Black Sox
affair reared its head in May. Banned player Oscar "Happy" Felsch went public with the allegation that in 1917 the White Sox bribed members of the
Detroit Tigers to lose four late-season games — back-to-back doubleheaders
in Chicago. Three stars remaining from that championship team — Eddie
Collins, Red Faber and Schalk — issued a denial. Money did change hands,
they said, but it was a reward for Detroit beating Boston, Chicago's closest
challenger in the standings, not for losing those games over Labor Day weekend. "I remember we contributed about $45 apiece for a pool to be offered
as a bonus to the Detroit pitchers if they defeated Boston in a series toward
the end of the season," Schalk said. "We thought nothing of it, as it was quite
a usual thing. All organized baseball knows that is often done." He further

recalled that Chick Gandil handled the money, which, Schalk assumed, was delivered.[17] When a reporter caught up with team owner Comiskey, the Old Roman dismissed Felsch's charge as too ridiculous to merit a response. Ban Johnson described the allegation as "nothing new," adding that information about the players' collection was prepared for the Black Sox trial but was never presented. Johnson said the matter was in the hands of Commissioner Landis.[18] Nothing further came of it — until Felsch resurrected the allegation nearly five years later, when Landis showed more interest.

20

Ray Down and Kid Out

The Schalk family — Ray, Lavinia, Pauline and Ray Junior — spent three months of the off-season of 1922–23 in Litchfield. That winter the family acquired a new member — a weeks-old puppy, a gift from a friend and admirer. Its first night in the Schalk basement, the puppy did not respond well to its new, cold and dark surroundings; about 2:30 in the morning, barks and yelps awakened everyone in the house — including Ray Junior, who contributed his own wails from the nursery upstairs. Ray Senior resolved the crisis by gathering up the puppy and his son and rocking them both to sleep.[1]

In addition to his domestic duties, Schalk aggressively worked out in preparation for his 12th season of major-league duty, ready to extend his record of 10 (and 10 consecutive) 100-game seasons. Before regular spring training in Seguin, Texas, pitchers and catchers convened about 150 miles south, in Marlin. The biggest excitement of the spring occurred off the field in Marlin, where fire broke out in the upper floor of Bule sanitarium, the team's temporary headquarters. Players, Sox officials and sportswriters rushed into the smoke-filled area and wheeled out the trunks containing the team's equipment before anything was lost.[2]

In Seguin, Kid Gleason's charges had trouble getting in much work because of cold, wet and windy weather. One rainy day, Gleason scouted around town and arranged the use of a cotton warehouse. The pitchers threw to Schalk and the other backstops for a half-hour. After the workout, the professionals played by climbing around on the mountain of cotton bales inside the warehouse.[3] On another day, at Baylor University in Waco, Schalk's day including catching some varsity hurlers along the sidelines. Some details of the story varied with time and the source — whether he was asked to do it by Baylor coach Frank Bridges, or whether Schalk requested a hurler or two to warm him up — the end result was that Schalk received several deliveries from a talented 22-year-old. After the workout, Schalk sent a telegram to team general manager Harry Grabiner, encouraging him to sign the right-hander before some other team beat the White Sox to it. Within days, Chicago had the right-hander's signature on a contract. His name: Ted Lyons. He remains the franchise's winningest pitcher (260) despite losing four seasons to military service. Lyons and the man credited with getting him on the White Sox, Schalk, entered the National Baseball Hall of Fame the same day in 1955. At the time of their selection for Cooperstown, Cracker joked that the team never reimbursed him for that timely and important telegram.[4]

As they had the previous spring, the White Sox and New York Giants, two-time defending World Series champions, agreed to a two-week barnstorming tour of exhibition games. Though he managed in the National League, the Giants' John McGraw saw Schalk in the 1917 World Series and the spring games in 1922 and 1923. As the exhibitions ended, he heaped praise on Schalk, describing him as "one of the best catchers I ever saw in my long experience as a player and manager."[5] The fiery backstop's standing among baseball's elite was further affirmed that spring when American League President Ban Johnson had a thank-you gift sent to the president of Mexico after the baseball executive visited south of the border. The token of appreciation was a silver statue depicting two ball players — St. Louis Browns star George Sisler and Schalk.[6]

Seeing their 1922 team nearly attain the first division, the top half of the eight-team American League, White Sox fans held out hope for better things in 1923. Though only three players from the 1917 champions remained on the roster, all were future Hall of Famers: Schalk, Red Faber and Eddie Collins. The team had another future Cooperstown inductee — Harry Hooper, acquired from Boston in 1921. In assessing the prospects of the White Sox, sportswriter Hugh Fullerton predicted, "It is a team to which almost anything may happen, excepting finishing last or first."[7] Fullerton was correct. By season's end, the Sox were neither first nor last.

After opening the 1923 regular season with four losses in Cleveland, the White Sox traveled to St. Louis. Some 20,000 fans jammed the Sportsman's Park seating area and another 4,000 stood in the outfield. When Schalk stepped up for his first at-bat of the game, a delegation from Litchfield presented him with a basket of roses. Schalk responded with a single and two runs batted in. His second RBI, coming on an eighth-inning squeeze bunt, was the final run in Chicago's 4–3 victory.

Several hours later, back in Chicago, a bomb thrown from a passing car caused minor damage to the exterior of Comiskey Park. The explosion shattered windows, demolished a sidewalk hot-dog stand and peeled fresh paint from the skin of the stadium. Team officials blamed labor unions. The White Sox and Cubs, whose ballpark had just sustained vandalism to its plumbing,

Eddie Collins (left) and William "Kid" Gleason, shown in 1921, preceded Schalk as White Sox manager. Gleason resigned after the 1923 season. Collins managed the Sox in 1925 and 1926 (Library of Congress, Prints & Photographs Division, Bain Collection, LC-B2-5256-13).

were the object of union pickets after they hired non-union firms for projects.[8] Six months later, the day before the Cubs were to host a City Series game, another bomb severely damaged ticket booths at Wrigley Field.[9]

The incident did not interfere with the White Sox home opener four days later. One feature introduced for Opening Day 1923 was a "radio concert"— piping in music through loudspeakers erected around Comiskey Park.[10] Shortly before Faber's first pitch against Cleveland, a gift basket of roses was presented to a man on the field. Such presentations were fairly common in those days, but this one was unusual in that the gift went to an *umpire*. The recipient was none other than Clarence Rowland, the manager of the 1917 champions, who had turned to umpiring. This was his first game in Chicago.[11] The roses cut the White Sox no favor with the rookie arbiter, and Cleveland won, 3–0. (As an umpire, Rowland was the target of more than the usual number of arguments; after five seasons, the American League dropped him.[12])

After losing their first two home games, the White Sox sat in last place with a 1–7 record, and it appeared that it would be an extremely long season for the South Siders. However, they edged back toward respectability. A doubleheader sweep in St. Louis on Independence Day pushed them above .500 for the first time all year (33–32) and found them in third place. It turned out to be the only day all season in which the White Sox had more victories than losses. The Sox would finish the year 69–85, seventh among the eight American League teams, and eight games worse than the season previous. Two days before they reached their high-water mark, star second baseman and captain Eddie Collins suffered a knee injury that cost him weeks of playing time. In a bit of baseball coincidence, future Hall of Famer Collins' twisted knee occurred in the game in which another future Hall of Famer made his major league debut. Ted Lyons, the boy from Baylor recommended by Schalk a few months earlier, reported after completing his college obligations and pitched a perfect eighth inning in a 7–2 loss at St. Louis.[13]

The 1923 season was the first in the majors for umpire Emmet "Red" Ormsby. Schalk and Ormsby had their moments. One year, after being called out at the plate on a close play, despite his head-first slide, Schalk arose and argued with Ormsby. After hearing enough squawking, the umpire told Schalk he was through for the afternoon. However, he did not emphasize the point with the dramatic signal common among umpires. Schalk returned to the bench and stayed there instead of heading to the locker room. He didn't tell his manager he had been ejected. When the next half-inning was to begin, Schalk, in catcher's gear, took his position behind the plate. Just before the first pitch, Ormsby called time. The catcher recalled the event: "He said to me, 'Schalk, you're out of this game and you know it.'" Only then did Cracker depart. The incident did not affect their friendship in later years. They lived only a couple of miles apart, and they often attended the same events and even served together on a fundraising committee for Saint Xavier College.[14]

Not all of Schalk's disagreements with umpires resulted in ejections, and some even provided lighter moments. One afternoon, he and umpire Dick Nallin just couldn't calibrate their definitions of the strike zone. Schalk began to hold his mitt in place whenever Nallin called a close pitch a ball. The Comiskey Park crowd took note, and when Schalk held the pose, White Sox

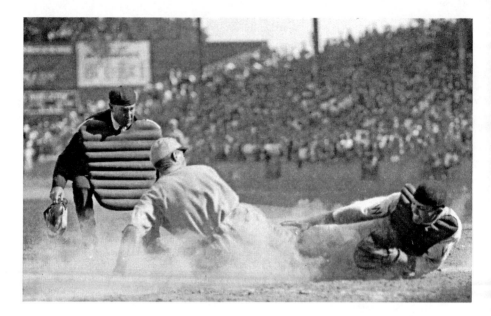

Umpire Dick Nallin, shown in 1924, umpired in the American League 18 years (1915–32), including Schalk's prime seasons. Nallin and Schalk had plenty of conversations about the arbiter's decisions (Library of Congress, Prints and Photographs Division, National Photo Company Collection, LC-F8-31541).

fans gave Nallin the business. The more Schalk did this, the more rancorous the crowd reaction. It continued throughout the game. In the eighth, after Nallin called a close delivery a ball, Schalk froze in position and the fans began hollering about Nallin's eyesight. The umpire removed his mask. He walked around faced Schalk, who was still holding the ball in position. Nallin leaned over, surveyed where Schalk held the ball, cupped his hands and bellowed, "It's still a ball!"[15]

On their first road trip, the White Sox visited New York's brand-new Yankee Stadium, dubbed the "House That Ruth Built." Babe Ruth had already christened the massive facility with a home run. Shortly afterward, a couple of unlikely visitors collected round-trippers. In the seventh inning of a 1–1 game June 6, Faber sent a pitch from lefty Herb Pennock into the left-field grandstand on one bounce for the first home run of his career.[16] (The rules at the time still awarded homers of the single-bounce variety.) The next afternoon, Schalk slammed a second-inning offering from Sam Jones into the left-field seats. His only round-tripper of 1923, the home run was the 10th of his career 11.

The homer was the offensive highlight for Schalk in a down year. He batted only .228 — down more than 50 points from the previous season and 25 points under his career average. His extra-base hits, stolen bases and on-base percentages likewise suffered. Yet, his 121 games extended his streak of 100 catching appearances to 11 campaigns — no small feat for a small man who had turned 31 years old. He was number one among the league's catchers for participation in double plays (20) and remained near the top in fielding percentage (.983), committing just 10 errors all year.

In the final week of the regular season, Schalk suffered a wrenched back. Some speculated that the injury would force him to miss the City Series against the Cubs. He was down but not entirely out. Of the six games in the series, Schalk sat out Game 3 and Game 5 and did not finish Game 2 and Game 6. He was not in the lineup when the White Sox staged their exciting comeback victory in the finale. The Cubs had won the first two City Series contests, but Faber's six-hit, complete-game victory in Game 3 seemed to shake the Sox out of their doldrums. In Game 4, on a Sunday afternoon with more than 41,000 fans jammed in Comiskey Park, Earl Sheely blasted a two-run homer in the ninth to knot the series. The South Siders claimed the next game for a 3–2 series lead and started Faber in Game 6 at Comiskey Park. The spitballer surrendered only two runs in seven innings, but the Cubs held a 3–1 lead when he exited. His batterymate, Schalk, was already out of the game. However, Cubs second baseman George Grantham committed an error in the ninth inning to open the door for the Sox, who scored twice to tie. In the 10th inning, when the Sox recorded nary a hit, Grantham's wild throw allowed the series-ending run to score.

While their fans outside Comiskey Park basked in the city title, the White Sox celebrated in their locker room. After a while, Manager Kid Gleason asked for quiet. To the shock of his players, Gleason announced his resignation. His boss, Comiskey, was not on hand and reportedly did not learn that he needed a new manager until he picked up a newspaper the next morning. The strain of the Black Sox scandal, the struggle of reconstructing the team and the downturn of the Sox in 1923 simply became too much for Kid, who was nearly 57 years old.[17] He returned home to the Philadelphia area. He came out of retirement after a couple of years and served as a coach for Connie Mack's Philadelphia Athletics for six seasons (1926–31). Gleason died on the second day of 1933.

Gleason's resignation sparked speculation over who would next manage the Chicago White Sox. Among the candidates was Ray Schalk. He wanted the job.

21

Passed Over, Battered and Benched

Charles Comiskey faced a dilemma in deciding who would manage his White Sox in 1924. It was not simply a matter of finding the best baseball man available, signing him and adjourning to his lodge in the Wisconsin woods. The Old Roman had to consider team politics and chemistry. Should he hire an "outsider" or go with one of his two internal candidates and risk bad relations with the man who was passed over? The top inside contender was one of the best minds in baseball, Comiskey's team captain, Eddie Collins. Nicknamed Cocky — he was anything but — Collins' name had often surfaced in connection with various managerial jobs. In 1922, when Miller Huggins appeared to be on his way out as skipper of the Yankees, reports had Collins becoming his successor. (Huggins not only kept his job in 1922, he managed the Yankees through several championship seasons — until his death in the final days of the 1929 campaign.)

Schalk was another internal candidate. In his analysis of Comiskey's options, *Tribune* sportswriter Irving Vaughan observed, "Schalk qualifies by the fact that he has long been a faithful employee — probably more so than any other man ever on Comiskey's payroll. He is a fighter, in the sense that he doesn't know what it is to quit." However, Vaughan also noted, "The one thing that might stand in the way of Schalk's promotion is that he never has minced words when dealing with pitchers. No hurler has been immune from Cracker's flow of language. But there never was anything personal in what he said. He howls at the slabbers because of his great desire to win, but the slabbers didn't always take it in the way it was given. Two of them even went so far during the last season as to say they couldn't pitch to him."[1] (The pair did not include Shovel Hodge, with whom Schalk came to blows in 1922, and was gone in 1923.)

However, if Comiskey chose either Schalk or Collins, would the loser in the managerial sweepstakes be able to continue with the White Sox without feeling resentment? Vaughan contended that both could, but recognized that it was Comiskey who had to be satisfied on that question. Whether he was answering that question, Comiskey did not say, but before the end of October, he selected an outsider as manager: Frank Chance, former player-manager of the Chicago Cubs and manager of the Yankees and Red Sox. Chance piloted the Cubs to four World Series in five seasons (1906–10), including the 1908 championship. Chicagoans revered the Peerless Leader. The *Tribune* interviewed five men on the street for their reaction. The "Inquiring Reporter" feature suggested that Comiskey hit a home run with his choice. John Anderson, a carpenter, said, "If baseball fans had been given a chance to have chosen the White Sox manager by popular election, Frank Chance would have been put into office, he's that popular. Tell Larry Graver that he did some good work." Graver was a former Sox ticket seller who became traveling secretary for Harry Frazee when the Chicago-based theater owner bought the Boston Red Sox in 1916. Frazee sold the team in July 1923, and Chance, who took over as Red Sox manager that season, departed at season's end. A friend of Schalk, Graver served as an intermediary as Comiskey and Chance negotiated contract terms.

After signing on as manager of the White Sox, Chance put his closest competitor for the job, Collins, on the trading block. The team captain learned about it from sportswriters. Collins expressed shock. "I liked Chicago and would have been delighted to play under Chance, but he is the boss and wants to get rid of me," he said. "Oh, well, that is all in the game. What else can I say?"[2] For a while, it appeared a lock that Collins would go to Washington and manage the Senators — but Chance and Washington's Clark Griffith couldn't strike a deal during the major leagues' winter meetings in Chicago.[3] Collins would report to the White Sox in 1924. But would Chance?

The specter of the Black Sox scandal resurfaced in early February 1924, when a Milwaukee jury heard Shoeless Joe Jackson's civil suit against the White Sox. Jackson sued for $18,500 — money he said the team owed him on his playing contract when he was suspended at the end of the 1920 season. He also wanted $1,500 from team owner Charles Comiskey, who, Jackson claimed, pledged that he would make up the difference between $5,000 and the 1917 World Series winner's share if his team beat the New York Giants in the Fall Classic. Comiskey failed to make good, Jackson said. Comiskey, sportswriter Hugh Fullerton and Faber were among the witnesses, but Schalk was not called. The jury issued a verdict in Jackson's favor, but the judge threw out the verdict, stating that jurors based the decision on Jackson's fraudulent testimony.

Frank Chance was ill during the winter meetings. After departing the session in wintry Chicago, the Peerless Leader retreated to Palm Springs, California, and then Hot Springs in hopes that warmer conditions would enhance his recovery from what was identified as asthma. Yet his condition deteriorated into pneumonia. In mid–February, still ill, he wired Comiskey with his resignation. The Old Roman wouldn't hear of it. He told Chance to rest and get well, and assured him that his managerial post would be waiting for him.

After this time, Schalk went to Hot Springs to prepare for official spring training; joining him were pitchers Leon Cadore and Red Faber. Other ballplayers sought out the spas and springs of the area. Among them were Walter Johnson and other members of the Washington Senators, who arrived about a week after Schalk. Schalk accompanied the Senators on a long hike, pointing out the best routes.[4]

Under the direction of Collins, Ed Walsh and newly signed coach Johnny Evers, training camp got off to a tough start. First, players arrived in Winter Haven, Florida, only to discover their hotel still under construction. They found quarters in Lake Alfred, about five miles away. Team officials arranged for a bus to transport the players between the hotel and training field, but Evers warned that loafing players would be made to walk the distance. Though two workouts a day were scheduled, only one round trip on the bus was offered. "The living arrangements are not so bad, as the food is good and the five-mile ride through the orange groves is a novelty," the *Tribune* noted. Then, with three coaches running the camp without a manager, players had trouble figuring out whose directions to follow. By mid–March, Chance told reporters he was feeling about ready for work but would wait until April 4, when he would meet his players as they headed north after training camp.

Chance managed the White Sox in only one game — an exhibition game at that. The weather was damp and chilly in Chicago on April 12 when the New York Giants came to town for a tune-up contest.[5] The poor weather dealt Chance's fragile health a setback, and he underwent emergency surgery within a week. The Peerless Leader never managed the White Sox during the regular season. Within five months, he was dead. He was 47.

Again passing over Collins and Schalk, Comiskey gave the managerial job to new coach Johnny Evers, the former star of the Cubs. However, after managing the first 21 games of the regular season, Evers suffered an appendicitis attack. While he recovered from surgery, Ed Walsh (three games) and Collins (27 games) managed the team. Despite the uncertainty of their managerial situation, the absence of injured star Faber and injuries to Schalk, the White Sox managed to play .500 ball until late July (44–44). They won some they should have lost and lost some they should have won. Amateur mistakes cost the White Sox here and there. In Boston on May 17, reserve Roy Elsh fell for the hidden-ball trick and was left red-faced at third base in a 5–4 loss.[6]

Cleveland held a 4–0 lead after six innings on an April Sunday in Chicago. Schalk doubled and scored in the seventh. In the eighth, future Hall of Famer Tris Speaker gave the White Sox a gift when he muffed an easy fly ball in center field. With a Comiskey Park crowd of some 32,000 now ignited, the Sox rallied for four runs for a 5–4 victory. The winning run came across when Schalk laid down a squeeze bunt to score Bill Barrett.[7]

A couple of weeks later, on a rainy May 6, Schalk registered the 11th and final home run of his major-league career — a fifth-inning shot over the left-field wall of Comiskey Park. The victim was Detroit's Lil Stoner, who nonetheless pitched a complete-game, 6–4 victory.[8]

Chicago let one get away in the first appearance of 1924 for Faber, who had to undergo early-season elbow surgery after it was discovered that his condition was misdiagnosed several months earlier. Entering in relief on June 18,

Pitching legend Walter Johnson (right) poses with Washington Nationals battery mate Herold "Muddy" Ruel in the Nationals' championship season of 1924. In Game 7 of the World Series that year, Ruel doubled and scored the winning run in the bottom of the 12th inning, and Johnson pitched the final four innings for the victory. By the mid–1920s, Ruel challenged Schalk's standing as the game's best catcher (Library of Congress, Prints and Photographs Division, National Photo Company Collection, LOT 12287).

he gave up just one hit to visiting Washington from the fifth through eighth innings. Faber was just one out from a 4–3 victory. Then his teammates failed to convert a fielder's choice. It was a close play. With the Comiskey Park crowd roaring, the usually quiet Eddie Collins went into such a tirade over the umpire's decision that he was thrown out of the game. The umpire was none other than his former manager, Clarence Rowland. When the game resumed, Faber fell behind Roger Peckinpaugh and then grooved a pitch. Peckinpaugh's two-run single put the Nationals ahead to stay, 5–4.[9]

Schalk was not involved in that loss. For the first time in his career, injury that season forced him to miss more games than he played. At least three times, foul tips caught his hand so severely he could not just shake off the pain. Schalk, who turned 32 years old during the campaign, logged catching appearances in barely one in three White Sox games. He suffered more broken digits and more lost time. Even before the season started, a sportswriter observed, "Ray Schalk is wearing out under the strain of catching more than 100 games for 11 consecutive seasons, and the time has come when a second-string backstop capable of receiving in at least 60 games is a dire necessity."[10] Clyde "Buck" Crouse, a late-season call-up in 1923, was the leading candidate.

The urgency of a quality back-up for Schalk became more apparent in Washington on May 25. The very afternoon in which Schalk reached his milestone 1,500th game caught, Cracker departed in the fourth inning when a foul tip smashed his thumb. However, Crouse was not available to step in; he was out with an injury suffered a few days earlier in Boston.[11]

At the time, Schalk's injury and the fortunes of the Windy City's baseball teams were far from foremost in the minds of Chicagoans. They were glued to developments in the murder of 14-year-old Bobby Franks, who was killed in the upscale Hyde Park district on his way home for supper. By the end of the month, Nathan Leopold and Richard Loeb, college students and lovers, themselves the products of well-to-do families, confessed to killing Franks just for the thrill of it. Only the impassioned plea of renowned attorney Clarence Darrow, whose closing argument lasted 12 hours, managed to spare his clients from the gallows. They were sentenced to life imprisonment. Twelve years later, Loeb died of five dozen razor cuts inflicted by his cellmate, James Day, who claimed self–defense against Loeb's sexual advances. That prompted Ed Lahey, of the *Chicago Daily News*, to write of the child-killer's death, "Richard Loeb, despite his erudition, today ended his sentence with a proposition."[12]

Meanwhile, the *Chicago Tribune* touted its latest technological advancement. It published the first photograph ever transmitted and received via telephone line. The image was a portrait of President Calvin Coolidge. The process — using a forerunner of the fax machine — required five minutes of telephone time for a single black-and-white image.[13]

Schalk's right thumb had barely recovered from his late–May injury when he suffered another. He missed at least two more weeks in June.[14] During his rehab, he spent some of his recovery time in his native downstate Illinois and, with Vin and his mother, paid a visit to friends Mr. and Mrs. Dick Large of Decatur.[15] By this time in his career, Schalk had suffered at least one broken bone to each digit of his throwing hand. The middle finger had been broken five times. The ring finger experienced three breaks, as had his thumb, and Schalk had lost every fingernail on that right hand at least once (four to the middle finger alone). Meanwhile, the hand covered by the catcher's mitt had escaped serious injury.[16]

Injuries continued to plague the Chicago catching corps. Crouse was backstopping during a late–August afternoon in Philadelphia, where the White Sox and Athletics were battling to see which of them would occupy the American League cellar. Chicago had already lost a dozen straight, and this game went a dozen innings. In the bottom of the 12th inning, with starter Faber still on the mound for the White Sox, Joe Hauser hit a foul tip that broke Crouse's thumb. Schalk donned the "tools of ignorance" and replaced Crouse — just long enough to be on the field when Hauser hit a walk-off homer.[17] Such was one of Schalk's 56 catching appearances in 1924. Now the losers of 13 straight, the White Sox, who went 7–20 in August, stayed in last place. In the final five weeks of the season, Philadelphia won just often enough to pass the struggling Red Sox and Indians, who made their own bids to free the White Sox from the cellar. Going into the final week of the campaign, the three teams were in a virtual tie for last. The White Sox appeared to be just going through the motions, perhaps biding their time until they could meet the Cubs in the Chicago City Series. "If there were any Cub spies on the grounds they surely will go back and tell (manager) Bill Killefer that there is nothing for him to worry about," the *Tribune*'s James Crusinberry wrote after Detroit battered Faber and Ted Lyons in the regular season's final weekend.[18] Chicago finished 1–5 to wind up 66–87. The next day, in a far-cical game, Boston whipped World Series–bound Washington, 13–1. Though the Red Sox started out playing seriously — after all, they didn't want to finish *last*— the champs' goofing-off became contagious. The game featured the antics of 48-year-old Washington coach Nick Altrock, who, in his only playing appearance in five seasons, hit a triple and pitched three innings. Despite a five-minute rain delay and 14 runs crossing the plate, the comedy lasted only 75 minutes.[19] The Red Sox laughed their way out of the cellar

(67–87), edging ahead of the White Sox by a half-game in the final standings.

The 1924 City Series of Chicago pitted two second-division teams. The Cubs finished fifth in the National League. A feature of the series was radio station WGN, recently acquired and renamed by the *Chicago Tribune* (nicknamed the World's Greatest Newspaper). The station became the first to provide a play-by-play broadcast of a major league game in Chicago when A.W. "Sen" Kaney described the action from his vantage point in the grandstand.[20] The White Sox could not defeat Cubs pitcher Grover Cleveland Alexander, who won Game 1 and Game 5, but the South Siders beat everyone else, taking yet another City Series in six games. Schalk, whose regular-season averages in batting (.196) and fielding (.959) were well below his norm, sat out Game 1. However, he started the final five battles, collecting two singles in 13 at-bats (.153). Manager Johnny Evers missed the final game of the series, staying at home with another round of the stomach troubles that plagued him throughout the season. Eddie Collins managed the team that afternoon. When the Sox recorded the final out of the series, Collins raced out of the dugout and hugged Harry Hooper like an excited schoolboy.[21]

A couple of days after the final out of the City Series, several White Sox players, including Red Faber, joined members of the New York Giants for barnstorming in Europe. If Schalk had any reservations about not going, they were short-lived. The tour was a bust — the low point came in Dublin, where only 20 paying spectators showed up — and organizers Comiskey and John McGraw aborted the exhibition after only a half-dozen contests.[22]

The arrival of Ray Schalk in his hometown always generated excitement, but perhaps never more than that a few days before the annual Schalk Day game. The baseball star was in Litchfield Bank and Trust Company to a visit his brother Leo, who was the cashier. Cracker unknowingly stepped on a button activating the burglar alarm. "The big gong outside rang, and all the riot guns were dusted off and detectives lost no time getting into the bank," the *Chicago Tribune* related. No shots were fired, and the bank and the rest of Litchfield soon returned to normal.

Schalk Day 1924 took on a special flavor. It became Schalk-Osborn Day. In addition to celebrating their veteran baseball star, Litchfield honored 25-year-old Harold Osborn. Born in the tiny community of Butler, just a half-dozen miles east of Litchfield, Osborn that spring set a world record for the high jump (6 feet, 8 inches). That summer, he became the first athlete to win Olympic gold in the decathlon and an individual event in the same Olympiad. With some 6,000 spectators on hand for the unusual combination of "athletics" and baseball, Osborn gave an exhibition of some field events, clearing

6-foot-5 in the high jump — a mere inch below his Olympic record. Osborn later joined fellow Olympian and Illinois native Joie W. Ray halfway through the mile run, pacing Ray to a 4:29 finish. Ray, standing 5-foot-5 and weighing 119 pounds, was considered America's first great miler. A few months after his Litchfield exhibition, Ray tied the world record for an indoor mile (4:12.0). The native of Kankakee remains the only U.S. Olympian to represent his country in the 1,500 meters (1920) and marathon (1928). In the 1970s, Ray and Osborn were enshrined in the National Track and Field Hall of Fame. After the track exhibition, fans watched the Litchfield team beat up on Mount Olive, 8–0. The home team's formidable lineup included three future members of the National Baseball Hall of Fame, Montgomery County products Red Ruffing, Jim Bottomley and Schalk.[23]

With the end of his injury-riddled 1924 campaign — as well as his record streak of 100-game seasons — Schalk found himself at a professional crossroads. In the next season, when he would turn 33 years old, could he be productive for the White Sox?

22

Cracker's Comeback

White Sox captain Eddie Collins, who served as interim manager for a month in the middle of 1924 after nearly being traded, received the job full-time for 1925. He replaced the oft-ill Johnny Evers. If Schalk, who had managerial aspirations of his own, was disappointed at being passed over, he did not disclose it. To do otherwise would have been unfair to his roommate and disloyal to Comiskey. And if Schalk was nothing else, he was loyal to Comiskey. "I am willing to do all I can to help Eddie get a start as a manager," he said. "He's a great fellow and I know every player on the team thinks the world of him and will hustle his head off to win. I think the spirit on the club this season will be great."

Red Faber was caught up in the spirit. Perhaps goaded by Crusinberry, the *Tribune* sportswriter from his hometown of Cascade, Iowa, Faber said that the 1925 White Sox, who finished last in 1924, would be better than the defending World Series champion Senators. "We have a better license to win a pennant than that bunch, and I think we will prove it this year."[1]

Schalk, meanwhile, aired his determination to rebound from a disappointing 1924. He planned to notch another 100-game season behind the plate. "I had a bum time of it last year with my hand," he told Crusinberry in mid–February. "I've decided I simply can't stick my fingers into those foul tips and get away with it, so I intend to avoid it this year." How he planned to accomplish that was not disclosed, but he added, "The old fingers are in fine shape now." Cracker stayed in shape by spending many afternoons at the Illinois Athletic Club, where handball was his preferred activity.[2] He probably found some time for bowling. He planned to join Faber in Hot Springs for extra conditioning before spring training. However, he had to cancel his trip to Arkansas. Schalk needed more time to wrap up affairs in his insurance business before hitting the ball diamond.[3]

After a less-than-satisfactory arrangements in Florida the previous year, Comiskey relocated the White Sox spring training camp to Shreveport,

As he had every off-season, Schalk worked out in a Chicago gymnasium during the winter of 1926–27, before his first season as player-manager of the White Sox. However, Schalk caught in only 15 games in 1927 and just one in his half-season of 1928 (Chicago History Museum, Chicago Daily News Collection, SDN-066450).

Louisiana. Schalk left Chicago a day or two before the team's southbound train so he could visit with family and friends in Litchfield. He caught the Sox train in St. Louis.[4] Collins ran a snappy camp, but it was not grueling. On a scheduled day off, he and Schalk played golf at Shreveport Country Club with Crusinberry and White Sox treasurer Louis Comiskey. Crusinberry modestly informed the entire *Tribune* readership that he "went out in 49 and came back in 50" for the foursome's low score of 99, followed by Collins (100) and Schalk (103). He added, "Mr. Comiskey went out in 60 and never came back."[5] The next day, after practice and lunch, Collins and Schalk were back at the links — this time with Commissioner Kenesaw Mountain Landis.[6] A few weeks earlier, coincidentally, the newspaper features service Associated Editors, Inc., asked Schalk to answer a reader's question, "Do you feel that playing a good deal of golf will interfere with playing good baseball?" Schalk replied no, if the player uses common sense — defined as not playing golf the morning of an afternoon baseball game.[7] On that, he and his new manager were in accord.[8]

Instead of playing its pre-season games against the Giants, as they had the previous couple of springs, the White Sox engaged only teams from colleges and the low minors. They went 19–0.[9] That only gave rise to speculation and debate on whether the White Sox were ready for American League competition or simply overconfident after their walk-overs against weak competition.

As the 1925 season approached, The Draper-Maynard Company featured Schalk in its advertisements for baseball gloves. Based in Plymouth, New Hampshire, the firm published a photo of Schalk in the catcher's crouch, his D&M No. 700 at the ready. The ad, targeted at young players across the country, stated, "Yes sir-ee! Nine out of every 10 players in the Majors use D&M gloves or mitts."[10] The endorsement represented a brand switch for Cracker. Four years earlier, his photo appeared, in full color, in a Wilson Athletic Equipment advertisement in the *Saturday Evening Post*. One of the featured Wilson items was the Ray Schalk Model catcher's mitt.[11]

The team spirit that Schalk predicted during the winter was evident as the regular season opened. Collins received much of the credit, but his veteran backstop did, too. "Ray Schalk's presence in the lineup ... peps up the team," the *Tribune* observed toward the end of April, a month when the Sox went 5–2. "All seem to be working hard for Collins, taking advantage of opportunities and making their hits count. The team shows more of the old White Sox spirit."[12]

Perhaps Schalk's most unusual exploit involving a baseball — with the possible exception of making that put-out at second base in 1918 — occurred at high noon on a chilly Monday, May 11, 1925. It took place not in a ballpark but on one of Chicago's busiest thoroughfares, Michigan Avenue. Thousands of lunch-hour spectators surrounded Schalk. Wearing street clothes and holding his trusty mitt, he attempted to catch a baseball dropped from the roof of the new Tribune Tower, a distance of 460 feet. Long-distance catches were sure-fire publicity-generators. In 1924, Babe Ruth caught a ball released by teammate Bob Meusel from the top of the Cohan Theater — a distance of just 130 feet; Babe dropped the first two. Schalk's effort would not challenge the distance record; three men, including Schalk's predecessor on the White Sox, catcher Billy Sullivan, once caught baseballs dropped from the Washington Monument, a distance of the 524 feet. (Before he made his catch in 1910, Sullivan missed 23 times.[13]) Traffic on Michigan Avenue was blocked for 20 minutes for the stunt, and policemen on horseback moved the crowd back so that the ballplayer would have room. Schalk stood at the ready and peered up 36 stories. Tribune Tower construction worker George Kersten had the honor of dropping the ball to the street below. The first ball blew into scaffolding along the Tower and never reached him. On the second try, Schalk nearly made a one-handed catch, but he bobbled the ball and dropped it. The third time was the charm. With a baseball hurtling toward him at an estimated 120 miles an hour, Schalk snared it. "Didn't sting me any more than one of those high fouls Babe Ruth used to hit," he said years later. The cheering crowd surged forward to congratulate Cracker. He posed for pictures and accepted a gift — a drawing of Tribune Tower — and headed for the ballpark, where the Sox had a 3 P.M. date with the Senators.[14]

One man was less than thrilled with Schalk's exhibition: Charles Comiskey. The Old Roman reportedly was unaware of his employee's stunt until it was over. It was a curious claim, considering that the *Tribune* promoted the event in at least two editions immediately before the event. Or maybe the Old Roman read only the *Chicago Daily News*, which published not a word about its competitor's publicity stunt involving the White Sox star.[15] Regardless, Schalk, who rarely missed a start, warmed the bench in Comiskey Park as Walter Johnson and the Senators blanked the White Sox, 9–0.[16] Schalk was back in action the next day, hitting a single and double and scoring twice in Chicago's 5–4 win over the Yankees. Bibb Falk delivered the winning blow — a two-out double in the 10th inning. The game was one of the 24 the White Sox played in Comiskey Park during May. The team had only two road contests all month. (The Sox then became nomads, playing 21 of 26 June games on the road.)

As Schalk was catching baseballs from skyscrapers, most Chicagoans went about their daily business. They shopped at National Tea Company, where Van Camp's pork and beans sold three cans for a quarter and two packages of Quaker Puffed Wheat set them back 21 cents. Clothier Maurice L. Rothschild, whose advertisement the morning after the *Tribune* Tower stunt featured a photo of Schalk at the event, featured socks — "the gayest kind of hose" — for 35 cents to $1.50 a pair. For entertainment, Chicagoans had a myriad of choices, including the Marx Brothers' latest movie, *I'll Say She Is*, at the Apollo; the stage production of *The Lady Next Door* at the Cort; and the Out-Door Life Exposition, featuring auto camping equipment, dude ranchmen and live game. Comiskey placed small ads promoting each afternoon's home game; it ran with the movie and theater ads under the general heading, "Amusements."[17] Meanwhile, another Chicago newspaper hosted a special event, "The Daily News School of Cooking and Home Economics." The free event was so popular — 6,000 women turned out for Day 1 alone — that it was staged at two sites in the city, the National Guard Armory on the north side and the massive Guyon's Paradise ballroom on the west side. (The owner of the latter venue, Louis Guyon, ran a conservative dance hall. He banned demonstrations of contemporary dances, including the current rage, the Charleston.[18])

A few days after his exploits outside Tribune Tower, Schalk participated in another event — but one of a more conventional nature. Cowboy actor Tom Mix visited Comiskey Park during a publicity swing for his movie, *Riders of the Purple Sage*. Dressed in a "two-quart sombrero and other striking sartorial creations," Mix made three or four pre-game tosses to Schalk. Team secretary Harry Grabiner could have used Mix or another such hero to catch a bad guy — the previous evening, his automobile was stolen from outside his home.[19]

Under Collins, the spirited Sox appeared poised for their first first-division finish since the Black Sox indictments. After sweeping the Tigers in their first four home games of the season, the Sox hosted Cleveland for a Sunday game. Comiskey Park was jammed by a city-record 44,000 fans, including about 8,000 who had to stand behind ropes on the outfield and near third base. However, Cleveland was poised to hand Chicago its first home loss of the year, holding a 7–2 lead with two out in the ninth inning. Willie Kamm hit an easy grounder to Indians shortstop Joe Sewell, who fired the ball to reserve first baseman Ray Knode with time to spare. With that, the spectators in the outfield crossed the ropes and streamed across the field toward the exits. They didn't notice that, somehow, Knode failed to have his foot on first base when he caught Sewell's throw. He wasn't even close. Umpire Billy Evans called the batter safe. Though the game was not officially over, thousands of fans, believing otherwise, massed on the field. "Even the umps couldn't find each other in the throng for some minutes," Crusinberry observed. When the umpires concluded that order could not be restored to resume the game, Cleveland received credit for a 9–0 victory by forfeit. The chief umpire was former Sox manager Clarence "Pants" Rowland.[20]

Schalk had a reputation for possessing one of the best baseball minds on the diamond. Sometimes, however, his thinking was too quick for the team's own good. In the top of the 11th inning in New York, with the score 3–3, Chicago's Bibb Falk opened with a walk. He advanced to second on a sacrifice bunt and stayed there during a strikeout. Schalk stepped to the plate, and Yankee manager Miller Huggins signaled for Herb Pennock to intentionally walk Cracker. However, Schalk surprised the Yankees by reaching out for the first wide pitch and slapping a single into right field. Unfortunately, Schalk's move also surprised baserunner Falk, who had no lead off second base when Schalk's bat met the ball and was thrown out at home in a close play. The

Yankees won in the bottom of the 11th, 4–3.[21] The victory was a rare positive for the slumping Yankees. Just a week or so earlier, Huggins endeavored to shake things up by benching his slumping veteran first baseman, Wally Pipp. His replacement was Lou Gehrig.[22] Once he got into the starting lineup, Gehrig proceeded to play in every single Yankee contest until April 1939 — 2,130 consecutive games, a major-league record until Cal Ripken passed him in 1995 on his way to 2,632 games.

Schalk came nowhere near suffering the number and severity of injuries he did the previous season, and he notched a 12th season of catching in at least 100 games (125). He had one of his best offensive seasons, batting .274. Schalk maintained his trademark energy and competitive spirit, sometimes with negative consequences. During the season, an umpire ejected him for the eighth and final time of his playing career.

Schalk continued to dash parallel to the first-base line to back up his infielders' play on grounders in case their throws eluded the first baseman. Though he was not the first catcher to do this,[23] Schalk was the first catcher to back up those plays as a matter of routine.[24] He pursued pop fouls with such intensity that it was common for him to crash into the backstop or grandstand rail. In a late–August contest in Washington, he took out a patron in a field box when he ran into the aisle to snare a foul off the bat of Sam Rice. Thus began another milestone game for Schalk — his 1,600th appearance as a catcher. "He was energetic and full of pep as if it had been his first," a Washington sportswriter noted.[25]

There was the story of the time Schalk chased to the backstop a pop foul that fell behind the screen. Said one spectator to another, "Schalk is losing a step."

Cracker *nearly* notched another milestone — catching another no-hit game. On September 19, Ted Lyons did not allow Washington a hit until two were out in the bottom of the ninth inning. With his own team's fans rooting for him to fail, pinch-hitter Bobby Veach looped a clean single into right field. Lyons retired the next batter and walked off the field with a 17–0 win. Had Lyons succeeded, Schalk would have shared the catching credit with Buck Crouse, who replaced Cracker during the lopsided affair.[26]

Chicago held third place for nearly four months. However, starting in late August they lost 11 of 13 games and fell to fifth. In late September, with their hopes of regaining the first division (and bonus money) slipping away, the White Sox visited the Yankees on an afternoon so chilly that it received comment in the newspapers. Twenty-first century players and fans who suffer through post-season games with wind-chills reaching the high 20s would be particularly interested to note that the low temperature that day was 49

Schalk waits for Johnny Mostil to cross the plate in Washington in 1925. Mostil's failed suicide attempt in 1927 added unexpected drama to Schalk's first spring training as White Sox manager. Mostil recovered but played a complete season just once afterward (Library of Congress Prints, and Photographs Division, National Photo Company Collection, LC-F8-36908).

and the high 62. In any case, with barely 1,500 shivering spectators on hand, New York emerged with a 7–6 victory. The game ended when Schalk tried to dash home from third on a pitcher-to-first fielder's choice. Pitcher Urban Shocker had looked Schalk back toward third before tossing to Lou Gehrig, whose relay throw to plate arrived in plenty of time. "Ray was out by 20 seconds, elapsed time," *The New York Times* quipped, "and there is grave doubt whether he has touched the plate yet."[27] The next afternoon, Chicago broke open a 2–2 game with three runs in the top of the 10th inning, but lost starting pitcher Faber when a pitch hit him on the knee. In the bottom of the 10th, the Yankees rallied against Faber's replacement, George Connally. They won it on a walk-off grand slam homer by Babe Ruth, who was mobbed by fans as he circled the bases. Sportswriter James B. Harrison began his game account in the *New York Times* by stating, "Ruth is stranger than fiction."[28] The White Sox finished the season 79–75, 18 games out of first and two games out of a coveted spot in the first division.

The 1925 City Series of Chicago again matched two second-division teams. The Cubs lost their season finale to come out on the short end of a three-team race for sixth place and fell into the National League cellar (68–86). The most dramatic game of the series was one that didn't count in the final standings. Pitching legend Grover Cleveland Alexander of the Cubs and 24-year-old right-hander Ted Blankenship of the White Sox battled through 19 innings at Comiskey Park. The score was 2–2 after five innings, and neither team scored after that. Alexander, 38 years old, gave up 20 hits, including a leadoff hit in every one of the final eight innings. The Cubs' final run crossed in the fifth on a sacrifice fly to right fielder Harry Hooper, who, as it turned out, was playing his last major-league competition. (The future Hall of Famer retired when Comiskey wanted to cut his salary in 1926.) It was a close play, and Schalk thought he tagged out Rabbit Maranville, but the plate umpire ruled to the contrary. The arbiter, again, was Schalk's former manager Clarence Rowland. The men considered themselves friends, and were on great terms throughout their lives — but not on this October afternoon. "Cracker thought he had tagged the man, and to emphasize his argument he jiggled Rowland's chest protector something awful," Crusinberry reported. Perhaps it was their friendship that kept Schalk from being excused from further proceedings. In the bottom of the 18th with two out, the Sox had the potential winning run on third base. Alexander endeavored to intentionally walk Schalk, who already had three hits, to force the pitcher Blankenship to win his own game. As he did earlier in the season against the Yankees, Schalk reached out for Alexander's wide offering and slapped it toward the right-field line. Cracker came within an inch of giving the game a surprise ending, but his stroke fell foul. Though the Cubs and Sox played the equivalent of more than two games — both using just their starting pitchers — the contest lasted just three hours and three minutes before Rowland and his fellow umpires ended the marathon due to darkness.[29] The Cubs went on to win four of the next five decisions to claim the series.

In divvying their City Series proceeds, the Sox voted a full share for a man who had not played an inning with them that season — and hardly at all the year before. Utility infielder Harvey McClellan, a Sox player since 1919, missed most of 1924 with stomach ulcers. After two surgeries early in the 1925 season, he was fighting for his life. In mid–July, when it was known that the battle would be lost, a delegation of his teammates visited McClellan in Chicago's Mercy Hospital. They wanted to tell him goodbye before he returned to his native Cynthiana, Kentucky, for the final time. McClellan died November 6, 1925. He was 30 years old.[30]

Rain and wet grounds postponed the annual Schalk Day exhibition, set

for a Sunday. Meeting at the Elks Club, event organizers and Schalk resched-
uled it for the following Thursday (October 22). Litchfield officials declared
that afternoon a half-day holiday.[31] A few days after the Litchfield game,
Schalk teamed with fellow future Hall of Famers Red Ruffing and Jim Bottomley in an exhibition in Nokomis.[32]

After an injury-riddled 1924, Schalk's comeback in 1925 was a success.
However, after 13 full seasons of major-league action, including a record-set-
ting workload of catching, the 33-year-old baseball veteran was laying the
foundation for the next phase of his life.

23

Transitions

Since November 1920, Schalk's off-season job had been selling insurance. As he approached his mid–30s, the conclusion of his playing career was on the horizon. He entered into new endeavors — coaching and commercial real estate. Schalk partnered with developer William J. Wightman on a block-long residential project on the west side of May Street between 83rd and 84th streets on Chicago's South Side. The site was a half-dozen miles south of Comiskey Park and described in their advertisement as "right in the heart of the most rapid growing business section of Chicago." The "million-dollar" project included a 40-flat residential building, 15 two-flat buildings and two 18-flat buildings. Wightman, who had real estate ventures all over town, probably didn't need Schalk's money or business acumen, but the publicity of having a famous ballplayer as a partner could not have hurt. The buildings are still home to hundreds of 21st century Chicagoans.[1] Meanwhile, Schalk continued in the insurance game.[2]

As the Wightman-Schalk project hit the newspapers, Schalk addressed a gathering of the Auburn Lions Club. His host at the meeting was future business partner Ben Stevenson. Cracker recounted his baseball career and defended Red Grange's controversial decision to enter professional football (then considered an endeavor of questionable repute). Schalk told the Lions, "If I should ever leave the White Sox I will quit baseball."[3] (Subsequent events would make him wrong on that point.) A few days later, Schalk agreed to serve as an assistant baseball coach for the University of Wisconsin, working indoors with the team in Madison for a month, until he departed for White Sox spring training.[4] After three days with the Badgers, Schalk noted their natural ability but "how far behind they are below the standard of the major leagues in baseball knowledge."[5] After accepting the coaching post, the Chicago branch of the University of Wisconsin Club staged a dinner in Schalk's honor.[6]

While coaching and insurance supplemented his baseball income, Schalk also parlayed some of his money into successful investments. While visiting over drinks with Ty Cobb one evening, Schalk received a stock tip. The Georgia Peach recommended buying shares in a Georgia-based company. Schalk did, held the stock and watched its value grow. The company was Coca-Cola.[7]

Cobb respected the Chicago catcher. "Ray Schalk was a little man, but one of the two or three greatest catchers who ever lived. He was a system man, but so clever at it that you had to study Schalk, and watch almost every pitch he called to get any kind of a line on him," he said in his autobiography. "For example, Ray would get his pitcher ahead of you on the ball-strike count by calling for fastballs. A curve seemed almost sure to come, but again there would be a fastball. And still another. Every fast one was a surprise, because you kept expecting something else. When you were absolutely certain that you'd get a curve or drop next — Ray would feed you another fastball. Then about the sixth pitch, he'd give you the twister — when you were fastball-happy and convinced he didn't have anything else in his pitcher's repertoire."[8]

By 1927, when Schalk began managing the White Sox and when this photograph was taken, his right hand showed the effects of catching more than 1,700 regular-season games. Schalk attributed many of the injuries to the spitball. He suffered at least a dozen broken bones and had lost every fingernail on the right hand at least once (four on the middle finger alone) (Chicago History Museum, Chicago Daily News Collection, SDN-066596).

Between his arrival in Shreveport on March 1 and the first spring-training workout, Schalk joined three team officials in nine holes at the local country club. "He didn't boast of the score," the *Washington Post* noted, "which was 57."[9]

A feature story on Schalk's career and advice to young catchers included this gem: "I have seen catchers lose their temper with their pitcher. This is all out of order. The pitcher becomes grouchy, loses his control and soon tells his manager he can not work with that catcher. I have heard this on many clubs." Indeed he had. Over the years, the fiery Schalk had cussed out many a pitcher — a few to the point that they didn't want to be his battery-mate.[10]

The 1926 White Sox, under the leadership of Eddie Collins for the second season, again appeared to have the makings of a first-division team. They held second place as late as Independence Day, when they were 42–35 and 9½ games behind the Yankees. Sitting in the runner-up position, the White Sox visited the City of Brotherly Love during a Philadelphia heat wave. They had games Thursday through Saturday and on Monday; Philadelphia still forbade baseball on Sundays. Several Chicago players spent their day off in Atlantic City. Collins, a former Athletics star who still lived in Philadelphia during the off-season, hosted Schalk to lunch at the Aronimink Golf Club.[11]

In the month after Independence Day, White Sox fortunes fell. By August 3, they were 52–52 and in sixth place in the eight-team American League. An eight-game winning streak advanced them into fifth, but that is where they finished the season (81–72). Though his batting (.265) and fielding (.977) averages did not fall off dramatically, Schalk was not the player he once was. His 100-game seasons were a thing of the past; he caught half the White Sox' games (80); Buck Crouse, Johnny Grabowski and Harry McCurdy shared the rest.

There were occasional embarrassments. "Ray Schalk dropped a pop foul

Detroit superstar Ty Cobb didn't have many friends in baseball, but Schalk was one of them. The Georgia Peach gave Cracker one useful tip: Buy stock in Georgia-based Coca-Cola. Schalk did, and it paid off handsomely. When Cobb died in 1961, Schalk was one of only three former players at his private funeral. Photograph dated 1914 (Library of Congress, Prints & Photographs Division, Bain Collection, LOT 11147-1).

right in his hands yesterday in the first inning of the opening game, hardly having to move out of the box for it," the *Washington Post* reported. "According to the Chicago scribes, this is the first time in years the veteran has been charged with an error on this kind of play."[12] Dick Nallin, who umpired in the American League for 18 seasons (1915–32) and worked four World Series,

When Schalk posed for this picture in 1926, he was in his final season as an active player. He appeared in only 23 games over the next three seasons. The gnarled fingers on his right hand give testament to his countless encounters with foul tips and spitballs (Chicago History Museum, Chicago Daily News Collection, SDN-066256).

exacted some measure of revenge as Schalk's playing days were winding down. Age and years of squatting behind the plate had sapped Schalk's legs of the speed that once allowed him to be a base-stealing threat. By this point in his career, whenever he hit an infield grounder, Schalk had to put his head down and give it his all to make it respectably close at first. After rapping one such ground ball, Schalk focused only on first base as he ran up the baseline. He was out by a mile — but he didn't realize it. By the time he raised his head after completing his run, all Schalk saw was the first baseman sauntering toward the first-base dugout to retrieve the ball. Schalk didn't realize that the first baseman had lost the ball only while preparing to return it to the pitcher. Schalk's baseball instincts took over, and he dashed for second base. The opponents picked up on Schalk's mistake and decided to magnify it. The first baseman purposely heaved high above second base and into center field, and so Schalk continued running to third. The outfielder then intentionally threw wildly to third as Schalk slid into the bag. Picking himself up, Schalk puffed toward home, where he slid across the plate well ahead of the throw. Thinking he had scored a most improbable four-base circuit on an infield roller, Schalk was shocked when Nallin hollered, "You're out! You were out at first base, you dope! How do you feel?!"[13] In August, there were rumors that the White Sox had sought waivers on Schalk. Asked about it, Collins was emphatic: "Just as long as I have anything to do with the Chicago team, Schalk will remain with it."[14]

Still, when he was in the game, Schalk was in the game. In Game 5 of the City Series against the Cubs, he blocked the plate against a hard-charging Hack Wilson, the Cubs' 190-pound outfielder. "Wilson hit Schalk at top speed and sent the little catcher head over heels into the dirt," the *Tribune* reported. "The shock evidently affected umpire Ernie Quigley as well as Schalk, because first he ruled Wilson safe and then called him out, and it wasn't five minutes afterwards that the fans became sure of what the umpire's decision was and they razzed him long and loudly." Schalk not only finished the game, won by Red Faber and the Sox, 3–1, he collected three hits, including an RBI single the inning after the collision.[15] The Sox reclaimed the city title with a Game 7 shutout in Wrigley Field, 3–0.

A month later, Charles Comiskey changed managers again. Comiskey gave the job to Schalk, who was present in team headquarters when the owner gave reporters the news. The owner unceremoniously (and coldly) released Eddie Collins (and his $35,000-a-year salary). The 39-year-old Collins, just returning home from a hunting trip, learned of his change in employment status only when a reporter read him Comiskey's announcement. On road trips, Collins and Schalk had been roommates for a decade.[16] After his release,

Kid Gleason (left), former White Sox coach and manager (1919–23), poses with Schalk, the new manager, in January 1927. When Schalk joined the White Sox in 1912, Gleason and catcher Billy Sullivan regularly worked with him on his defense (Chicago History Museum, Chicago Daily News Collection, SDN-066343).

Tribune readers learned that Collins failed to control his players — getting them to run out easy grounders, for example — and that they laughed at Cocky's propensity for playing hunches in making managerial decisions. For his part, Comiskey didn't appreciate Collins' public complaints about the quality of players the front office provided him.[17] Still, some thought that

Collins got a raw deal, noting that Comiskey saved lots of salary money by releasing the future Hall of Famer.[18] The release of Collins (174–160 in two-plus seasons as Sox manager), permitted him to return to his original team, Connie Mack's Philadelphia Athletics, with whom he finished his career as a part-time player.

Comiskey's selection of Schalk was viewed as the owner's "reward for long and faithful service," noted Harry Neily of the *Chicago American*. The *Tribune*'s Crusinberry added, "After his long and untiring service with the club, it was fitting that he be given a chance as manager."[19] Schalk's loyal service apparently included not telling all he knew while Comiskey was trying to keep a lid on the Black Sox episode. Observers predicted great things for Cracker. "Ray Schalk, both in personality and in temperament, has the qualities for a successful baseball manager," offered the *Tribune*'s Harvey Woodruff. "'Cracker' is a fine little gentleman off the field and a fiery little pepperbox on the field. This latter attribute is what probably has earned him his position as leader of the White Sox crew when it was decided to change pilots." Describing Schalk as a popular player who will be one of the boys but also a "strict disciplinarian," Woodruff added, "He will command their respect as well as their liking."[20] The 34-year-old Schalk hired two coaches: Frank Roth, a 48-year-old former catcher, and 40-year-old Russell "Lena" Blackburne, a former infielder whom the Sox sent to the minors in the deal to acquire Schalk in 1912.[21]

In reply to a letter of congratulations from Moe Berg, then a White Sox reserve infielder, Schalk wrote, "I feel confident that all the boys will help me and do their utmost towards having a winner for the Sox. I know it is the ambition and desire of all of us to have a winning club, if that is possible, and it is my intention to leave nothing undone to accomplish that end."[22] Schalk tried to trade for someone to succeed Eddie Collins at second base, but the other clubs expected too much. "The Yanks would gladly have given Aaron Ward, but they wanted either Ted Blankenship or Ted Lyons," *The Sporting News* reported. "They might just as well have asked for the entire ball club."[23] Eventually, the Yankees came around a few weeks later, giving up Ward for Johnny Grabowski and Ray Morehart.

By this time, the Schalks resided in an apartment at 6818 Paxton Avenue, about five miles from Comiskey Park and a few blocks west of the exclusive South Shore Country Club. In the building next door, at 6820 Paxton, lived the family of Louis Comiskey, son of the Old Roman. The Schalks spent the holidays back home in Litchfield, but Ray's visit was interrupted by an old nemesis.

Black Sox conspirator Swede Risberg revived the allegation that during

Schalk, who dropped out of high school after a year or two, tends to paperwork in early 1927, before his first season as White Sox manager. Over the years, Schalk received loads of fan mail and did his best to accommodate autograph-seekers (Chicago History Museum, Chicago Daily News Collection, SDN-067099).

the 1917 pennant race the White Sox bribed members of the Detroit Tigers to throw back-to-back doubleheaders. Those four victories over Labor Day weekend helped extend the lead of the White Sox, who already held a 4½-game advantage over Boston. Nearly each of the Chicago players contributed $45 — worth about $750 in 2008 — toward a gift for the Tigers. All claimed it was to make good on a promise, made during the Labor Day series, to reward the Tigers if they defeated the Red Sox later in the month. On September 19–20, Detroit took all three games in Boston, positioning the White Sox to clinch the pennant the next day in Fenway Park. Commissioner Kenesaw Mountain Landis was already investigating charges of game-fixing by two of the game's leading lights, Tris Speaker and Ty Cobb, and Risberg saw his opportunity. He detailed his allegation in a two-hour meeting with Landis on New Year's Day 1927. He specifically implicated pitcher Red Faber, who struggled in both ends of one day's doubleheader, and then-manager Clarence

Rowland. Fellow Black Sox figure Happy Felsch backed much of Risberg's story. However, he said that Rowland was not involved, the "doings" were orchestrated by Chick Gandil, and everyone but Weaver and pitcher Reb Russell paid into the pool.[24] (Instead of cash, Buck Weaver reportedly made his gift a handbag for Detroit infielder Oscar Vitt.) Gandil took out an affidavit swearing that the money was used to reward the Tigers after losing those four games to the White Sox, with Detroit pitcher Bill James accepting the cash.[25] Risberg further intimated that late in 1919 the pennant-winning White Sox, appreciative of Detroit's cooperation two years earlier, laid down against the Tigers so that they might move up in the standings and thus improve their cut of World Series proceeds.[26] (The Tigers easily made the first division in 1919, but finished a half-game behind third-place New York.)

Former players from both teams denied the accusations. The commissioner summoned about three dozen of the principals, including Schalk, to a hearing in Chicago. Four were excused when Landis realized that they played for neither the White Sox nor Tigers in 1917. Ed Walsh came all the way from Connecticut to point out that fact to Landis, who apologized to the former pitching great for his inconvenience. Not everyone complied with the order to appear. One was Jack Lapp, who was out of the major leagues in 1917. What's more, Lapp died in 1920. Landis was powerful, certainly, but not powerful enough to bring back the dead.

The day of the hearing, Landis' large office on Michigan Avenue was packed. Ballplayers and nearly 40 reporters filled all the chairs and stood in the aisles. Cigarette smoke created a haze. Landis sat and simmered for a half-hour after the scheduled starting time until Risberg appeared. Seated together near the front of the room were the previous and current managers of the White Sox, Eddie Collins and Ray Schalk. The commissioner began by questioning Risberg. Over the next hour, Swede gave a performance that Don Maxwell of the *Tribune* described as "fumbling and feeble." For the next four hours, 25 men denied Risberg's allegation. First up was Rowland, who opened, "It's a damned lie!" An outraged Eddie Collins, who at the time made his $45 contribution belatedly and reluctantly, told Landis, "It's a God-damned lie!" Schalk was the next to testify, and he repeated that the money was to reward Tigers pitchers for good work against Boston. After Cracker came Cobb, who was already on the hot seat because of the alleged game-fixing with Speaker; he denied knowledge of a payoff and said that he remembered no details about the quality of play in Detroit's series against Chicago nine years earlier. Throughout the hearing, Risberg sat back, smoked cigarettes and grinned when witness after witness call him a liar. Pittsburgh manager Donie Bush, who was a Tigers player in 1917, shook his fist in Risberg's face and challenged him to a fight. Bill James, who accepted the delivery of the cash, said it was promised during the Labor Day weekend — but for future Tiger victories over the Red Sox; for a while after the Tigers tamed Boston, players joked the White Sox would not make good. The money was not collected until the end of September, more than a week after Detroit's sweep in Boston, and more than three weeks after the Tigers' Labor Day weekend series against Chicago.

Soon after the dramatic hearing, Landis dropped the matter. He ruled that there was insufficient evidence, and he indicated that he was less concerned about events that occurred before he took office in late 1920 than those occurring on his watch.[27] However, Landis made it clear that side-deal "gifts" of this sort were hereafter prohibited. Asked for his reaction, Schalk said, "That's just the way I knew it would finish. He could not have decided otherwise on the evidence submitted. Now we'll get ready for the battles on the ball field."[28] (In addition, Cobb and Speaker escaped the game-fixing charge and secured free-agent status. Both played two more seasons. Cobb joined Eddie Collins on the Philadelphia Athletics while Speaker went to Washington for 1927 and to the Athletics in 1928.)

Spring training 1927 opened in Shreveport, Louisiana, with Schalk in charge for the first time. Most of the players had signed their contracts, but there were some holdouts, including rookie Charlie Barnabe. The left-handed pitcher arrived in Shreveport to learn that the team policy was not to pick up the meal tab for players who were not signed. Barnabe refused to pay for his own meals. After about 24 hours without food, the recruit was invited into a contract negotiating session with Schalk and Lou Barbour, traveling secretary. The manager and paymaster then engaged in a side conversation about food, describing in delicious detail their favorite dishes. The mental imagery was too much for Barnabe, who signed his contract and hustled off to the Youree Hotel dining room, the Marble Cafe.[29]

The White Sox, like most major league teams, lacked a formal organization for scouting new talent. Comiskey apparently told one prospect, a lad named J.H. Ridgeway, he could try out with the Sox if he got himself to Shreveport at his own expense. Ridgeway took up the Old Roman on the offer and presented himself in the Sox clubhouse. Sportswriter Westbrook Pegler told the story. "He addressed Ray Schalk as Mr. Chalker, which was encouraging, and when trainer and equipment manager William Ananias (Buckner) assembled him a uniform from the remnants about the club house, he asked for a pair of garters. This made Mr. Schalk suspect that the new boy was not quite ready for work in the major leagues." Pegler said Schalk gave Ridgeway a look like a manager might give a prospect who said, "I'm a stranger on these grounds; could you tell me which way is left field?" After watching his players shell Ridgeway over three or four innings of a pick-up game, Schalk thanked the lad for his efforts and excused him for the day. He was never seen again.[30]

During morning batting practice a few days later, outfielder Johnny Mostil, walking onto the field, took a line drive to the middle of his chest. Mostil was already the team hypochondriac. "It is stated that if there is typhoid in Alaska or an epidemic of hang nail in the Dantzig corridor, Mr. Mostil will turn up with symptoms of his own," Pegler wrote, "and today's smack on the chest is expected to get him off with a rousing start."[31] In fact, Mostil's health complaints were already under way. As soon as he arrived in Shreve-

Three members of the 1927 Chicago White Sox (from left), coach Lena Blackburne, outfielder Bill Barrett and player-manager Ray Schalk, prepare to board their train for spring training. Schalk's first training camp as manager, in Shreveport, Louisiana, was marred by the failed suicide attempt of player Johnny Mostil, whose despondency was linked to losing his fiancée to Barrett (Chicago History Museum, Chicago Daily News Collection, SDN-066772).

port, Mostil told Schalk, "I'm sick and I'm worried and I'm boiling up inside." A physician named Dr. Slicer was summoned, and he found Mostil nervous, complaining of wisdom-tooth pain and experiencing elevated blood pressure. "That boy is in bad shape," Slicer told Schalk. The next day, when rain washed out practice, most of the players killed time in the hotel. Team booster Pat Prunty returned to his room to discover his friend Mostil, unconscious and bleeding from deep slashes in his wrists, on the bathroom floor. Hoping to avoid publicity, team personnel used the downtown hotel's back door to deliver the 30-year-old into an ambulance. At Schumpert Hospital, he received the Roman Catholic sacrament of Last Rites. After several tense hours, doctors determined that Mostil would survive.

Despite the team's attempt to squelch the news of Mostil's "little accident," the story immediately topped the front pages of the Chicago papers. Various rumors and theories surfaced regarding Mostil's motivation for his desperate act, including depression over ongoing dental problems and unease over his playing contract. Another theory claimed distress over discovery of his affair with the wife of teammate Red Faber; the rumor was that when Red found out about his Irene and Mostil, he threatened to kill his teammate, who then slashed his own wrists. The pitcher's only son — his mother was Red's second wife — scoffed at the notion of Red Faber threatening Mostil over Irene. "My father didn't have a jealous bone in his body," Urban C. Faber II said.[32] The Fabers remained married until Irene's death 16 years later, and Red and Mostil remained teammates for several seasons after the incident.

A love triangle existed, but it did not involve the Fabers. Mostil became despondent when he learned that his girlfriend — Margaret Carroll, of Hammond, Indiana — had dumped him for his teammate and spring training roommate, Bill Barrett.[33] Carroll, quoted immediately after the incident as Mostil's near-fiancée, later became Mrs. William Barrett.[34] Mostil escaped death and recovered sufficiently to play some late-season games.

Meanwhile, Schalk needed to deal with the fallout of the Mostil incident, which dealt a blow to team morale, and establish himself as a manager. Despite his pre-season optimism about team unity, Schalk's fiery, all-business approach to baseball sparked push-back from some players, starting with Barrett. Irving Vaughan of the *Tribune* reported, "Barrett, whose idea of life is to laugh it off, hadn't been playing in a manner indicating undivided attention to business on his part. He has done such things before, so it required no time for Schalk to observe the objectionable mental attitude." There were other objectors. "Schalk's 'ride' of Barrett bears out stories from the South that some of the players on the team were heated under the collar because of the new pilot's stern attitude. They are said to have complained lustily, but even though this may be true, it doesn't necessarily mean that any harm will result." Vaughan added, "When Collins was manager, he was inclined to be mild mannered in giving his orders. Some of the men took advantage of him and the team suffered accordingly. Hence nobody can blame Schalk if he gets a bit wrathy."[35] Though he was reducing his playing role, Schalk continued to work out and see action. He suffered yet another broken finger in Wichita Falls, Texas, on March 21, when a foul tip (again) caught the middle finger of his throwing hand.[36]

Chicago baseball fans found it easier to follow their favorites in 1927. WGN radio announced it would broadcast every home game of both the Cubs and White Sox. The American League had previously banned broadcasts of its games, and in 1926 the *Tribune*-owned station delivered accounts of only the National League Cubs' weekend home games. Quin Ryan provided the play-by-play for WGN.[37] Meanwhile, the Chicago *Daily News*' station, WMAQ, prepared for its third season of broadcasting Cubs' home games and its inaugural season with the Sox. Sportswriter Hal Totten returned to the WMAQ microphone. The same edition of the *Daily News* carried an article concerning the future of collegiate football. Two faculty members from Big Ten institutions predicted that it would wither and die within five years. "Student ills, such as poor scholarship, low morals of student bodies, the sacrifice of the physical training of the student body at large for the benefit of the few and a loss of objective in higher education are some of the reasons why college presidents will ask that the old athletic rivalry in the most important of college sports shall cease."[38]

Other changes awaited the White Sox. The team renovated and expanded Comiskey Park. Built in 1910 with a seating capacity of 41,000 patrons — its record was 43,825 in the 1925 City Series — the ballpark could now seat 55,000 and shoehorn in some 5,000 more.[39] The project cost Charles Comiskey $600,000 — all of it his own money. A renovated ballpark, expanded radio coverage and the land development Greater Chicago Acres — $350 an acre, payable at $10 a month — were not the only changes in the Windy City. On the same afternoon Schalk managed his first official game (in Cleveland), William Hale Thompson officially returned as Chicago mayor. Big Bill, mayor from 1915 to 1923, served again until 1931.

Festivities for White Sox Opening Day 1927 included a welcoming ceremony and gifts for Schalk, a pre-game parade from downtown Chicago south to the ballpark, brass bands and the debut of the White Sox Rooters Association.[40] Johnny Mostil, still recovering from his wounds, made an appearance on the field.[41] Though Comiskey hoped for a sell-out, the afternoon was breezy and cold; temperatures sat in the low 40s. The *Tribune*

As new player-manager of the White Sox, Schalk is feted before Opening Day 1927 in Comiskey Park. The baby is Charles Comiskey II, grandson of the team owner and himself a future vice president of the club. The message on the floral tribute reads, "Success to Ray." However, success didn't happen, and Schalk was fired the next season (Chicago History Museum, Chicago Daily News Collection, SDN-066578).

reported attendance of 30,000, while the *American* said it was closer to 40,000. Thousands of others stayed inside and listened to the game on the radio. In Schalk's first home game as manager — the team opened 3–5 on the road — Cleveland defeated Ted Lyons, 5–4. The new manager put himself in the lineup and, after accepting a warm ovation before his first at-bat, singled to right. He played half the game.[42] That night, both teams went to the McVickers Theater, where they saw Hollywood's newest baseball movie, *Slide Kelly Slide*.[43]

In the opening third of the season, Schalk's charges won nearly two out of three contests. A 12–2 streak moved them into second place, just a game behind the Yankees, in early June. Sportswriters took notice. Alan J. Gould, sports editor of The Associated Press, wrote a complimentary article, crediting the team's success to sound fundamentals and Schalk's leadership. The new manager told Gould, "The entire outfit is pulling together. I've never seen any greater teamwork than this bunch is showing. They are on their toes every minute." Schalk also stated that he intended to stay active as a player "at least once in a while."[44]

However, Schalk appeared on the field wearing the "tools of ignorance" only 15 times in 1927 — and at least one of those appearances was brief. In the second inning July 22, New York rookie Julian Wera, attempting to score on a sacrifice fly, crashed into Schalk. The Chicago player-manager was knocked unconscious but somehow held onto the ball to complete the double play. The collision hurt Wera, too, but he stayed until the eighth inning. However, Cracker's day was done; he departed Comiskey Park for examination at a hospital. The badly shaken Schalk suffered a concussion, broken thumb and bruised nose, but he was released to recuperate at home.[45] A full month after the incident, he was still experiencing dizzy spells.[46]

Five weeks earlier, as the AP feature story appeared in U.S. newspapers, Schalk's crew had arrived in New York for a four-game series. The Yankees won the opener, but Chicago's team spirit was evident. "The White Sox spilled pepper all over the lot and chattered constantly from the field and bench," the *New York Times* noted. "Ray Schalk has hypnotized the athletes into believing that they have a chance to win the pennant. Great thing, hypnotism."[47] The comment might have broken the spell. In Game 2, despite two Tony Lazzeri homers off Faber, the Sox took an 11–6 lead into the bottom of the ninth inning. Then the Yankees erupted. Faber retired only one Yankee, gave up three runs and had a runner on first when he headed for the showers. Still, the Sox held an 11–9 lead. Lazzeri proceeded to place a delivery by reliever George Connally just inside Yankee Stadium's right-field foul pole (295 feet away) and just over the 4-foot-high wall. It was Lazzeri's third homer of the game, and the two-run shot propelled the Yankees to an electrifying win in 11 innings, 12–11.[48] This loss hurt. "Schalk says that in his 16 years of big league baseball he never has seen a defeat that so cast down an aggregation supposed to be hard boiled in such matters," Edward Burns told *Chicago Tribune* readers. "He admits it has had him on the ropes."[49] The Yankees won three of four. Schalk left town complaining that Yankee Stadium, with its short fence in right, was a "trick field" tailored for New York's lefty sluggers, particularly Babe Ruth.[50]

Including the heartbreaker in New York, the White Sox went 9–14 the rest of June. During that slide, Schalk experienced his only ejection as a manager. When umpire Brick Owens ruled an apparent homer by Alex Metzler a foul ball, Schalk charged from the dugout and, during the argument, kicked dirt on Owens. (That tantrum also earned Schalk a three-game suspension from American League President Ban Johnson. The severity of the punishment was among the "final straws" as unhappy league owners pressured Johnson to finally step aside.[51]) With Cracker absent, the White Sox rallied for three runs in the bottom of the ninth to edge Cleveland, 8–7. The rally featured acting manager Blackburne, 40 years old, inserting himself as a pinch-hitter. In his first major-league appearance in eight years, Blackburne singled and soon afterward scored the winning run on a sacrifice fly.[52]

Despite that excitement, by mid–July, the White Sox had dropped to fifth place in the American League, some 15 games behind the powerful Yankees, who were making it a runaway. Team spirit and positive feelings faded. Observers criticized Schalk for overworking his pitchers. "At the beginning of this season the White Sox big four — Ted Lyons, Alphonse Thomas, Ted Blankenship and Red Faber — alone carried the Chicago club to victory," the *Washington Post*'s Frank H. Young wrote. "But Schalk frequently used his men for relief work between their regular assignments, and, as a result, the whole four are only ordinary pitchers now. And that Schalk has not learned a lesson yet is indicated by the fact that in the last series with the Nats, he called on Blankenship in two games and used Lyons as relief man one day and then started him the next."[53] It didn't help that Faber, 38 years old, was ineffective on the mound and missing starts due to a bum knee. Barely two months after sports fans across the country read of the unity and spirit on the White Sox, rumors of internal strife were rampant. Schalk tried to refute those reports, stating that the team was in accord and in pursuit of a first-division finish.[54]

Still, the team was in trouble. Front-office interference emerged as a reason. "Charles A. Comiskey apparently doesn't believe in letting a manager be the real boss of the team," wrote Don Maxwell in the *Chicago Tribune*. "He wants a figurehead, a field foreman instead of a field marshal." Maxwell recalled an exchange between Schalk and a reporter who asked whether the Sox had purchased a particular player: "How would I know? You'll have to find out from the 35th Street office." Davis J. Walsh of the International News Service said that when a recovering Johnny Mostil showed up to work out with the team, Schalk was as surprised as anyone; Comiskey didn't think it neces-

A major-league manager had the opportunity and obligation to meet with vis-iting celebrities. On this afternoon in 1927, the guest is U.S. Vice President Charles Dawes (Chicago History Museum, Chicago Daily News Collection, SDN-066503).

sary to notify his manager.[55] Maxwell added, "Schalk wasn't complaining. He was merely explaining what is becoming more and more apparent. The man-ager of the White Sox isn't supposed to rule. He's expected to carry out the instructions from Chicago." It didn't help team morale that administration engaged in espionage. Comiskey ordered traveling secretary Tip O'Neill to send him a telegram daily, detail how a game was lost and what a player who committed a miscue had for dinner and what time he retired for the night. Walsh noted, "What Comiskey apparently is doing to Schalk is only what he did to Eddie Collins, Johnny Evers and other men who handled the club." In Maxwell's analysis, Schalk deserved a share of the blame. Entering the job expected to be a take-charge guy — and appearing to be just that early on — Schalk had become lax on discipline. His failure to get tough with disenchanted outfielder Bibb Falk was presented as just one example. "Maybe Schalk is too easy on fellows of Falk's type," Maxwell wrote.[56]

One of Schalk's positive personnel decisions was the result of a misunderstanding. In late July and early August, Chicago's catching corps was depleted due to injury. Schalk was still experiencing dizzy spells from his collision with Wera a few weeks earlier, and his thumb was not healed. Buck Crouse was nursing banged-up fingers. In Boston on August 5, the only available member of Chicago's banged-up receivers, Harry McCurdy, suffered an injury in the second inning but stayed in the game. The story goes that in the dugout Schalk commented, to no one in particular, that the team would be in a bad way if McCurdy couldn't continue. In so many words, reserve infielder Moe Berg told his manager, "What are you worrying about? You've got a great catcher sitting here on the bench." As baseball fate would have it, in the very next inning a collision at home plate knocked out McCurdy. Schalk then turned to Berg and said, "All right, you asked for it. Go in and catch." The 25-year-old performed adequately and took another turn behind the bat two days later. Immediately afterward, Berg declared that he was now a catcher — and he remained one for the duration of his career. Only later was it disclosed that when Berg mentioned to Schalk that the team had another fill-in catcher, he was not referring to himself. The man Berg had in mind was first baseman Earl Sheely. Somewhere along the line, Berg got the idea that Sheely had caught in the Pacific Coast League.[57] (If Sheely ever caught, the occasion must have been extremely rare; he starred in the PCL at first base.) In any case, Berg, highly educated and a genius, is among the most interesting and intriguing Americans ever — in any field of endeavor. His 15 seasons as a reserve in the majors — nearly all of them as a catcher — were but a chapter in a colorful life story that included spying for the U.S. government.

After going 40–32 through June (.556), the White Sox faded terribly, posting a 30–51 (.370) record from July to the season's merciful end. In late August, the *Tribune* observed, "About the toughest job left in the league for this year rests on the shoulders of Ray Schalk. There is no doubt the team's spirit is shattered. The men simply are discouraged over their blowup after the fine start and for Schalk to rally them is almost an impossibility."[58] The comment was on target, as the team lost 14 of 15 contests during one stretch of September.

The White Sox did not even get a chance to redeem themselves in the City Series. The Cubs chose not to follow tradition and issue a challenge to the defending city champ for another series. Apparently, the Cubs were piqued that the South Siders cheered each time the Cubs took a loss in their drive for the National League pennant. The Cubs in the World Series would mean no City Series — and thus no share of gate receipts for the Sox. Comiskey's crew cheered often. The North Siders held a two-game lead entering September, but they swooned (12–18) as Pittsburgh, St. Louis and New York surged past them in the standings. On September 19, the fading Cubs, already in fourth place, exacted some revenge by announcing there would be no City Series. "The season of 1927 contained so many splendid possibilities that any series other than a world's series would be an ill-fitting climax," explained Cubs President William Veeck. Further, Veeck also wanted to get started on renovations at Wrigley Field. Comiskey had no choice but to go along — but not without a dig at the North Siders: "As far as we are concerned, nothing is to be gained by the Sox defeating the Cubs in another City Series."[59]

Thus the off-season of 1927–28 began, as did speculation over Schalk's future.

24

⋄⋄⋄⋄

Goodbye

At the close of the 1927 season, Harvey T. Woodruff of the *Chicago Tribune* gave Schalk a vote of confidence. He noted that the White Sox were not really expected to finish in the first division anyway — and that was before losing the services of Johnny Mostil to a failed suicide attempt. "He is entitled to another year's leadership," Woodruff said of Schalk, "and even then he must have more playing strength under him to figure among the leaders."[1]

Apparently, the only person whose opinion counted, team owner Charles A. Comiskey, was not convinced. In October, the Old Roman hosted Schalk at his Wisconsin estate for two long weeks — and even then there followed no announcement whether Schalk would return as manager. Cracker remained in limbo another month, and his prospects appeared dim in late November when the team did not include him on the travel itinerary for the minor-league winter meetings in Dallas. A few days later, after meeting with Comiskey at the ballpark, Schalk was hired for the 1928 season at a salary of $25,000. They celebrated with a dinner hosted by the Old Roman's son Lou, after which the younger Comiskey and Schalk took in a night of boxing at the Coliseum.

"All last season Cracker obviously was hampered by the 'I knew him when...' attitude of some of the players," the *Tribune* observed. "With the vote of confidence shown by reappointment, Schalk probably will have a sterner mein and other desirable attitudes resulting from his year's experience."[2] A tougher Schalk was the theme of Hot Stove League sports stories. Meanwhile, the Sox hired retired spitballer Ed Walsh (Hall of Fame Class of 1946) as their pitching coach, succeeding Frank Roth.[3]

The White Sox found familiar surroundings for spring training 1928 — Shreveport, Louisiana. They secured Biedenharn Park for workouts and returned to the massive Youree Hotel. However, the Youree added a stipulation to its new contract with the Sox — no animals in guest rooms. That development seriously disappointed relief pitcher George Connally. A pet lover,

Schalk conducts a spring training workout in Shreveport, Louisiana, in 1928. As a player-manager, he caught just one game that season — the major-league debut of Ed Walsh Junior, on the same day Schalk departed as manager (Chicago History Museum, Chicago Daily News Collection, SDN-067324).

Connally the previous year brought to his room in the Youree a hound dog, rabbit, two guinea pigs and a pair of pigeons. His roommate, coach Lena Blackburne, moved out when the barking became too much.[4]

Schalk's new contract apparently so energized him that during spring training the player-manager aired his intention to catch most of the team's games. However, he suffered another injury during spring training and stuck to the bench, with a couple of exceptions, for the Chicago duration of his White Sox career. Comiskey did little to improve the team, aside from overpaying ($123,000) for Chalmer "Bill" Cissell, a shortstop from the Pacific Coast League. He sold off veteran Aaron Ward and bid Roger Peckinpaugh *adieu* as he became manager in Cleveland. Johnny Mostil had returned late the previous year. After that, management did little but issue optimistic statements about the team's prospects for 1928. John C. Hoffman of the *Chicago Daily News* stated, "It is difficult to discover with the naked eye any phenomenal changes for the better in Schalk's corps of flingers, of course, providing the available talent is not trying to 'kid' the laymen," adding, "Manager Schalk will find the going no easier than it was last season."[5] Paid to find a silver lining, Schalk told a United Press reporter, "We'll bear watching for three reasons: 1. Youth, 2. Speed, 3. Hustle."[6] That was the best he could muster. John Kieran of the *New York Times* said of the White Sox, "All in all, it isn't a team that looms up as a serious threat to the Yankees, ... but it has possibilities. Which means it may go up or may go down."[7]

In their final pre-season game, the Sox defeated the minor-league team of Springfield, Illinois, 45 miles north of Litchfield. Many of the 1,500 shivering fans were on hand to honor their hometown hero.[8] They presented him a 6-foot-tall grandfather clock.[9] Two days later, when the White Sox hosted Cleveland, Ray Schalk was not in the Opening Day lineup for the first time in 16 seasons.

In the first month of the season, the White Sox dropped into the American League cellar. "The club that hasn't finished out of the second division for eight years is as poorly a balanced team as a management could provide," *Tribune* sports editor Don Maxwell stated in a lengthy analysis of the team. "Everyone except Harry Grabiner, the hard working secretary, admits it. He continues to talk about Mr. Comiskey's 'fine club.'" Maxwell concluded, "Schalk deserves less talk about a 'fine club' and more effort to find him some one who can pitch nine fairly creditable innings. Of course, the White Sox were hard hit by the scandal of 1919, but Chicago's fans rate more than an eighth-place team nine years afterward."[10]

The *Tribune*'s Irving Vaughan also cited front-office interference as contributing to the team's malaise. Vaughan reported a player's claim that he saw a telegram from the Sox office instructing Schalk to use a particular pitcher on just two days' rest — all to an unsatisfactory result.[11] The pitcher apparently was Alphonse "Tommy" Thomas, who started May 4 and again May 7. To that point in the season, no other Chicago pitcher started on two days' rest.[12]

Still, Schalk searched for answers. Following the lead of his counterpart on the North Side, Cubs manager Joe McCarthy, Schalk started holding regular morning practices.[13]

A couple of days later, the White Sox beat Cleveland, 4–3, on Willie Kamm's bases-loaded single in the bottom of the 10th. The Sox might have won it in regulation, if not for a miscue by their manager. The White Sox loaded the bases with no one out. Schalk stood on second base; he had walked and advanced on another walk. The next hitter, Bud Clancy, lofted a shallow fly to Cleveland left fielder Charlie Jamieson, who made the catch and threw home to easily nail baserunner Johnny Mann. Catcher Luke Sewell then

Radio was only in its infancy, but broadcasts of baseball games were popular with listeners. The American League did not permit broadcasts until 1927. Here, in 1928, manager Schalk (left) answers a question for *Chicago Daily News* sportswriter Hal Totten over WMAQ, the *Daily News'* station (Chicago History Museum, Chicago Daily News Collection, SDN-067100).

spotted Schalk trying to advance to third. Sewell fired to third baseman John Hodapp, who tagged Schalk in a rundown to complete the triple play.[14] Kamm's hit in the next inning spared the White Sox further embarrassment.

Bearing more troubles than "an armless man at a picnic," as Vaughan described him, Schalk was losing control of his team. By early June, he benched two of his better hitters, outfielders Bibb Falk and Bill Barrett, for dogging it. Vaughan offered the opinion that fines were in order. "When a manager is so lenient that his men become possessed of the idea they are bigger than the boss, it is time for the boss to show them the error of their way and there is nothing like a slice off the pay check when it comes to doing that."[15] Chicago went 12–13 in June and escaped the cellar — Detroit (8–17) was the new occupant — but that was no comfort for the team and especially its rooters.

On the eve of their Independence Day doubleheader in Chicago, the White Sox announced that recently acquired Ed Walsh Jr., the 23-year-old son of their pitching coach, would start the opener against the St. Louis Browns the next day. It would be a historic day for the White Sox. How historic, few were aware.

In the clubhouse less than a half-hour before the 1:30 P.M. start of the doubleheader, Schalk called together his players. His trembling hands holding a letter, he started to read:

"Under my hand writing, this day July 4th, 1928, I turn in my resignation as Manager of the Chicago White Sox Base Ball Club of this great Chicago town.

"It has been mutually agreed between Mr. Comiskey and I that I resign. The Club has been going bad; the results have not been satisfactory, so I step out as Manager of the Club, leaving it to him to appoint someone else to take my place."

Schalk could not finish. He broke into tears. Players gathered around to console him and to see what else was contained in his letter. As Schalk shuffled to his locker and inspected his bats while trying to regain his composure, the players read on:

> Mr. Comiskey and I have always been the best of friends; wonderful man; more than an employer to me; and a friend and advisor; and I have nothing but the highest regard for him. The Club at the present is in a sort of experimental stage, and a change in the management might be helpful to the situation.
> TO THE BASE BALL FANS OF THIS GREAT CITY, THE PUBLIC AND THE PRESS:
> I wish to take this opportunity of expressing my appreciation for their loyalty and ardent support. These sixteen years of my life have been a source of great pleasure to me, and I am stepping out with the friendliest feelings toward my employer and Chicago.
> My residence in Chicago has been permanently established, and while my connection in Base Ball remains in the balance, I trust I will not lose my identity with same for some years to come. I am by no means through with Base Ball — my love for the game will be ever-lasting and will keep me at it as long as I am capable — plans for the moment are a little indefinite, but my present intention is to remain as a player, and whoever succeeds me I most sincerely wish them the best of everything.[16]

Schalk's resignation did not take effect instantly. That afternoon, he still had a job to do. He composed himself and took the field for his last appearance in a White Sox uniform. Sixteen years earlier, in his debut, he caught Ed Walsh. In his final game with the White Sox he caught the debut of Ed Walsh, Jr. Schalk's appearance in the lineup was mostly symbolic. It was the only catching he did in all of 1928.

The departure was no surprise. The *Tribune*'s Irving Vaughan revealed, "He was inclined to be lenient with his players and they took advantage of it. Some of them talked back when he gave orders. Some openly ridiculed his efforts. Such conditions brought on the inevitable shattering of morale and the team fell to pieces, also to eighth place."[17] A writer in *The Sporting News* stated that Schalk "was not temperamentally fitted for the role of a leader and the job became doubly difficult because he was unfortunate enough to have among his players a few who were inclined to imagine that a touch of indifference was a sign of intellect." Giving up the managership was for the best: "He'd have worried himself into a toupee had he hung on for the remainder of the season."[18]

The White Sox were now under the command of Lena Blackburne, a former Sox player and current coach. He made it clear that the Schalk manner of doing things was in the past. The 41-year-old ruled through hard words, hard work and continual threats of $50 fines against transgressors. He eschewed "small ball" in favor of big innings. The Sox initially responded, going 9–3 — all on the road — before cooling off. Nonetheless, the White Sox under Blackburne played .500 ball (40–40) and finished fifth in the American League.

Upon his departure, Schalk became the subject of published tributes celebrating his career. "There will be discussion from time to time in the future, as there has been in the past, as to the identity of the greatest outfielder, the four best infielders, or the king of pitchers," the *Chicago Tribune* observed. "But there can be no real dispute concerning the catcher. In the light of Schalk's record, the second-best can hardly be discerned." In addition to his ironman record —12 out of 13 seasons with at least 100 catching appearances, including 11 consecutive campaigns — Schalk was noted for his ability to cut down basestealers, handle pop-ups and take charge of his team's defense.[19]

After a few days of public speculation, the University of Wisconsin, which a couple of years earlier hired him to assist the baseball team during its winter workouts, denied rumors that Schalk would take over the Badger program.[20]

Schalk expressed an interest in remaining with the White Sox — or any team that would have him — as a player, but no teams were interested in a

35-year-old whose body had been battered by more than 1,700 games behind the plate — not even the White Sox. When his former charges and teammates completed their doubleheader split in Chicago and headed east on a road trip, Schalk was not on the train. A week later, the White Sox released him. Grabiner sent him a telegram stating only, "Waivers have been secured. You are at liberty to negotiate with any Club for your services."[21] That was it. Not even a "sincerely yours." Such was the lot of White Sox managers. Eight of the 11 had been fired; of the three others, two resigned and the third, Frank Chance, died before managing an official game. The cold manner in which Eddie Collins was sent packing in 1926 won Comiskey no admirers, and Schalk's departure also raised eyebrows.

By the end of July, it became public knowledge — if there were doubts — that Schalk's resignation was hardly voluntary. On July 27, Schalk stated he might sue the Old Roman for unpaid salary related to his role as a player. Sure, he stepped down as manager, but he still wanted to play. "While he was willing to give up the managership at $25,000 (a year), he fully expected to resume his catcher's status at $15,000," the *Tribune* revealed. "He could go to another team — he had two offers — but for sentimental reasons he'd rather battle for the good old nine — at $15,000 per." Comiskey's response was that "a resignation is a resignation" but he'd be willing to pay $6,000 — but no more — for Schalk's services as a benchwarmer backstop.[22] (A subsequent report set the offer at $7,500. "I didn't mind a cut," Schalk said, "but I certainly wasn't going to take an amputation."[23]) The Old Roman said, "The Schalk matter is a closed incident as far as the White Sox or myself is concerned."[24]

Though Comiskey deservedly had a reputation for being excessively tight with a dollar, to pay $15,000 for a light-hitting, soon-to-be 36-year-old who had but 16 catching appearances the previous 1½ seasons would have been foolhardy. At that time, even half that would have been generous. (Comiskey also had a generous side that received less visibility. Former major leaguer Billy Sullivan, Jr., the son of the star catcher who helped Schalk break into the majors, revealed to baseball researcher Norman Macht that when it became time for his brothers Joseph and Stanley to attend college, the Old Roman paid all their expenses for their four years at Notre Dame. The younger Sullivan, who said Commy did the same for Ed Walsh, Jr., did not accept the same offer — he also went to Notre Dame — because he didn't want to be committed to sign with the White Sox. However, he opened his major-league career with the Sox but played for six other teams.[25])

Comiskey knew the value of education. And he knew the value of a benchwarmer. That no other team signed him after his release a couple of weeks later shows other owners shared the Old Roman's analysis of Schalk's current market value. Any hard feelings between the loyal catcher and owner apparently soon dissipated. In fact, Schalk continued his August tradition of sending birthday flowers to team executive J. Louis Comiskey, the Old Roman's son.[26] It was time to move on.

25

❖

A New Role

In the fall of 1928, for the first time in 18 seasons, Ray Schalk was not associated with professional baseball. The paychecks from the White Sox stopped, but the husband of Lavinia and father of 10-year-old Pauline and 7-year-old Ray Jr. was not relegated to any unemployment line. He still had his off-season job of insurance sales, his housing venture with William J. Wightman and a new endeavor with businessman Ben Stevenson.

Months before Schalk left the White Sox, he and Stevenson commissioned construction of a bowling and billiards emporium on East 79th Street near Cottage Grove Avenue, about five miles due south of Comiskey Park. Stevenson and Schalk Recreation featured 20 lanes for bowling, 17 pool tables, five billiards tables, "space for golf nets," putting greens, soda fountain and even "check room and rest room for the ladies." Bowling was more than a business investment for Schalk; he enjoyed ten-pins for recreation. The grand opening was Saturday night, September 22, 1928. The event featured a speech by U.S. Senator Charles S. Deneen, a billiards demonstration and lecture by cuemaster David McAndless, an exhibition bowling match and appearance by Lena Blackburne and Ted Lyons of the White Sox, who that afternoon had defeated the Yankees, 5–2. Stevenson and Schalk marketed their facility as a classy enterprise. "A special invitation is extended to the ladies of the district who are interested in bowling and golf," one their advertisements stated. "You will receive a welcome at any time of the day or evening and always find an atmosphere of the highest respect."[1] The Stevenson & Schalk Bowling Alley Company was incorporated for $20,000 and granted a charter by the Illinois secretary of state. Listed as incorporators were Ben and Bina Stevenson and Ray and Lavinia Schalk.[2]

A Norwegian orphan who came to the United States at age 16, Ben Stevenson started out as a heating contractor before entering the real estate business. The same year he opened the bowling center with Schalk, Stevenson made his mark in amateur golf circles by winning the Dixie Amateur and

Hialeah championships — no small feat considering that he had taken up the game just four years earlier, at age 38.[3]

Almost immediately, Stevenson and Schalk Recreation made a name for itself in competitive bowling. The center's five-man team won the state title in 1929.[4] Somewhere along the line, Clarence "Jersey" Schalk became associated with one or more of his brother's bowling enterprises, both as an employee and a competitor. Jersey was an outstanding bowler — better than his famous brother. One February evening in 1936, he rolled a 279 in league play at Stevenson and Schalk Recreation.[5] More than two decades later, when Ray sold his last enterprise, Jersey stayed on the payroll.

Though he was now in the bowling business, Schalk had not given up on baseball. And baseball had not given up on Schalk — if not as a player, at least as a coach. The New York Giants, Detroit Tigers and at least one other club showed interest.[6] Schalk preferred Detroit, not only to stay in the American League, but to work with friend Bucky Harris, who had just been hired as Tigers manager. To join the Tigers, he was willing to take less than the others offered. "I would like very much to have Schalk as an assistant," Harris told reporters, "for he is a smart veteran and would prove a big help in rounding out my battery men." Harris indicated it would come down to money — how much owner Frank Navin would offer.[7] Navin's answer was insufficient or tardy; a couple of weeks later, Schalk signed a one-year deal with John McGraw's New York Giants of the National League. He replaced 49-year-old Roger Bresnahan, the catcher on McGraw's championship teams in the century's first decade. Schalk would serve as pitching coach, run the team in McGraw's absence, coach at third base and, should circumstances warrant, don the "tools of ignorance" and catch. United Press reported that his salary would be $12,000 a year.[8] McGraw hired former major-league infielder and minor-league manager Bert Niehoff as his other coach.

Spring training 1929 challenged Schalk. He was to learn and follow McGraw's system and get to know a new team in San Antonio. However, McGraw was not present; he was on vacation in Cuba the first couple of weeks of camp. He placed Schalk in charge of the Giants, but sent Cracker extensive instructions by cable every day. "What all these instructions were Schalk did not feel himself in a position to disclose," the *New York Times* reported, "but that certain drastic changes in training are contemplated." The Giants abruptly dropped from two workouts a day to one, but added practices on Sundays, which were traditional days off.[9] While supervising practices, Schalk also worked out. Picking up where he left off in the Chicago gymnasium during the winter, he took batting practice, ran out his hits, warmed up pitchers and shagged flies. He wanted to be ready for game action, should the need

In 1929, when Schalk was a player-coach for the New York Giants, Lavinia brought their children Pauline and Ray Jr. from their Chicago home to visit in New York. This photograph was taken in the Polo Grounds (photograph courtesy Lillian Hendricks).

arise.[10] An added challenge for Schalk during the spring was seeing his former team, the White Sox, in a handful of exhibition games.

Chicago Cubs president William Veeck and his organization recognized a prime marketing opportunity in Schalk's first baseball appearance in the Windy City since leaving the White Sox. The Cubs declared Ray Schalk Day for Monday, June 3. It was advertised as the first such "day" conducted at Wrigley Field. (The Schalks maintained their residence in Chicago, on the South Side, at 6818 Paxton Avenue). About 2,000 South Siders swelled the attendance at Wrigley Field to 12,000. In a pre-game ceremony, Schalk graciously accepted a traveling bag and golf bag from the Cubs. On the field, Schalk accommodated his well-wishers by making his first catching appearance of the season (only his second since 1927). He caught the first three innings and went hitless in his only plate appearance; the Giants won easily, 8–1.[11] The next evening, Schalk and the Giants' Fred Lindstrom, a Chicago native, were the guests of honor at a banquet at the Midland Club.[12]

The 1929 campaign was disappointing for the Giants, who finished third in the National League, 13½ games behind the champion Cubs. One of the livelier incidents of the campaign came July 6, when rookie umpire George Magerkurth ejected McGraw in the eighth and a short time later gave Schalk the thumb.[13] Aside from three innings on his "day" in Chicago, Schalk played in only four other games. They were short stints; he recorded only three putouts over those four games. The last of those three represented his final appearance as a major-league player. His performance in St. Louis on September 15, 1929, was hardly noteworthy. He caught the bottom of the eighth after starting catcher James "Shanty" Hogan departed for a pinch-runner in the top of the frame. Since the Cardinals held onto their 6–4 lead after 8½ innings, there was no bottom of the ninth for Schalk to catch.[14] After 1,762 games, and 1,727 defensive appearances (all behind the plate), Ray Schalk's playing days ended. He hit .253 and fielded at a .981 average over those 18 seasons.

In early November 1929, just days after the Stock Market Crash, McGraw fired Schalk and Niehoff. The coaches didn't get along well. McGraw didn't explain himself. He didn't have to. The coaches had one-year contracts, and he was in charge. The Giants' pitching staff, under Schalk's responsibility, posted a 3.97 earned-run average, worse than the 1928 team's 3.67 but exactly the same as its 1927 mark. McGraw hired former Giants star and Boston Braves manager Dave Bancroft to replace Schalk.[15] Another former Giant, Emil "Irish" Meusel, took Niehoff's place.

Schalk was not out of baseball long. Schalk confirmed that he was under consideration to manage the Brooklyn Dodgers — an interesting possibility

Schalk joined John McGraw's New York Giants as a player-coach in 1929. He played in five games; they were his only National League appearances and the last of his 18-year major-league career. Schalk and fellow coach Bert Niehoff didn't get along, and McGraw released them both after one season (Chicago History Museum, Chicago Daily News Collection, SDN-068385).

Schalk visits with Philadelphia Athletics star Jimmie Foxx (in uniform) before a 1929 World Series game in Chicago's Wrigley Field. A future Hall-of-Famer, Foxx batted .350 in the series as the Athletics defeated the Cubs in five games (Chicago History Museum, Chicago Daily News Collection, SDN-069146).

in light of the fact that Wilbert Robinson had managed the team since 1914 and had not been released; as it played out, Robinson would continue to manage the team through 1931.[16] By Christmas 1929, however, Schalk signed on as a coach for manager Joe McCarthy's defending National League champion Chicago Cubs. That he could continue in the game and keep his family in Chicago — albeit with a longer commute to Wrigley Field, on the North Side — no doubt made the Cubs' offer especially attractive. About this time, the Schalk family moved from Paxton Avenue, where Louis Comiskey lived next door, to an apartment at 6830 Chappel Ave. The coach's drive to Wrigley was no shorter; the new residence was just three blocks west of the former apartment.[17] By mid–January 1930, Schalk was working out with Cubs catcher Gabby Hartnett, who was coming back from shoulder problems, in the Illinois Athletic Club gym.[18] Nine years later, Hartnett broke Schalk's major-league record for career catching appearances.

If Schalk planned to play a key role in running the Cubs, McCarthy had other ideas. By season's end, the *Tribune* said that under McCarthy, Schalk had been "little more than a bat boy." One of Cracker's assignments was to represent the team at the funeral of 38-year-old starting pitcher Harold Carlson, who suddenly experienced internal bleeding and died May 28. The 1930 Cubs fought to win the National League pennant and a return trip to the World Series. Despite the death of Carlson and the loss of star infielder Rogers Hornsby to a broken ankle two days later, Chicago rode Hack Wilson's hot hitting in August to grab the top spot in the National League. On his way to a league-record 56 homers, Wilson hit 13 of them in August. During the season, the Elgin National Watch Company, based in suburban Chicago, gave a wrist watch to every Cub after he hit a home run. Before Wilson hit No. 30, Schalk told him, "Hacky Smacky, when you hit your 45th, I want the watch." Wilson replied, "I'll give you two." When the time came, he kept his word.[19] Wilson, stocky and strong, was one of the most talented and troubled men in baseball history. Through the 2008 campaign, he still holds the major-league record for runs batted in (191 in 1930). Alcohol was his undoing. It is said that McCarthy once tried to demonstrate for Wilson the dangers of the demon rum. The manager dropped a worm in a glass of water, where the worm wriggled and survived. McCarthy then dropped a worm in a glass of booze, where the worm immediately shriveled and died. "What does that tell you, Hack?" the manager asked. Replied Wilson: "If I keep drinking I won't get worms."[20]

Chicago entered the final month of the season with a five-game lead over New York, with Brooklyn and St. Louis (23–9 in August) close behind. In the heat of the pennant drive, the Cubs cooled off. Over the first three weeks of September they went 9–13. The Cardinals found a higher gear in September, winning 21 out of 25 to bring the pennant to St. Louis. With four games to play, and his team yet to be officially eliminated from the pennant race, a frustrated Veeck announced that in 1931 infielder Rogers Hornsby would replace Joe McCarthy as manager. McCarthy, whose team had just won two straight and sat three losses behind the Cardinals with four games remaining, initially planned to complete the season but then asked to be released from that responsibility. Under Hornsby, the team swept its final four games, but it was too little too late. The Cubs finished second, two games behind the Cardinals.

After winning those final six regular-season games, the Cubs won the City Series in six games. They beat the White Sox in Game 5 and Game 6 by identical 6–4 scores, with Wilson hitting homers in each contest. The finale was in Comiskey Park, where Sox fans occasionally tossed fruit at Wilson. Entering the ninth, the Sox held a 4–3 lead. In the top of that frame, Wilson, who homered in the fifth, ripped a key single that set up a game-tying sacrifice fly. The Cubs scored twice more and sent the fruit-throwers home disappointed. The City Series title brought each member of the Cubs an additional $1,235.71. The Sox had to settle for $769.35.[21]

McCarthy's departure was probably a positive for Schalk. It meant he would have more responsibility. Hornsby asked Schalk to stay on as a coach for 1931 and work with the pitchers.[22] His starters were Charlie Root, Bob Smith, Pat Malone and Guy Bush. Meanwhile, McCarthy landed on his feet. He managed the New York Yankees from 1931 until early in 1946, during which time his teams appeared in eight World Series — and won seven of them.

Schalk's off-season included a visit to the Tivoli Theater, about 16 blocks from his bowling emporium on the South Side, where he was guest of honor. Several Cubs players, including Wilson, Hartnett and Kiki Cuyler, were appearing as a "revue." The feature film at the Tivoli was *The Spoilers*, starring Gary Cooper.[23] Schalk's city was becoming a more violent place. Prohibition-era bootlegging was rising and the economy declining. The newspapers routinely published accounts of shootings and raids on liquor violators. Chicago's homicide rate, 10.5 per 100,000 residents in 1920, had jumped to 14.6 by 1930. By 1940, after Prohibition had been gone a half-dozen years, the homicide rate had dropped by more than half (7.1).[24]

After their pennant in 1929 and fade into second in 1930, the 1931 Cubs could not muster another pennant drive. A "highlight" of the season for Schalk came in Chicago July 18, when he raised such a fuss over umpire Ted McGrew's fair-foul call on a grounder that he not only received an ejection but a $50 fine from the league. (Hornsby received the same punishment for the same incident.)[25] The team imploded under internal strife. Hard-drinking Hack Wilson, a headache for Hornsby throughout the year, in early September was suspended for the balance of the season. The final straw was Wilson standing by while one of Schalk's pitchers, Pat Malone, pummeled two sportswriters at a Cincinnati railroad depot. The victims were Harold Johnson of the *Chicago American* and Wayne K. Otto of the *Herald-Examiner*. Said Hornsby, "Malone's attack on two baseball writers was one of the most disgraceful I have ever encountered in the game." Neither Malone nor Wilson appealed his suspension.[26] The 1931 Cubs finished third, 17 games behind the Cardinals, who repeated as National League champs and avenged their World Series loss to Connie Mack's Philadelphia Athletics. The Cubs, 84–70 in the regular season, were favored in the City Series against the White Sox, who finished last in the American League (56–97). Schalk hardly recognized his former team. The 1931 White Sox roster included only a half-dozen players who were on the team when he exited as manager in 1928, including lifelong friends Red Faber and Ted Lyons. In the series, Faber won twice as the White Sox surprised the Cubs in seven games.

After two seasons coaching for the Cubs, Schalk resigned. He set his sights on new opportunities.

26

❖

Shuffle Off to Buffalo

After he left the Cubs, Schalk wanted to buy a minor-league club. Pants Rowland, his friend and former manager, had purchased the Reading (Pennsylvania) ballclub of the International League in late 1930, and some speculated that Schalk would invest in the Reading operation or buy the bankrupt Toledo Mud Hens of the American Association.[1] Cracker attended the minor leagues' winter meeting, where he offered $150,000 for the last-place Mud Hens providing he didn't have to assume any of the current ownership's debts.[2] If he bought the team, his first order of business would be to hire a manager, since Casey Stengel, who had piloted the Mud Hens the previous six seasons, departed to coach in Brooklyn. Schalk's bid for Toledo fell short. The Cleveland Indians bought the team on a one-year option, giving the Indians their first farm team.[3]

Schalk found another opportunity. Frank Offerman, owner of the last-place Buffalo Bisons of the International League, hired Schalk as manager. Apparently learning his lesson from his lax administration of the White Sox, Schalk put his players on notice. "There will be no loafing among the Bisons and indifferent work will not be tolerated," he said. The 39-year-old Schalk added that, if needed, he would fill in as catcher. Buffalo's downfall in 1931 was pitching, and that was where Schalk could be expected to help. Assisting Schalk would be coach Jocko Munch.[4] Schalk also hired Alfred J. Ferry as a scout. Schalk respected Ferry's judgment; after all, in 1911 it was Ferry who first recommended to the Detroit Tigers a teen-age catcher named Schalk.[5] The Buffalo roster included one familiar name: The catcher was Schalk's former backup with the White Sox, Buck Crouse.

The 1932 Bisons improved under Schalk, advancing from worst in the International League to pennant contender before slipping to third place (91–75). Buffalo fans and Offerman were thrilled. On Labor Day, the team staged Ray Schalk Day. A couple of weeks later, Schalk signed to manage the Bisons two more seasons.[6]

The Schalk Family (from left): Ray Jr., Ray, Lavinia and Pauline. The happy occasion might have been Ray Schalk Day in Buffalo, at the conclusion of the 1932 campaign, Ray's first as manager of the Bisons (*Buffalo News*).

Schalk and his family returned to Chicago for the winter of 1932–33. Just after New Year's Day, he received word from Philadelphia that Kid Gleason, former White Sox coach and manager, died at age 66. The occasion was particularly emotional for Schalk. As a White Sox rookie, he learned the finer points of catching from Gleason, then a coach and later manager. That winter also marked the death of Chicago Mayor Anton Cermak, who in Miami died of a gunshot intended for President-elect Franklin D. Roosevelt. On his way to the hospital, the critically wounded Cermak said to FDR, "I'm glad it was me and not you."[7]

During spring training 1933 in Fort Lauderdale, Schalk crossed paths with *Chicago Tribune* sportswriter Harvey T. Woodruff. The two men sat and reminisced for a while, and Schalk did something rare — discuss the Black Sox series of 1919. Unfortunately, or perhaps by agreement, Woodruff printed nothing from the conversation.[8] However, Woodruff shared some insight on the personal impact of national and international events. The Great Depression was in full force, with some 13 million Americans unemployed. Inaugurated as president earlier in the month, Roosevelt declared a "bank holiday" to stop panic-fueled runs on banks and to sort out which financial institutions would survive. "Daughter Alberta ... sent us an air mail special delivery letter saying the Evanston bank in which were deposited the family funds to run the cottage during our absence and to provide for our return trip has not gone back to work after the holiday," Woodruff wrote. "She said $30 was due the maid, $15 to the laundress, and she had no money, so what should she do. We had no idea, so we wired her, 'Just be brave and you'll grow up a good woman.'"[9]

In early April, Schalk paid a call upon President Roosevelt. He secured FDR's autograph on his special baseball. The signatures of William Howard Taft, Warren G. Harding, Calvin Coolidge and Herbert Hoover already appeared on the ball.[10] More signatures awaited.

After vaulting into respectability the previous season, the 1933 Buffalo Bisons (83–85) slipped to second in their half of the two-division International League regular-season standings. But they made the four-team playoffs, and they made the most of it, beating Baltimore before topping Rochester in the championship round. With a city-record 24,000 fans jamming the home ballpark, Schalk's Bisons swept Rochester for the International League crown and the right to face Columbus, the American Association champion, in the best-of-nine Little World Series. Buffalo's magic ran out, and Columbus prevailed in eight games.

After the season, Schalk was back in Chicago. In early October, he attended the funeral of Cubs president William L. Veeck, who as sportswriter Bill Bailey led the wedding-gift fund drive for Ray and Vin back in 1916. Meanwhile, Cracker might have taken in a game or two of the 1933 City Series, where the Sox swept the Cubs. Later that month, his parents visited from Litchfield to take in the massive Chicago World's Fair.[11] In addition to looking after his bowling center, Schalk found time to relax with friends. He attended Chicago Blackhawks hockey games regularly; former White Sox associates Louis Comiskey and Rowland occasionally went along.[12] That winter, he attended a Hot Stove League banquet at the Palmer House, playfully entering the banquet hall arm-in-arm with his friend and long-time batterymate Red Faber.[13]

Coming off their International League playoff championship, the 1934 Bisons failed to post a winning record (76–77) or make the post-season. Still, owner Offerman offered Schalk another contract. Probably in light of the Depression economy and the team's slip in the standings, the contract was for one season only and at a salary below Schalk's previous two-year deal.[14]

In the winter of 1934–35, Schalk made an early departure for Florida, where he served on the faculty of Max Carey's baseball school in Miami.[15] Vin and their children joined him for part of Buffalo's 1935 spring training in the Sunshine State. One day, Schalk's business partner Ben Stevenson visited Cracker in Florida. Driving back to his hotel, Stevenson crashed into some cows standing on the roadway. The car careened into a Florida swamp, but Stevenson escaped serious injury.[16]

The Bisons manager expected lots of fight in his players, and he didn't hesitate to provide an example. On May 11 in Buffalo, Schalk and Baltimore manager Guy Sturdy engaged in a first-inning fistfight at the edge of the visitors' dugout. In the top of the first, Sturdy complained that Buffalo pitcher Ed Holley tried to hit Irv Jeffries. As Schalk walked to the third-base coach's box for the bottom of the first, the managers exchanged words. The 5-foot-7 Schalk moved the argument to the edge of the Baltimore dugout, where he and the 6-foot Sturdy got physical. "It was a typical ball players fight — plenty of swinging and cussing, but no damage," reporter Frank Wakefield mused.[17] Both managers were ejected, and Sturdy picked up a $50 fine for what the umpire termed "obstreperous conduct" before exiting.[18] It would not be the last time Schalk used his fists on a ball field. The 1935 Bisons fought their way to third place in the International League (86–67) before bowing out in the first round of the playoffs. Their manager was hired back for 1936.

The Schalks kept their Chicago apartment but lived in Buffalo during the summer, after the children's school year ended. Eighteen-year-old Pauline and 14-year-old Ray Jr. received positive treatment in a 1936 *Buffalo Times* feature story on the family. That the siblings were civil to each other in the presence of reporter Ethel M. Hoffman means they either masked their real feelings or their decades-long estrangement had yet to bloom. A student at University of Chicago High School, Pauline indicated that her career options included being an athletic director. However, the star of the feature story was Vin. "You like her instantly. Her handclasp is warm and her dark eyes are friendly," Hoffman wrote. "Her black bob is streaked with grey and she looks a little like (evangelist) Aimee Semple McPherson minus the angel toga." The man of the house was not around for the interview. He was at work at the Buffalo ballpark, and Lavinia was missing the day's game because she didn't like streetcars and the family auto was not available.

Mrs. Schalk offered some insight on her emotions as a baseball wife. "One of the first things I learned after I married Mr. Schalk was that I would have to sit back and listen to people booing the team and not boo back. It seems hard, too. In the theater, if you don't like the stars' performance, you get up and leave. If you tried any other means of criticism, the ushers would act. But in baseball, the fans are always right. I still blaze inside, however, when people boo the boys. They're doing their best — every one of them. And they can hear a good deal of what is being said about them in the grandstand, too." A doorbell interrupted the Depression-era interview. "A beggar was at the door," Hoffman wrote. "He went away palming some silver. 'That's the third one today. I suppose they have this house marked, but somehow I can't turn them away,' said Mrs. Schalk, rather apologetically." The article also revealed that Vin was an avid (thrice-weekly) bowler, a knitter and a movie-goer. Further, she was prone to car-sickness. Though she considered the people of Buffalo friendly, Vin Schalk admitted she was anxious to get home to Chicago. One complication, she confessed, might be dealing with their land-lord when the family returned to town with a dog — a gift from a Buffalo fan.[19]

On June 29, 1936, the Bisons were 43–31, in third place and 4½ games behind Newark. During July, they gained a place in the standings but lost a game to the new league leader, Rochester. Then the Bisons staged a breath-taking rally in the pennant drive. They posted a 22–4 mark over a three-week stretch and grabbed the International League regular-season title, extending their lead over Rochester to 8½ games before coasting to a 94–60 finish, 5½ games ahead.[20]

In the league playoffs' best-of-seven semifinals, Buffalo defeated Newark in five games. In the finals, the Bisons battled Baltimore — figuratively and literally. Schalk was in the middle of it. Buffalo was losing 8–6 and down to its final out in Game 4 in Baltimore. The Orioles were in the process of bring-ing in a relief pitcher for starter Cliff Melton, who had been the target of Schalk's taunts from the third-base coach's box all game. Schalk hollered something more at Melton, and the Baltimore hurler hurled the baseball at Schalk. He missed, but he immediately afterward connected with a fist to Schalk's face. The 44-year-old manager tangled with the 24-year-old Melton, who stood nearly a foot taller. Players from both teams rushed in, and soon there were fans streaming onto the field. Melton and Schalk were ejected. It took about 15 minutes, and police intervention, before the game resumed long enough for the Orioles to collect the game's final out for a series-tying victory.[21] After the skirmish, Melton displayed on his shoulder bite marks; he claimed they came from Schalk. (It was Melton's second melee of the post-season, the first having come a week earlier against Rochester.)

Eventually, Buffalo defeated Baltimore in the series to earn another trip to the Little World Series, against Schalk's team of long ago, the Milwaukee Brewers. In an apparent move to save time and travel expenses, the schedule for the best-of-seven series put the first three games in Wisconsin. Before the opener, long-time Milwaukee fans, recalling that a quarter-century earlier they cheered for a teenage catcher named Schalk, presented Cracker with a

Two managers who brought championships to the state of New York in 1936 are
honored at a banquet. Joe McCarthy (left), a Buffalo resident in the off-season,
managed the New York Yankees to American League and World Series titles,
while Schalk guided Buffalo to an International League championship. Schalk
coached for McCarthy's Cubs in 1930 (*Buffalo News*).

floral tribute. There, the hospitality stopped. The Brewers beat Buffalo all
three games in Milwaukee. The Bisons staved off a series sweep with a 2–1
win in New York, but the Brewers wrapped up the Little World Series the
next night, 8–3. One oddity of the series' five games was that it featured two
triple plays, one by each team.

    While his Bisons staged one of the game's best stretch runs anywhere, a
Schalk business endeavor back in Chicago was taking root. In partnership with

retired meat dealer George Foell, he commissioned construction of a one-story business block. The site, on the northwest corner of 94th and Ashland, included four stores and a bowling facility. The project's cost was estimated at $140,000. Schalk and Foell's general contractor was William Wightman, who partnered with Schalk on a housing project a decade earlier.[22] On October 25, 1936, a rainy Sunday, nearly 1,000 people turned out for the formal opening of Beverly Recreation bowling center.[23] In 1938, the partners hired Lou Barbour, former White Sox traveling secretary.[24] Schalk sold his interest in the Beverly Recreation operation to Foell in 1940. In January 1943, fire struck the bowling alley. The flames and a subsequent explosion killed six people and injured at least 73, including the owner's wife, Helen Foell.[25] The toll would have been lower if many of the victims had not stayed inside to watch the early stages of the fire.[26]

A few days before Beverly Recreation's 1936 grand opening in Chicago, Schalk was in Buffalo for a banquet honoring a former boss, manager Joe McCarthy. His Yankees that month beat the Giants for another World Series title. McCarthy owned a home in Buffalo and was extremely popular with the locals. The banquet featured George M. Cohan as master of ceremonies and Warren Brown, the Chicago sportswriter and McCarthy friend, was toastmaster. Also in attendance were Yankees star Lou Gehrig; Dr. Allan Roy Dafoe, who gained fame in 1934 as the obstetrician who delivered the Dionne quintuplets; and Buffalo native and polo star Shorty Knox.[27]

Tobacco smoke created a haze throughout the banquet hall. Schalk no doubt contributed with the byproduct of his cigars. Smoking at athletics-based events was not considered unusual, and athletes routinely endorsed tobacco products. R.J. Reynolds Tobacco Co. placed a large notice in *The Sporting News* featuring leading athletes espousing the benefits of smoking: "For Digestion's Sake ... Smoke Camels!" Golfer Tony Manero, bowler Johnny Murphy and multi-sport athlete Mary Carter offered testimonials how cigarettes eased their digestion. "Since I've learned how pleasant Camels make my mealtime, I wouldn't be without them," stated Ms. Carter. "They never get on my nerves."[28]

Schalk's sixth and final season in Buffalo, 1937, was a let-down from the previous campaign's championship excitement. The Bisons went 74–79 to finish fifth and out of the playoffs. Schalk resigned. His contract was up anyway, and new challenges awaited.

27

Indianapolis and Milwaukee

Once again, Schalk was not out of a baseball job long. On Thanksgiving Eve 1937, he signed a one-year contract with Norman A. Perry to manage the Indianapolis Indians of the Class AA American Association. Two days later, Leo T. Miller resigned as Buffalo's business manager and followed him to Indianapolis.[1] Schalk succeeded Wade "Red" Killefer — his brother Bill was a former manager of the Chicago Cubs — to return to the West and become general manager of Hollywood in the Pacific Coast League.

Schalk inherited a team that in 1937 finished sixth in the eight-team league (67–85).[2] During the winter he put his new charges on notice: At training camp, wives and automobiles would be off-limits.[3] Schalk's Indians trained in Bartow, Florida.[4] When they opened the regular season at home, pre-game festivities included about 100 people parading around the field and displaying a banner, "RAY SCHALK'S BOOSTERS OF CHICAGO." The new manager's fans were treated to an exciting Opening Day in Indianapolis. With his team trailing Minneapolis 4–2 in the bottom of the ninth, pinch-hitter Buck Fausett hit a two-run, inside-the-park homer to tie the game. Later, Glenn Chapman, who needed a double to hit for the cycle, settled for a game-winning single.[5] Minneapolis enjoyed payback in mid–July, when Stanley Spence hit a long drive that tucked inside the foul pole for a game-winning homer. Schalk, coach Wes Griffin and several Indianapolis players surrounded umpire Charley Johnson and vehemently argued that the ball was foul. The argument included some shoving. When American Association President George M. Trautman heard about it, he suspended Schalk for three games. Trautman also fined Griffin, third baseman Steve Mesner, catcher Bill Baker and first baseman Bob Latshaw; the sum of the four men's fines was $35.[6] Schalk found himself on the outs with umpires later in the season. Described by Chicago sportswriter Arch Ward as "one of the quietest chaps in the game," he received ejections twice in a single week.[7]

After the Independence Day games, Indianapolis topped the American

Association by a half-game over St. Paul and two games over Kansas City. However, things started to unravel later in the month, when the Indians showed the effects of several key injuries and the loss of leading pitcher Vance Page, who was traded to the Chicago Cubs.[8] Instead of contending for the league title, the Indians were just hoping to hold onto a first-division finish and a spot in the playoffs. They caught a break when Trautman removed a Toledo victory from the official standings; it came in a make-up of a late-season game originally rained out in Louisville. Toledo and last-place Louisville played the game in Toledo as part of a doubleheader. Trautman threw out the Mud Hens' victory because the arrangements for the make-up game lacked league approval; the decision hurt Toledo's playoff bid.

Schalk resigned after six seasons managing Buffalo (1932-37). Within a couple of months, he agreed to manage the Indianapolis Indians of the American Association (photograph courtesy Lillian Hendricks).

For much of the season, the Indianapolis manager had a special assistant—his son and namesake. Ray Jr., who was making a name for himself on prep ball fields, accompanied his dad on many road trips.[9] The Indians nearly blew a six-run lead in their final game, but held on to win the contest and to edge Toledo by a half-game for the last playoff berth.[10] Trautman's decision to remove that Toledo victory in the make-up contest made the difference. In the playoffs, however, Indianapolis fell to Kansas City in six games.[11]

Schalk's success in Buffalo and Indianapolis raised the possibility of him returning to manage in the major leagues. He interviewed for the job of leading the hapless St. Louis Browns. The location, near his hometown, had a special appeal for Schalk. However, the rebuilding task would be formidable. As sportswriter Joe Williams described the Browns, "They can't do anything that is going to hurt them, they are that bad." Yet Browns owners Donald Barnes and William DeWitt would offer Schalk no more than a one-year contract to get it done. He turned them down and returned to Indianapolis.[12] Fred Haney took the job running the 1939 Browns, and the team responded by going 43–111 in 1939—among the 10 worst records of the 20th century.

Indianapolis was back in the American Association pennant chase in 1939. However, Schalk and the front office were not seeing things eye-to-eye. Yet, that friction did not seem to affect the team. In one stretch, from late June to mid–July, Indianapolis went 17–6 and won seven straight.[13] An entry went into the league record books July 10 when the Indians recorded only one assist in their win over Milwaukee.[14] The hot streak pulled Indianapolis into third place (49–43). Right then, at the league's All-Star break, Schalk resigned, citing differences with his bosses. (Some reports pointed to Leo Miller, who had been elevated from business manager to president of the Indians, but others stated Schalk was forced out over Miller's objections. It should be noted that Schalk agreed to work for Miller again a decade later. More likely, the source of Schalk's discontent was owner Norman Perry.[15]) In any case, as coach Wes Griffin took over the club, Schalk returned to his home in Chicago. The *Daily News* the next day carried a photo of the former manager relaxing (wearing suit and tie) in his living room, with a smiling Vin resting her hand on his left shoulder and daughter Pauline lighting his cigar.[16]

Schalk's abrupt departure brought him attention from reporters, and he used the opportunity to express his opinion that baseball lacked a sufficient supply of capable ball players — especially catchers. "There's a terrible lack of good ball players in the minor leagues all over the country," he said. He added that the situation was becoming apparent in the big leagues. "When I was playing, the American League alone had Cy Perkins, Steve O'Neill, Muddy Ruel, Wally Schang, Johnny Bassler and Bill Carrigan," he told the *Los Angeles Times*. "Now they have (Bill) Dickey."[17] Had he assessed the National League side of the ledger, Schalk might have mentioned Chicago's Gabby Hartnett. Schalk's employment status allowed him to be present at Wrigley Field to personally offer Hartnett congratulations for breaking his major-league record for catching appearances. (As it turned out, *The Sporting News* discovered that the celebration was premature. Somewhere along the line, someone miscalculated. Hartnett's games as a pinch-hitter were somehow lumped in with his catching appearances, and someone forgot to include Schalk's five appearances in the National League in 1929. Thus, Hartnett needed another 10 catching appearances to break Schalk's record of 1,727.[18] He got them, and went on to register 1,792 games behind the plate.[19])

Schalk's open schedule might have allowed him to pay a few visits on Ray Jr., who, in the fall of 1939 entered DePauw University in Greencastle, Indiana, about 50 miles west of Indianapolis. After an outstanding pitching career at Hyde Park High School, young Ray earned DePauw varsity letters in baseball three seasons (1941–43) as an outfielder and pitcher.[20]

Old Ray apparently learned a lesson from his 1928 salary dispute with

Charles Comiskey after his forced resignation as White Sox manager. The Indians agreed to keep sending him paychecks for the balance of the 1939 season (unless another baseball job came along).[21] That fall, he was considered for a vacancy to manage the Eastern League team at Williamsport (Pennsylvania), a Philadelphia Athletics farm team.[22] That did not occur — former Phillies infielder and future Dodgers general manager Fresco Thompson got the job — and Schalk spent the first half of the 1940 season on the sidelines.

In July 1940 in the seventh inning of a 6–5 loss to visiting Columbus, Milwaukee Brewers manager Mike Heath assigned himself to pinch-hit for his pitcher. He went down on strikes, disputing the calls of an umpiring nemesis, one Mr. Teban. Heath put up such a squawk that Teban tossed him from the game. Immediately afterward, Heath resigned as manager of the last-place team. His departure could not have been voluntary or a surprise to Milwaukee management. Between Heath's termination and the next afternoon's contest, Schalk was signed, brought to town for pictures and fitted for a uniform. A year and three days after abruptly leaving Indianapolis, Schalk was back in the game and back in Milwaukee, the city from which he made his jump to the major leagues in 1912. His contract covered the balance of the 1940 season.[23]

If Brewers boosters expected Schalk to work miracles in the second half of the season, they were disappointed; the residents of Borchert Field went 24–44 on his watch and stayed in the American Association basement. His stint in Milwaukee ended. Succeeding him was former Chicago Cubs manager Bill Killefer, the brother of the man Schalk had succeeded in Indianapolis, Wade Killefer.[24]

Now 48 years old, Schalk turned his full attention to his business endeavors and family milestones.

28

Businessman, Volunteer and Celebrity

Soon after completing his fill-in stint as manager of the Milwaukee Brewers, Schalk learned of the death of friend Charley Straight, a noted composer, pianist and orchestra leader. The Chicagoan performed around the world and produced such contemporary hits as "My Rose of Old Kildare," "I Love You Sunday," and "Everybody Calls Me Honey." However, the Depression and slow bookings in September prompted Straight to take a temporary job as a water sampler for the Chicago Sanitary District. Working near a manhole on a Sunday evening, Straight was struck by a 19-year-old's vehicle and killed. Straight was also a baseball fan, and he became friends with several White Sox figures, including Red Faber, Pants Rowland and Schalk, who lived less than a mile from the Straight apartment.[1]

Ray and Lavinia Schalk's daughter, Pauline, married Harry T. Osolin. By January 1941, the couple had set up housekeeping at 8233 Ingleside, just a 10- to 15-minute drive from her parents' residence.[2] Before their first anniversary, the United States entered World War II. Osolin served in the Army and as late as March 1946 he was a captain stationed in Paris. While he was overseas, Pauline lived with her parents and worked as a service representative for Illinois Bell Telephone Co.[3] At some point afterward, Pauline and Harry's marriage failed.

In 1941, the year after selling his interest in the Beverly Recreation Center, Schalk built bigger and better. He constructed a massive complex at 95th Street and Maplewood Avenue in the Chicago south suburb of Evergreen Park. Covering a full block, the facility included three dozen bowling lanes, a dozen billiards tables, lounge, restaurant and space for shops and offices. It was built in less than five months and opened September 19. Though his new recreation facility consisted of only one level, Schalk named it Evergreen Towers.

While workers constructed Evergreen Towers, Ray and Vin moved from an apartment at 6830 Chappel Avenue, near their first bowling alley, to 9229

Damen Avenue, about seven miles south and west. The residence was in the Beverly neighborhood (also known as Beverly Hills). With its newer construction and tree-lined streets, Beverly was an area to which many middle-class families aspired. The Schalks lived on Damen a couple of years and then move to a single-family home in Beverly, 8945 S. Oakley Avenue. It would be his final address.

Out of professional baseball for the time being, Ray devoted much of his energy toward Evergreen Towers. It became a popular site for league play, tournaments and charity exhibitions. His brother "Jersey" never found his way to a career, so Ray found a spot for him on the bowling alley payroll.[4] Jersey had the same girlfriend for two or three decades, but never married.[5] Ray found time to volunteer in support of baseball, kibitz with his cronies and get involved in community projects and events. He staged and played in many celebrity bowling exhibitions, and enjoyed rounds of golf at the Beverly Country Club and other South Side courses.

Schalk was a regular guest at service, civic and business club meetings. Speaking to a businessmen's group in 1941, he rated Ed Walsh the best pitcher he ever caught, followed by his friend Faber and Black Sox figure Eddie Cicotte.[6] Schalk was a regular (often with Faber) at Hot Stove League banquets, including those staged by the Old Timers' Baseball Association of Chicago and Chicago Baseball Writers. In 1947, he and former Cubs catcher Jimmy Archer were the featured guests at the Old Timers' 29th annual banquet.[7] He joined the advisory board of the Metropolitan Amateur Baseball League, whose commissioner was Archer. Another member of the advisory panel was a former New York Giants outfielder who made his mark in another sport: George Halas, founder of the National Football League and the Chicago Bears.[8] Cracker visited hospital patients, especially men wounded in the war, and backed boys' baseball and girls' softball activities. He got back into uniform and visited Comiskey Park in July 1944 when he, along with Faber and other former White Sox greats, sold war bonds. That same month, he and ex-batterymate Joe Benz played a few innings of softball with the Longwood Tavern team, which squeaked out a 23–22 win over the squad from Mike King's Tavern; the celebrity appearance swelled the crowd to an estimated 600.[9]

While continuing most of those activities, Schalk reconnected with professional baseball in mid-1944, when he signed on as a scout for the Chicago Cubs. Later that season, he saw his American League record for most catching appearances in a season (151 out of 154 games in 1920) broken by Frank Hayes of Philadelphia (all 155, including one tie contest).[10] In 1946, Schalk went to New York City to manage a national group of young all-stars in a benefit game staged by the *New York Journal-American* in the Polo Grounds. Before a crowd of nearly 16,000, his team lost to retired star Rabbit Maranville's squad in 11 innings. Bill Klem served as an umpire. In the post-game ceremony, 18-year-old Dimitrios "Jim" Baxes, of San Francisco, accepted the Most Valuable Player trophy from the widow of Lou Gehrig.[11] Despite this national notoriety, Baxes did not reach the major leagues until he was 30 years old, in 1959, when he saw limited action with the Los Angeles Dodgers and then Cleveland.

Meanwhile, in her spare time, Vin volunteered with an organization supporting Chicago's Martha Washington Home for Dependent Crippled Children. In the 1940s, she served several terms as a vice president.[12] She also helped Ray with the business end of his bowling enterprises.[13]

During the winter of 1946–47, an official of the Purdue University athletic department called Schalk with a question. Did he know someone who might be interested in serving as an assistant coach for the university's baseball program? When the men talked again a few days later, Schalk answered yes, he had a suggestion: Ray Schalk. In early March 1947, Athletic Director Guy Mackey hired him to be a part-time assistant coach on Mel Taube's staff.

In 1947, Schalk and former Cubs catcher Jimmy Archer were the honored guests at the annual banquet of the Old Timers' Baseball Association of Chicago and Chicago Baseball Writers (Old Timers Baseball Association of Chicago).

A multi-sport star at Purdue who became head basketball coach the year before, Taube was now adding baseball to his coaching chores. Taube needed the help. At the initial tryout for the 1947 season, some 200 players showed up. "This is not a baseball squad," Schalk quipped, "it's an army."[14] The Purdue opportunity involved his temporary relocation to West Lafayette, Indiana, some 115 miles from home, for three months each spring, during which Vin stayed in Chicago. Ray enjoyed campus life and working with collegiate players. His initial three-month appointment paid $2,000.[15] The arrangement suited him, and Purdue officials liked his work, even though their baseball teams rarely had winning seasons. After nearly a decade with Purdue, Schalk expressed some disappointment that he had been unable to develop an outstanding catcher to reach the major leagues.[16] The best player to emerge from the Boilermakers program was Chicago native Bill "Moose" Skowron, who went on to a 14-year major-league career that included eight World Series and four All-Star games.

Schalk assisted at Purdue for 18 springs. He was known to get into uniform hours before practices, anxious to get back onto the ball field. After four baseball seasons at Purdue (52–40–3), Taube departed for Carleton College in Minnesota. His successor at Purdue had something in common with Assistant Coach Schalk: Each became a Hall of Famer. Schalk entered Cooperstown in 1955. The head coach? He is enshrined in another Hall. The coach was Hank Stram, a Purdue assistant football coach who went on to coach a Super Bowl winner (Kansas City Chiefs, 1969–70). Stram entered the Pro Football Hall of Fame in 2003. He and Schalk remained close throughout Cracker's lifetime. By the mid–1960s, when Schalk was in his 70s and Stram was winning American Football League titles, a vote of the Purdue trustees was required to approve the part-time assistant's continued employment because he had passed official retirement age.[17] Schalk's presence on campus was not limited to the baseball season. Ray and Lavinia rarely missed Boilermakers football games.

After his fourth spring with Purdue, in 1950, Schalk received a call to return to the professional ranks. His former team in Buffalo was having a first-to-worst season. The Bisons had won the International League under Paul Richards but were now in the cellar under Frank Skaff, whose team was 15–32 and had lost 10 of its previous 13 contests.[18] In mid–June, Schalk's former general manager from his days in Buffalo and Indianapolis, Leo Miller, decided to replace Skaff. As he had nearly a decade earlier in Milwaukee, the 57-year-old Schalk agreed to fill out one season as manager. He inherited a last-place team and emerged at the end of the season with ... a last-place team. The Bisons had a .319 winning percentage under Skaff; under Schalk they improved slightly (.386). That stint concluded Schalk's official connection to professional baseball. In a letter to friends after the season, he let it be known that he was not returning to Buffalo in 1951; whether that was his decision or Miller's, he did not say.[19]

Schalk was not much for public pronouncements on politics, but in 1950 he did join former Notre Dame football star Ziggy Czarobski in endorsing John J. Duffy, Democratic candidate for president of the Cook County (Illinois) Board. Though it seems unheard-of today, after decades of Daley Democrats' dominance in Chicago politics, Duffy did lose the race to the Republican, William Erickson. Still, backing the Democrat could not have hurt Schalk's chances when Mayor Richard J. Daley needed someone to run his Youth Foundation's baseball program.

Meanwhile, Schalk's Evergreen Towers bowling center remained a viable enterprise, and the owner took an active role. Lou Barbour, former traveling secretary of the White Sox, hired in 1939, was his No. 2 man; and Schalk's brother Jersey helped out in the office. The morning of June 7, 1948, minutes after the enterprise opened for the day, a half-dozen men walked in through the back entrance. They approached soda fountain and checkroom clerk Dorothy Hoffman and asked for Schalk by name. When she told them that he was in his office, they pulled out guns. They demanded that Hoffman take them to him.

Thus began an hour-long drama in which more than 50 men and women were held hostage. While some of his compatriots stood guard and rounded up prisoners, the ringleader pointed his gun at Schalk and demanded that he open the safe. The plot stalled when Schalk convinced the robbers that he did not know the safe's combination; no one on site did. Only Barbour, who had yet to arrive for work, knew the secret numbers. "We'll wait for Lou," the robber in charge stated. "Just behave yourselves and no one will get hurt." While the 36-year-old Mrs. Hoffman was allowed to sit, Schalk and three male employees — the alley man, porter and handyman — were made to stand with their faces to the office wall. Meanwhile, out in the bowling center, other robbers herded about two dozen terrified pin boys into the basement, where they were locked into an air-tight liquor vault. Other people walking into Evergreen Towers immediately found themselves staring into the barrel of a pistol and following the bearer's orders. The roster of prisoners ushered into Schalk's office included a cook, bartender, refuse collector, ice man, the facility's restaurant owner and his sister, Schalk business partner Grover Lutgert and even the postal carrier on his morning rounds. After a while, Vin Schalk arrived; she, too, was ordered into the office. (Newspaper accounts did not mention whether Jersey Schalk was on the premises.) Eventually, the office became so crowded, the robbers moved some hostages into the basement, where they were locked in a storage room.

The wait continued.

When an unsuspecting Barbour arrived for work, the robbers ordered him to open the safe. They cleaned it out. They also broke open strong boxes in the restaurant and the cocktail lounge. They got $250 from Lutgert's wallet. And they took from Schalk the keys to his 1947 Buick. Issuing the standard warning to stay put and not call authorities, the robbers fled in Schalk's sedan. The take was an estimated $2,450 in cash plus the car. After a few minutes of hearing no activity upstairs, the pin boys, panicked by their airtight surroundings in the liquor vault, broke down the door. They freed the captives in the storage room and cautiously ascended the stairs. No one was hurt in the episode. Later that day, Schalk and Barbour posed for a *Chicago Tribune* photographer. Cigar clenched in his teeth, Schalk crouched by the safe and held a damaged box while Barbour thoughtfully peered over his shoulder. Despite investigations by police and postal inspectors — imprisoning the mail carrier on his rounds was a federal offense — no arrests resulted.[20]

On March 6, 1950, retired umpire Bill Guthrie, who "called 'em as he saw 'em" in the American League (1928–32) and minor leagues for three decades, was found dead in his Halwood Hotel room on the South Side. In poor health for several years, Guthrie, who eked out a wage as a boiler operator for the Chicago Police Department, died of a heart attack. He was 63 — and destitute. His body was removed to a funeral chapel, but there was no one to pay for burial.[21] In stepped Schalk and a handful of other retired ball players. They put up some of their own money and got the American League to donate toward Guthrie's funeral. The former umpire's sorry circumstances inspired Schalk to form Baseball Anonymous, an organization to quietly help down-on-their luck former sports professionals. Less than a month after Guthrie's death, Schalk hosted an organizational meeting at his bowling alley; he was elected Baseball Anonymous president.[22] Friends and ex–Sox Red Faber, Tony Piet and Joe Benz were charter members. Dues were $2 a year. The organization did not limit its assistance to baseball men; it recruited Red Grange and George Halas as board members to represent pro football in Chicago.[23]

In addition to Faber and Benz, Schalk remained close to another former Chicago teammate, Buck Weaver. He was kicked out of baseball for life by Commissioner Landis for having knowledge of the 1919 World Series fix — he sat in on the conspirators' meetings — but was never accused of playing anything less than his best against the Cincinnati Reds that October. Even during the brief period when Schalk revealed anything about the scandal,

Cracker considered only seven players traitors to the White Sox — the eighth man was Buck Weaver. While trying in vain to win reinstatement into baseball's good graces, Weaver occasionally attended the same Hot Stove League events in Chicago as Schalk and Faber.[24] He, Faber and Schalk got together on or near the announcement of Cracker's election to the Hall of Fame. A year later, on the last day of January 1956, Weaver collapsed on a Chicago street and died of a heart attack. He was 65. Schalk expressed regret at his friend's passing but refused to discuss Weaver's link to the Black Sox affair. (Meanwhile, Ty Cobb expressed his opinion that Weaver got a raw deal when banned for life.[25]) Schalk served as a pallbearer for the man he described as the best third baseman he had ever seen.[26]

Within a year of its founding, the Baseball Anonymous roster showed nearly 700 members. Most of the group's acts of assistance and kindness were, as its name suggested, handled anonymously. Its most public — and possibly touching — endeavor came in 1958, when they brought former White Sox pitching great Ed Walsh back to Chicago for an appearance at Comiskey Park. Walsh was 77 years old, in poor health and hurting financially. Back at the site of his pitching heroics, and hearing the cheers of the White Sox fans, Walsh accepted a Baseball Anonymous check.[27] In 1912, when Schalk was a 19-year-old acquisition from Milwaukee, Ed Walsh put him to the test. Skeptical during a practice session that a teenager could handle his spitball and fastball, Walsh offered to start by tossing in easy ones. "Never mind me," Schalk replied sharply. "If you have any speed, I'd like to see it."[28] Ed Walsh Day was one of the last projects of Baseball Anonymous, which faded as player salaries improved and as its mainstays grew older.

29

Turmoil on the Home Front

After three decades in the bowling business, Schalk in 1958 sold his final location, Evergreen Towers, which he opened 17 years earlier. His brother Clarence stayed on as an office assistant. "Jersey" was on the job later that year when he died of a heart attack. He was 59.[1] The youngest of the Schalk siblings was the first to go. The last, Walter, a retired railroad machinist who lived in Alton, Illinois, near St. Louis, died in mid–1984 at age 93.[2] In between them were Leo C. (1883–1968), retired president of the Litchfield Bank and Trust; Minnie Schalk (1885–1967), who never married; and Theresa Schalk Hinton (1887–1976), an employee in the Litchfield city clerk's office.[3]

Back in Litchfield, their parents lived long lives. Their daughter Minnie, described as outspoken and a "typical old maid," resided with them and made their care her full-time occupation. Herman and Sophia's marriage lasted nearly 64 years — until October 1945, when he died at age 89. His widow lived until July 1953, when she was 93. Minnie then moved in with her sister and brother-in-law and later resided in long-term-care accommodations at St. Francis Hospital. Minnie refused to apply for Social Security assistance, telling her siblings in so many words, "I took care of our parents all these years, and now you can take care of me."

When Mr. and Mrs. Ray Schalk visited their hometowns, it was a Big Deal. Trips to Litchfield and Farmersville gave him a chance to show off his new car or the latest jewelry item he had purchased for Vin and to catch up with family and friends. As a young woman who had just married into the family, Lillian Hendricks recalls that, in January 1951, her first impression of the former baseball star was less than positive. Ray was unsmiling and "distant" and apparently irked that his nephew Karl Hendricks' bride was ignorant or unappreciative of his fame. That coolness quickly melted away, helped in part by Lillian's skill in the kitchen. Karl was a hunter, and Lillian's wild duck dinners were a big hit with Ray. After a meal featuring duck, sauerkraut, mashed potatoes and homemade ice cream, he would declare, "That is a Big League dinner!" The evening usually ended with a spirited game of gin rummy.[4]

Though they were for the most part common people, Ray and Vin were also products of his athletic and business success. They had money, and it influenced Vin's views on some issues, such as women working outside the home. Vin opposed it. One evening, after one of her trademark wild duck dinners and a few hands of cards, Lillian announced that she had to turn in because she had to go to work in the morning. Vin challenged her. "Why do you have to have a job? You don't need to work." The wife of her nephew, a Chevrolet dealer, replied that maybe Vin didn't know her financial circumstances and whether she had to work. Decades later, Lillian, who thought the world of Vin, said, "It was her only remark that didn't make sense." Further, Vin was not one to push her children to work or forge their own trails.[5]

Even as adults, Pauline and Ray Jr. did not get along. It was not a relationship one might write off as tensions or rivalries common among juvenile or teen siblings. For that matter, "estranged" described Pauline's relationship with virtually everyone. A relative put it bluntly: "She was a hellcat. She thought everybody else should dance to her tune," a relative observed. Pauline's parents were not immune to her wrath. "She'd rip her mother up one side and down the other."[6]

Sometime after returning from wartime service in Europe, her first husband, Harry Osolin, threw in the towel on the marriage. She begged him not to leave, but he had had enough. By the mid–1950s, Pauline was married to another military veteran, Robert Brinson. He was a partner in his family's business, Brinson Manufacturers Sales, which sold automobile dashboard dials.[7] Pauline and Bob lived in south suburban Palos Park and worshipped at the local Presbyterian church. Bob was involved in the community. In 1960, he accepted the chairmanship of the Palos-Orland YMCA, which set its sights on building its own facility. In the mid–1960s, he became a director of Northlake Bank in suburban Melrose Park. In later years, Bob and Pauline relocated to north suburban Barrington. The Brinsons adopted a son, Roy. Pauline was a stern and possessive mother. "Whatever he did, it wasn't right," the relative recalled. During their visits downstate, mealtimes were punctuated by Pauline's constant admonitions of her young son. "Roy! ... Roy! ... Roy!" No one dared say a thing because, after all, it involved Pauline and she was always right. "It was very sad for all of us to watch."[8] As Roy became an adult, his mother's personality and possessiveness tended to keep prospective girlfriends at a distance.[9] Pauline complained frequently and bitterly that her brother received more attention and consideration from her parents. About that, she actually was right. "It was true. It was so obvious," a relative said. "Vin thought the sun rose and set with him (Ray Junior)."[10]

The younger Ray Schalk had issues of his own, including alcoholism, domestic violence and career frustrations. All that was yet to surface in August 1942, when he enlisted in the U.S. Army Reserve, with induction deferred until he finished college. Ray Junior returned to Indiana for his senior year at DePauw University. An economics major pursuing minors in psychology and history, he lived in the Beta Theta Pi fraternity house and played on the baseball team. DePauw was not a baseball hotbed; its record during Ray Junior's four years was 26–35–1, with no winning campaigns. His senior season, he switched from pitcher to outfield and earned his third straight varsity letter.[11] As the end of the baseball season and spring semester approached, Ray Junior, never a Dean's List performer, found himself one course short of the graduation requirements. (Another member of DePauw Class of 1943 was James Quayle, whose son Dan served as U.S. vice president from 1989 to 1993.) Over the summer and early fall of 1943, Ray Junior fulfilled the requirements for Econ 440, the senior seminar. DePauw awarded his Bachelor of Arts degree off-cycle, in early November 1943; the university accelerated his coursework so he could begin his military service.[12]

Shortly afterward, in a Chicago railroad depot as he was heading to boot camp, Ray Junior met an attractive young woman.[13] Her name was Geraldine Hudson. Like Ray, she was 22. Geraldine was a veteran professional entertainer — one-half of the sister act of acrobatic dancers billed as the Hudson Wonders. From the late 1920s, when they were pre-teens, into the mid–1940s, Chicagoans Helene "Ray" and Geraldine Hudson earned favorable notices across the United States and 40 countries. They entertained in clubs, motion pictures and vaudeville theaters in New York, Chicago, Los Angeles and cities in between. The daughters of a quintessential stage mother, Ray and Geraldine received an early break in 1929, when they secured a long-term contract at the Folies Bergère in Paris; the sisters wound up performing in Europe for two years. A New York entertainment writer in 1935 said of the Hudson Wonders, "Their small-time tag is the only thing not big-time about 'em."[14] He later called them the "two greatest girl eccentric dancers I've ever seen."[15] The reporter became known to millions of Americans as host of a long-running variety show on national television. His name was Ed Sullivan. (Some time later — hopefully, several years later, as Geraldine was but 14 years old on the occasion of those write-ups — Sullivan dated Geraldine a time or two.[16]) In the *Washington Post*, Nelson Bell described the Wonders as "two feminine acrobatic dancers who haven't heard about the law of gravity."[17] Among their Hollywood credits were Cecil B. DeMille's, *Four Frightened People* (1933) and

Edward F. Cline's *See My Lawyer* (1945). They also performed on Broadway; their credits included *Star and Garter* (1942), starring Gypsy Rose Lee. Many nights, they were part of a stage show preceding a theater's screening of a motion picture.

Meanwhile, Ray Junior went to war. The Army private served in the Pacific. He and Gerry corresponded throughout his time in the military. Sometime after his discharge, he married the Geraldine half of the Hudson Wonders. (As it happened, the bride then had multiple Rays in her life — her husband, her father-in-law and her sister.) Unfortunately, theirs was a troubled marriage. He was abusive and alcoholic. Gerry was a vivacious and outgoing woman who nonetheless possessed a down-to-earth quality. Geraldine liked to drink, too, and she had bouts with mental illness. When Ray Junior and Gerry drank, they fought. His downstate Illinois relatives, Ray, Vin, and others, became aware of their "knock-down, drag-out" rows.[18] Those problems were either concealed or yet to emerge when the couple adopted two infants — James in 1959 and Diane in 1960. (The Cook County judge who signed the adoption papers was Otto Kerner, a future Illinois governor and

Lavinia and Ray, shown in August 1961, occasionally attended White Sox games at Comiskey Park (photograph courtesy Lillian Hendricks).

federal judge who would serve prison time on a bribery charge.) When Ray Junior and Gerry brought home their newly adopted Jim, she joined Alcoholics Anonymous. Though she regularly attended AA, her son said, she developed a dependency on medications. Some were prescribed for her emotional problems and some might have been intended to mitigate the physical toll her show-business career took on her body.

Ray Junior enjoyed working at his father's bowling establishments. It gave him a chance to roll a few games, have a few drinks and hang out with the guys. He also liked roofing and other construction work; as a college student on summer break, he helped build Evergreen Towers. Either occupation would have satisfied him. His parents — Ray especially — had other ideas. They wanted him to put his economics degree to use — insurance sales, for example. After all, his father did well in insurance when he was the same age. Eventually, around the time he and Gerry were in the adoption process, Ray Junior acquiesced. He became an agent for Metropolitan Life Insurance Company. But his heart was never in it.

Because of their son and daughter-in-law's problems, Vin and Ray played an important and ongoing role in their grandchildren's lives. More than once, when Ray Junior and Gerry were having an episode of some sort, they drove to their son's home — in south suburban Oak Lawn and then nearby Palos Heights — to retrieve the children. Vin made sure they got to and from school, and Ray took Jim to many of his speaking engagements, baseball clinics and trips to Comiskey Park. As a Little Leaguer, Jim received instruction from two Hall of Famers, his grandfather and Red Faber. Looking back, Jim said he and his sister enjoyed a "sort of storybook relationship" with their Schalk grandparents, who never raised their voices to the children and made their time together "seem like a summer vacation." During actual summer vacation, Ray and Vin took Jim and Diane to their grandparents' old stomping grounds in Litchfield and Farmersville. Grandpa Schalk loved his cigars. But when the smoke bothered Diane and she asked him to put them out, he did so without a fuss. As a young boy, Jim a few times visited the National Baseball Hall of Fame with his grandfather. On one such excursion, Jim and other young relatives of inductees got together by themselves and enjoyed the amenities of the hotel's fancy restaurant. They marveled that relatives of famous ballplayers didn't need money; they just had to tell the waiter who they were. Ray found out about it and explained to young Jim the hard facts: Grandpa would indeed have to pay that bill. Jim visited Cooperstown several times, before and after his grandfather's death. How special those opportunities were, he said, "didn't sink in as much then as they did later on."[19]

As hard as their grandparents tried, though, they could not completely

mask the reality of the children's troubled existence. When she was in condition to do so, Geraldine occasionally volunteered her expertise to perform
in or choreograph church and community productions.[20] Otherwise, she was
a stay-at-home mom (as her mother-in-law wished). She had psychological
problems. Ray Junior was unhappy with his job, unhappy with his marriage
and drinking too many martinis. It was a situation ticketed for tragedy.

30

Cooperstown Calls

When he joined the Chicago White Sox in 1912, Schalk carried the expectation that he would be an outstanding catcher. Before his first full season in Chicago ended in 1913, he attracted accolades. *Baseball Magazine* placed the rookie on its second team for its American League "All-America Club."[1] In just another year or two, Schalk earned mentions as the best catcher currently on a ball field. *Baseball Magazine* promoted him to first team in 1915 and made him a unanimous selection in 1916.[2] Legendary sportswriter Grantland Rice made Schalk a member of his personal all-star team in 1920.[3] Irwin M. Howe, *Chicago Tribune* reporter and the American League's statistician, gave Cracker a similar nod in 1921.[4] Before long, many experts put him in a class of his own — arguably the best player to ever don shin guards, chest protector and mask. As Brian Bell of the *Washington Post* put it a few years after the star's playing days ended, "Schalk is the yardstick by which most catchers are measured nowadays."[5] It was a belief expressed in many quarters over many years during and after his playing career.

An impressive array of athletes, managers, sportswriters and umpires lauded Schalk and placed him on their "all-time" rosters. The list of players includes Hall of Famers Ty Cobb, Babe Ruth, Hugh Jennings and Sam "Wahoo" Crawford, as well as Muddy Ruel, Duffy Lewis and Bill Wambsganss (whose claim to fame was recording the only unassisted triple play in World Series history). Chicago sportswriters Ring Lardner and Warren Brown rated Schalk as arguably the best ever.

Billy Evans, a veteran American League umpire, frequently boosted Cracker in his syndicated newspaper column. In 1930, several years after Schalk played regularly, Evans wrote about the 10 best catchers he had observed in his quarter-century in baseball. He rated Schalk No. 1. "He did not have a great arm, but he was tough to steal against because he had a master mind. Nine times out of 10 he would pick the proper spot for the pitch out. He wasn't a good hitter, but in the pinch was mighty dangerous. However, he came close to being the perfect receiver. He was grace personified back of the bat, rated his pitchers beautifully, was without a peer in catching foul flies and no catcher in all baseball ever put the ball on the runner better than Schalk. He was mighty smart."[6] In another column, Evans explained that Schalk was a "thinker" who was constantly assessing not only his own position and role but those of everyone else on the field.[7]

In one of his books, Ty Cobb stated, "On my All-Time team, I want two catchers, and they are Ray Schalk and Mickey Cochrane. I have to give Bill Dickey almost an equal nod here. All three, tremendous handlers of pitchers, students of batters, and directors of the defense. If Schalk had hit a bit higher, I would have to rank him in a class by himself."[8] Ah, his offense. Would his career batting average of just .253 be too much of an obstacle to win him a place in the National Baseball Hall of Fame?

The Hall inducted its first class in 1936, three years before the dedication of the facility in Cooperstown, New York; baseball mythology says the game was invented there. Three of the five charter inductees were American Leaguers whose careers overlapped Schalk's — Ruth, Cobb and Walter Johnson. (The other two were National League stars Christy Mathewson and Honus Wagner.)

To win election by the writers, players must be retired at least five years but have been active players within the previous 20 years. Active players or those retired less than five years who die are similarly eligible. Inductees are selected by veteran members of the Baseball Writers' Association of America. They set their standards high: "Candidates shall be chosen on the basis of playing ability, integrity, sportsmanship, character, their contribution to the team on which they played and to baseball in general." A former player has to be selected on at least 75 percent of the ballots.[9]

Who is "Hall worthy?" The question makes for interesting and impassioned debates among baseball experts and fans. Since the inception of the Hall of Fame, the official and unofficial standards regarding eligibility — for electors and for honorees — have been moving targets. Members of the Baseball Writers' Association of America — tough graders, by the way — have been involved from the start. Running on a parallel track, there have been an Old-Timers Committee, a Centennial Commission, Veterans Committee and, more recently, Negro Leagues Committee. Their lack of consensus (to put it mildly) on who deserves a place in the Hall of Fame created a double standard that frustrated electors, baseball men and fans. BBWAA electors hardly let anybody in; the complaint was that the Old-Timers let everybody in. Both views were not exactly correct. Many men whose places in Cooperstown are considered "natural" picks fell short of induction the first time their names went before the writers — and, in some cases, many times after that. Nap Lajoie, Cy Young and Tris Speaker had to wait; they entered one year after the charter class. Joe DiMaggio? Say it ain't so — even the Yankee Clipper could not attract 75 percent in 1954. Cubs great Frank Chance, the Peerless Leader, topped the balloting two consecutive years in the mid–1940s but fell short of the magical 75 percent. Jackie Robinson barely slid into Cooperstown in 1962, qualifying with just 2 percent to spare. "The electoral process moves with the approximate speed of a glacier," elector Arthur Daley of the *New York Times* observed. "That's as it should be, however, because Cooperstown loses its value once it becomes as simple as joining the Elks."[10]

In December 1935, less than a decade after Schalk retired as a player, the names of 33 "immortals" were announced for the ballot to be the Hall's inaugural class. Schalk's name was absent. The only catchers listed were Roger Bresnahan, whose playing career spanned 1897–1915, Lew Criger (1896–1912) and Mickey Cochrane, an active player who had just completed his 11th year in the majors.[11] A week later, apparently in response to public criticism of the list, the ballot added seven players; Schalk was among the additions. (Of the seven, four were catchers from Chicago: Johnny Kling, Gabby Hartnett, Billy Sullivan, and Schalk.) It didn't matter much; none of the seven won selection as an "immortal." Poll director Henry P. Edwards defended the electoral process, stating that any player in any position was eligible; all he needed for admission to the Hall was 75 percent of the votes.[12]

In 1953, the Baseball Hall of Fame Committee on Veterans replaced the Old-Timers Committee. This new committee would consider veterans of at least 10 seasons who played before World War II (plus 1942) and who had been retired as players at least 21 years.[13] In its first election, to the chagrin of the writers, the new Veterans Committee packed another half-dozen into the Hall (including umpire Bill Klem). After that, the Veterans Committee was limited to two picks every other year. Schalk would remain on the writers' ballot through 1955, but the Veterans Committee represented an alternative route to Cooperstown. Considering his low batting average, he would need it.

It is a cliché, perhaps, but it's true: Much of Schalk's contribution to the White Sox did not show up in box scores. The bases that opponents didn't steal, because they knew it was risky to run on Cracker. The extra bases that weren't lost when a Chicago infielder's throw eluded the first baseman, because Schalk was running along and backing up the play. The cajoling and coaching he gave White Sox pitchers, and whose pitch calls helped his hurlers escape trouble. The games he played with broken or jammed his fingers, or with ringing ears after having the daylights knocked out of him in a collision with a baserunner intent on scoring. His ironman records — for games caught in a single season and in a career — had been eclipsed. His 30 steals in a single season — a long-standing record for a catcher — was broken in 1982. He still holds the record for career double plays by a catcher (226), but that is not a statistic that attracts lots of Hall of Fame votes.[14]

The closest Schalk came to winning election the hard way was in 1955, when the writers knew it was his last year of eligibility; even then, he received only 45 percent and finished eighth. His second- and third-best percentages were 31 in 1947 and 22.7 in 1942. After falling short in his final go-around with the writers — in 1955, they elected Joe DiMaggio and three others — his name immediately transferred to the 11-member Veterans Committee. Its members included chairman J.G. Taylor Spink, publisher of *The Sporting News*; Warren Giles, president of the National League; Will Harridge, American League president; Paul S. Kerr, the Hall's vice president and treasurer; retired Detroit star Charlie Gehringer; and Chicago sportswriter Warren Brown, a Schalk booster.

On January 31, 1955, just five days after his final strikeout with the writers, Ray Schalk connected. The Veterans Committee chose him for the National Baseball Hall of Fame. He and the committee's other pick, John F. "Home Run" Baker, would enter Cooperstown with the writers' choices: DiMaggio, Ted Lyons, Clarence "Dazzy" Vance and Charles "Gabby" Hartnett. Schalk had connections with three of his five fellow inductees. As Philadelphia's third baseman in 1912, Baker robbed Schalk of a base hit in Cracker's first at-bat with the White Sox, and they saw plenty of each other through Baker's final season in 1922. After a 1923 tryout of Lyons, then a college pitcher, Schalk recommended that the White Sox brass grab him, and they were teammates for six seasons, including Schalk's time as Sox manager. Hartnett and Schalk were star catchers in the Windy City. Their careers overlapped in the first half of the 1920s and they were teammates on the Cubs in the early 1930s, when Schalk was a coach. In 1939, Hartnett surpassed Schalk's major-league record for career appearances as a catcher.

For more than a half-century, writers, researchers or bloggers wanting to criticize the Hall of Fame selection process, or to make the case for this player or that, frequently mention Ray Schalk. After all, his career batting average is only .253 — the lowest of any position player enshrined in Cooperstown. That is all most need to know to write off Schalk as a bad choice. In the 1990s, leading baseball historian and statistician Bill James criticized the selection process in general and cited the induction of Schalk (among others) as an example of a bad pick. James said there are players with comparable (or better) records who didn't make Cooperstown, including Luke Sewell, Rollie Hem-

Schalk beside his plaque at the National Baseball Hall of Fame in Cooperstown.
In inscribing this photo for his grandson Roy Brinson, he signed it "Popoo"
(photograph courtesy Lillian Hendricks).

sley, Jack O'Connor, Muddy Ruel and Steve O'Neill. James noted that Schalk was an outstanding defensive player, but believes that his candidacy got a boost because he was an honest player during the 1919 Black Sox episode and because Warren Brown was on the Veterans Committee. (James was similarly critical of the 1964 selection of Schalk's friend Red Faber.)[15] A few years later, James ranked Schalk No. 35 among catchers (including those whose careers preceded, paralleled and followed Schalk's). Among those who caught before and during Schalk's prime, James ranked just five catchers ahead of Cracker: Mickey Cochrane (1925–37), Hartnett (1922–41), Roger Bresnahan (1897–1915), Buck Ewing (1880–97) and Wally Schang (1913–31). Using the Win Shares system he devised, James calculated that Schalk would have won the American League Gold Glove for catchers nine times in a 10-season span, from 1913 to 1922; his only "miss" was the war year of 1918. James described Schalk's selection to Cooperstown as coming on the "whim" of the Veterans Committee.[16] It didn't matter whether contemporary or subsequent critics agreed. (And many agreed: New York columnist Dan Daniel, for example, said the selection of Baker and Schalk was overdue.[17]) Like an umpire's decision on a close play, the Veterans Committee's decision was final: Ray Schalk was in the National Baseball Hall of Fame.

Somehow, a reporter phoned Schalk before Cooperstown did. The call interrupted Cracker's afternoon nap. Told the news, he didn't believe it at first. It seems that in years past, some friends would place similar calls as a prank. Finally convinced it was true, Schalk said, "You've taken my breath away. Hold the phone. I want to tell my wife." With Vin's elation audible in the background, he resumed what would be the first of countless phone calls that day. Well-wishers phoned and stopped by the Oakley Avenue residence, as did reporters and photographers. "It's something every ball player living thinks about and hopes for," he said. "When it happens, well, you're just very, very happy."[18] The phone call that touched Schalk the most came from friend and former adversary Ty Cobb, who phoned from Nevada. The conversation lasted about 20 minutes. Concerned about the expense to be borne by the Georgia Peach, Schalk suggested that they wrap it up, noting, "This is not a nickel phone." Cobb playfully shot back, "Listen, you little squirt! I've known you for 40 years and you are still trying to tell me what to do!" That evening, instead of bowling as planned, Ray appeared on *Chicago Tribune* sports editor Arch Ward's television program on *Tribune*-owned WGN.[19]

The previously scheduled annual dinner of the Old Timers' Baseball Association of Chicago, held three days after his selection, was particularly festive. Hartnett, elected a week ahead of Schalk, was the guest of honor at the corned-beef-and-cabbage banquet in the Hotel Sherman. An association vice president, Schalk was among several who had already kicked in to allow the Fox De Luxe beer to flow all evening without charge.[20] Cracker was introduced and roundly cheered by the 1,500 in attendance for attaining Cooperstown. A few weeks later, when he returned to Purdue University for another season as assistant coach, little Ray Schalk was a Big Man on Campus. His new status rekindled newspaper features and special appearances throughout the six months between his election and induction. One article detailed Schalk having dinner in Chicago with Roy Campanella, the star catcher of the Dodgers, and other baseball men. When the conversation came around to the 1919 World Series, Schalk said he knew nothing about the Black Sox plot and had no reason to suspect anything. The newspaper account did not state whether Schalk said it with a straight face and with fingers crossed.[21] The attention gave Schalk an audience as he embellished other stories — like the joke about his strategy to keep Cobb from stealing third: When the Georgia Peach was on first and took off to steal second, throw to third — lest he take two bases.[22] On Opening Day 1955, it was only fitting that the White Sox invited their two Hall of Famers–elect, Ted Lyons and Schalk, to handle First Pitch duties.[23] Cracker also caught the First Pitch from National Association President George Trautman when Lafayette (Indiana) made its debut in the Mississippi-Ohio Valley League.[24]

Cooperstown hosted the 1955 Hall of Fame ceremony on July 25. Among those in the Schalk contingent checking into the Otesaga Hotel were Ray and Vin; their children, Ray Junior and Pauline; and Ray's brothers Clarence, Walter and Leo. The proceedings had a Chicago theme, as three of the six inductees (Hartnett, Lyons and Schalk) were stars in the Windy City. But there was no question that it was Joe DiMaggio's day. The Yankee Clipper, looking handsome and fit at age 40, attracted most of the ink and fan attention.

Called forward to receive their plaques in the order in which they entered the major leagues, Schalk was up second — perhaps his highest spot in a batting order ever. Following Baker to the podium, an emotional Schalk choked up. "It's a dream that has come true," he told the assemblage. "I thank God for giving me strength to carry on."[25] He added his thanks to Vin. Schalk's plaque at the Hall of Fame reads:

RAYMOND WILLIAM SCHALK
CHICAGO A.L. 1912 TO 1928
NEW YORK N.L. 1929
HOLDER OF MAJOR LEAGUE RECORD FOR
MOST YEARS LEADING CATCHER IN FIELDING,

Ray's three brothers attended his 1955 induction into the National Baseball Hall of Fame. Posing in Cooperstown are (from left) Leo, Walter, Ray and Clarence (Bottomley-Ruffing-Schalk Museum, Nokomis, Illinois).

EIGHT YEARS; MOST PUTOUTS, NINE YEARS;
MOST ASSISTS IN ONE MAJOR LEAGUE (1810);
MOST CHANCES ACCEPTED (8965). CAUGHT
FOUR NO-HIT GAMES INCLUDING PERFECT
GAME IN 1922.

A few minutes later, Lyons thanked Schalk, the man who recommended that the White Sox hire him. After the ceremony and picture-taking, Hall of Famers 74 through 79 proceeded to Doubleday Field, where they were re-introduced before the Hall of Fame Game. In the exhibition, the Boston Red Sox beat the Milwaukee Braves, 4–2. Ted Williams hit a two-run homer in the top of the first inning. Williams and three men on the Braves roster that afternoon — Hank Aaron, Warren Spahn and Eddie Mathews — would later enjoy a more prominent role in festivities at Cooperstown.

In appreciation of what baseball had done for him, Schalk donated a baseball to the Hall of Fame. Not just any baseball — the ball bearing the autographs of several U.S. presidents. It bore the signatures of William Howard Taft, Warren G. Harding, Calvin Coolidge, Herbert Hoover, Franklin D. Roosevelt and Harry S Truman. With the exception of FDR — whose autograph Schalk secured personally in April 1933 — the autographs were arranged through emissaries (on three occasions, it was the Senators' Clark Griffith). Schalk's baseball was in Woodrow Wilson's White House for 10 days, but he was too ill to fulfill the request. After the ball entered its collection, the National Baseball Hall of Fame arranged to have President Dwight D. Eisenhower (in 1956) and President John F. Kennedy (in 1961) add their signatures.[26]

His highest place in baseball history secured, Schalk stayed in New York a few more days and appeared at Old Timers Day in Yankee Stadium.[27] Then the newest Hall of Famer returned to Chicago and resumed his life.

31

Final Inning

In 1958, the year Schalk got out of the bowling business and turned 66, he accepted a new job — supervisor of boys' baseball for the Mayor Daley Youth Foundation, Richard J. Daley's outreach program. He conducted clinics and oversaw program administration. He succeeded Rogers Hornsby in the position. Schalk didn't necessarily need the money. He had invested well — Ty Cobb's tip about Coca-Cola stock helped — and his bowling enterprise had been successful. A *Tribune* columnist made wry reference to Cracker filling his time helping out at Purdue University part-time and "clipping coupons from his gilt-edged bonds."[1]

Schalk's friend Cobb died July 17, 1961, in Georgia. When he was laid to rest in Royston, only three men from professional baseball — Mickey Cochrane, Nap Rucker and Schalk — were on hand. Some cited that as evidence that Cobb was held in low regard in the baseball fraternity. The Georgia Peach, a hard-bitten player and manager who became additionally somber and sullen in his final years, had plenty of detractors and made plenty of enemies. However, that was partly his mystique. The reality is that the Cobb funeral was a private service and few were invited. Further, many of Cobb's contemporaries were already dead. During their playing days, Schalk once told a reporter, "I have watched some wonderful hitters in the American League. I have fooled some, and have the dope on practically all of them. I have detected a weak spot in every one except Ty Cobb. I confess that I have been unable to find Cobb's weakness as a batter or a base runner."[2] Former sportswriter Sid Keener, then a Hall of Fame official, represented Cooperstown at the service. A few weeks later, in a personal letter to Keener, Schalk said, "The Greatest of the Great is at rest in his own Little Hall of Fame at Royston. May his soul rest in peace."[3]

In 1959, his native Harvel held a ceremony to rename the town ball field after Schalk. He traveled to downstate Illinois for the occasion and brought along his friend Guy Mackey, Purdue athletic director.[4] A few months later, after the White Sox won their first pennant in 40 years, the team invited Schalk and Red Faber to throw out the First Pitch before Game 1 against the Dodgers. As the current and future Hall of Famers did their thing — Faber, the spitballer, delighted the crowd by pretending to "load up" — White Sox manager Al Lopez quipped, "I wish they were in shape. I'd leave them in the whole game."[5]

Faber and Schalk received another honor in 1963. They were among the 13 players named to the all-time Chicago baseball team, selected in a poll of Chicago members of the Baseball Writers' Association of America. Only four of the 13 were White Sox stars; the other two were pitcher Ted Lyons and shortstop Luke Appling.[6] Schalk made another of his several trips to Cooperstown for the Hall of Fame induction ceremony in 1964, when Appling and Faber were enshrined.

Faber was on hand in August 1962, when Schalk was the guest of honor at a surprise 70th birthday party in the Club Martinique in Evergreen Park. About 100 folks turned out, including his wife, children and siblings. Mackey was there, as were neighbor and former major leaguer Tony Piet and retired umpire Red Ormsby. Also present was Sharkey Colledge, who was hired as a White Sox clubhouse "boy" in 1906 and was still in the team's employ as equipment manager on his way to an amazing six decades with the team.[7] That birthday celebration was small potatoes compared to the 50th wedding anniversary bash thrown for Ray and Vin on October 25, 1966. Up to 400 relatives and friends attended the event, also at the Martinique and organized by their children. (If they were true to their personalities, Pauline took charge of arrangements and Ray Junior got to help pay for it.) Baseball figures on hand to celebrate the Schalks' milestone included Pants Rowland; Charlie Grimm; Lew Fonseca; Lou Boudreau; Will Harridge, former American League president; Tony Piet; Chuck Comiskey; and Bill "Moose" Skowron, the best player out of Purdue University during Schalk's years as an assistant coach. Purdue was well represented with the presence of former football coach Stu Holcomb (then at Northwestern), Mackey and the Purdue Glee Club, which provided entertainment. Warren Brown, the sportswriter whose presence on the Veterans Committee sealed Cracker's selection into the Hall of Fame, assisted with arrangements.[8] The Hall of Famer's anniversary party was such an event that it received a mention in *The Sporting News*.[9]

By then, Schalk had stepped down as part-time assistant coach at Purdue. He called it quits before preparation for the 1965 season began. For three months every year since 1947 — 18 seasons — he had lived in Lafayette, Indiana. Now 72 years old, he explained that it was time to stop being separated from his beloved Vin for such long stretches and, besides, he wanted to devote more of his attention to his duties with the Mayor Daley Youth Foundation.[10] In honor of his service, Purdue made Schalk an honorary member of the P-Men lettermen's club and its Class of 1920. "I guess I could be one high school dropout who made out pretty good," he joked.[11]

Cracker still found time for a round for golf now and then — even when conditions were less than ideal. In April 1967, his home course, Beverly Country Club, sustained damage in a tornado that killed 33 in the Chicago area and injured hundreds more. Nonetheless, Schalk and Chris Smits showed up the next day and played a round, despite damaged buildings and uprooted trees and debris littering the course.[12]

On the home front, Ray and Vin also devoted time and attention to Ray Junior's children, Jim and Diane. It was not simply a matter of being attentive grandparents; it was a matter of necessity. Their son's excessive drinking and abusive outbursts were increasingly problematic. Meanwhile, Geraldine also drank and struggled with her own mental health; she entered hospitals from time to time. "They practically raised us," Jim said of his Schalk grandparents. He described Lavinia as the linchpin for the family, including Ray. "Vin was his right-hand man and his left-hand man," he said.[13]

Professional baseball observed its centennial in 1969, and Major League Baseball, individual teams and other baseball-related organizations planned special activities to mark the occasion. As a Hall of Famer, Schalk was invited

Celebrating their 50th wedding anniversary in October 1966, Ray and Lavinia Schalk pose with his three of his four living siblings. From left are Leo, Theresa (Hinton), Ray, Vin, and Walter. His sister Minnie died in 1967 after an extended illness (Bottomley-Ruffing-Schalk Museum, Nokomis, Illinois).

to many events and took part in several — as his schedule, health and interest allowed. That February, he traveled to New York City to accept the Retroactive Award from the state's chapter of the Baseball Writers Association. The year 1969 also marked the 50th anniversary year of the Black Sox World Series, and the Retroactive Award was a nod to Schalk's integrity in the face of his teammates' crookedness. His efforts to report and thwart the scandal were revealed in Eliot Asinof's 1963 book, *Eight Men Out*. Schalk had refused to cooperate with Asinof. As recounted earlier, at a New York banquet a half-dozen years after the book's release, Joe DiMaggio, with Asinof in tow, tried to reintroduce the author and Schalk, to no avail. Other honorees at the dinner included Detroit's 31-game winner Mickey Lolich, who received the Babe Ruth Award, and Cubs favorite Ernie Banks, who accepted the Ben Epstein Good Guy Award. Also introduced was Stan Musial, newly elected to the National Baseball Hall of Fame. They also received enthusiastic applause from the crowd of 1,500-plus.

Clearly, it was an audience rooted in the present. "When Ford Frick announced that Waite Hoyt and Stan Coveleski had been named for the honors at Cooperstown (the previous day, courtesy of the Veterans Committee), there was only mild applause," a sportswriter noted. "'Who are those guys?' the majority seemed to be saying. The same lack of response greeted an award to Ray Schalk, who was not only one of the great catchers of his period but an honest member of the Chicago White Sox of 1919...."[13] A few months later, the White Sox demonstrated that they hadn't forgotten (yet): They invited Schalk and his boss, Sox fan Mayor Richard J. Daley, to take part in First Pitch ceremony on Opening Day 1969 at Comiskey Park.[14] That year Schalk also attended the Hall of Fame induction ceremony in Cooperstown, a Centennial banquet in Washington ($35 a plate!), and the St. Louis Cardinals' Hall of Fame Day.

He might have taken part in more events if not for health setbacks. Vin, 75 years old, was briefly hospitalized that spring. That summer, Ray encountered serious health issues of his own. A lifelong cigar smoker, he had experienced minor throat problems previously. Now, it was serious: cancer of the esophagus. In the final week of January 1970, he and Lou Boudreau were honored at halftime of the Northwestern-Purdue basketball game in Chicago. Within a few days, however, the 77-year-old entered Chicago's Wesley Memorial Hospital.[15] Soon, his health was not his family's foremost concern.

By late February, in the depths of a dark Chicago winter, Ray Junior felt the world closing in on him. His father had been in the hospital a month, and probably would never recover. His wife, Geraldine, who struggled with her mental well-being, experienced another episode requiring hospitalization.

She was a patient in the same hospital as her father-in-law. Meanwhile, he hated his job selling insurance but had two young children to raise. That was enough. After the children went to bed, Ray Junior entered the bedroom of his Palos Heights home. Still wearing his shirt, pants and shoes, he reclined on the bed and pulled out a 20-gauge shotgun. He pointed the weapon at his head and steadied it between his knees. Then Ray Schalk Junior pulled the trigger. He was 48 years old.

The next morning, 11-year-old Jim and 9-year-old Diane Schalk awoke and discovered the bloody scene in their parents' room. The boy phoned Palos Heights police. The story was in all the papers the next day.[16] That her estranged brother took his own life on her birthday, Pauline viewed as a calculated — and final — jab at her.[17] His father was released from the hospital long enough to attend the funeral but Geraldine was absent.[18]

Though relatives publicly described Ray Senior's condition as "not serious," the reality was that the Hall of Famer was starving to death. The cancer in his esophagus made nourishment extremely difficult.[19] By the second week of May, in his fourth month of hospitalization, pneumonia set in.

At 1:30 P.M. Tuesday, May 19, 1970, Hall of Famer Ray Schalk died. He was 77.

That evening, before the last-place White Sox managed just two hits in their 3–0 loss to the California Angels, everyone in Comiskey Park observed a moment of silence.

So many mourners showed up for the wake that Thompson Funeral Home in south suburban Oak Lawn opened all four of its viewing rooms. The day of their grandfather's funeral, Jim and Diane Schalk counted 168 vehicles in the procession to the cemetery.[20] The pallbearers included two friends from Ray's days at Purdue, football coach Hank Stram and assistant director Guy Mackey.[21]

Newspapers across the country published obituaries and tributes to the star catcher of a bygone era. Most pointed out that Schalk had broken the mold, proving that a slightly built but aggressive receiver could handle the rigors of professional baseball as well as the prototypical burly catchers. Articles recounted the many accolades he received over the years — considered the game's best catcher by Babe Ruth and others — as well as his honesty and his refusal to discuss the 1919 World Series. Ray Schalk took what he knew about the Black Sox scandal to his grave.

Epilogue

In downstate Illinois, baseball fans in the tiny coal-mining town Nokomis (population 2,265[1]) established a baseball history museum — actually, a window display in a diner — in 1981. Soon, the organization occupied its own building. The museum was named after two National Baseball Hall of Fame honorees with the distinction of growing up in Nokomis: Red Ruffing (1967) and Jim Bottomley (1974). A couple of years later — and over some objections within the membership — the museum added Schalk's name.[2] Some members' reluctance apparently had to do with the fact that, unlike the other two stars, Schalk was not raised in Nokomis but in the Montgomery County communities of Harvel and Litchfield. In 2008, the museum reopened in a new building three years after sustaining collateral damage when an adjacent building burned. The modest facility's exhibits honor not only its namesakes but the region's other baseball stars and teams. Schalk's relatives, especially Violet Schalk, the widow of Ray's brother Walter, donated photos and other memorabilia. Walter, the last survivor among Ray's siblings, died in 1984 at age 94. Their sister Theresa Hinton died in mid–1976.

After the death of her son and husband in the first half of 1970, Lavinia helped her daughter-in-law Geraldine with her young children, Jim and Diane, as much as she could. Geraldine, who married attorney Dale Broder in 1974, died 20 years later at age 72. Ray and Vin's daughter, Pauline Brinson, died in 1985 at age 67. Four years later, on March 5, 1989, Lavinia Graham Schalk died in a suburban Chicago nursing home; the Hall of Famer's widow was 95. Ray and Vin had only three grandchildren. Pauline's son Roy died in October 2008 after several years of illness. Meanwhile, Ray Junior's son Jim resided in Florida and his daughter Diane in her native Illinois.

In the days and weeks following his death in May 1970, Schalk's name showed up in a sports column or article now and then. If baseball fans had forgotten (or never knew) the stars of the Deadball Era (and early Lively Ball period), as a Hartford sportswriter lamented in 1969, the same could be said of the scribes. Only the eldest in the sportswriting fraternity had ever seen the likes of Babe Ruth or Lou Gehrig or Ray Schalk compete. Who was left to write their stories?

Schalk's name occasionally surfaces. It hit the papers in 1982 when John Wathan of the Kansas City Royals broke Cracker's major league record for stolen bases by a catcher in a season (30); the mark stood 65 years. Buffalo inducted the former Bisons manager into its baseball Hall of Fame. In 1989 the White Sox gave fans attending a particular game a photo showing three of their catching greats: Schalk, Carlton Fisk and Sherman Lollar. Schalk's name surfaces among memorabilia collectors and, of course, when a sports expert or blogger needs an example of a ballplayer who doesn't "belong" in Cooperstown. (The .253 batting average is all the "evidence" they need.)

With each passing season, his name becomes less familiar. When the Chicago White Sox adorned their outfield wall with the images of their former "greats," they did not include that of Schalk, choosing to go with some ex-players who did not attain Cooperstown status. (Red Faber suffered similar treatment.) In Litchfield, there is no sign at the city limits informing visitors that it is the hometown of a Hall of Famer; the only mention is his last name on a backstop screen at the city ball fields.

On a sunny Sunday afternoon in May 2007 in rural Illinois, a men's slow-pitch softball league scheduled a couple of games on Ray Schalk Field in the municipal park in Harvel, population 228. The diamond was not in the best shape. Surrounding the field were a scattered array of houses and then farmland. Lots of farmland. A visitor, wanting a glimpse of the field named in honor of the Hall of Famer, approached two men in their mid–20s. They were in uniform and waiting for their game to begin. The visitor asked, "Do you know who Ray Schalk was?" One man was stumped. "Can't say." His teammate gamely tried to help. "I think he was a ballplayer. From somewhere around here."[3]

Appendix

Raymond William Schalk

Chicago White Sox (AL) 1912–28
New York Giants (NL) 1929

Inducted into the National Baseball Hall of Fame (1955)

Nickname: Cracker
Born: August 12, 1892, Harvel, Illinois.
Died: May 19, 1970, Chicago, Illinois.
Buried: Evergreen Cemetery (Oakland Section), Evergreen Park, Illinois.
Bat: Right.   **Throw:** Right.
Height: 5–9.   **Weight:** 165.
Played First Major League Game: August 11, 1912.
Final Game: September 15, 1929.
First Game Managed: April 12, 1927.
Last Game Managed: July 4, 1928.

Batting

Year Team	G	AB	R	H	2B	3B	HR	RBI	BB	SO	HBP	SAC	SB	CS	AVG
1912 CHI (AL)	23	63	7	18	2	0	0	8	3	—	4	3	2	—	.286
1913 CHI (AL)	129	401	38	98	15	5	1	38	27	36	3	14	14	—	.244
1914 CHI (AL)	136	392	30	106	13	2	0	36	38	24	8	21	24	11	.270
1915 CHI (AL)	135	413	46	110	14	4	1	54	62	21	3	17	15	18	.266
1916 CHI (AL)	129	410	36	95	12	9	0	41	41	31	6	15	30	13	.232
1917 CHI (AL)	140	424	48	96	12	5	2	51	59	27	7	17	19	—	.226
1918 CHI (AL)	108	333	35	73	6	3	0	22	36	22	3	15	12	—	.219
1919 CHI (AL)	131	394	57	111	9	3	0	34	51	25	2	14	11	—	.282
1920 CHI (AL)	151	485	64	131	25	5	1	61	68	19	2	21	10	4	.270
1921 CHI (AL)	128	416	32	105	24	4	0	47	40	36	7	9	3	4	.252
1922 CHI (AL)	142	442	57	124	22	3	4	60	67	36	3	22	12	4	.281
1923 CHI (AL)	123	382	42	87	12	2	1	44	39	28	4	17	6	4	.228
1924 CHI (AL)	57	153	15	30	4	2	1	11	21	10	2	6	1	5	.196
1925 CHI (AL)	125	343	44	94	18	1	0	52	57	27	3	14	11	5	.274
1926 CHI (AL)	82	226	26	60	9	1	0	32	27	11	2	8	5	1	.265
1927 CHI (AL)	16	26	2	6	2	0	0	2	2	1	0	1	0	0	.231
1928 CHI (AL)	2	1	0	1	0	0	0	1	0	0	0	0	1	0	1.000
1929 NY (NL)	5	2	0	0	0	0	0	0	0	1	0	0	0	0	.000
Total (18 years)	1,762	5,306	579	1,345	199	49	11	594	638	355(i)	59	214	176	69(i)	.253

World Series

Year Team	G	AB	R	H	2B	3B	HR	RBI	BB	SO	HBP	SAC	SB	CS	AVG
1917 CHI (AL)	6	19	1	5	0	0	0	0	2	1	0	0	1	1	.286
1919 CHI (AL)	8	23	1	7	0	0	0	2	4	2	1	0	1	1	.304
Total (2 Series)	14	42	2	12	0	0	0	2	6	3	1	0	2	2	.286

KEY: G — Games. AB — At bats. R — Runs scored. H — Hits. 2B — Doubles. 3B — Triples. HR — Home runs. RBI — Runs batted in. BB — Walks. SO — Strikeouts. HBP — Hit by pitch. SAC — Sacrifices. SB — Stolen bases. CS — Caught stealing. AVG — Batting average. (i) = incomplete data.

Fielding
(All games as catcher)

Year Team	G	PO	A	E	DP	PB	AVG
1912 CHI (AL)	23	115	40	14	4	0	.917
1913 CHI (AL)	**125**	599	154	15	18	15	.980
1914 CHI (AL)	**125**	613	183	21	20	12	.974
1915 CHI (AL)	**134**	655	159	13	8	12	**.984**
1916 CHI (AL)	124	653	166	10	25	3	**.988**
1917 CHI (AL)	**139**	624	148	15	18	8	**.981**
1918 CHI (AL)	106	**422**	114	12	15	8	.978
1919 CHI (AL)	129	551	130	13	14	4	.981
1920 CHI (AL)	**151**	581	138	10	**19**	6	.986
1921 CHI (AL)	126	453	129	9	19	11	.985
1922 CHI (AL)	**142**	591	150	8	16	3	**.989**
1923 CHI (AL)	121	481	93	10	20	3	.983
1924 CHI (AL)	56	176	55	10	8	5	.959
1925 CHI (AL)	125	368	99	8	15	5	.983
1926 CHI (AL)	80	251	45	7	6	3	.977
1927 CHI (AL)	15	24	8	0	1	0	1.000
1928 CHI (AL)	1	4	0	0	0	0	1.000
1929 NY (NL)	5	7	0	0	0	0	1.000
Total (18 years)	1,727	7,168	1,811	175	226	98	**.981**

World Series

Year Team	G	PO	A	E	DP	PB	AVG
1917 CHI (AL)	6	32	6	2	1	1	.950
1919 CHI (AL)	8	29	15	1	1	0	.978
Total (2 Series)	14	61	21	3	2	10	.965

KEY: G — Games. PO — Putouts. A — Assists. E — Errors. DP — Double plays. AVG — Fielding average. **Bold type** indicates league leader.

Major League Managerial Record

Year Team	G	W	L	PCT	RS	RA	PL
1927 CHI (AL)	153	70	83	.458	662	708	5
1928 CHI (AL)	75	32	42	.432	309	362	6(a)
Total (2 years)	228	102	125	.449	971	1070	

KEY: G — Games. W — Wins. L — Losses. PCT — Percentage of games won. RS — Runs scored. RA — Runs allowed. PL — Place in standings (of 8 teams). (a) — Place at time of release July 4, 1928.

Major League Franchises, 1912–29

American League

Boston (Red Sox)
Chicago (White Sox)
Cleveland (Naps, Indians)
Detroit (Tigers)
New York (Highlanders, Yankees)
Philadelphia (Athletics)
St. Louis (Browns)
Washington (Nationals, Senators)

National League

Boston (Braves)
Brooklyn (Superbas, Robins, Dodgers)
Chicago (Cubs)
Cincinnati (Reds)
New York (Giants)
Philadelphia (Phillies)
Pittsburgh (Pirates)
St. Louis (Cardinals)

Chapter Notes

Chapter 1

1. *Litchfield (Illinois) Daily News*, July 19, 1911.
2. Article quoted by C.C. Johnson Spink, *The Sporting News*, March 28, 1962.
3. Autobiographical article, undated, 1927.
4. *The Sporting News*, March 28, 1962.
5. *Litchfield (Illinois) Daily News*, August 1911.
6. Munsell, *Historical Encyclopedia of Illinois*, 1918.
7. Farrell, *My Baseball Diary.*
8. *Litchfield (Illinois) News-Herald*, circa 1970. Ted Simmons column.
9. Harvel Centennial book, 1973.
10. Herman Schalk's age in the 1900 census was listed as 41. In 1910, it was 56 and in 1920, it was 63. That enumerators called in the spring of the census year should not have been a factor, as Herman was said to have been born in December, long after the enumerators visited.
11. *Chicago Daily News*, May 21, 1970.
12. U.S. Census, 1890.
13. Schalk said his father came to the U.S. aboard a steamship and his mother via sailboat. Quote appeared in tribute article published in the *Chicago Daily News*, May 21, 1970.
14. U.S. Census, 1880.
15. *Centennial History of Litchfield*, 1953.
16. National Register of Historic Places Internet site.
17. *Centennial History of Litchfield*, 1953; U.S. Census records, 1910 and 1920; James T. Farrell, *My Baseball Diary.*
18. *Litchfield (Illinois) News-Herald*, circa 1970. Ted Simmons column.
19. *Ibid.*
20. *Decatur (Illinois) Review*, March 1, 1909.
21. *Litchfield (Illinois) Daily News*, July 25, 1955. Two Litchfield newspapers, the *Daily News* and *Herald*, merged in 1913.
22. *Litchfield (Illinois) Daily News*, August 10, 1912.

23. *Chicago Tribune*, February 4, 1955.
24. Autobiographical article, undated, 1927.
25. Undated article, circa 1926–27.
26. Correspondence from Jarrell Jarrard to sportswriter Larry Tate, May 10, 2007.
27. *Litchfield (Illinois) Daily Herald*, 1909.
28. An undated autobiographical article, circa 1926–27.
29. *Litchfield (Illinois) Daily News*, October 25, 1916.
30. *Chicago Daily News*, May 21, 1970.
31. *Decatur (Illinois) Review*, October 24, 1910.
32. *Litchfield (Illinois) Daily News*, April 13, 1911.
33. *Litchfield (Illinois) Daily News*, April 18, 1911.
34. *Janesville (Wisconsin) Gazette*, April 9, 1915.
35. *Decatur (Illinois) Review*, December 7, 1910.
36. *Ibid.*
37. Box score, National Baseball Hall of Fame archives.
38. *Litchfield (Illinois) Daily News*, July 4, 1911.
39. *Litchfield (Illinois) Daily News*, July 11, 1911
40. Retrosheet.org.
41. Joe Vila column, circa 1928, National Baseball Hall of Fame archives.
42. *Washington Post*, April 16, 1932.
43. *Litchfield (Illinois) Daily News*, July 8, 1911.
44. Joe Vila column, circa 1928, National Baseball Hall of Fame archives.
45. National Baseball Hall of Fame archives.
46. *Litchfield (Illinois) Daily News*, July 19, 1911.

Chapter 2

1. *Milwaukee Journal*, July 19, 1911.
2. Ibid.

3. *Milwaukee Sentinel,* July 23, 1911.

4. Podoll, *The Minor League Milwaukee Brewers,* page 106.

5. *Chicago Tribune.* June 20, 1909. The ballpark was constructed for the Chicago Whales of the short-lived Federal League (1914–15). The Cubs moved there in 1916.

6. *Leslie's Illustrated Weekly,* July 8, 1909.

7. Reprinted in the *Litchfield (Illinois) Daily News,* August 6, 1911.

8. *The Sporting News,* October 5, 1911.

9. *Chicago Tribune,* April 14, 1912. Britton inherited the Cardinals from her uncle, M. Stanley Robison.

10. *Washington Post,* April 12, 1912.

11. *The Sporting News,* May 16, 1912.

12. *The Sporting News,* May 23, 1912.

13. Podoll, *The Minor League Milwaukee Brewers,* page 157.

14. *The Sporting News,* May 16, 1912.

15. *Total Baseball, Total Football II* and *Chicago Tribune,* November 7, 1920. The team's only season in the American Professional Football Association, forerunner of the National Football League, was 1920. In 1921, George Halas (who also played professional football and baseball) moved his Decatur Staleys to the Windy City.

16. *Milwaukee Journal,* July 1912.

17. Society for American Baseball Research Biography Project and *Chicago Tribune,* April 23, 1915.

18. *Milwaukee Sentinel* article reprinted in *Litchfield (Illinois) Daily News,* April 10, 1912.

19. Podoll, *The Minor League Milwaukee Brewers,* page 156.

20. *Ibid.*

21. *Chicago Tribune,* May 4, 1913.

22. Hamann and Koehler, *The American Association Milwaukee Brewers,* page 20.

23. *The Sporting News,* June 20, 1912.

24. Podoll, *The Minor League Milwaukee Brewers,* page 157.

25. *Milwaukee Journal,* July 15, 1912.

26. *Milwaukee Journal,* July 19, 1912.

27. *Milwaukee Journal,* July 15, 1912.

28. *Atlanta Constitution,* August 1, 1912.

29. *Boston Globe,* July 19, 1912.

30. *Ibid.*

31. *Litchfield (Illinois) Daily News,* July 10, 1912; *Milwaukee Journal,* July 18, 1912; *Boston Globe,* August 4, 1912; Undated newspaper article, "Pirates After Star Catcher," in National Baseball Hall of Fame archives.

32. *Milwaukee Journal,* July 18, 1912; Hedges' attendance confirmed in *Washington Post,* August 6, 1912.

33. *Milwaukee Journal,* July 19, 1912.

34. *Boston Globe,* July 18, 1912.

35. *Milwaukee Journal,* August 9, 1912.

36. *Chicago Tribune,* August 10, 1912.

37. Berran recorded a hit in his first major-league at-bat in Game 1 on August 11, 1912. He went hitless in three at-bats in Game 2. He never appeared in another major-league contest.

38. *Chicago Tribune,* August 11, 1912.

39. Retrosheet.org.

40. *Ibid.*

41. *Chicago Inter-Ocean,* August 10, 1912.

42. National Baseball Hall of Fame archives; *The Sporting News,* August 15, 1912.

43. *Chicago Inter-Ocean,* August 11, 1912.

44. *Milwaukee Journal,* August 10, 1912.

Chapter 3

1. *Chicago Tribune,* August 11, 1912.

2. *Ibid.*

3. *Chicago Tribune,* September 6, 1918.

4. Schalk's recollection, shared with Auburn Park Lions Club. *Southtown Economist,* January 12, 1926.

5. *Chicago Daily News,* May 20, 1970.

6. *Ibid.*

7. *Chicago Tribune,* February 1, 1955.

8. *The Sporting News,* February 9, 1955; *Chicago Daily News,* February 1, 1955; *Chicago Tribune,* February 1, 1955.

9. *Chicago Tribune,* September 11, 1911. Advertisements for White Sox games were grouped with theater ads and typically were the smallest notices on the page.

10. *Chicago Daily News,* May 20, 1970

11. *Southtown Economist,* January 12, 1926.

12. *Chicago Inter-Ocean,* August 12, 1912.

13. *Ibid.*

14. *Chicago American,* August 12, 1912.

15. *Hartford Courant,* May 17, 1912.

16. Initial newspaper articles spelled the patron's last name as Lucker.

17. *Boston Globe,* May 12, 1912.

18. *Atlanta Constitution, Chicago Tribune* and *New York Times,* May 22, 1912.

19. *New York Times,* May 19, 1912.

20. Retrosheet.org.

21. John Kieran column, *New York Times,* September 9, 1937.

22. "In My Day, Catchers Could Take It," by Schalk, *Chicago Times,* April 11, 1937.

23. *Decatur (Illinois) Review,* September 18, 1912, quoting a statement by White Sox trainer William Buckner to Schalk acquaintance Grover Hoover, of Taylorville, Illinois, who paid a visit to Comiskey Park.

24. *Chicago Tribune,* September 2, 1912.

25. *Decatur (Illinois) Herald,* September 21, 1912.

26. *Chicago Tribune,* September 27, 1912.

27. *Chicago Tribune,* September 28, 1912.

28. *Chicago Tribune,* September 27–29, 1912.

29. Lindberg, *The White Sox Encyclopedia*, page 464; *Chicago Tribune* article under Chance's byline, October 19, 1912.

30. Lindberg, *The White Sox Encyclopedia*, page 19.

31. *The Sporting News*, July 3, 1913.

32. *Evening Standard*, Ogden City, Utah, October 15, 1912.

33. *Chicago Daily Defender*, May 30, 1936. Among Petway's credits is nailing Ty Cobb on 10 attempted steals in Havana in 1909–10.

34. *Chicago Tribune*, May 4, 1913.

35. *Chicago Tribune*, January 15, 1913.

Chapter 4

1. *Litchfield (Illinois) News-Herald*, 1970.

2. David Condon column, *Chicago Tribune*, May 20, 1970.

3. Paso Robles Inn (www.pasoroblesinn. com).

4. *Chicago Tribune*, March 9, 1913.

5. *Chicago Tribune*, March 7, 1913.

6. *Chicago Tribune*, March 3, 1913.

7. *Chicago Tribune*, March 26, 1913.

8. *The Sporting News*, April 25, 1912.

9. Retrosheet.org.

10. *Chicago Tribune*, April 12, 1913.

11. *Ibid.*

12. *Chicago Tribune*, April 18, 1913.

13. *Chicago Defender*, May 24, 1913.

14. Sam Weller, *Chicago Tribune*, April 14, 1913.

15. *Chicago Tribune*, April 24, 1913.

16. *Baseball Magazine*, May 1913, pages 71–72.

17. *Chicago Tribune*, May 4, 1913.

18. *Chicago Tribune*, May 18, 1913.

19. Retrosheet.org and *Chicago Tribune*, September 21, 1901.

20. *Washington Post* and *Chicago Tribune*, May 18, 1913.

21. *Chicago Daily Defender*, May 24, 1913.

22. *Washington Post* and *Chicago Tribune*, June 15, 1913.

23. *The Sporting News*, June 19, 1913.

24. In 1950, Schalk told a sportswriter that the umpire was Bill Guthrie. However, Guthrie first umpired in the American League only part of 1922, when Schalk was in his 11th big-league season, and did not become full-time in the circuit until 1928, when Schalk was managing.

25. John P. Carmichael column, *Chicago Daily News*, May 21, 1970.

26. *Chicago Tribune*, February 19, 1914.

27. *The Sporting News*, June 19, 1913.

28. *Chicago Tribune*, June 24, 1913.

29. Retrosheet.org credits Schalk with 18 double plays. *Baseball Magazine* of December 1913 said he took part in 21.

30. *Chicago Tribune*, June 21, 1913.

31. *Chicago Tribune*, September 18, 1913.

32. *Chicago Tribune*, October 9, 1913.

33. *Chicago Tribune*, October 13, 1913.

34. *Chicago Tribune*, October 15, 1913. According to U.S. Bureau of Labor Statistics estimates, in 1915 the average American earned $687. Figure from a U.S. Census Bureau press release, August 9, 2006, citing "Historical Statistics of the United States: Colonial Times to 1970."

Chapter 5

1. Elfers, *The Tour to End All Tours*, page 12.

2. *Ibid*, page 26.

3. *Chicago Tribune*, October 20, 1913.

4. *Chicago Tribune*, November 10, 1913.

5. *Chicago Tribune*, October 21, 1913.

6. Callahan's successor, Clarence Rowland, quoted in the *Chicago Tribune*, December 27, 1954; *The Sporting News*, January 3, 1962.

7. *Chicago Tribune*, October 27, 1913.

8. *Dubuque (Iowa) Times-Journal*, Oct. 27, 1913.

9. *New York Times*, October 28, 1913.

10. Elfers, *The Tour to End All Tours*.

11. *Chicago Tribune*, October 30, 1913.

12. Elfers, *The Tour to End All Tours*, page 61.

13. McGraw column, *New York Times*, November 9, 1913.

14. *Chicago Tribune*, November 5, 1913.

15. McGraw column, *New York Times*, November 7, 1913.; *Chicago Tribune*, November 6, 1913.

16. *Chicago Tribune*, November 6, 1913.

17. *Chicago Tribune*, November 7, 1913.

18. *Chicago Tribune*, November 8, 1913.

19. *Los Angeles Times*, November 10, 1913.

20. Elfers, *The Tour to End All Tours*.

21. *Chicago American*, November 20, 1913.

22. McGraw column, *New York Times*, November 11, 1913.

23. Elfers, *The Tour to End All Tours*, pages 77–78.

24. *New York Times*, November 16, 1913.

25. *New York Times*, August 27, 1921. Lobert's record stood for 11 years.

26. *New York Times*, November 16, 1913; Elfers, *The Tour to End All Tours*, pages 80–81.

27. "Dav's Day Dreams," *Chicago American*, November 6, 1913.

28. *Medford (Oregon) Evening Telegram*, November 19, 1913.

Chapter 6

1. *Decatur (Illinois) Review*, January 31, 1914.
2. *Decatur (Illinois) Review*, February 17, 1914.
3. *Washington Post*, November 10, 1918.
4. *Chicago Tribune*, February 19–21, 1914.
5. *New York Times*, April 19, 1914; *Hartford Courant*, September 7, 1914.
6. *Chicago Tribune*, February 21, 1914.
7. *New York Times*, February 14, 1914.
8. *Chicago Tribune*, February 22, 1914.
9. *Chicago Tribune*, February 24, 1914.
10. *Los Angeles Times*, February 25, 1914.
11. *Chicago Tribune*, March 2, 1914.
12. *Chicago Tribune*, March 8, 1914.
13. *Chicago Tribune*, March 27, 1914.
14. *The Sporting News*, March 12, 1914.
15. *The Sporting News*, March 26, 1914.
16. *Chicago Tribune*, March 30, 1914.
17. *Chicago Tribune*, April 2, 1914.
18. *Chicago Tribune*, April 6, 1914.
19. *Chicago Tribune*, April 10, 1914.
20. *Chicago Tribune*, April 12, 1914.
21. Ibid.
22. *Chicago Tribune*, April 14, 1914; Britannica.com.
23. *Chicago Tribune*, April 27, 1914.
24. *Chicago Tribune*, May 1, 1914.
25. *Chicago Tribune*, June 1, 1914.
26. *Chicago Tribune*, June 13, 1914.
27. *Chicago Tribune*, June 14, 1914.
28. John P. Carmichael, *Chicago Daily News*, May 27, 1946.
29. *The Sporting News*, June 25, 1914.
30. *Dubuque (Iowa) Telegraph-Herald*, June 24, 1914.
31. *Chicago Tribune*, June 22, 1914.
32. *Chicago Tribune*, August 26, 1914.
33. *Chicago Tribune*, July 26, 1914.
34. *Chicago Tribune* and *Washington Post*, September 3, 1914.
35. *Chicago Tribune* and *Washington Post*, September 3, 1914.
36. *Chicago Tribune*, September 8, 1914.
37. *Chicago Tribune*, September 9, 1914.
38. "In the Wake of the News," *Chicago Tribune*, September 9, 1914.
39. *Chicago Tribune*, October 16, 1914.
40. *New York Times*, October 17, 1914.
41. *Boston Globe*, October 14, 1914.

Chapter 7

1. *Washington Post*, November 1, 1914; *Los Angeles Times*, November 20, 1914.
2. *Chicago Tribune*, December 31, 1914, stated Gleason coached for Callahan in 1913 and 1914.
3. *Boston Globe*, October 24, 1914 (concerning Walsh); *Hartford Courant*, December 2, 1914 (concerning Jones).
4. *Chicago Tribune*, December 9, 1914.
5. *Boston Globe*, December 9, 1914.
6. *Baseball Magazine*, February 1915.
7. *Los Angeles Times*, December 25, 1914.
8. *Baseball Magazine*, March 1915.
9. *Chicago Tribune*, December 18, 1914.
10. *Chicago Tribune*, December 26, 1954.
11. *Waterloo (Iowa) Evening Courier*, February 9, 1915.
12. *Chicago Tribune*, December 31, 1914.
13. U.S. Census Bureau.
14. Undated article, January 30, 1915. Publication unknown.
15. Undated article by George C. Rice, apparently published during off-season of 1914–15.
16. *Chicago Tribune* and *Los Angeles Times*, March 13, 1915.
17. *Chicago Tribune*, March 30, 1915.
18. *Chicago Tribune*, April 3, 1915.
19. *Chicago Tribune*, April 23, 1915.
20. *Chicago Tribune*, May 2, 1915.
21. *Chicago Tribune*, May 10, 1915.
22. *The Sporting News*, January 29, 1947.
23. *Chicago Tribune*, May 13, 1915.
24. *Ibid.*
25. *Washington Post*, May 15, 1915.
26. *Chicago Tribune*, May 15, 1915.
27. *Dubuque (Iowa) Telegraph-Herald*, May 16, 1915.
28. *Chicago Tribune*, May 15, 1915.
29. *Chicago Tribune*, February 16, 1930.
30. *Chicago Tribune*, May 22, 1915.
31. *Chicago Tribune*, May 23, 1915.
32. *The Sporting News*, undated article, circa 1940.
33. *The Sporting News*, circa 1940; Farrell, *My Baseball Diary*, "The Perfect Catcher."
34. *Chicago Tribune*, July 15, 1915.
35. *Chicago Tribune*, July 26, 1915.
36. *Chicago Tribune*, October 11, 1915.
37. James, *The New Bill James Historical Baseball Abstract*, page 395.
38. *Chicago Tribune*, October 11, 1915.
39. Hourly temperature readings, *Chicago Tribune*, October 8–10, 1915.
40. *Decatur (Illinois) Review*, October 16, 1915.
41. *Litchfield (Illinois) Daily News*, October 25, 1915; *Decatur (Illinois) Review*, December 2, 1915.
42. *Decatur (Illinois) Review*, October 26, 1915; *Litchfield Daily News*, October 25, 1915.
43. *Litchfield (Illinois) Daily News*, October 25, 1915.

Chapter 8

1. *Chicago Tribune*, March 10, 1916.
2. *Chicago Tribune*, March 12, 1916.
3. In the *Chicago Tribune* on March 19, 1916, Sanborn did not identify the players who defied Comiskey's wishes.
4. *Boston Globe*, April 6, 1916.
5. *Chicago Tribune*, April 13, 1916.
6. *Chicago Tribune*, March 10, 1916.
7. *Chicago Tribune*, April 25, 1916.
8. *New York Times*, April 26, 1916.
9. *New York Times*, *Washington Post* and *Chicago Tribune*, June 10, 1922.
10. *Chicago Tribune*, April 30, 1916.
11. *Chicago Tribune*, May 7, 1916.
12. *Janesville (Wisconsin) Gazette*, May 1, 1916.
13. *Chicago American*, May 3, 1916; *Decatur (Illinois) Review*, May 1, 1916.
14. *Chicago Tribune*, May 4, 1916.
15. Ibid.
16. *New York Times* and *Chicago Tribune*, July 8, 1916.
17. *Decatur (Illinois) Herald*, July 13, 1916.
18. *The Sporting News*, July 20, 1916.
19. *Chicago Tribune*, June 26, 1916.
20. Among the papers publishing the article, without a byline, were the *Lincoln (Nebraska) Daily News* on August 21, 1916, and *Hamilton (Ohio) Evening Journal*, August 25, 1916. The piece might have been written by George S. Robbins, of the *Chicago Daily News*.
21. James, *The New Bill James Historical Baseball Abstract*, page 395.
22. Quoted in the *San Antonio (Texas) Light*, August 27, 1916.
23. Undated newspaper article, 1917, National Baseball Hall of Fame collection.
24. *Litchfield (Illinois) Daily News*, October 23, 1916.

Chapter 9

1. James Schalk, phone interview, May 15, 2008.
2. *Chicago American*, October 24, 1916.
3. *Chicago American*, October 25, 1916.
4. *Chicago American*, October 26, 1916.
5. *Chicago Tribune* advertisement, October 26 and 30, 1916.
6. *Chicago Tribune*, October 31, 1916.
7. *Ibid.*
8. *Chicago Evening Post*, October 31, 1916.
9. *Litchfield (Illinois) Daily News*, October 25, 1916.
10. *Litchfield (Illinois) Daily News*, February 27, 1918; *Chicago Tribune*, February 28, 1918.
11. Social Security Death Index.
12. Shriners publication, 1970.

13. *Chicago Tribune*, various articles from the 1940s and 1950s.
14. *Chicago Tribune*, October 25, 1916.

Chapter 10

1. *Chicago Tribune*, April 12, 1917.
2. *Chicago Tribune*, April 15, 1917.
3. *New York Times*, May 6, 1917; *Chicago Tribune*, May 7, 1917.
4. *Chicago Tribune*, April 20, 1917.
5. *Chicago Tribune*, April 28, 1917.
6. *Chicago Tribune*, August 18, 1917.
7. *Boston Globe*, June 17, 1917.
8. *Chicago Tribune*, June 18 and 19, 1917.
9. *The Sporting News*, June 21, 1917.
10. *Cascade (Iowa) Pioneer*, June 17, 1917.
11. *Chicago Tribune*, July 22, 1917.
12. *The Sporting News*, August 16, 1917.
13. *Chicago Tribune*, September 4, 1917.
14. Thebaseballpage.com.
15. *The Sporting News*, September 27, 1917.
16. *Washington Post*, September 27, 1917.
17. Lindberg, *The White Sox Encyclopedia*.
18. Asinof, *Eight Men Out*, pages 21–22.
19. *Los Angeles Times*, September 18, 1917.
20. Undated New York newspaper clipping, September-October 1917.
21. Undated newspaper article, September-October 1917.
22. *Baseball Magazine*, November 1917.

Chapter 11

1. *Chicago Tribune*, October 6–7, 1917; Farrell, *My Baseball Diary*.
2. *Chicago Tribune*, October 4, 1917.
3. "Voice of the People," *Chicago Tribune*, October 5, 1917.
4. *Chicago Tribune*, October 4, 6 and 7, 1917. Ticket value estimate made using cost of living calculator on American Institute for Economic Research web site.
5. *The Sporting News*, November 21, 1940.
6. *Chicago Tribune*, October 7, 1917.
7. *New York Times*, October 7, 1917.
8. *The Sporting News*, October 11, 1917.
9. *Chicago Tribune*, October 7, 1917.
10. Ibid.
11. Urban Faber. Undated newspaper article.
12. *New York Times* and *Chicago Tribune*, October 8, 1917.
13. Clarence Rowland, as told to Jack Ryan, *Chicago Daily News*, February 12, 1945.
14. Urban Faber, as told to Hal Totten, "My Three Wins in '17 Series." *Baseball Digest*, February 1948.

15. *The Sporting News*, October 18, 1917.
16. Lindberg, *The White Sox Encyclopedia*.
17. Clarence Rowland, as told to Jack Ryan, *Chicago Daily News*, February 12, 1945.
18. *Chicago Herald*, October 18, 1917.
19. *The New York Times* and *Chicago Herald*, October 16, 1917; *The Sporting News*, October 18, 1917.
20. *Chicago Tribune*, October 17, 1917.
21. Graham, *McGraw of the Giants*.
22. *The Sporting News*, October 11, 1917.
23. *New York Times*, October 18, 1917; *Dubuque (Iowa) Telegraph-Herald*, October 18, 1917; *Chicago Daily Journal*, October 16, 1917.
24. Baseball-almanac.com.
25. *Chicago Tribune*, October 18, 1917.
26. *Dubuque (Iowa) Telegraph-Herald*, October 17, 1917.
27. *Chicago Tribune*, October 17, 1917.
28. *Chicago Herald* and *Chicago Tribune*, October 18, 1917.
29. Malcolm McLean, *Atlanta Constitution*, March 31, 1918.
30. *Litchfield (Illinois) Daily News*, October 22, 1917.

Chapter 12

1. *Cascade (Iowa) Pioneer*, December 20, 1917.
2. *Chicago Tribune*, January 29, 1918.
3. *Chicago Tribune*, February 1, 1918.
4. Schalk told Manager Clarence Rowland of his draft status. *Chicago Tribune*, January 31, 1918.
5. *Litchfield (Illinois) Daily News*, February 27, 1918; *Chicago Tribune*, February 28, 1918.
6. *Chicago Tribune*, January 31, 1918.
7. *Chicago Tribune*, March 16, 1918.
8. Baseball researcher Peter Morris, citing a comment by I.E. Sanborn of the *Chicago Tribune*.
9. *Boston Globe*, January 1, 1918.
10. Brown, *The Chicago White Sox*, page 116; Thorn, *The Armchair Book of Baseball*.
11. *Chicago Tribune*, March 21, 1918.
12. *Chicago Tribune*, March 26, 1918.
13. *Chicago Tribune*, March 19, 1918.
14. *Atlanta Constitution*, May 14, 1918.
15. *Chicago Tribune*, January 1, 1919.
16. *Chicago Tribune*, March 27, 1918.
17. *Chicago Tribune*, March 23, 1918.
18. *Chicago Tribune*, March 27, 1918.
19. *Chicago Tribune*, April 2, 1918.
20. *Chicago Tribune*, April 15, 1918.
21. *Chicago Tribune*, April 17, 1918.
22. *Christian Science Monitor*, May 23, 1918.
23. *Washington Post*, June 22, 1918.
24. *New York Times*, June 22, 1918.
25. *Chicago Tribune*, May 16, 1918.

26. *Ibid.*
27. *The Sporting News*, June 18, 1918.
28. *Chicago Tribune*, June 14, 1918.
29. *Chicago Tribune*, June 11, 1918.
30. *Chicago Tribune*, June 13, 1918.
31. *Chicago Tribune*, June 18, 1918.
32. *Chicago Tribune*, June 26, 1918.
33. Jim Nitz, Felsch Biography Project article, Society for American Baseball Research.
34. *Chicago Tribune*, May 16, 1918.
35. *Kansas City Star*, July 20, 1915.
36. Play-by-play summary in *Chicago Daily News*, June 28, 1918.
37. *Chicago Daily News*, June 28, 1918; *Chicago Tribune*, June 29, 1918.
38. *The Sporting News Guide*. The play occurred June 28, 1964.
39. Macht, *Connie Mack and the Early Years of Baseball*, page 253.
40. Article under Schalk's byline. *New York Journal-American*, August 28, 1955. A *Baseball Digest* article (January-February 1955) stated that one of the victims at first was Charlie Jamieson of Cleveland in 1920.
41. *Chicago Tribune*, July 2, 1918.
42. *Chicago Tribune*, January 1, 1919.
43. Fleitz, *Shoeless: The Life and Times of Joe Jackson*, page 153.
44. *Christian Science Monitor*, July 2, 1918.
45. *Washington Post*, July 2, 1918.
46. *Chicago Tribune*, August 6, 1918.
47. *Chicago Tribune*, July 15, 1918.
48. Retrosheet.org.
49. *Chicago Tribune*, July 22, 1918.
50. *Chicago American*, July 20, 1918.
51. *Chicago American*, July 20 and 23, 1918.
52. *Chicago Tribune*, July 21, 1918.
53. *Chicago Tribune*, July 27, 1918.
54. *Boston Globe*, September 3, 1918.
55. *Chicago Tribune*, September 2, 1918.
56. *Chicago Tribune*, September 3, 1918.
57. *Chicago Tribune*, September 15, 1918.
58. *Chicago Tribune*, September 10 and 16, 1918.
59. *Chicago Tribune*, October 7, 1918.
60. *Chicago Tribune*, October 27, 1918.

Chapter 13

1. *Chicago Tribune*, January 1, 1919.
2. Ibid.
3. Ibid.
4. Bill Veeck, *The Hustler's Handbook*. Quotes from team secretary Harry Grabiner's journal.
5. *Chicago Tribune*, February 11, 1919.
6. *Chicago Tribune*, March 22, 1919.
7. *Chicago Tribune*, March 21, 1919.
8. *Chicago Tribune*, March 23, 1919.

9. *Washington Post*, various articles between May 29 and July 5, 1918.
10 *Chicago Tribune*, March 29, 1919.
11 *Atlanta Constitution*, April 13, 1919.
12 *Chicago Tribune*, April 21, 1919.
13 Asinof, *Eight Men Out.*
14. *Ibid.*
15. Fleitz, *Shoeless: The Life and Times of Joe Jackson*, page 154.
16. Thorn, *The Armchair Book of Baseball.*
17. Brown, *The Chicago White Sox,* page 117.
18. Asinof, *Eight Men Out.*
19. *Chicago Tribune*, May 28, 1919.
20. *Chicago Tribune*, June 1, 1919.
22. *Chicago Tribune*, June 8, 1919.
22. *Chicago Tribune*, June 4, 1919.
23. *Chicago Tribune*, June 22, 1919.
24. *Chicago Tribune*, June 29, 1919
25. *Chicago Tribune*, August 10, 1919.
26. *Chicago Tribune*, August 3, 1919.
27. *Chicago Tribune*, July 22, 1919. In both games, Dickie Kerr earned victories in relief, 7–6 and 5–4. The doubleheader started at 2 P.M.
28. *Washington Post*, September 10, 1919.
29. *Chicago Tribune*, July 27, 1919.
30. *Chicago Tribune*, August 17, 1919.
31. *Atlanta Constitution*, August 24, 1919.
32. *Boston Globe*, September 16, 1919.

Chapter 14

1. Quoted by Asinof, *Eight Men Out.*
2. Syndicated article published in hundreds of newspapers, including the *Kansas City Star*, September 26, 1919.
3. *Atlanta Constitution*, August 24, 1919.
4. *Atlanta Constitution*, August 31, 1919.
5. *Chicago Tribune*, September 24, 1919.
6. On November 25, 2007, the *Chicago Tribune* posted some heretofore missing documents related to the Black Sox conspiracy, including a copy of the notice calling a special meeting.
7. *Chicago Tribune*, September 17, 1919.
8. *Chicago Tribune*, November 25, 2007, reporting on the discovery of heretofore missing documents related to the Black Sox conspiracy. At the time, reports appeared in many newspapers, including the *Washington Post*, September 18, 1919.
9. *Chicago Tribune*, September 17, 1919.
10. *Chicago Tribune*, September 29, 1919.
11. Dellinger, *Red Legs and Black Sox,* page 228; Society for American Baseball Research biography of Collins.
12. Asinof, *Eight Men Out*, page 70.
13. Asinof, *Eight Men Out,* page 41.
14. Dellinger, *Red Legs and Black Sox,* page 201.
15. "I Recall," by Hugh Fullerton, *The Sporting News*, October 17, 1935, page 5.
16. Dellinger, *Red Legs and Black Sox,* page 202; Asinof, *Eight Men Out*, page 46.
17. Asinof, *Eight Men Out*, Page 46.
18. Fullerton, *The Sporting News*, October 17, 1935.
19. *Ibid.*
20. Dellinger, *Red Legs and Black Sox,* page 207; Leventhal, *Take Me Out to the Ballpark*, pages 64–65.
21. Dellinger, *Red Legs and Black Sox,* page 210.
22. *New York Times*, October 2, 1919.
23. Dellinger, *Red Legs and Black Sox,* page 214.
24. Published in the *Atlanta Constitution*, October 17, 1919, and other U.S. newspapers.
25. *New York Times*, October 2, 1919.
26. *Chicago Tribune*, October 2, 1919.
27. *New York Times*, October 2, 1919.
28. Dellinger, *Red Legs and Black Sox,* page 234.
29. Fleitz, *Shoeless: The Life and Times of Joe Jackson*, page 178, citing Bob Broeg's *Super Stars of Baseball*, page 40.
30. Fullerton, *The Sporting News*, October 17, 1935.
31. Asinof, *Eight Men Out*, page 72.
32. Associated Press report carrying a Memphis dateline, published in the *Chicago Tribune*, February 14, 1937.
33. Dellinger, *Red Legs and Black Sox,* page 228.
34. Asinof, *Eight Men Out*, pages 66–67.
35. *Boston Globe*, October 3, 1919.
36. Dellinger, *Red Legs and Black Sox,* page 234.
37. Neale was a multi-sport athlete. He played on Jim Thorpe's football team, the Canton Bulldogs, before joining the Reds in 1916. Even before he left major-league baseball, Neale returned to the gridiron as a coach. His underdog Washington & Jefferson College (Washington, Pennsylvania) battled California to a scoreless tie in the 1922 Rose Bowl. Later, he coached the Philadelphia Eagles to two National Football League titles. In 1969, Neale entered the Pro Football Hall of Fame.
38. *Boston Globe*, October 3, 1919.
39. Dellinger, *Red Legs and Black Sox,* page 210.
40. Asinof, *Eight Men Out*, pages 88–89.
41. Asinof, *Eight Men Out*, page 90; Carney, *Burying the Black Sox*, page 81.
42. Werber and Rogers, *Memories of a Ballplayer,* page 9.
43. Dellinger, *Red Legs and Black Sox,* page 341.
44. *Chicago Tribune*, October 4, 1919.

45. The article carried Gleason's byline, but he no doubt had assistance from a ghostwriter. *Chicago Tribune*, October 4, 1919.
46. *Washington Post*, October 5, 1919.
47. *New York Times*, October 5, 1919.
48. *Chicago Tribune*, October 5, 1919.
49. "In the Wake of the News" column, *Chicago Tribune*, October 5, 1919.
50. Baseball-Almanac.com.
51. "In the Wake of the News" column, *Chicago Tribune*, October 8, 1919.
52. Asinof, *Eight Men Out*, page 115.

Chapter 15

1. Carney, *Burying the Black Sox*, page 50.
2. *Ibid*, page 49.
3. Asinof, *Eight Men Out*, pages 93–94.
4. *Atlanta Constitution* and others, October 10, 1919.
5. *Chicago Tribune*, October 21, 1919.
6. *Collyer's Eye*, December 13, 1919.
7. I.E. Sanborn in the *Chicago Tribune*, September 20, 1919.
8. *Chicago Tribune*, September 25, 1919.
9. *The Sporting News*, December 25, 1919, page 4.
10. *The Sporting News*, January 8, 1920.
11. Carney, *Burying the Black Sox*, page 259.
12. Asinof, *Bleeding Between the Lines*, pages 93–96.
13. *Ibid*.
14. Most likely, it was February 1969, when the New York chapter of the Baseball Writers Association of America presented Schalk the Retroactive Award. Schalk might not have liked sportswriters, but not so much that he wouldn't accept their awards.
15. Asinof, *Bleeding Between the Lines*, page 97.
16. *Ibid*.

Chapter 16

1. *The Sporting News*, October 7, 1920.
2. *Chicago Tribune*, February 21, 1920.
3. Asinof, *Bleeding Between the Lines*, Page 94.
4. *Chicago Tribune*, November 28, 1920; *Collyer's Eye*, December 13, 1919.
5. *Chicago Tribune*, February 3, 1920. Also on the program was Joe Farrell, White Sox booster and member of Comiskey's Woodland Bards.
6. Levitt, Armour and Levitt, "History versus Harry Frazee: Re-revising the Story," *The Baseball Research Journal* (2008), pages 26–41.
7. *The Sporting News*, February 3, 1921.
8. Mahl, *The Spitball Knuckleball Book*, pages 91–95.

9. *The Sporting News*, November 21, 1940.
10. *New York Times*, January 11, 1920.
11. *Chicago Tribune*, May 21, 1920.
12. Richard C. Lindberg, *The White Sox Encyclopedia*.
13. Fleitz, *Shoeless: The Life and Times of Joe Jackson*, page 209.
14. *The Sporting News*, October 7, 1920.
15. Lindberg, *The White Sox Encyclopedia*.
16. *Chicago Tribune*, April 15, 1920.
17. *Chicago Tribune*, April 18, 1920.
18. *Chicago Tribune*, April 22, 1920.
19. *Chicago Tribune*, April 25, 1920.
20. *Chicago Tribune*, April 28, 1920.
21. Asinof, *Eight Men Out*.
22. Asinof, *Bleeding Between the Lines*, pages 93–94.
23. *The New York Times* and *Chicago Tribune*, May 13, 1920.
24. *Chicago Tribune*, May 18 and 20, 1920; *Boston Globe* and *New York Times*, May 22, 1920; Minneapolis statistics courtesy of Stew Thornley.
25. *Chicago Tribune*, May 15, 1920.
26. *Chicago Tribune*, June 6, 1920.
27. *New York Times*, August 4, 1920.
28. *Chicago Tribune*, August 10, 1920.
29. *Chicago Tribune*, August 5, 1920.
30. *Chicago Tribune*, "Wake of the News" column, June 24, 1920. Verse credited to "Em Ef."
31. *Chicago Tribune*, June 19, 1920.
32. Cottrell, *Blackball, the Black Sox and the Babe*, pages 175–176, citing *Baseball Magazine*.
33. *Chicago Tribune*, August 3, 1920.
34. *Chicago Daily News*, July 1, 1920.
35. *Chicago Tribune*, July 5, 1920.
36. *Washington Post*, August 10, 1920.
37. *Chicago Tribune*, August 21, 1920.
38. "Notes of the Sox," *Chicago Tribune*, August 28, 1920.
39. "Risberg and Weaver were the best players New York had today," stated the *Chicago Tribune* after the game of August 28, 1920.
40. Fleitz, *Shoeless: The Life and Times of Joe Jackson*, page 217.
41. *Chicago Tribune*, September 1, 1920.
42. Fleitz, *Shoeless: The Life and Times of Joe Jackson*, pages 218–219, citing *Baseball Digest*, June 1949.
43. *Chicago Tribune*, September 5, 1920.
44. *Washington Post* and *Chicago Tribune*, September 13, 1920.
45. *Chicago Tribune*, September 14, 1920.
46. *Chicago Tribune*, August 31, 1920.

Chapter 17

1. *Boston Globe*, September 19, 1920.
2. *Boston Globe*, September 24, 1920.

3. *Boston Globe*, September 23, 1920; *Chicago Tribune*, September 25, 1920.

4. *Chicago Tribune*, September 14, 1920.

5. *Chicago Tribune*, September 28, 1920; Asinof, *Eight Men Out*, page 168.

6. Synopsis of Cicotte's testimony before the Cook County Grand Jury, September 28, 1920. The document, for decades believed lost, surfaced in late 2007 and was posted on the *Chicago Tribune* web site.

7. James L. Kilgallen, United News correspondent. Column published in the *Atlanta Constitution*, October 31, 1920.

8. Brown, *The Chicago White Sox*, page 110.

9. Asinof, *Eight Men Out*, pages 170–172.

10. Correspondence with the author, December 18, 2008.

11. *Boston Globe*, September 29, 1920.

12. Asinof, *Eight Men Out*, page 174.

13. *Chicago Tribune*, May 21, 1970, taken from a 1940 interview with the *Tribune*'s Ed Burns.

14. *Chicago Tribune*, September 29, 1920.

15. Lindberg, *The White Sox Encyclopedia*, page 29.

16. Cottrell, *Blackball, the Black Sox and the Babe*, page 228, citing a *New York Tribune* article of October 1, 1920.

17. *Boston Globe*, October 2, 1920.

18. United Press International feature story carried in many papers, including the *Daily Inter Lake*, Kalispell, Montana, August 12, 1954.

19. *Chicago Tribune*, October 5, 1920.

20. *Chicago Tribune*, October 18, 1920.

21. *New York Times*, October 1, 1920.

Chapter 18

1. *Chicago Tribune*, November 28, 1920 and January 16, 1921.

2. *Chicago Tribune*, March 5, 1921.

3. *Chicago Tribune*, January 28, 1921.

4. *Chicago Tribune*, February 16, 1921.

5. Retrosheet.org.

6. *Chicago Tribune*, January 29, 1921.

7. *Chicago Tribune*, April 12, 1921.

8. *Chicago Tribune*, March 27, 1921; Sagert, *Joe Jackson: A Biography*, page 135.

9. Asinof, *Eight Men Out*, page 232.

10. *Chicago Tribune*, June 28 and 29, 1921.

11. Asinof, *Eight Men Out*, pages 242–243.

12. *New York Times*, July 12, 1921.

13. In *The Sporting News* of August 4, 1921, Oscar C. Reichow referred to Schalk being present but contended that the fraternization never happened.

14. Asinof, *Eight Men Out*, pages 242–243.

15. Wire-service account. *Dubuque (Iowa) Telegraph-Herald*, August 3, 1921.

16. Asinof, *Eight Men Out*, page 227.

17. *Chicago Tribune*, July 30, 1921.

18. *The Sporting News*, August 4, 1921.

19. Sagert, *Joe Jackson: A Biography*, page 136.

20. *Chicago Tribune*, July 29, 1921.

21. *Ibid.*

22. *Chicago Tribune*, August 4, 1921.

23. *Chicago Tribune*, May 21, 1970.

24. *Chicago Tribune*, August 4, 1921.

25. *New York Times*, August 8, 1921.

26. *Chicago Tribune*, August 9, 1921. DePauw University records confirm the birthdate as August 8, 1921.

27. *Chicago Tribune*, August 12, 1921.

28. *Chicago Tribune*, August 7, 1921.

29. *Chicago Tribune*, July 6, 1921.

30. *Washington Post*, December 30, 1921.

31. *Chicago Tribune* and *Boston Globe*, August 21, 1921.

32. *Chicago Tribune*, October 1, 1921.

33. *New York Times*, October 2, 1921.

34. "In the Wake of the News," *Chicago Tribune*, October 5, 1921.

35. *Litchfield (Illinois) Daily News*, October 24, 1921; *Decatur (Illinois) Review*, October 22, 1921.

36. *New York Times*, November 3, 1921.

37. *Chicago Tribune*, December 30, 1921.

Chapter 19

1. *Chicago Tribune*, January 1, 1922.

2. *Chicago Tribune*, March 19, 1922, and April 9, 1922.

3. *Chicago Tribune*, February 24, 1922.

4. "In the Wake of the News," *Chicago Tribune*, April 16, 1922.

5. *Chicago Tribune*, April 17, 1922.

6. *Chicago Tribune*, May 1, 1922.

7. Jack Laing column, quoting Schalk, published May 29, 1968, in the *Syracuse (New York) Post-Standard*.

8. *Chicago Tribune*, May 2, 1922.

9. He lost credit for the first of those four years later, when record-keepers rescinded credit for Jim Scott, who blanked Washington through nine innings in 1914. However, the contest went into the 10th inning, and Scott gave up two hits in a 1–0 loss.

10. *Chicago Tribune*, September 8, 1922.

11. *Chicago Tribune*, August 16, 1922.

12. *The Sporting News*, August 17, 1922.

13. *Chicago Herald-Examiner*, August 2, 1922.

14. *Chicago Tribune*, August 29, 1922.

15. Society for American Baseball Research Baseball Records Committee; Retrosheet.org.

16. *Chicago Tribune*, September 22, 1922.

17. *Chicago Tribune*, May 12, 1922.
18. *Decatur (Illinois) Review*, May 13, 1922.

Chapter 20

1. *Atlanta Constitution*, February 12, 1923.
2. *Chicago Tribune*, March 5, 1923.
3. *Chicago Tribune*, March 28, 1923.
4. Lyons' personal account, stating Bridges asked Schalk to catch a few Baylor pitchers, appeared in the *Chicago Tribune*, April 14, 1932. Schalk, who told the story many times, stated for the *Chicago Tribune* of February 1, 1955, that he asked Bridges for a pitcher to warm him up.
5. *Los Angeles Times*, March 26, 1923.
6. *New York Times*, April 24, 1923.
7. *Chicago Tribune*, April 2, 1923.
8. *Chicago Tribune*, April 23, 1923.
9. *Chicago Tribune*, October 15 1923.
10. *Chicago Tribune*, April 26, 1923.
11. *Chicago Tribune*, April 27, 1923
12. *Washington Post*, February 18, 1928.
13. *Chicago Tribune*, July 3, 1923.
14. *Southtown Economist*, Chicago, February 16, 1955.
15. Shirley Povich column, *Washington Post*, October 15, 1939.
16. *New York Times*, June 7, 1923.
17. *Chicago Tribune*, October 17, 1923.

Chapter 21

1. *Chicago Tribune*, October 26, 1923.
2. *Chicago Tribune*, December 11, 1923.
3. *Chicago Tribune*, December 12, 1923.
4. *Washington Post*, February 23, 1924.
5. *Chicago Tribune*, April 13, 1924.
6. *New York Times*, May 18, 1924.
7. *Chicago Tribune* and *Washington Post*, April 21, 1924.
8. *Chicago Tribune*, May 7, 1924; SABR home run log.
9. *Chicago Tribune*, June 19, 1924.
10. *Chicago Tribune*, March 4, 1924.
11. *Washington Post*, May 26, 1924.
12. University of Missouri-Kansas City "Famous Trials" web pages; Swanson, *Chicago Days*.
13. *Chicago Tribune*, May 22, 1924.
14. Associated Press report, *Alton (Illinois) Telegraph*, June 12, 1924.
15. *Decatur (Illinois) Review*, June 24, 1924.
16. *Chicago Tribune*, May 17, 1925.
17. *Chicago Tribune*, August 27, 1924.
18. *Chicago Tribune*, September 27, 1924.
19. *Washington Post*, October 1, 1924.
20. *Chicago Tribune*, October 2, 1924.
21. *Chicago Tribune*, October 7, 1924.

22. *Washington Post*, November 4, 1924.
23. *Chicago Tribune*, October 27, 1924.

Chapter 22

1. *Chicago Tribune*, March 6, 1925.
2. *Chicago Tribune*, February 13, 1925.
3. *Chicago Tribune*, February 21, 1925.
4. *Chicago Tribune*, February 28, 1925.
5. *Chicago Tribune*, March 9, 1925.
6. *Chicago Tribune*, March 10, 1925.
7. *Los Angeles Times*, February 22, 1925.
8. *Chicago Tribune*, December 26, 1924.
9. Lindberg, *White Sox Encyclopedia*, Page 34.
10. *The Youth's Companion*, March 26, 1925.
11. *Saturday Evening Post*, April 2, 1921.
12. *Chicago Tribune*, April 28, 1925.
13. *Chicago Tribune*, June 20, 2004.
14. Arch Ward's "Wake of the News," *Chicago Tribune*, February 8, 1955.
15. *Chicago Daily News*, May 12, 1925.
16. *New York Times* and *Chicago Tribune*, May 12, 1925.
17. *Chicago Tribune*, May 12, 1925.
18. Kenney, *Chicago Jazz: A Cultural History 1904–1930*, page 70.
19. *Chicago Tribune*, May 16, 1925.
20. *Chicago Tribune*, April 27, 1925.
21. *New York Times* and *Chicago Tribune*, June 20, 1925.
22. *The Sporting News*, June 11, 1925.
23. Macht, *Connie Mack and the Early Years of Baseball*, page 253.
24. *Chicago Tribune*, August 13, 1925.
25. *Washington Post*, August 31, 1925.
26. *Chicago Tribune*, September 20, 1925.
27. *New York Times*, September 24, 1925.
28. *New York Times*, September 25, 1925.
29. *Chicago Tribune*, October 8, 1925.
30. *Chicago Tribune*, November 7, 1925.
31. *Chicago Tribune*, October 19, 1925.
32. *Chicago Tribune*, October 26, 1925.

Chapter 23

1. Google Maps street views.
2. *Chicago American*, November 12, 1926.
3. *Southtown Economist*, Chicago, January 12, 1926.
4. *Washington Post*, January 10, 1926; *Chicago Tribune*, January 15, 1926.
5. *Ibid*.
6. *Chicago Tribune*, January 16, 1926.
7. James Schalk interview, May 15, 2008.
8. Cobb with Stump, *My Life in Baseball*, pages 158–159.
9. *Washington Post*, March 2, 1926.

10. *Galveston (Texas) Daily News*, May 16, 1926.

11. *Chicago Tribune*, July 11, 1926.

12. *Washington Post*, August 27, 1926.

13. Shirley Povich column, *Washington Post*, October 15, 1939.

14. Daniel M. Daniel syndicated column. *Oakland (California) Tribune*, December 7, 1926.

15. *Chicago Tribune* and *Los Angeles Times*, October 5, 1926.

16. Daniel M. Daniel syndicated column. *Oakland (California) Tribune*, December 7, 1926.

17. Don Maxwell analysis, *Chicago Tribune*, November 16, 1926.

18. Norman E. Brown, sports editor of the *Sarasota (Florida) Herald*, said that Comiskey saved at least $20,000 by firing Collins.

19. *Chicago Tribune, Chicago American* and *New York Times*, November 12, 1926.

20. "In the Wake of the News," *Chicago Tribune*, November 14, 1926.

21. *Chicago Tribune*, December 12, 1926.

22. Personal letter on White Sox stationery, dated November 16, 1926, on file at National Baseball Hall of Fame.

23. *The Sporting News*, December 23, 1926.

24. *Chicago Tribune*, January 2, 1927.

25. *Chicago Tribune*, January 7, 1927.

26. *Chicago Tribune*, January 6, 1927.

27. Asinof, *Eight Men Out*, pages 284–5.

28. *Chicago Tribune*, January 13, 1927.

29. *Chicago Tribune*, March 8, 1927.

30. *Chicago Tribune*, March 5, 1927.

31. *Chicago Tribune*, March 8, 1927.

32. Urban C. Faber II, telephone interview with author, November 22, 2004.

33. Sox catcher Bucky Crouse gave an interviewer the details more than a quarter-century afterward. Murdock, *Baseball Players and Their Times: Oral Histories of the Game, 1920–1940*.

34. *Boston Globe*, January 27, 1951.

35. *The Sporting News*, April 14, 1927.

36. *New York Times*, March 22, 1927.

37. *Chicago Tribune*, April 3, 1927.

38. *Chicago Daily News*, April 11, 1927.

39. *Chicago Tribune*, April 19, 1927.

40. *Chicago Tribune*, April 20, 1927.

41. *Chicago Tribune*, April 21, 1927.

42. Ibid.

43. *Chicago Evening Post*, April 19, 1927.

44. The article likely appeared in hundreds of newspapers. Among them were the *Washington Post* on June 8, 1927, and *Atlanta Constitution* on June 12, 1927.

45. *Chicago Tribune*, July 23, 1927.

46. *Los Angeles Times*, August 21, 1927.

47. "Pickups and Putouts," *New York Times*, June 8, 1927.

48. *New York Times*, June 9, 1927.

49. *Chicago Tribune*, June 21, 1927.

50. *New York Times*, June 16, 1927.

51. *The Sporting News*, July 14, 1927.

52. *Chicago Tribune*, June 29, 1927.

53. *Washington Post*, July 24, 1927.

54. *Chicago Tribune*, August 16, 1927.

55. "Charles Comiskey wants to run club but keeps manager," *Lima (Ohio) News*, August 20, 1927.

56. *Chicago Tribune*, August 17, 1927.

57. Compiled from Retrosheet.org; *Chicago Tribune*, August 6, 1927; *Washington Post*, August 7, 1937.

58. *Chicago Tribune*, August 28, 1927.

59. *Chicago Tribune*, September 20, 1927.

Chapter 24

1. *Chicago Tribune*, September 29, 1927.

2. *Chicago Tribune*, December 1, 1927.

3. *Chicago Tribune*, February 4, 1928.

4. *Chicago Tribune*, December 25, 1927.

5. *Washington Post*, March 27, 1928.

6. *Lincoln (Nebraska) State Journal*, March 31, 1928.

7. *New York Times*, March 15, 1928.

8. *Chicago Daily News*, April 10, 1928.

9. Undated article from a Litchfield newspaper.

10. *Chicago Tribune*, May 5, 1928.

11. *Chicago Tribune*, May 17, 1928.

12. Retrosheet.org. Game log of White Sox 1928 season.

13. *Atlanta Constitution*, May 23, 1928.

14. *Chicago Tribune*, May 24, 1924; Retrosheet.org.

15. *The Sporting News*, June 7, 1928.

16. Letter from Schalk dated July 4, 1928, National Baseball Hall of Fame archives, Cooperstown, N.Y.

17. *Chicago Tribune*, July 5, 1928.

18. *The Sporting News*, July 12, 1928.

19. *Chicago Tribune*, July 8, 1928.

20. *Chicago Tribune*, July 8 and July 12, 1928.

21. Western Union telegram, dated July 13, 1928, addressed to Schalk's home in Chicago, National Baseball Hall of Fame archives, Cooperstown, N.Y.

22. *Chicago Tribune*, July 28, 1928.

23. United Press. *Lincoln (Nebraska) Evening State Journal* and *Daily News*, November 21, 1928.

24. Associated Press dispatch dated July 27, 1928, National Baseball Hall of Fame archives.

25. Norman Macht interview notes shared with the author, July 4, 2008. Macht was a personal friend of the younger Sullivan (1910–1994), who himself played in the majors a dozen seasons.

26. *Chicago Tribune*, August 12, 1932.

Chapter 25

1. *Southtown Economist,* September 21 and 28, 1928.
2. *Chicago Tribune,* October 23, 1928.
3. *Chicago Tribune,* December 20, 1967.
4. Illinois Bowling Association web site.
5. *Chicago Tribune,* February 9, 1936.
6. *Chicago Tribune,* November 13, 1928.
7. *Washington Post,* October 31, 1928.
8. United Press. *Lincoln (Nebraska) Evening State Journal and Daily News,* November 21, 1928.
9. *New York Times,* February 17, 1929.
10. *New York Times,* February 19, 1929.
11. *Southtown Economist,* May 10 and May 29, 1929; *Chicago Tribune* and *New York Times,* June 4, 1929.
12. *Chicago Tribune,* June 3, 1929.
13. *New York Times,* July 7, 1929.
14. *New York Times,* September 15, 1929; Retrosheet.org.
15. *Washington Post,* November 5, 1929.
16. Associated Press story, published in the *Washington Post,* November 5, 1929.
17. Advertisement in *Chicago Tribune,* February 28, 1931. That the residence was an apartment was mentioned in a *Buffalo (New York) Times* feature story in 1935.
18. *Chicago Tribune,* January 17, 1930.
19. Jack Laing column. *Post-Standard,* Syracuse, New York, October 9, 1965.
20. Parker, *Fouled Away: The Baseball Tragedy of Hack Wilson,* page 49.
21. *Chicago Tribune,* October 17, 1930.
22. *Chicago Tribune,* September 24, 1930.
23. *Southtown Economist,* October 31, 1930; *Chicago Tribune,* November 2, 1930.
24. *Encyclopedia of Chicago,* Chicago Historical Society.
25. *Los Angeles Times,* July 21, 1931.
26. *Washington Post,* September 9, 1931.

Chapter 26

1. *New York Times,* November 7 and 18, 1931.
2. *Washington Post,* December 2, 1931.
3. *Washington Post,* January 8, 1932.
4. *The Sporting News,* March 10, 1932.
5. *Chicago Tribune,* April 16, 1932.
6. *New York Times,* September 25, 1932.
7. Swanson, *Chicago Days,* page 145.
8. "In the Wake of the News," *Chicago Tribune,* March 21, 1933.
9. "In the Wake of the News," *Chicago Tribune,* March 31, 1933.
10. *Washington Post,* April 9, 1933.
11. *Chicago Tribune,* October 22, 1933.

12. *Chicago Tribune,* February 3, 1934.
13. *Chicago Tribune,* December 13, 1933.
14. *New York Times,* October 24, 1934.
15. *Washington Post,* February 19, 1935.
16. *Chicago Tribune,* March 20, 1935.
17. *The Sporting News,* May 23, 1935.
18. *New York Times,* May 12, 1935.
19. *Buffalo (New York) Times,* circa 1936.
20. *The Sporting News,* August 3 and 24, 1936.
21. *New York Times,* September 22, 1936.
22. *Chicago Tribune,* July 30 and August 9, 1936.
23. *Chicago Tribune,* October 26, 1936. Weather: *Chicago Daily News,* October 26, 1936.
24. Undated article, Hall of Fame archives, August 1940; *The Sporting News,* November 21, 1940.
25. *Chicago Tribune,* January 6, 1943.
26. *New York Times,* January 7, 1943.
27. *New York Times,* October 20, 1936.
28. *The Sporting News,* October 1, 1936.

Chapter 27

1. *New York Times,* November 25 and 27, 1937.
2. *The Sporting News,* September 16, 1937.
3. "In the Wake of the News," *Chicago Tribune,* February 18, 1938.
4. *The Sporting News,* March 17, 1938.
5. *The Sporting News,* April 21, 1938.
6. United Press article. *Corpus Christi (Texas) Times,* July 20, 1938.
7. *Chicago Tribune,* September 5, 1938.
8. *Chicago Tribune,* July 31 and August 1, 1938.
9. *Southeast Economist* (Chicago), March 16, 1939.
10. *The Sporting News,* September 15, 1938.
11. *The Sporting News,* September 29, 1938.
12. Joe Williams column, *New York World-Telegram,* October 31, 1938.
13. *Chicago Tribune,* July 18, 1939.
14. *The Sporting News,* July 20, 1939.
15. Initial reports carried by The Associated Press, *Chicago Tribune* and others, specified Miller. A year later, the *Milwaukee Journal* cited Perry. On September 26, 1940, W. Blaine Patton reported in *The Sporting News* that Miller opposed his friend Schalk's ouster.
16. *Chicago Daily News,* July 19, 1939.
17. *Los Angeles Times,* July 30, 1939.
18. *The Sporting News,* September 14, 1939.
19. Retrosheet.org.
20. DePauw University Web site listing baseball letter-winners; *The Sporting News,* March 18, 1943; *Chicago Tribune,* March 7, 1943; undated article, May 20, 1943.

21. *The Sporting News*, July 27, 1939.
22. *New York Times*, November 7, 1939.
23. *Milwaukee Journal*, July 21, 1940.
24. *Los Angeles Times*, December 3, 1940.

Chapter 28

1. *Daily Southtown* (Chicago), September 26, 1940, and Google.
2. *Chicago Tribune* (Southwest edition), January 5, 1941.
3. *Southtown Economist* (Chicago) of March 6, 1946, included several of these details after Pauline suffered a few bumps in a minor traffic accident.
4. *Chicago Tribune*, November 8, 1958, and author's interview with James Schalk, 2008.
5. Lillian Hendricks interview, May 6, 2007.
6. *Southtown Economist* (Chicago), October 22, 1941.
7. *The Sporting News*, February 12, 1947.
8. *Chicago Tribune*, March 2, 1941.
9. *Southtown Economist* (Chicago), July 19, 1944.
10. *Washington Post*, October 2, 1944.
11. *New York Times*, August 16, 1946.
12. *Chicago Tribune*, January 31, 1943; March 25, 1946.; April 21, 1948; December 12, 1949.
13. James Schalk interview, May 15, 2008.
14. "In the Wake of the News," *Chicago Tribune*, April 15, 1947.
15. Purdue University Board of Trustee Minutes, June 14, 1947, page 588.
16. *New York World-Telegram and Sun*, July 25, 1955.
17. Purdue University Board of Trustee Minutes, May 5, 1965, page 398.
18. *The Sporting News*, June 21, 1950.
19. *New York Times*, November 14, 1950.
20. *Chicago Daily News*, June 7, 1948; *Chicago Tribune*, June 8, 1948.
21. *Chicago Tribune*, March 7, 1950.
22. *Chicago Tribune*, March 29, 1950.
23. *The Sporting News*, April 5, 1950.
24. A photo from the 27th annual Old Timers' banquet shows a group that included Schalk, Faber and Weaver.
25. Associated Press article datelined San Francisco. *Chicago Tribune*, February 3, 1956.
26. *Chicago Tribune*, February 1, 1956. Pallbearer information from Black Sox expert Gene Carney.
27. *The Sporting News*, July 2, 1958.
28. The story was told countless times. Irwin M. Howe included it in a profile of Schalk for his series on the 10 best players he had ever seen, *Chicago Tribune*, April 14, 1930.

Chapter 29

1. *Chicago Tribune*, November 8, 1958.
2. Undated article, likely from a Litchfield newspaper.
3. Litchfield centennial book, 1953.
4. Author's interviews with Lillian Hendricks, March 26 and May 6, 2007.
5. Author's interview with Lillian Hendricks, December 4, 2008.
6. Author's interview with Lillian Hendricks, December 4, 2008.
7. Deborah Brinson, widow of Schalk grandson Roy Brinson, correspondence with author dated October 6, 2007.
8. Author's interview with Lillian Hendricks, December 4, 2008.
9. Correspondence with Deborah Brinson, October 6, 2007.
10. Author's interview with Lillian Hendricks, December 4, 2008.
11. *The Sporting News*, March 18, 1943, and DePauw University web site.
12. Registrar's Office, DePauw University, 2008.
13. Author's interview with Jim Schalk, son of Geraldine Hudson Schalk, December 3, 2008.
14. *New York Times*, June 7, 1935.
15. *New York Times*, July 19, 1935.
16. Author's interview with Jim Schalk, December 3, 2008.
17. *Washington Post*, October 11, 1941.
18. Author's interview with Lillian Hendricks, December 4, 2008.
19. Author's interview with Jim Schalk, May 15, 2008.
20. Author's interview with Lillian Hendricks, December 4, 2008.

Chapter 30

1. *Baseball Magazine*, December 1913.
2. *Baseball Magazine*, December 1915 and December 1916.
3. Cottrell, *Blackball, the Black Sox and the Babe*, page 212, citing the *New York Tribune*, September 14, 1920.
4. *Washington Post*, December 30, 1921.
5. Brian Bell, *Washington Post*, February 28, 1930.
6. Syndicated column carried in newspapers nationwide, including the *Jefferson City (Missouri) Post-Tribune*, February 6, 1930.
7. Syndicated column. *Alton (Illinois) Telegraph*, January 29, 1923.
8. Cobb with Stump, *My Life in Baseball*, page 266.
9. National Baseball Hall of Fame.

10. *New York Times*, January 17, 1955.
11. *Los Angeles Times*, December 25, 1935.
12. *New York Times*, January 1, 1936.
13. National Baseball Hall of Fame.
14. Society for American Baseball Research, *The SABR Baseball List & Record Book*, page 301.
15. James, *Whatever Happened to the Hall of Fame?*, page 111.
16. James, *The New Bill James Historical Baseball Abstract*, page 395.
17. *New York World-Telegram and Sun*, February 1, 1955.
18. United Press article, *Litchfield (Illinois) Daily News*, February 1, 1955.
19. *Chicago Tribune*, February 1, 1955.
20. Old Timers' Baseball Association of Chicago Annual Reunion and Dinner program, February 3, 1955.
21. Bill Roeder article in the *New York World-Telegram and Sun*, June 21, 1955.
22. "In the Wake of the News," *Chicago Tribune*, October 6, 1955.
23. *The Sporting News*, April 19, 1955.
24. *The Sporting News*, May 10, 1955.
25. Associated Press article, *Chicago Tribune*, July 26, 1955.
26. National Baseball Hall of Fame archives.
27. *New York Times* and *Chicago Tribune*, July 31, 1955.

Chapter 31

1. *Chicago Tribune*, June 3, 1957.
2. *Boston Globe*, May 14, 1919.
3. Handwritten letter from Schalk to Keener, National Baseball Hall of Fame archives.
4. Harvel Centennial book, 1973.
5. *Chicago Tribune*, October 2, 1959.
6. *Chicago Tribune*, December 15, 1963.
7. *Lafayette (Indiana) Journal and Courier*, August 1962.
8. *Chicago Tribune*, October 26, 1966; *Litchfield (Illinois) News-Herald*, October 29, 1966.

9. *The Sporting News*, November 5, 1966.
10. *Chicago Tribune* and *Washington Post*, February 4, 1965.
11. Associated Press article, carried in the *Hartford Courant* and hundreds of other papers, May 20, 1970.
12. *Daily Southtown*, Chicago, April 21, 2007.
13. Author's interview with Jim Schalk, December 3, 2008.
14. Bill Lee, *Hartford Courant*, February 4, 1969.
15. *Chicago Tribune*, April 17, 1969.
16. *Chicago Tribune* columnist Robert Wiedrich encouraged readers to send Schalk get-well cards. January 28, 1970.
17. *Chicago Sun-Times* and *Chicago Tribune*, February 28, 1970.
18. Author's interview with Lillian Hendricks, May 6, 2007.
19. Author's interview with Lillian Hendricks, December 4, 2008.
20. *Chicago Tribune*, February 28, 1970; Hendricks interview.
21. James Schalk, interview with author, May 15, 2008.
22. Associated Press photo, published in the *Alton (Illinois) Telegraph*, May 23, 1970.

Chapter 32

1. Estimated July 2007, down 4.6 percent since the 2000 census.
2. Joe Kempe Memoir, University of Illinois at Springfield, 1986–87. As he told it, he was the only one to show up for a scheduled board meeting. He moved, seconded and voted to add Schalk's name to the museum. Though some members were upset, the organization declined to rescind the action.
3. Author's personal experience, May 13, 2007.

Bibliography

Books

Asinof, Eliot. *Eight Men Out.* New York: Holt, Rinehart and Winston, 1963.

_____. *Bleeding Between the Lines.* New York: Holt, Rinehart and Winston, 1979.

Axelson, G.W. *Commy* (1919). Jefferson, N.C.: McFarland, 2003.

Brown, Warren. *The Chicago White Sox* (1952). Kent, Ohio: Kent State University Press, 2007.

Carney, Gene. *Burying the Black Sox: How Baseball's Cover-Up of the 1919 World Series Fix Almost Succeeded.* Dulles, Va.: Potomac, 2006.

Carroll, Bob, et al. *Total Football II.* New York: HarperCollins, 1999.

Cooper, Brian E. *Red Faber: A Biography of the Hall of Fame Spitball Pitcher.* Jefferson, N.C.: McFarland, 2007.

Cottrell, Robert C. *Blackball, the Black Sox and the Babe: Baseball's Crucial 1920 Season.* Jefferson, N.C.: McFarland, 2002.

Creamer, Robert W. *Stengel: His Life and Times.* New York: Simon & Schuster, 1984.

Dellinger, Susan. *Red Legs and Black Sox: Edd Roush and the Untold Story of the 1919 World Series.* Cincinnati: Emmis Books, 2006.

Elfers, James E. *The Tour to End All Tours.* Lincoln: University of Nebraska Press, 2003.

Farrell, James T. *My Baseball Diary* (1957). Carbondale: Southern Illinois University Press, 1998.

Fleitz, David L. *Shoeless: The Life and Times of Joe Jackson.* Jefferson, N.C.: McFarland, 2001.

Forker, Dom, Michael J. Pellowski, and Wayne Stewart. *Baffling Baseball Trivia.* New York: Sterling, 2004.

Gilbert, Brother, CFX. *Young Babe Ruth: His Early Life and Baseball Career, from the Memoirs of a Xaverian Brother.* Harry Rothgerber, editor. Jefferson, N.C.: McFarland, 1999.

Graham, Frank. *McGraw of the Giants: An Informal Biography.* New York: G.P. Putnam's Sons, 1944.

Hamann, Rex, and Bob Koehler. *The American Association Milwaukee Brewers.* Charleston, S.C.: Arcadia, 2004.

Historical Encyclopedia of Illinois. Chicago: Munsell, 1918.

Holmes, Dan. *Ty Cobb: A Biography.* Westport, Connecticut: Greenwood, 2004.

Huhn, Rick. *Eddie Collins: A Baseball Biography.* Jefferson, N.C.: McFarland, 2008.

Hurd, Owen. *Chicago History for Kids.* Chicago: Chicago Review Press, 2007.

Husman, John R. *Baseball in Toledo.* Charleston, S.C.: Arcadia, 2003.

James, Bill. *The New Bill James Historical Baseball Abstract.* New York: Simon & Schuster, 2001.

_____. *Whatever Happened to the Hall of Fame? Baseball, Cooperstown, and the Politics of Glory.* New York: Simon & Schuster, 1995.

_____, and Rob Neyer. *The Neyer/James Guide to Pitchers.* New York: Simon & Schuster, 2004.

Kenney, William Howland. *Chicago Jazz: A Cultural History 1904–1930.* New York: Oxford University Press, 1994.

Leventhal, Josh. *Take Me Out to the Ballpark: An Illustrated Tour of Baseball Parks Past and Present.* New York: Leventhal Publishers, 2003.

Lindberg, Richard C. *The White Sox Encyclopedia.* Philadelphia: Temple University Press, 1997.

Litchfield Centennial, Inc. *Centennial History of Litchfield.* 1953.

Lowry, Philip J. *Green Cathedrals: The Ultimate Celebration of Major League and Negro League Ballparks.* New York: Walker, 2006.

Macht, Norman L. *Connie Mack and the Early Years of Baseball.* Lincoln: University of Nebraska Press, 2007.

Mahl, Tom E. *The Spitball Knuckleball Book.* Elyria, Ohio: Trick Pitch Press, 2009.

Murdock, Eugene Converse. *Baseball Players and Their Times: Oral Histories of the Game, 1920–1940.* Westport, Conn.: Meckler, 1991.

Parker, Clifton Blue. *Fouled Away: The Baseball Tragedy of Hack Wilson.* Jefferson, N.C.: McFarland, 2000.

Podoll, Brian A. *The Minor League Milwaukee Brewers, 1859–1952.* Jefferson, N.C.: McFarland, 2003.

Reichler, Joseph L., editor. *The Baseball Encyclopedia,* 7th edition. New York: Macmillan, 1988.

Sagert, Kelly Boyer. *Joe Jackson: A Biography.* Westport, Conn.: Greenwood, 2004.

Simons, William M., and Alvin L. Hall. *The Cooperstown Symposium on Baseball and American Culture, 2001.* Jefferson, N.C.: McFarland, 2001.

Skipper, John C. *Wicked Curve: The Life and Troubled Times of Grover Cleveland Alexander.* Jefferson, N.C.: McFarland, 2006.

Society for American Baseball Research. *Deadball Stars of the American League.* David Jones, editor. Dulles, Va.: Potomac, 2007.

_____. *Deadball Stars of the National League.* Tom Simon, editor. Dulles, Va.: Brassey's, 2004.

Stump, Al. *Cobb: The Life and Times of the Meanest Man Who Ever Played Baseball.* Chapel Hill, N.C.: Algonquin, 1994.

Swanson, Stevenson, editor. *Chicago Days: 150 Defining Moments in the Life of a Great City.* Chicago: Cantigny First Division Foundation, 1997.

Thorn, John, and Pete Palmer, editors. *Total Baseball.* New York: Warner Books, 1989 and 1999.

Thorn, John, and James Stevenson. *The Armchair Book of Baseball.* New York: Galahad Books, 1997.

Werber, Bill, and C. Paul Rogers III. *Memories of a Ballplayer: Bill Werber and Baseball in the 1930s.* Cleveland, Ohio: Society for American Baseball Research, 2001.

Wilbert, Warren N., and William C. Hageman. *The 1917 White Sox: Their World Championship Season.* Jefferson, N.C.: McFarland, 2000.

Periodicals

Alton (Illinois) Telegraph.
Atlanta Constitution.
Baseball Magazine.
Boston Globe.
Buffalo (New York) Times.
Cascade (Iowa) Pioneer.
Chicago American (and *Chicago's American*).
Chicago Daily Journal.
Chicago Daily News.
Chicago Daily Defender.
Chicago Evening Post.
Chicago Herald.
Chicago Herald-Examiner.
Chicago Inter-Ocean.
Chicago Sun–Times.
Chicago Times.
Chicago Tribune.
Christian Science Monitor.
Collyer's Eye.
Connellsville (Pennsylvania) Daily Courier.
Corpus Christi (Texas) Times.
Daily Inter Lake. Kalispell, Montana.
Decatur (Illinois) Herald.
Decatur (Illinois) Review.
Dubuque (Iowa) Telegraph-Herald.
Dubuque (Iowa) Times-Journal.
Evening Standard. Ogden City, Utah.
Galveston (Texas) Daily News.
Hamilton (Ohio) Evening Journal.
Hartford (Connecticut) Courant.
Janesville (Wisconsin) Gazette.
Jefferson City (Missouri) Post-Tribune.
Kansas City (Missouri) Star.
Leslie's Illustrated Weekly.
Lima (Ohio) News.
Lincoln (Nebraska) Daily News.

Lincoln (Nebraska) State Journal.
Litchfield (Illinois) Daily News.
Litchfield (Illinois) News-Herald.
Los Angeles Times.
Medford (Oregon) Evening Telegram.
Milwaukee (Wisconsin) Journal.
Milwaukee (Wisconsin) Sentinel.
Muscatine (Iowa) Journal.
Newark (New Jersey) Daily News.
The New Republic.
New York Times.
New York Journal-American.
New York World-Telegram.
New York World-Telegram and Sun.
San Antonio (Texas) Light.
Sarasota (Florida) Herald.
Southeast Economist (Chicago).
Southtown Economist (Chicago).
Sports Illustrated.
State Journal-Register. Springfield, Illinois.
The Sporting News.
Syracuse (New York) Post-Standard.
Washington Post.
Waterloo (Iowa) Evening Courier
The Youth's Companion.

Articles

Chicago History. "The Names of Chicago Baseball Teams." No. 11, Vol. 8 (Spring 1969).

Daniel R. Levitt, Mark L. Armour and Matthew Levitt. "History versus Harry Frazee: Re-revising the Story." *The Baseball Research Journal*, Volume 37 (2008).

Schimler, Stuart. "Jack Pfiester." The Baseball Biography Project of the Society for American Baseball Research, www.bioproj.sabr.org.

Sullivan, Frank R. Interview with Mark Johnson, 1978–79. Oral History Office, Sangamon State University, Springfield, Illinois.

Voigt, David Quentin. "The Chicago Black Sox and the Myth of Baseball's Single Sin." *Journal of the Illinois State Historical Society.* Fall 1969.

Other Sources

Baseball-Almanac.com

Ballparks of Baseball.com.

BaseballLibrary.com.

Burgess, William Morton III. Databases of various experts' all-star selections and sportswriters.

Carney, Gene. www.baseball1.com/carney/

Encyclopedia of Chicago web site, hosted by the Chicago History Museum, Newberry Library and Northwestern University.

Google. Map street views.

Illinois Bowling Association.

Macht, Norman. Notes of interview with Billy Sullivan Junior.

Paso Robles Inn. www. pasoroblesinn.com

Polk, R.L & Co., *Chicago City Directory*, 1928.

Retrosheet.org. Some information in this book was obtained free of charge from, and is copyrighted by, Retrosheet, 20 Sunset Road, Newark, Delaware.

Society for American Baseball Research, various publications.

Thebaseballpage.com

University of Illinois at Springfield Norris L. Brookens Library. Oral History archives. Memoirs of Joe Kempe (1986–87) and Frank R. Sullivan (1979).

Index

Numbers in ***bold italic*** indicate pages with photographs.

Aaron, Hank 291
Abilene, Texas 49–50, 75
Adams, Joe 13
Agnew, Sam 76
Alexander, Grover Cleveland 12, 174, 189, 197, 212, 221
Altrock, Nick 115, 211
American Association 14–16, 18, 21–22, 132, 167, 182, 259, 261, 266–269
American Giants, Chicago 31, 90, 167
American League 16, 27–28, 34, 57, 71, 77, 81, 141–142, 162, 184, 203, 235, 286, 293
American Red Cross 96, 122
Anderson, John 207
Appling, Luke 293
Archer, Jimmy 10, 42, 93, 129, 271
Arcos, Litchfield, Illinois 5, *6*, 7
Armour Square Park, Chicago 105
Aronimink Golf Club, Philadelphia 225
Asinof, Eliot 133, 143, 150, 153, 159–161, 166, 176, 295
Associated Press 108, 237
Athletic Park, Milwaukee 17
Atlantic City, New Jersey 178
Attell, Abe 142, 149, 183
Austin, Jimmy 40, 76, 166
Austrian, Alfred 175–176
Automobiles 45, *92*, *94*, 118, 121, 141, 180, 217, 262
Ayers, Yancey "Doc" 62

Baer, Bugs 31
Bailey, Bill *see* Veeck, William, Sr.
Bain, Mary 38
Baker, Bill 266
Baker, Frank "Home Run" 26, 128, 286, 288–289
Baker, Newton D. 84, 122
Baltimore Orioles 145, 175, 263
Bancroft, Dave 253
Banks, Ernie 295
Barbour, Lou 232, 265, 274–275

Barnabe, Charlie 232
Barnes, Donald 267
Barnett, Illinois 10
Barrett, Bill 209, ***233***, 234, 245
Barrett, Jimmy 15–16
Barrett, Margaret Carroll 234
Barrington, Illinois 278
Barry, Jack 99
Bartow, Florida 266
Baseball Anonymous 275–276
Baseball Magazine 37, 45, 72, 104, 158, 283
Baseball Players Fraternity 37
Baseball Writers Association of America 284, 293
Bassler, Johnny 195, 268
Battle Creek, Michigan 197
Baxes, Jim 272
Baylor University 200
Beaumont, California 57
Bell, Brian 283
Bell, Nelson 279
Bender, Charles "Chief" 26
Bene, Jake 5
Benton, John "Rube" 110–112
Benz, Joe 23, 43, 63, 66, 68, 81–82, 93, 117, 128–129, 271, 275
Berg, Moe 229, 240
Beta Theta Pi 279
Beverly Country Club 271, 294
Beverly Recreation Center 270
Biedenharn Park, Shreveport, Louisiana 242, ***243***
billiards 167, 250, 270
Bisbee, Arizona 50
Black Sox 2–3, 101, ***119***, 120, ***123***, ***127***, 133, 140–154, ***157***, 158–160, 162–163, ***164***, 166, 173, 176, 178, 181–182, 184–185, ***186***, 187, 189, 198, 205, 207, 218, 229, 260, 271, 276, 288–289, 295–296
Blackburne, Russell "Lena" 21, 63, 65, 75, 229, ***233***, 238, 243, 247, 250
Blair, James H. 38

Blankenship, Ted 221, 229, 238
Block, James "Bruno" 21
Bodie, Frank "Ping" 31, 58, 59, 171
Bonham, Texas 49
Borchert Field, Milwaukee 269
Borton, Babe 37
Boston Braves 70, 83, 100, 253
Boston Globe 19, 99, 149
Boston Red Sox 30, 39, 65, 77, 79–80, 83,
    88–89, 99–101, *102*, 108, 113, 124, 126, 131,
    135, 138, 155, 162, 181, 187, 195–196, 207,
    211, 230, 232, 290, 301
Bottomley, Jim 178, 213, 222, 297
Boudreau, Lou 293
bowling 141, 167, 214, 250–251, 257, 261, 265,
    270–272, 274–275, 277, 281, 288, 292
Brandt, William 86
Bresnahan, Roger 80, 251, 285, 288
Breton, John "Jimmy" 68
Bridges, Frank 200
Brinson, Robert 278
Brinson, Roy 278
Britton, Helen Hathaway 16
Broder, Dale 297
Brooklyn, New York 11
Brooklyn Dodgers (and Superbas) 15, 253,
    269, 289
Brown, Warren 265, 283, 286, 288, 293
Brown Shoe Company, Litchfield, Illinois 178
Buckner, William 35, 42, 59, 69, 75, 118, 120,
    195, 232
Buffalo, New York 14, 37, 103, 262–265, 298
Buffalo Bisons 14, 259–266, 273–274
Buffalo (New York) Times 262
Burke, Jimmy 125
Burns, Bill "Sleepy" 143, 175
Burns, Ed 187
Burns, George 109
Bush, Donie 165, 231
Bush, Guy 257
Butler, Illinois 212

Cadore, Leon 208
Cairo, Illinois 16
California Angels 296
Callahan, James "Nixey" 24, *24*, 26–27, 31,
    33, 35, 38, 44, 46, 48, 50–51, 54–55, 59–
    60, 66, 70–72, 170
Campanella, Roy 289
Cantillon, Joe 181–182
Capron, Ralph 17
Carey, Max 262
Carleton College 273
Carlson, Harold 256
Carney, Gene 142, 159, 176
Carrigan, Bill 268
Carter, Mary 265
Cascade, Iowa 65, 77, 83, 100, 155, 180, 214
Cermak, Anton 260
Cerny, Jimmy 132

Chance, Frank 30–31, 37–38, 207–208, 248,
    285
Chapman, Glenn 266
Chapman, Ray 20, 34–35, 87, 170
Chappell, Larry 55, 59
Chase, Hal 37, 52, 126, 163, 183
Cheney, Larry 42
Chicago American 52, 90, 92, 167, 229, 258
Chicago Baseball Writers 271
Chicago Bears 271
Chicago Blackhawks 261
Chicago Board of Trade 86
Chicago Cardinals 17
Chicago City Series 30–31, 42–43, 69–71, 73,
    80–81, 89–90, 178, 189, 197, 202, 205, 211–
    212, 221, 227, 235, 240–241, 257–258, 261
Chicago Cubs 10, 16, 17, 30, 31, 37, 38, 42,
    43, 56, 57, 60, 69, 70, 71, 80, 81, 84, 89,
    90, 92, 93, 108, 121, 127, 129, 130, 163, 174,
    177, 178, 180, 183, 189, 197, *198*, 201, 202,
    205, 207, 208, 211, 212, 221, 227, 235, 240,
    241, 244, 253, 256, 257, 258, 259, 261,
    266, 267, 269, 271, 285, 286, 295, 301
Chicago Daily News 125, 210, 217, 235, 243,
    327
Chicago Evening Post 93, 140
Chicago Herald 113, 114, 196
Chicago Inter-Ocean 13, 108
Chicago Journal 74
Chicago Orphans 38
Chicago Police Department 275
Chicago River 22, 80, 167
Chicago Tigers 17
Chicago Whales 60
Chill, Oliver 85, 135, 137, 171, 172
Cicotte, Eddie 30, 42, 56, 59, 69, 70, 79, 89,
    98, 101, *107*, 108, 109, 110, 115, 118, 124, 132,
    133, 134, 142–148, *145*, 150–151, 153, 156,
    158, 162–163, 165–166, 172, 174–176, 271
Cincinnati, Ohio 140, 142, *143*
Cincinnati Reds 2, 132, 139–155, 275
Cissell, Chalmer "Bill" 243
Clancy, Bud 244
Clark, Harry 18
Cleveland Indians (and Naps) 13, 34, 40, 62–
    63, 84, 86, 91, 164, 166, 170, 174, 175, 178,
    189, 195, 197, 201, 202, 209, 218, 236, 238,
    244, 259, 272, 301
Cleveland Spiders 13, 145
Cline, Edward F. 280
Cobb, Ty 2, 15, 17, 26, 27, 37, 68, 69, 76, 88,
    120, 124, 128, 165, 170, 194, 224, *225*, 230,
    231, 232, 276, 283, 284, 288, 289, 292
Coca-Cola 224, 292
Cochrane, Mickey 284, 285, 288, 292
Coffeyville, Kansas 48
Cohan, George M. 149, 265
Cole, Bert 194
Colledge, Sharkey 293
Collins, Eddie 72, 77, 79, 84, 87, 102, *111*,

111–113, 121, 124–126, 133, 137, 139, 145–146, 148, 156, 162, 164–166, 175, 177–178, 181, 184, 196, 198, 201, *202*, 203, 206, 210, 212, 214, 225, 227, 229, 231–232, 239, 248

Collins, John "Shano" 31–32, 37, 42, 76–77, 79, 112, 120, 142, 144, 168, 177–178, 181, 185

Collyer's Eye 88, 156, 158–159, 161, 163

Columbus, Ohio 261, 269

Comiskey, Charles A. 2, 12, 20, 22, 37, 44, *53*, 53–54, 70–73, 80, 83–84, 87–88, 92, 96, 103, 106, 108, 114, 117, 122, 126, 130–131, 133, 141–142, 144, 148, 156, 161–163, 175–176, 178, 183–184, 196, 199, 206–208, 217, 227, 229, 232, 235, 238, 242, 248–249, 269

Comiskey, Charles, II *236*, 293

Comiskey, J. Louis 44, 114, 175, 215, 229, 249, 256, 261

Comiskey, Nancy Kelly 44

Comiskey Park 22–23, 26, 34, 37, 42, *61*, 61, 66, 70, 75–76, 79–80, 84, 91, 98, 105–106, 108–110, 121, 127–128, 135, 137–138, 155, 165, 170, 174, 182, 188, 201–202, 205, 209, 218, 223, 229, 235, *236*, 257, 271, 276, 281, 295, 296

Connally, George 220, 237, 242–243

Connolly, Tommy 67–68

Cook, Luther "Doc" 66

Coolidge, Calvin 211, 261, 291

Coombs, Cecil 67

Corey, Ed 120

Courtney, Harry 170

Coveleski, Harry 76

Coveleski, Stan 295

Crabb, Frank 11

Craig, Ted 105

Crawford, Sam "Wahoo" 44, 50, 68–69, 283

Cree, William "Birdie" 66

Criger, Lew 285

crime and civil unrest 2, 7, 61, 99, 108, 137, 274–275

Crosley Field, Cincinnati *see* Redland Field

Crouse, Clyde "Buck" 210–211, 219, 225, 240, 259

Crowder, Enoch H. 121

Cruce, Lee 48

Crusinberry, James 66–70, 77, 99, 108, 113, 117, 138, 151, 153, 155, 161, 165, 174–175, 182, 185, 211, 214–215, 218, 221, 229

Cuba 251

Cummings, Minnie 38

Cuyler, KiKi 257

Cynthiana, Kentucky 221

Czarobski, Ziggy 274

Dafoe, Allan Roy 265

Daley, Arthur 285

Daley, Richard J. 274, 292

Dallas, Texas 242

Daly, Tom 51–53, 62, 65, 77, 177

dances 56

Danforth, Dave 98, 118

Daniel, Dan 288

Daniel, Harry 26

Danville, Illinois 16

Darrow, Clarence 210

Daubert, Jake 144

Dauss, Herb 166

Davenport, Iowa 86

Dawes, Charles *239*

Day, James 210

Daylight Saving program 121

deadball 2, 35, 162, 297

Decatur, Illinois 13

Dellinger, Susan 143, 148

DeMille, Cecil B. 279

Demmitt, Ray 62–63, 66, 69, 115, 125

Dempsey, Jack 32

Deneen, Charles S. 250

Denver Bears 22

DePauw University 268, 279

Derrick, Claud 70

Des Moines, Iowa 46, 53, 183

Detroit Tigers 13–14, 26–27, 29, 36–37, 62, 66, 76, 79, 83–84, 88, 100–101, 120, 128, 138, 165, 175, 178, 192, 194–195, 197–198, 209, 211, 230–232, 246, 251, 259, 286, 295

DeWitt, William 267

Dexter Park, Chicago 108

Dickey, Bill 268, 284

DiMaggio, Joe 160, 285–286, 289, 295

Dinneen, Bill 172

Divernon, Illinois 5

Donlin, Mike 51

Donovan, Fred 13

Doolan, Mickey 46

Doran, Lewis 12

Dougherty, Tom 18

Douglas, Arizona 50

Draper-Maynard Company, Plymouth, New Hampshire 216

Dreyfuss, Barney 144

Dryden, Charles 156

Dublin, Ireland 212

Dubuc, Jean 29

Dubuque, Iowa 12, 44, 46, 65, 72, 75, 77, 86

Dubuque (Iowa) College 86

Duffy, Hugh 16

Duffy, John J. 274

Duluth-Mesaba League 128

Duncan, Louis "Pat" 144

Dunn, James 84, 134

Dunn Park, Cleveland 84

Dunne, Edward F. 38, 46

Easterly, Ted 27

Eastern League 269

Eastland excursion boat 80

Edwards, Henry P. 285

Ehmke, Howard 194

Eisenhower, Dwight D. 291
Eldredge, W.S. 52
Elgin (Illinois) National Watch Company 256
Eller, Horace "Hod" 150
Ellerbe, Frank 172
El Paso, Texas 32, 50, 59, 60
Elsh, Roy 208
Empress of Japan 54
Ens, Mutz 21
entertainment 18, 56, 114, 144, 155, 202, 217–218, 237, 263, 279, 280
Epstein, Ben 295
Erickson, William 274
Evans, Billy 87, 140, *141*, 148, 218, 283–284
Evans, Steve 49–50
Evergreen Park, Illinois 270, 293
Evergreen Towers 270–271, 274, 277, 281
Evers, Johnny 56, 108, 192, 208, 212, 214, 239
Ewing, Buck 288

Faber, Irene 234
Faber, Urban "Red" 2, 12, 46, 52, 62, 65, 76, 77, 83, 87, 89, 100, *109*, 110, 111, 117, 118, 122, 129, 133, 148, 155, 159, 161, 168, 177, 180, 181, 188, 196, 198, 201, 208, 212, 214, 227, 230, 234, 238, 258, 261, 270, 275, 281, 288, 293, 298
Faber, Urban C., II 234
Fairbanks, Douglas 32
Falk, Bibb 197, 217, 218, 240, 245
Fallon, William J. 183
fan behavior 18, 20, 27, 38, 50, 63, 68, 70, 76, 80, 84, 99, 106, 113–114, 135, 138, 146, 165, 168, 171, 180, 194, 204, 218, 220, 227, 257, 263
Farmersville, Illinois 11–12, 55, 91, 93, 95, 277, 281
Farnsworth, W.A. 155
Federal League 37, 56, 60, 71–73, 120
Felsch, Oscar "Happy" 79, 109, 112, 124, 126, *127*, 130–131, 135, 138, 151, 153, 165–166, 172, 198–199, 231
Fenway Park, Boston 99–100, 173, 230
Ferdinand, Archduke Franz 74
Ferguson, Charlie 38
Ferry, Alfred J. 13, 259
fights and altercations 27, 85, 87, 112, 134, 135, 150, 172, 196, 263
fines 27, 197–198, 249, 260, 264, 268
Finney, Ed 75
Fisk, Carlton 298
Flagstead, Ira 165, 192
Fletcher, Artie 108, 112
Foell, George 265
Foell, Helen 265
Foley, Matt 26
Follies Bergere 279
Fonseca, Lew 293
football 17, 46, 149, 223, 235, 271, 273–275, 293, 296

Fort Lauderdale, Florida 260
Foster, Eddie 67
Foster, Rube 167
Fournier, Jack 58, 66–68, 77, 85
Foxx, Jimmie *255*
Franks, Bobby 210
Frazee, Harry 99, *102*, 141, 162, 207
Frick, Ford 295
Friend, Hugo 184
Fromme, Art 54
Fullerton, Hugh 103, 143–146, 155–156, 158, 201, 207

Galesburg, Illinois 12
Galva, Illinois 197
gambling 2, 27, 99, 100, 138, 139, 141, 143, 144, 146, 150, 153, 156, 163, 166, 173, 174, 175, 178, 183, 185, 186, 198
Gandil, Arnold "Chick" 63, 67, 98, 112, 113, 118, *119*, 125, 126, 133, 134, 139, 149, 156, 163, *164*, 177, 199, 231
Garden City, New Jersey 113
Garden City semi-pro team 129
Gardner, Larry 166
Gehrig, Lou 219–220, 265, 272, 298
Gehringer, Charlie 286
Gharrity, Edward "Patsy" 172
Giles, Warren 286
Gillespie, Illinois 189
Gleason, William "Kid" 26, 28, 31, 37, 56, 57, 58, 71, 72, 73, 74, 120, 130, *131*, 132, 135, 145, 146, 148, 149, 150, 151, 153, 158, 167, 168, 171, 176, 181, 182, 184, 185, 188, 189, 195, 196, 200, *202*, 205, *228*, 260
golf 50, 118, 120, 215, 224, 250, 253, 271, 294
Goodyear Tire blimp 137
Gossett, John "Dick" 33
Gould, Alan J. 237
Grabiner, Harry 56, 132, 162, 200, 218, 244
Grabowski, John 225, 229
Graham, Frank 113
Graham, Hannah McConnell 91
Graham, James 91
Graham, Mae 91
Graham, Roy V. 192
Graney, Jack 62, 85, 98, 135
Grange, Harold "Red" 223, 275
Grantham, George 205
Graver, Larry 91, 93, 155, 207
Great Western Smelting Company, Chicago 128, 131
Griffin, Wes 266, 268
Griffith, Clark C. 28, 67, 115
Griffith Park, Washington, D.C. 28, 138
Grimm, Charlie 293
Groh, Henry "Heinie" 144, 149, 151, 153
Groom, Bob 90, 98
Guthrie, Bill 275
Guyon, Louis 218

Halas, George 271, 275
Haney, Fred 267
Hannah, James "Truck" 124
Hannibal, Missouri 12
Hansen, Roy 132
Harding, John P. 92, 106
Harding, Warren G. 261, 291
Harridge, Will 286, 293
Harris, Bucky 251
Harrison, Carter, Jr. 34
Harrison, James B. 220
Hartnett, Charles "Gabby" 256–257, 268, 285–286, 288–289
Harvel, Illinois 8, 10–11, 292, 297–299, 327
Hauser, Joe 211
Havenor, Agnes 15–16
Havenor, Charles 15–16
Hayes, Bryan 135
Hayes, Frank 271
Heath, Mike 269
Hedges, Robert L. 19
Heilmann, Harry 165, 194
Hemsley, Rollie 286, 288
Henagow, Isaac 61
Hendricks, Karl 277
Hendricks, Lillian 277
Hendrix, Claude 174
Hendryx, Tim 125
Herrin, Illinois 20
Herrmann, August "Garry" 122, 148
Herzog, Charles "Buck" 113, 180
Heydler, John 148
Hildebrand, George 121
Hillsboro, Illinois 115
Hilltop Park, New York 26
Hinton, Theresa Schalk 8, 297
Hodapp, John 245
Hodge, Clarence "Shovel" 195–196, 206
Hoffman, Dorothy 274
Hoffman, Ethel M. 262
Hoffman, John C. 243
Holcomb, Stu 293
Holke, Walter 81, 109, 112
Holley, Ed 262
Hollocher, Charlie 197
Hollywood, California 266
Hooper, Harry *102*, 181, 201, 212, 221
Hoover, Herbert 261, 291
Hornsby, Rogers 256–258, 292
Horstmann, Oscar 74
Hot Springs, Arkansas 208, 214
hotels 26, 32, 90, 93, 106, 113, 118, 120, 142–143, *143*, 146, 162, 178, 186, 208, 232, 234, 242, 261, 275, 289
Houston, Texas 49
Howard, Ivan 87
Howe, Irwin M. 188, 283
Hoyt, Waite 295
Hudson, Helene 279
Hudson Wonders 279–280

Huerta, Victoriano 60
Huggins, Miller 135, 168, 196, 206, 218
Humphries, Bert 42, 70

Illinois Athletic Club, Chicago 22, 214, 256
Illinois Bell Telephone Company 270
Illinois-Missouri League 12–14
Illinois Trust and Savings Bank 137
Independence Day 170, 188, 203, 225, 246, 247, 266, 299, 301, 327
Indianapolis, Indiana 165
injuries 38, 42, 48, 49, 55, 59, 63–66, 69, 75, 84, 85, 103, 118, 120, 124, 131–133, 135, 137, 181, 190, 196, 204, 209, 211–212, 239, *224*, *226*, 242, 245, 267
International League 81, 122, 259, 261–263, 273
Irving, Illinois 10
Isbell, Frank 51

Jacksboro, Texas 120
Jackson, "Shoeless" Joe 2, 34, 81, 85, 87, 90, *97*, 109, 111, 118, 122–123, *123*, 125, 130, 138, 144–145, 150–151, 153, 158, 172, 182, 207
James, Bill (baseball statistician) 81, 88, 286
James, Bill (player) 101, 153, 232
Jamieson, Charlie 244
Jarrard, Roy 10
Jasper, Henry 63, 65, 77
Jeffries, Irv 262
Jemison, Dick 132, 140
Jenkins, Joe 135
Jennings, Hugh 283
Johnson, Ban 27, 57, 71, 84, 96, 122, 141, 148, 174, *183*, 183–184, 196, 199, 201, 238
Johnson, Ernie 184
Johnson, Harold 258
Johnson, Hickory 13
Johnson, Walter 39, 48, 67, 77, 87, 124, 128, 208, *209*, 217, 284
Johnston, Doc 62
Johnston, Johnny 40
Joliet, Illinois 180
Jones, Fielder 71, 125
Jones, Sam 204
Jonnard, Clarence "Bubber" 178
Joplin, Missouri 48
Joss, Addie 195
Judge, Joe 138

Kamm, Willie 218, 244
Kaney, A.W. "Sen" 212
Kankakee, Illinois 213
Kansas City, Missouri 46, 48, 56, 57, 89, 121, 267, 273, 298
Kansas City Chiefs 273
Kansas City Royals 298
Keener, Sid 292
Kelley, Henrietta 175
Kennedy, John F. 291

Kerner, Otto 280
Kerr, Dickie 133, 146, 168, 171, 175, 177–178, 181, 192
Kerr, Paul S. 286
Kersten, George 217
Kewanee, Illinois 33
Kilgallen, James L. 175
Killefer, Bill **198**, 211, 266, 269
Killefer, Wade "Red" 266
King, Mike 271
Kinsella, Dick 13
Klein, Frank 156
Klem, Bill 21, 50–54, 112, 272, 285
Kling, Johnny 10, 285
Knode, Ray 218
Knox, Seymour "Shorty" 265
Kohn, Maurice 38
Koob, Ernie 98
Kopf, Larry 145
Kuhn, Walt "Red" 27, 28, 31, 33, 35, 58

Labor Day 100–101, 128, 198, 230, 232, 259
Lait, Jack 151, 153, 155
Lajoie, Nap 40, 62, 285
Lake Alfred, Florida 208
Lake Shore League 188
Landis, Kenesaw Mountain 142, 163, 182, 199, 215, 230–232, 275
Lapp, Jack 65, 231
Lardner, Ring 31, 59, 69, 155, 283
La Salle Street Station, Chicago 114, 132, 137
Latshaw, Bob 266
Lazzeri, Tony 237
League Park, Cleveland 84
Lees, George 187
Lehman, Dodo 168
Leibold, Harry "Nemo" 125, 141, 177, 181, 185
Leonard, Hubert "Dutch" 101
Leopold, Nathan 210
Lewis, Duffy 108, 283
Lewis, Phil 18
Lincoln Park, Chicago 121
Lindstrom, Fred 253
Links, Ottmar J. 22
linotype 11
Litchfield, Illinois 5, **6**, 7–8, 10–14, 24, 30–31, 46, 54–55, 65, 70, 81–83, 86, 90–91, 93–94, 100, 113–115, 117, 121, 131–132, 170, 178, 189–190, 197, 200–201, 212–213, 215, 222, 229, 244, 261, 277, 281, 297–298, 327
Little Rock, Arkansas 49
Lobert, Hans 53
Loeb, Richard 210
Logan Squares 129
Lolich, Mickey 295
Lollar, Sherman 298
London, Jack 52
London, England 62
Lopez, Al 293
Loras College, Dubuque, Iowa 86

Lord, Harry 37, 40, 126
Los Angeles, California 32, 51, 56, 57, 58, 59, 72, 74, 75, 103, 105, 268, 272, 279
Los Angeles Angels 74
Los Angeles Dodgers 125, 293
Los Angeles Times 51
Louisville, Kentucky 267
Lowdermilk, Grover 76, 128, 133, 167
Lueker, Claude 27
Lutgert, Grover 274
Lynn, Byrd 103, 122, 135, 171, 178
Lyons, Ted 201, 203, 211, 219, 229, 236, 238, 250, 258, 286, 289, 293

Macbeth, Bill 155
Macht, Norman 248
Mack, Connie 42, 72, 79, 171, 205, 229, 258
Mackey, Guy 272, 292–293, 296
MacLean, Malcolm 138, 140
Madison Square Garden, New York 108
Magee, Lee 51, 163
Maggert, Hal 75
Maharg, Bill 175
Malone, Pat 257–258
Manero, Tony 265
Mann, Johnny 244
Maranville. Rabbit 1, 221, 272
Marlin, Texas 192, 200
Marshall, William Riddle "Doc" 15
Marshall Field & Company 134
Martha Washington Club, Chicago 94, 272
Marx Brothers 217
Mathews, Eddie 291
Mathewson, Christy 21, 45, 52, 77, 139, 143–146, 163, 284
Mattick, Wally 34, 40
Maxwell, Don 231, 238, 244
Mayer, Wally 66
Mayor Daley Youth Foundation 292, 294
Mays, Carl 124, 135, 170–171, 194
Mays, Willie 126
McAndless, David 250
McBride, George 108
McCarthy, Joe 244, 256–257, **264**, 265
McCarty, Lew 109, 112
McClellan, Harvey 178, 184, 221
McClusky, Illinois 55
McCormick, Barry 99
McCurdy, Harry 225, 240
McGraw, John 13, 42, 44, 103, 104, 139, 192, 201, 212, 251
McGrew, Ted 257
McIntyre, Matty 327
McMullin, Fred 99, 120, 140, 149, 171, 183
McNally, Augustine J. 100
McPherson, Aimee Semple 262
Melton, Cliff 263
Mercy Hospital, Chicago 221
Mergenthaler, Ottmar 11
Merkle, Fred 17

Mesner, Steve 266
Metropolitan Amateur Baseball League 271
Metropolitan Life Insurance Company 281
Metzler, Alex 238
Meusel, Bob 168, 196, 216
Meusel, Emil "Irish" 253
Meyers, John "Chief" 52
Midland Club, Chicago 253
military 48, 50, 60, 96–97, *97*, 100, 113, 115, 117, 121–122, 124, 128, 130, 201, 271, 278–280
Miller, Elmer 124
Miller, Leo T. 266
Milliken, Stanley T. 68
Milwaukee, Wisconsin 126
Milwaukee Braves 290
Milwaukee Brewers 14, 263–264, 269–270
Milwaukee Journal 15, 18, 19, 20, 21
Milwaukee Sentinel 15
Mineral Wells, Texas 83, 97, 118, 120, 121, 132, 163
Minneapolis, Minnesota 7
Minneapolis Millers 18, 167, 182, 266
Mississippi-Ohio Valley League 289
Mitchell, Mike 67
Mix, Tom 218
Moeller, Danny 63
Montgomery County, Illinois 7–8, 178, 213, 222, 297
Moran, Pat 142–145
Morehart, Ray 229
Morgan, Ray 67
Moriarty, George 36–37, 137
Morris, Nelson 181
Morse Code 108
Mostil, Johnny 185, 195, 196, *220*, 233, 234, 235, 238, 242, 243
Mount Olive, Illinois 12, 90, 115, 178, 213
Mulligan, Joe 81, 90
Munch, Jocko 259
Murphy, Charles W. 31, 56
Murphy, Eddie 79, 177–178
Murphy, Johnny 265
Murrin, M.L. 106
Musial, Stan 295
music 18, 114, 144, 155, 202
Muskogee, Oklahoma 49
Myers, Edward 186

Nallin, Dick 76, 87, 98, 194, 203–204, *204*, 225, 227
National Baseball Hall of Fame 1, 28, 104, 197, 201, 213, 281, 283–291, *287*, *290*, 295, 297, 299, 327
National Commission 106, 122, 142, 148, 163
National Guard Armory, Chicago 217
National League 16, 100, 127, 142, 145, 148, 162, 235, 286
National Tea Company 217
National Track and Field Hall of Fame 213

Navin, Frank 14, 251
Navin Field, Detroit 194
Neale, Alfred "Greasy" 149
Neily, Harry 229
Neuberger, Franklin J. 181
New York, New York 7, 271, 295
New York Giants 13, 42, 44, 81, 83, 103, 105–116, 120, 192, 201, 207–208, 212, 251, *252*, *254*, 271, 299
New York Times 86, 113, 163, 184, 187, 220, 237, 244, 251, 285
New York Yankees 27, 31, 34, 37–38, 66, 69, 80, 87, 124, 135, 137, 142, 162, 164, 167–168, 170–172, 174–175, 187–189, 194, 196–197, 206–207, 217–221, 225, 229, 237–238, 244, 250, 257, *264*, 265, 301
Newport, Kentucky 143
Niehoff, Bert 251, 253
no-hitters 62–63, 98, 195, 219
Noel, Bruce 17
Nokomis, Illinois 222, 297
Northlake Bank, Melrose Park, Illinois 278
Northwestern League 44

Oakland, California 32
O'Connor, Jack 288
O'Day, Hank 56–57
Offerman, Frank 259
Old Timers' Baseball Association of Chicago 271, *272*
O'Loughlin, Frank "Silk" 27, 34, 38–40, 62, 65, 76
Olson, Ivy 40
O'Neill, Joe "Tip" 56–58, 60, 91, 239
O'Neill, Steve 101, 268, 288
Oneonta, New York 187
Opening Day 12, 28, 34, 62, 75, 165, 202, 235, *236*, 244, 266, 289, 295
Ormsby, Emmet "Red" 203, 293
Orr, Heidie 11
Osborn, Harold 212
Osborne, Ernie 197
Oshkosh, Wisconsin 17
Osolin, Harry T. 270
Otto, Wayne K. 258
Ottumwa, Iowa 46
Owens, Brick 101, 121, 135, 165, 167, 238
Oxnard, California 52

Pacific Coast League, 32, 57, 58, 74, 130, 162–163, 196, 240, 243, 266
Page, Vance 267
Palm Springs, California 208
Palos Heights, Illinois 281, 296
Palos Park, Illinois 278
Paris, France 57, 279
Paso Robles, California 32–33, 56, 58–59, 74
Pass, Sam 91, 115, 142, 170, 174, 183
Peckinpaugh, Roger 86, 210, 243
Pegler, Westbrook 232

Pennock, Herb 204, 218
Peoria, Illinois 46, 72–73
perfect game 195
Perkins, Cy 268
Perritt, William "Pol" 110
Perry, Norman A. 266
Petway, Bruce 31
Pfiester, Jack 17
Philadelphia Athletics 23, 39, 65, 70, 72, 79, 126, 205, 219, 225, 229, 232, *255*, 258, 269
Philadelphia Phillies 46, 53, 71, 103, 174, 269, 301
Piet, Tony 275, 293
Pipp, Wally 219
Pittsburgh Pirates 17
Plank, Eddie 85
Plymouth, New Hampshire 216
Polo Grounds, New York 86, 110–111, 114, 167, 170, 187, 194, 272
Portland, Oregon 54
Prohibition 163, 191, 257
Prunty, Pat 234
Purdue University 159, 272–273, 289, 292–296

Quayle, Dan and James 279
Quigley, Ernie 227
Quin, Harry D. 15
Quinn, Jack 128, 142

railroads 7, 10, 26, 49, 55–57, 59, 68, 84, 111, 114–115, 121, 187, 258, 279
Rariden, Bill 111–112, 151
Rath, Morrie 35, 144, 149, 151
Ray, Joie W. 213
Raymond, Illinois 10
Reading, Pennsylvania 259
Redland Field, Cincinnati 144, 153
Redlands, California 75
Reichow, Oscar C. 159, 185, 196
Replogle, Hartley 174–175
Rice, George C. 74
Rice, Grantland 83, 87, 104, 283
Rice, Sam 219
Richards, Paul 273
Rickey, Branch 75
Ridgeway, J.H. 232–233
Rigler, Cy 151, *152*
Ripken, Cal 219
Risberg, Charles "Swede" 98, 125, 133, 140–141, 145–146, 149, 151, *157*, 164, 166, 172, 229–231
R.J. Reynolds Tobacco Co. 265
Robbins, George 100
Robertson, Charlie 194–195
Robertson, Dave 109, 112
Robinson, Jackie 118, 285
Robinson, Wilbert 256
Roche, Jack 90
Rochester, New York 81, 261, 263

Rommel, Eddie 194, 197
Roosevelt, Franklin D. 260, 291
Roosevelt, Theodore 32
Roosevelt Newsboys Club, Boston 177
Root, Charlie 257
Roseboro, Johnny 125
Roth, Frank 229
Roth, Robert "Braggo" 69–70, 81, 90–91
Rothstein, Arnold 183
Roush, Edd 143–144, *147*, 148, 150, 153
Rowland, Ann 91, 114
Rowland, Clarence "Pants" 12, 19, 46, 53, 72–77, *73*, 79–81, 84, 87–89, 91–93, 97, *97*, 99, 101, 103, 106, *107*, 108, 110–114, 117, 121–122, 126, 128, 130, 132, 170, 203, 210, 218, 221, 231, 259, 261, 270, 293
Royston, Georgia 292
Rucker, Nap 292
Ruel, Herold "Muddy" 82, *209*, 268, 283, 288
Ruether, Walter "Dutch" 144, 185
Ruffing, Charles "Red" 213, 222, 297
Ruppert, Jacob 141
Russell, Ewell "Reb" 48, 76, 89, 93, 110, 231
Ruth, George "Babe" 3, 101–102, 131–132, 138, 162, 164, 166–168, *169*, 170, 174, 187–188, 197, 204, 216–217, 220, 238, 283–284, 295–296, 298
Ryan, Quin 235

Saier, Vic 70
St. Joseph's College, Dubuque, Iowa 86
St. Louis, Missouri 7, 11, 13, 16, 19, 30, 34–35, 40, 49, 51, 75–76, 81, 85–86, 90, 97–98, 101, 121, 125, 128, 132, 135, 138–139, 143, 156, 166, 170, 172, 175, 177–178, 183–184, 197, 201, 203, 215, 241, 246, 253, 256, 267, 277, 295, 301
St. Louis Browns 19, 30, 40, 75–76, 82, 85, 90, 98, 121, 125, 128, 135, 158, 170, 172, 177, 197, 201, 246, 267, 301
St. Louis Cardinals 13, 16, 49, 253, 257–258, 295
St. Louis Globe-Democrat 82
St. Mary's Training School, Des Plaines, Illinois 170
St. Paul, Minnesota 7, 267
Saint Xavier College, Chicago 203
Sallee, Harry "Slim" 108–109, 146, 149
San Antonio, Texas 251
Sanborn, Irving E. 30, 39, 56, 65, 84–85, 97, 120, 171
San Diego, California 52
San Francisco 32, 46, 53–55, 58–59, 196, 272
Saturday Evening Post 216
Schaefer, William "Germany" 71
Schalk, Clarence "Jersey" 8, 181–182, 251, 277, *290*
Schalk, Diane 280
Schalk, Ferdinand 8

Schalk, Geraldine Hudson 279–280, 282, 294–297

Schalk, Herman 7, 8, 11, 327

Schalk, James 280

Schalk, Lavinia Graham 12, 30–31, 55, 91–92, 94–96, 114, 117, 142, 161, 167, 187, 200, 211, 250, *252*, *260*, 261–263, 268, 270, 272–274, 277–281, *280*, 288, 289, 293–295, 297

Schalk, Leo 8, *9*, 11, 212, 277, 289, *290*, *294*

Schalk, Pauline 94, 117, 121, 161, 167, 197, 200, 250, *252*, *260*, 262, 268, 270, 278, 289, 293, 296–297

Schalk, Ray, Jr. 94, 187, 200, 250, *252*, *260*, 267–268, 278–282, 289, 293–296

Schalk, Roy 182

Schalk, Sophia Brandt 8, 277

Schalk, Theresa 8, *294*, 297

Schalk, Violet 297

Schalk, Walter 8, *9*, *290*, *294*

Schalk, Wilhelmina 8

Schalk Day 82, 90, 115, 125, 170, 178, *179*, 189, 212, 221, 253, 259

Schang, Wally 60, 196, 268, 288

Schauer, Alexander "Rube" 98

Schorling Park, Chicago 31

Schumpert Hospital, Shreveport, Louisiana 234

Schupp, Ferdinand "Ferdie" 110

Scott, Everett 196

Scott, Jim 48, 52, 59, 62–63, 70, 98, 100

Seattle, Washington 54

Seguin, Texas 192, 200

Sewell, Luke 244, 286

Shanks, Howie 39, 63, 67

Shean, Dave 135

Sheboygan, Wisconsin 188

Shedd Aquarium, Chicago 95

Sheely, Earl 194, 197, 205, 240

Sheridan, J.B. 81–82, 164

Shibe Park, Philadelphia 171, 194

Shocker, Urban 135, 197, 220

Shotton, Burt 85, 124

Shreveport, Louisiana 214–215, 224, 232, 234, 242

Siekmeyer, E.L. 188

Sioux City, Iowa 105

Sisler, George 128, 197, 201

Skaff, Frank 273

Skowron, Bill "Moose" 273, 293

Slattery, William Paul 77

Slight, Andy 52

Smith, Bob 257

Smith, Ed W. 92

Smith, Harry 126, 219

Smith, Jimmy 145

Smith, Wally 68

Smits, Chris 294

Sousa, John Philip 144

South Main Street Park, Tulsa 48

Spahn, Warren 291

Spalding, A.G. 44

Speaker, Tris 44, 88–89, 134, 164, 189, 209, 230, 285

Spence, Stanley 266

Spink, Taylor J.G. 286

Sporting News 16–17, 33, 45, 65, 87, 96, 100, 113, 158–160, 164, 229, 247, 265, 268, 286, 293, 327

Sportsman's Park, St. Louis 75–76, 201

sportswriters 32, 60, 62, 83, 92–93, 113, 127, 132, 142, 151, 153, 155–156, 159, 166, 220, 232, 235, 244

Springfield, Illinois 11, 178, 244

Staunton, Illinois 115

Stengel, Casey 259

Stephenson, Harry 118, 184

Sterrett, Charles "Dutch" 19

Stevenson, Ben 223, 250, 262

Stevenson and Schalk Recreation 250–251

Stockton, California 75

Stoneham, Charles A. 192

Stoner, Lil 209

Straight, Charley 270

Stram, Hank 273, 296

Strunk, Amos 173, 177

Sturdy, Guy 262

Styles, William "Lena" 171

Sullivan, Billy, Jr. 248

Sullivan, Billy, Sr. 28, 31, *33*, 33–34, 65, 72, 216, 285

Sullivan, Ed 196, 279

Sullivan, Joseph 248

Sullivan, Stanley 248

Sullivan, Ted 19, 44

Sullivan, Indiana 184

suspensions 2, 27, 76, 177–178, 182, 240, 260, 268

Sweeney, Bill 70

Sweeney, Jeff 39

Syracuse, New York 26

Taft, Charles P. 57

Taft, William Howard 28, 261, 291

Tampico, Mexico 61

Taube, Mel 272

taverns 7, 8, 79, 81, 191, 271

Taylor, Chester 48

Taylorville, Illinois 8, 10–11

Terry, Zebulon "Zeb" 87, 177

Texas League 44

theaters 91, 93, 108, 216–217, 237, 242, 257

Thomas, Alphonse "Tommy" 238, 244

Thomas, Chester "Pinch" *102*

Thompson, Fresco 269

Thompson, William Hale 81, 167, 170, 178, 235

Thormahlen, Hank 124

Thorpe, Jim 44

Three-I League 12–13, 65, 72

3-M League 12

ticket prices and scalpers 61, 106, 110, 140, 165
Times Square, New York 108
Tinker, Joe 89
Toledo Mud Hens 20, 259
Totten, Hal 235, *245*
Trautman, George M. 266
Tribune Tower 2, 167, 216–218
triple plays 85, 245, 264, 283
Trolley League 11
Truman, Harry S 291
Tulsa, Oklahoma 48–49

umpires 2, 16, 18, 20–21, 27, 39, 50–54, 56, 62,
    67–68, 75–76, 85, 98–99, 101, 112, 115, 121,
    128, 130, 135, 137, 139–140, *141*, 148, 151, *152*,
    160, 165, 167, 171, 188, 194, 196, 203–204,
    204, 210, 218–219, 221, 227, 238, 253, 257,
    262, 266, 272, 275, 283, 285, 288, 293
uniforms *6*, 27, 38, 42, 45–46, 53, 59, 62,
    84, 96–97, 108, 115, 120, 124, 133, 187, 232
University of Chicago High School 262
University of Wisconsin 223, 247

Vance, Dazzy 286
Vaughan, Irving 166, 194, 206, 234, 244, 247
Veach, Bobby 165, 219
Veeck, William, Sr. 52, 241, 253
Veiock, Jack 104
Venice (California) Tigers 57
Victoria, British Columbia, Canada 54
Vila, Joe 175, 247
Virden, Illinois 11
Vitt, Oscar 231
Vosburg, William R. 22

Wabada Graduates, St. Louis 81
Waco, Texas 163, 200
Waddell, George E. "Rube" 18
Wagner, Eugene 50
Wagner, Honus 284
Wakefield, Frank 262
Walsh, Davis J. 238
Walsh, Ed, Jr. 246
Walsh, Ed, Sr. 24, 187, 208, 276
Walters, Alfred "Roxy" 137
Wambsganss, Bill 283
war 37, 55, 74, 95–97, 108, 117, 121–122, 124,
    128, 131, 270–271, 280
Ward, Aaron 229, 243
Ward, Arch 266, 288
Washington Nationals (and Senators) 26, 28,
    39, 62–63, 66–68, 71, 76–77, 82, 84, 87–
    88, 102–103, 124, 132, 138, 170, 172, 173,
    184–185, 207–208, *209*, 210–211, 214, 217,
    219, *220*, 232, 291
Washington Park, Los Angeles 57
Wathan, John 89, 298
Waugh, William F. 23
Waxahachie, Texas 181
Weatherford, Texas 118

Weaver, Buck 2, 34–35, 40, 51, 66–68, 70,
    76–77, 85, 87, 90, 98–99, 101, 109, 112, 117,
    121, 131–132, 138, 153, 156, 165–166, 172,
    184, *186*, 231, 275–276
Weeghman, Charles 84
Weilman, Carl 75
Weller, Sam 32, 93
Wera, Julian 237
Werber, Bill 150
Wesley Memorial Hospital, Chicago 295
West Lafayette, Indiana 273
Western League 46
Western Union 17
WGN 212, 235, 288
Wheeler, Pete 105
White, Guy Harris "Doc" 24, *25*, 36, 57
White Sox Rooters Association 235
Wichita Falls, Texas 235
Wightman, William J. 223, 250
Wilkinson, Roy 178, 184
Willett, Ed 29
Williams, August "Gus" 76
Williams, Claude "Lefty" 89, 122, 124, 130,
    132–133, *134*, 148, 151, 156, 165–166, 172,
    176, 186
Williams, Eugene 135
Williams, Harry A. 51, 72, 103
Williams, Ted 290
Williamsport, Pennsylvania 269
Willson, Frank "Kid" 127
Wilson, Frank 188
Wilson, Hack 227, 256, 258
Wilson, Woodrow 61, 95, 127, 291
Wilson Athletic Equipment 216
Wingo, Ivy 51
Winter Haven, Florida 208
WMAQ *245*
Wolfgang, Mel 90
Woodland Bards 84, 106, 142
Woodruff, Harvey T. 35, 142, 168, 192, 229,
    242, 260
World Series 2, 42, 70, 89, 103, 105–114, *107*,
    123, *134*, 140–155, *145*, *147*, 255
World Tour of 1913–14 44–57, 62, 71
Wrigley Field, Chicago 16, 201–202, 241, 253,
    256, 268

Yankee Stadium, New York 204, 237, 291
Yaryan, Clarence "Yam" 184, 189, 195
Young, Cy 285
Young, Frank H. 238
Young, Ralph 166
Youree Hotel, Shreveport, Louisiana 232,
    242–243
Yuma, Arizona 57, 59

Zeider, Rollie 37
Zelser, David 183
Zimmerman, Henry "Heinie" 109, 111
Zork, Carl 183